THE COMPLETE STYLIST AND HANDBOOK

30%

WORDINESS

H	1	2	3	4	5	6	7	8	9
	Counting Words	Is and Was	Of and Which	The Use of	There Is, It Is	Jargon	Distinctions, Definitions	Passive Voice	Noun Habit
	163–164	167–168	170–171	172–173	169	450–451	177–178	165–168	173–176

EVIDENCE

I	1	2	3	4	5	6	7	8	9
	Facts, and Degrees of Belief	Assumptions	Definitions	Proof	Fallacies	Citing Authority	Induction	Deduction	Induction-Deduction
	104–108	108–109	110–113	115–116	115–125	116–117	120–127	127–128	129–131

GRAMMAR

J	1	2	3	4	5	6	7	8
	Parts of Speech	The Simple Sentence: Three Forms	Compound, Complex Sentences	Shifts in Structure	Agreement: Subject-Verb	Tense	Mood	Irregular Verbs
	332–335	335–336	337	338–339	340–342	342	345	346–349

	9	10	11	12	13	14	15	16
	Pronouns: Subject and Object	Possessive Pronouns with Gerunds	Pronouns and Antecedents	Adjectives vs. Adverbs	Squinting Modifiers	Comparisons	Dangling Constructions	Restrictives, Nonrestrictives
	350–355	355	356–358	359–360	361	361–362	363–364	370–372

MECHANICS

PUNCTUATION

K	1	2	3	4	5	6	7	8	9
	The Comma: Introductory Phrases	The Comma: Between Clauses	The Comma: Inserted Phrases	The Comma: Items in Series	Fragment	Comma Splice	Run-on	Semicolon	Colon
	366–368	368–370	370–372	374–375	375–376	376–378	376	381–382	384–385

	10	11	12	13	14	15			
	Parenthesis	Dash	Brackets	Quotation Marks	Italics	Ellipsis			
	388–390	388–389	390–391	391–394	393–394	394–396			

SPELLING

L	1	2	3	4	5	6	7	8	9
	Some Principles	Troublesome Words	Apostrophe	Hyphen	Virgule (Slash)	Diacritical Marks	Numbers	Abbreviations	Capitalization
	398–400	401–403	406–408	409–411	412	412–413	413–414	414–416	417–419

*The letter-and-number coding can serve as pointers to weaknesses in your papers; for example, your instructor's marking of "H8" in a page margin would send you to pp. 165–168 in the text, to review the excesses of the passive voice.

**The page numbers in the boxes refer to the main text discussions; additional references appear in the Index.

THE COMPLETE STYLIST AND HANDBOOK

SECOND EDITION

SHERIDAN BAKER

The University of Michigan

1817

HARPER & ROW, PUBLISHERS, New York

Cambridge, Hagerstown, Philadelphia, San Francisco,
London, Mexico City, São Paulo, Sydney

Sponsoring Editor: Phillip Leininger
Developmental Editor: Walter Brownfield
Project Editor: Robert Ginsberg
Designer: T.R. Funderburk
Production Manager: Marion Palen
Compositor: P & M Typesetters
Printer and Binder: Book Press

THE COMPLETE STYLIST AND HANDBOOK, Second Edition

Library of Congress Cataloging in Publication Data

Baker, Sheridan Warner.
    The complete stylist and handbook.

    Includes index.
    1. English language—Rhetoric.   I. Title.
PE1408.B283   1980   808'.042   79-17621
ISBN 0-06-040452-3

PREFACE

Since 1976, teachers and students in thousands of classrooms have tested *The Complete Stylist and Handbook*. Their suggestions, reinforcing my own experience, have prompted this second edition. My first edition was, of all things, too wordy! At least, it lingered too long on certain tangents, trying too hard to be complete. Now, the basic *Rhetoric* reduces 14 chapters to 12; the *Handbook*, 6 sections to 5, reorganizing for clarity and economy. I have refreshed everything. Though I have also added a number of examples and exercises—some poems in the "Literature" chapter, how to answer an essay question, how to describe a process, an analysis of a short story—you now have in sum a leaner and cleaner book, especially strengthened in the all-important early chapters on the practical problems that confront the beginning writer.

In the *Rhetoric*, I now move more rapidly, and, I think, more efficiently, from the search for a thesis into the essay's basic structure and on to the main rhetorical unit, the paragraph, in its three general manifestations—beginning, middle, and end. In Chapter 2, "Basic Structure," I have condensed the former full chapter on outlines—jotted, topic, and sentence—into an extension of the basic pro–con tactics I advocate for young writers. I had previously treated the varieties of middle paragraphs as both "orders" and "modes." Eliminating this overlap, reducing two chapters to one, now simplifies the presentation with no loss of substance (Chapter 4). Then I have moved up "Straight and Crooked Thinking: Handling the Evidence" as Chapter 5 to cap this speedier progression through the essay as a whole. I have also rewritten and reorganized the chapters on the research paper, unearthing from the back of the *Handbook* my former guide to the library and making it new, and setting up a new sample term paper as an improved working model. The whole section on research is as up to date as I can make it, with fuller examples of basic research, note-taking, and formal documentation.

But the basic approach, as in my short rhetoric, *The Practical Stylist*, remains the same, since, in almost two decades, it has proven itself fundamental. It stresses rhetoric as the art of communication and persuasion. It emphasizes argument as the quickest and clearest teacher of rhetorical principles. It begins with the two primal elements, inner idea and outer form, thesis and structure. It proceeds step by step with the progressively smaller and more powerful units—paragraphs, sentences, words. Then the rhetorical process culminates in "Writing About Literature," now thoroughly overhauled, and the research paper.

The *Handbook*, as before, begins with a short chapter on "The English Language," and covers grammar, spelling, punctuation, and usage, all newly considered. The *Handbook* reinforces chapters in the *Rhetoric*, offering material the teacher may integrate with assignments or assign separately and the student may use for constant and ready reference. In particular, I have reconsidered the comma, that key to meaning, now describing it in terms students have found clearer: the Introducer, the Coordinator, the Inserter, and the Linker. And I have amplified the treatment of those perpetual headaches, the run-on, the comma splice, and the fragment.

I have revised the *Instructor's Manual* to match, again adding possibilities for other angles and alternate uses and solutions for exercises, with new diagnostic tests to help set priorities for assignments.

The Complete Stylist and Handbook again strives to show the student how important writing is in coming to grips with our ideas and ourselves, to demonstrate that writing is really our only steady means of getting our thinking straight and clear. Throughout, I urge students to see that style is both personal and public, a matter of finding one's self in language— one's own personality written into reason and looking its best.

Sheridan Baker

CONTENTS

THE
RHETORIC

1 SUBJECT AND THESIS   3

THE STYLISTIC APPROACH   3
WHAT SHALL I WRITE?   4
WHERE ESSAYS FAIL   5
THE ARGUMENTATIVE EDGE   6
  Find your thesis. Sharpen your thesis. Use your title.
Exercises   9
  Believe in your thesis. Persuade your reader.
Exercises   12
ATTITUDE   13
  Don't take yourself too seriously. Consider your readers.
THE WRITTEN VOICE   15
  Make your writing talk.
Exercise   17
  Don't apologize. Consider your pronouns. Plan to rewrite.

A NOTE ON MECHANICS   23
A FIRST PAPER   24
Exercise   26

2 BASIC STRUCTURE   27

BEGINNING, MIDDLE, END   27
MIDDLE TACTICS   28
    Arrange your points in order of increasing interest.
Exercises   29

    Acknowledge and dispose of the opposition.
Exercises   33

    Run comparisons point by point.
Exercise   36

OUTLINING   37
    Begin your paper with a jotted outline. Outline your exam
    answers.
Exercises   40

    Proceed to the topic outline. Check your outline for
    balance. Refine with the sentence outline. Observe the
    basic rules of outlining.
Exercises   45

3 PARAGRAPHS: BEGINNING, MIDDLE, END   50

THE STANDARD PARAGRAPH   50
    Plan for the big paragraph.
BEGINNING PARAGRAPHS: THE FUNNEL   52
    State your thesis at the END of your beginning paragraph.
Exercises   55

MIDDLE PARAGRAPHS   55
    Make your middle paragraphs full, and use transitions.
    Check your paragraphs for clarity and coherence.
    Accustom yourself to the transitional tags. Lead your
    reader with specific details.

Exercises   63

END PARAGRAPHS: THE INVERTED FUNNEL   65
> Reassert your thesis.

Exercises   67

MORE ON MECHANICS, PARAGRAPHS, AND LONG
  QUOTATIONS   68

THE WHOLE ESSAY   69

Exercises   75

**4 PARAGRAPHS: DESCRIPTIVE, NARRATIVE,
   EXPOSITORY   76**

DESCRIPTIVE PARAGRAPHS   76
> Put your perceptions into words. Guide some descriptions
>   through time.

Exercises   80

NARRATIVE PARAGRAPHS   81
> Narrate to illustrate.   81

Exercises   83

EXPOSITORY PARAGRAPHS   86
> Develop most paragraphs by examples.

Exercises   87

> Cause and effect: trace back or look ahead.

Exercises   91

> Problem and solution: follow the natural order.

Exercises   93

> Comparison and contrast: run similarities side by side.

Exercises   96

> Comparison and contrast: develop differences point by
>   point.

Exercises   99

> Natural divisions: use the natural joints.

Exercises   101

> Describing a process: follow the natural steps.

Exercises   103

5 STRAIGHT AND CROOKED THINKING: HANDLING THE EVIDENCE   104

FACTS, AND DEGREES OF BELIEF   104
Write as close to the facts as possible. Believe what you write—but learn the nature of belief. Don't mistake opinion for fact. Dispute your preferences with care.
ASSUMPTIONS AND IMPLICATIONS   108
Check your statements, root and branch.
Exercises   109

DEFINITION   110
Clear up your terms. Try different kinds of definition. Cover all the angles. Beware of cracks in your logic.
Exercises   114

LOGICAL FALLACIES   115
Trust your common sense. Cite authorities reasonably.
Exercises   117

Handle persistences as you would authorities. Inspect your documentary evidence before using.
Exercises   120

INDUCTIVE FALLACIES   120
Keep your hypothesis hypothetical. Use analogies to clarify, not to prove. Look before you leap.
Exercises   123

DEDUCTIVE FALLACIES   124
Establish your premise. Check for the classic fallacies.
Exercises   125

THE INDUCTIVE ESSAY   125
Try some reverse English.
Exercises   127

THE DEDUCTIVE ESSAY   127
Hang your essay from your Big Idea.
Exercises   128

THE DEDUCTIVE-INDUCTIVE ESSAY   129
Try a question for a thesis.
Exercises   131

6 WRITING GOOD SENTENCES   134

THE SIMPLE SENTENCE   135
>Use the simple active sentence, loosely periodic.

Exercises   136

COMPOUND AND COMPLEX SENTENCES   137
>Learn the difference between compound and complex sentences. Avoid simple-minded compounds. Try compounding with semicolon and colon.

Exercises   140

>Learn to subordinate.

Exercises   143

>Try for still closer connections: modify.

Exercises   145

Exercises   149

Exercises   151

PARALLEL CONSTRUCTION   152
>Use parallels to strengthen equivalent ideas. Repeat your paralleling connectives. Watch the paralleling of pairs. Learn to use paralleling coordinators.

Exercises   157

THE LONG AND SHORT OF IT   159
>Experiment with the fragment. Develop a rhythm of long and short.

Exercises   162

7 CORRECTING WORDY SENTENCES   163

>Count your words.

Exercises   164

>Shun the passive voice.

Exercises   168

>Check the stretchers. Beware the of-and-which disease.

Exercises   171

>Beware "the use of." Break the noun habit.

Exercises 176

Give your writing warmth. Avoid excessive distinctions and
definitions.
Exercises 178

8 WORDS 181

WORDS AND THINGS 182

Learn the multiple meanings of words. Try a little punning.
Exercises 184

VOCABULARY 184

Build your vocabulary.
Exercises 187

ABSTRACT AND CONCRETE 188
Exercises 190

METAPHOR 191
Exercises 195

ALLUSION 196
Exercises 197

DICTION 197
Exercises 200

9 WRITING ABOUT LITERATURE 201

EXPLICATION 202
Exercises 206

STEPS AND QUESTIONS 208

To summarize, paraphrase. To search out style, imitate with
parody.
Exercises 211

Explain the metaphors.
Exercises 213

VERSIFICATION 215

Find the sound in poetry.

Exercises 217

> Determine the genre.

Exercises 219

THE NOVEL AND THE DRAMA   222

> Analyze titles, names, allusions. Look for symbols. Identify the written voice: point of view. Identify the written voice: tone and style. Determine the setting. Describe the plot. Distinguish plot and plotting. Characters: individuals or stereotypes? Analyze characterization. Describe the author's blend of narration and scene. Consider structure. Note the similarities and differences of drama and fiction.

Exercises 233

EVALUATION   235

> Evaluate firmly—reach a judgment. In criticism, write in the present tense. Describe and explain.

Exercises ("Evangelist," by Joyce Cary, with analysis)   **240**

10 BEGINNING RESEARCH: USING THE LIBRARY   245

CHOOSING YOUR SUBJECT   246

> Pick something that interests you. Find a thesis. Persuade your reader that you are right. Pick an argument.

ORGANIZING YOUR RESOURCES   248

> Getting around. Getting equipped. Analyze the problem. Distinguish your sources: primary, secondary, tertiary. Get acquainted with the tools. Follow a basic strategy.

Exercises 256

INSIDE THE SYSTEM   258

> Understand the machinery. Learn how libraries alphabetize.

Exercises 263

MAKING YOUR CARDS   263

> Take brief notes. Take care against plagiarism.

Exercises 269

11 WRITING THE RESEARCH PAPER 270

YOUR FIRST DRAFT 270
Plot your course. Outline more fully, if you wish. Put in your references as you go.
YOUR FINAL DRAFT 272
Reset your long quotations. Allow space for notes at the foot of the page. Make and punctuate your footnotes meticulously.
Exercises 279

Abbreviate your references after the first full citation.
Exercises 282

Abbreviate books of the Bible, even the first time. Abbreviate plays and long poems after the first time. Match your bibliography to your footnotes.
Exercises 285

12 THE FULL RESEARCH PAPER 287

THE
HANDBOOK

SECTION A THE ENGLISH LANGUAGE 307

THE INDO-EUROPEANS 308
THE ANGLO-SAXONS (449) 310
ANGLO-SAXON BORROWINGS 311
MIDDLE ENGLISH (1100–1500) 314
MODERN ENGLISH (1500 onward) 318
AMERICAN ENGLISH 320
Exercises 325

SECTION B   A WRITER'S GRAMMAR   330

GRAMMAR AS THERAPY   330
GRAMMAR AS MEANING   331
> Know the basic parts of speech.

SENTENCES   335
> Learn to identify the simple subject and its verb. Know the structure—and modifications—of the simple sentence.

Exercises   338

SUBJECTS   338
> Avoid awkward changes of subject in midsentence. Avoid illogical shifts in person and number.

Exercises   340

VERBS   340
> Keep your verb and its subject in agreement. Use the tense that best expresses your idea. Avoid unnecessary shifts in tense, voice, and mood. Master the tenses of the troublesome verbs.

Exercises   349

PRONOUNS AS SUBJECTS AND OBJECTS   350
> Match a pronoun's form to its function. Use subjective pronouns for subjective functions. Use objective pronouns for objective functions. Use a subjective pronoun for the subject of a noun clause. Use the possessive pronoun before a gerund.

Exercises   355

PRONOUNS AND THEIR ANTECEDENTS   356
> Keep your antecedents specific, unambiguous, and close at hand. With an indefinite antecedent, use a singular pronoun.

Exercises   358

MODIFIERS MISUSED AND MISPLACED 359
Learn the difference between adjectives and adverbs. Put your modifiers where their meaning is clear. Make your comparisons complete.
Exercises 362

DANGLING VERBAL CONSTRUCTIONS 363
Connect a modifier clearly to what it modifies.
Exercises 364

SECTION C PUNCTUATING THE SENTENCE 366

THE COMMA 366
The INTRODUCER, the COORDINATOR, the INSERTER, the LINKER.
Exercises 368

Exercises 370

Exercises 373

Exercises 375

FRAGMENTS, COMMA SPLICES, AND RUN-ONS 375
Beware the comma splice, and the run-on.
Exercises 379

THE SEMICOLON 381
Use the semicolon as a coordinator only where you could also use a period, unless desperate.
Exercises 383

THE COLON 384
Use a colon as a green light, or arrow. Use the colon to introduce quotations.
Exercises 385

THE PERIOD 386
Use a period after an indirect question. Use a period after a polite command or request; use exclamations sparingly.

Exercises 387

PARENTHESIS AND DASH   388
Exercises 390

BRACKETS   390
Exercises 391

QUOTATION MARKS AND ITALICS   391
Exercises 397

ELLIPSIS   394
Exercises 397

SECTION D   **SPELLING, WORD-PUNCTUATION,
CAPITALIZATION   398**

SPELLING IT OUT   398
Exercises 405

APOSTROPHE   406
Exercises 408

Exercises 409

HYPHEN   409
Exercises 411

VIRGULE   412
DIACRITICAL MARKS   412
NUMBERS   413
ABBREVIATIONS   414
Exercises 416

PROBLEMS IN CAPITALIZATION   417
Exercises 419

SECTION E   **USAGE   421**

A GLOSSARY OF USAGE AND COMMON
ERRORS   424

INDEX   481

THE
RHETORIC

Chapter 1

SUBJECT AND THESIS

THE STYLISTIC APPROACH

Style in writing is something like style in a car, a gown, or a Greek temple—the ordinary materials of this world nicely aligned, standing out from the daily scene, compelling a second look. Your materials are our daily language. But your own voice outlines your style, and then your writing smoothes its alignment. Your writing chips out all the uncertainties, all the hems and haws and "you knows" of talk. Your written page seems to speak the common language uncommonly well.

That is the style to aim for: your spoken voice at its best, your best thoughts well said. It requires something of the craftsman in you, as you discover the knots and potentials in your material and come to like words as some people like polished wood or stones. You may even learn to enjoy phrasing and syntax, and the very punctuation that keeps them straight, since writing well is a labor of love, and like love it can bring unexpected pleasure and satisfaction.

Style is not for the gifted only. Quite the contrary. Everyone, indeed, already has a style, and a personality, and can develop both. The stylistic side of writing is, in fact, the only side that can be analyzed and learned. The stylistic approach is the practical approach: you learn some things to do and not to do, as you would learn strokes in tennis. Your ultimate game is up to you, but you can at least begin in good form. Naturally, it takes practice. You have to keep at it. Like the doctor and the lawyer and the golfer and the tennis player, you just keep practicing—even to write a practically perfect letter. But if you like the game, you can probably learn to play it well. You will at least be able to write a respectable sentence, and to express your thoughts clearly, without puffing and flailing.

In the essay, as in business, trying to get started and getting off on the wrong foot account for most of our lost motion. So you will start by learning how to find a thesis, which will virtually organize your essay for you. Next, you will study the relatively simple structure of the essay, and the structure of the paragraph—the architecture of spatial styling. Then, for exercise, you will experiment with various styles of sentence, playing with length and complexity. And finally you will get down to words themselves. Here is where writing tells; and here, as in ancient times, you will be in touch with the mystery. But again, there are things to do and things not to do, and these can be learned. So, to begin.

WHAT SHALL I WRITE?

First you need a subject, and then you need a thesis. Yes, but *what shall I write?* That is the question, persisting from the first Christmas thank-you letter down to this very night. Here you are, an assignment due and the paper as blank as your mind. The Christmas letter may give us a clue. Your mother probably told you, as mine did, to write about what you had been doing. Almost anything would do—Cub Scouts, Brownies, the birthday party, skating—so long as you had been doing it. As you wrote, it grew interesting all over again. Finding a mature subject is no different: look for something you have experienced, or thought about. The more it matters to you, the more you can make it matter to your readers. It might be skiing. It might be dress. It might be roommates, the Peloponnesian War, a political protest, a personal discovery of racial tensions, an experience as a nurse's aide. But do not tackle a big philosophical abstraction, like Freedom, or a big subject, like the Supreme Court. They are too vast, your time and space and knowledge all too small. You would probably manage no more than a collection of platitudes. Start rather with something specific, like baby-sitting, and let the ideas of freedom and justice and responsibility arise from there. An abstract idea is a poor beginning. To be sure, as you move ahead through your course in writing, you will work more directly with ideas, with problems posed by literature, with questions in the great civilizing debate about what we are doing in this strange world and universe. But again, look for something within your concern. The best subjects lie nearest at hand, and nearest the heart.

Suppose we start simply with "The Teen-Ager." That, in the recent past, is certainly close enough. Moreover, it will illustrate admirably how to generalize from your own experience, and how to cut your subject down to manageable size. Your first impulse might be to describe the temptations of theft, or drugs, or first cars, and the realities of breaking the law. Were you to write this in the first person, it might be amusing, especially to your acquaintances and friends. But it would remain merely personal; it would still lack an important ingredient of adulthood. You would still be working in that bright, self-centered spotlight of consciousness in which we live before we really begin to grow up, in which the child assumes that all his experiences are unique. If you shift from "me" to "the teen-ager," however, you will be stepping into maturity: acknowledging that others have gone through exactly the same thing, that your particular experiences have illustrated once again the general dynamics of youth and the group. So you will write not "I was afraid to say anything" but:

> **The teen-ager fears going against the group more than death itself. When the speedometer hits 100, silence is the rule, though the heart is screaming in every throat.**

By generalizing your private feelings, you change your subject into a thesis. You simply assume you are normal and fairly representative, and you then generalize with confidence, transposing your particular experiences, your particular thoughts and reactions, into statements about the general ways of the world. You might want to sharpen your statement a little more, as you turn your subject into a thesis, asserting something like: "The thrilling high-speed ride, if survived, will probably open the teen-ager's eyes to the dynamics of the group." Put your proposition into one sentence. This will get you focused. And now you are ready to begin.

WHERE ESSAYS FAIL

You can usually blame a bad essay on a bad beginning. If your essay falls apart, it probably has no primary idea to hold it together. "What's the big idea?" we used to ask. The phrase will serve as a reminder that you must find the "big idea" behind your several smaller thoughts and musings before you start to write. In the beginning was the _logos,_ says the Bible—

the idea, the plan, caught in a flash as if in a single word. Find your *logos,* and you are ready to round out your essay and set it spinning.

The big idea behind our ride in the speeding car was that in adolescence, especially, the group can have a very deadly influence on the individual. If you had not focused your big idea in a thesis, you might have begun by picking up thoughts at random, something like this:

> **Everyone thinks he is a good driver. There are more accidents caused by young drivers than any other group. Driver education is a good beginning, but further practice is very necessary. People who object to driver education do not realize that modern society, with its suburban pattern of growth, is built around the automobile. The car becomes a way of life and a status symbol. When teen-agers go too fast they are probably only copying their own parents.**

A little reconsideration, aimed at a good thesis-sentence, could turn this into a reasonably good opening paragraph, with your thesis, your big idea, asserted at the end to focus your reader's attention:

> **Modern society is built on the automobile. Children play with tiny cars; teen-agers long to take out the car alone. Soon they are testing their skills at higher and higher speeds, especially with a group of friends along. One final test at extreme speeds usually suffices. It is usually a sobering experience, if survived, and can open one's eyes to the deadly dynamics of the group.**

Thus the central idea, or thesis, is your essay's life and spirit. If your thesis is sufficiently firm and clear, it may tell you immediately how to organize your supporting material. But if you do not find a thesis, your essay will be a tour through the miscellaneous. An essay replete with scaffolds and catwalks—"We have just seen this; now let us turn to this"— is an essay in which the inherent idea is weak or nonexistent. A purely expository and descriptive essay, one simply about "Cats," for instance, will have to rely on outer scaffolding alone (some orderly progression from Persia to Siam) since it really has no idea at all. It is all subject, all cats, instead of being based on an idea *about* cats, with a thesis *about* cats.

THE ARGUMENTATIVE EDGE

Find your thesis.

The *about*-ness puts an argumentative edge on the subject. When you have something to say *about* cats, you have found your underlying idea. You have something to defend, something to fight about: not just "Cats," but "The cat is really a person's best friend." Now the hackles on all dog people are rising, and you have an argument on your hands. You have something to prove. You have a thesis.

"What's the big idea, Mac?" Let the impudence in that time-honored demand remind you that the most dynamic thesis is a kind of affront to somebody. No one will be very much interested in listening to you deplete the thesis "The dog is a person's best friend." Everyone knows that already. Even the dog lovers will be uninterested, convinced they know better than you. But the cat. . . .

So it is with any unpopular idea. The more unpopular the viewpoint and the stronger the push against convention, the stronger the thesis and the more energetic the essay. Compare the energy in "Democracy is good" with that in "Communism is good," for instance. The first is filled with platitudes, the second with plutonium. By the same token, if you can find the real energy in "Democracy is good," if you can get down through the sand to where the roots and water are, you will have a real essay, because the opposition against which you generate your energy is the heaviest in the world: boredom. Probably the most energetic thesis of all, the greatest inner organizer, is some tired old truth that you cause to spurt with new life, making the old ground green again.

To find a thesis and to put it into one sentence is to narrow and define your subject to a workable size. Under "Cats" you must deal with all felinity from the jungle up, carefully partitioning the eons and areas, the tigers and tabbies, the sizes and shapes. The minute you proclaim the cat the friend of humanity, you have pared away whole categories and chapters, and need only think up the arguments sufficient to overwhelm the opposition. So, put an argumentative edge on your subject—and you will have found your thesis.

Simple exposition, to be sure, has its uses. You may want to tell someone how to build a doghouse, how to can asparagus, how to follow the outlines of relativity, or even how to write an essay. Performing a few exercises in simple exposition will no doubt sharpen your insight into the problems of finding orderly sequences, of considering how best to lead your readers through the hoops of writing clearly and accurately. It will also illustrate how much finer and surer an argument is.

You will see that picking an argument immediately simplifies the problems so troublesome in straight exposition: the defining, the partitioning, the narrowing of the subject. Not that you must be constantly pugnacious or aggressive. I have overstated my point to make it stick. Actually, you can put an argumentative edge on the flattest of expository subjects. "How to build a doghouse" might become "Building a doghouse is a thorough introduction to the building trades, including architecture and mechanical engineering." "Canning asparagus" might become "An asparagus patch is a course in economics." "Relativity" might become "Relativity is not so inscrutable as many suppose." Literary subjects take an argumentative edge almost by nature. You simply assert what the essential point of a poem or play seems to be: "*Hamlet* is essentially about a world that has lost its values." You assume that your readers are in search of clarity, that you have a loyal opposition consisting of the interested but uninformed. You have given your subject its edge; you have limited and organized it at a single stroke. Pick an *argument*, then, and you will automatically be defining and narrowing your subject, and all the partitions you don't need will fold up. Instead of dealing with things, subjects, and pieces of subjects, you will be dealing with an idea and its consequences.

Sharpen your thesis.

Come out with your subject pointed. Take a stand, make a judgment of value, make a *thesis*. Be reasonable, but don't be timid. It is helpful to think of your thesis, your main idea, as a debating question—"Resolved: Welfare payments must go"—taking out the "Resolved" when you actually write your thesis down. But your resolution will be even stronger, your essay clearer and tighter, if you can sharpen your thesis even further—"Resolved: Welfare payments must go because————." Fill in that blank, and your worries are practically over. The main idea is to put your whole argument into one sentence.

Try, for instance: "Welfare payments must go because they are making people irresponsible." I don't know at all if that is true, and neither will you until you write your way into it, considering probabilities and alternatives and objections, and especially the underlying assumptions. In fact, no one, no master sociologist or future historian, can tell absolutely if it is true, so multiplex are the causes in human affairs, so endless and tangled the consequences. The basic assumption—that irresponsibility is growing—may be entirely false. No one, I repeat, can tell absolutely. But by the same token, your guess may be as good as another's. At any rate, you are now ready to write. You have found your *logos*.

Now you can put your well-pointed thesis-sentence on a card on the wall in front of you to keep from drifting off target. But you will now want to dress it for the public, to burnish it and make it comely. Suppose you try:

Welfare payments, perhaps more than anything else, are eroding personal initiative.

But is this fully true? Perhaps you had better try something like:

Despite their immediate benefits, welfare payments may actually be eroding personal initiative and depriving society of needed workers.

This is your full thesis, and you can write that down on a scrap of paper too.

Use your title.

After your thesis, think of a title. A good title focuses your thinking even more sharply and catches your reader's thoughts on your finished paper. Your title is your opening opportunity. It is an integral part of your paper. Don't forget it.

Work up something from your thesis. It will be tentative, of course. Your thinking and your paper may change in the writing, and you will want to change your title to match. But a good title, like a good thesis, has a double advantage: (1) it helps you keep on track as you write; (2) it attracts and helps keep your reader on track as he reads. It is the first step in your persuasion. So try something attractive:

Welfare Not Warfare

Farewell to Welfare

Whom Does Welfare Benefit?

You can probably do better. You will do better when you finish your paper. But don't forget your title as a starter, both for your writing and for your written paper. Capitalize all significant words (see pp. 417–418 for details). Titles do not take periods, but do take question and exclamation marks if you need them.

EXERCISES

1. *Below I have listed a series of subjects about which you might write. Transform each into an assertion, a thesis. Start by trying to transform some of the subjects into debating propositions. For example, "Welfare payments" becomes, "Resolved: Welfare payments must go." Having done that, you might take it a step further by supplying a reason. For example, "Resolved: Welfare payments* *must go because they are sapping people's initiative." Now you have a clear thesis, although it may be a bit mechanical in form. All that remains is to dress it up for public appearance. "Welfare payments, perhaps more than anything else, are eroding personal initiative and destroying the work-instinct." Supply a thesis statement and a title for each of the following subjects:*

1. Abortion laws
2. The appearance of our campus
3. Student housing
4. Weight-lifting
5. Five-mile, cross-country run
6. Modern aristocracy
7. A novel you have read. For example, Joseph Heller's *Catch-22*
8. Unequal distribution of blacks and whites in occupational groups
9. Half-day sessions in elementary schools
10. The tourist trade

2. *The following sentences are all thesis statements taken from actual students' papers. As you can see, the authors did not spot the built-in weaknesses. Explain what, if anything, you think wrong with each of these as thesis-statements. Then revise them as best you can.*

1. I think we should all insist on the retention of the present abortion laws.
2. The campus of———University (College) is unique in many ways.
3. With the increasing enrollment at this university (and with the larger number of married students) steps need to be taken to increase student housing.
4. From experience, I would believe that weight-lifting can be helpful to a growing young man in more ways than one.
5. The five-mile, cross-country run is one of the most challenging of track events. It requires speed, endurance, and strategy.
6. No matter how it used to be in this country, we have an aristocracy of money now.
7. Joseph Heller's *Catch-22* is not great literature. Indeed, the book is not really a novel at all; it is just a series of little stories.
8. I believe, and will try to show, that the unequal distribution of blacks and whites in occupational groups revealed in the last Census is the result of two problems: inferior education for blacks and discriminatory hiring by white employers.
9. Could half-day sessions in elementary schools provide the same quality of education as provided by full-day sessions?
10. The tourist trade is good for people.

Believe in your thesis.

Notice how your assertion about welfare mellowed as you revised. And not because you have resorted to cheap tactics, though tactics may get you to the same place, but rather because you brought it under critical inspection, asking what is true in it: what can (and cannot) be assumed true, what can (and cannot) be proved true. And you have asked yourself where you stand.

You should, indeed, look for a thesis you believe in, something you can even get enthusiastic about. Arguing on both sides of a question, as debaters do, is no doubt good exercise, if one can stand it. It breaks up old ground and uncovers what you can and do believe, at least for the moment. But the argument without the belief will be hollow. You can hardly persuade anyone if you can't persuade yourself. So begin with what you believe, and explore its validities.

Conversely, you must test your belief with all the objections you can think of, just as you have already tested your first proposition about welfare payments. First, you have acknowledged the most evident objection—that the opposition's view must have some merit—by starting your final version with "Despite their immediate benefits . . . ." Second, you have gone a little deeper by seeing that in your bold previous version you had, with the words *are eroding,* begged the question of whether responsibility is in fact undergoing erosion; that is, you had silently assumed that responsibility *is* being eroded. This is one of the oldest fallacies and tricks of logic. To "beg the question," by error or intent, is to take for granted that which the opposition has not granted, to assume as already proved that which is yet to be proved. But you have saved yourself. You have changed *are eroding* to *may be eroding.* You have gone farther in deleting the *perhaps more than anything else.* You have come closer to the truth.

You may wonder if it is not astoundingly presumptuous to go around stating theses before you have studied your subject from all angles, made several house-to-house surveys, and read everything ever written. A natural uncertainty and feeling of ignorance, and a misunderstanding of what truth is, can well inhibit you from finding a thesis. But no one knows everything. No one would write anything if he waited until he did. To a great extent, the writing of a thing is the learning of it—the discovery of truth.

So, first, make a desperate thesis and get into the arena. This is probably solution enough. If it becomes increasingly clear that your thesis is untrue, no matter how hard you push it, turn it around and use the other end. If your convictions have begun to falter with:

> **Despite their immediate benefits, welfare payments undermine initiative. . . .**

try it the other way around, with something like:

> **Although welfare payments may offend the rugged individualist, they relieve much want and anxiety, and they enable many a fatherless family to maintain its integrity.**

You will now have a beautiful command of the major objections to your new position. And you will have learned something about human fallibility and the nature of truth.

Persuade your reader.

Once you believe in your proposition, you will discover that proving it is really a venture in persuasion. *Rhetoric* is, in fact, the art of persuasion, of moving the reader to your belief. You have made a thesis, a hypothesis really—an opinion as to what the truth seems to be from where you stand, with the information you have. Belief has an unfolding energy. Write what you believe. You may be wrong, of course, but you will probably discover this as you probe for reasons, and can then reverse your thesis, pointed with your new conviction. The truth remains true, and you must at least glimpse it before you can begin to persuade others to see it. So follow your convictions, and think up reasons to convince your reader. Give him enough evidence to persuade him that what you say is probably true; find arguments that will stand up in the marketplace and survive the public haggle. You must find public reasons for your private convictions.

EXERCISES

3. *Look over the thesis-statements you devised in Exercise 1. Which is most likely to have the reader nodding in agreement even before he finishes the sentence? And which of your thesis-statements seems to be most interesting and exciting? Which seems to have the best argumentative edge? After having identified the most interesting and the least interesting of your thesis-statements, briefly explain what you think generates the greater interest in the one than in the other. The topics themselves? Your interest in the topics? The way you have stated the thesis? Try to be as specific as possible.*

ATTITUDE

Writing well is a matter of conviction. You learn in school by exercises, of course; and exercises are best when taken as such, as body-builders, flexions and extensions for the real contests ahead. But when you are convinced that what you write has meaning, that it has meaning for you—and not in a lukewarm, hypothetical way, but truly—then your writing will stretch its wings and have the whole wide world in range. For writing is simply a graceful and articulate extension of the best that is in you. Writing well is not easy. It does not come naturally, though your natural endowments will certainly help. It takes unending practice, each essay a polished exercise for the next to come, each new trial, as T. S. Eliot says, a new "raid on the inarticulate."

In writing, you clarify your own thoughts. Indeed, you probably grasp them for the first time. Writing is thinking. The process of writing not merely transcribes but actually creates thought, and generates your ability to think. Through writing, you discover thoughts you hardly knew you had; through writing, you come to know what it is that you know. All kinds of forgotten impressions, lost facts, and surprising updrafts of words and knowledge support your flight. As you test your thoughts against their opposites, as you answer the questions rising in your mind, your conviction grows. You learn as you write. In the end, after you have rewritten and rearranged for your best rhetorical effectiveness, your words will carry your readers with you to see as you see, to believe as you believe, to understand your subject as you now understand it.

Don't take yourself too seriously.

Take your subject seriously—if it is a serious subject—but take yourself with a grain of salt. Your attitude is the very center of your prose. If you take yourself too importantly, your tone will go hollow, your sentences will go moldy, your page will go fuzzy with *of's* and *which's* and nouns clustered densely in passive constructions. In your academic career, the worst dangers lie immediately ahead. Freshmen usually learn to write tolerably well, but from the sophomore to the senior year the academic damp frequently sets in, and by graduate school you can often cut the gray mold with a cheese knife.

You must constantly guard against acquiring the heavy, sober-sided attitude that makes for wordiness and its attendant vices of obscurity, dullness, and anonymity. Do not lose your personality and your voice in the monotone of official prose. You should work like a scholar and scientist, but you should write like a writer, one who cares about the economy and beauty of language, and has some individual personality. Your attitude, then, should form somewhere between a confidence in your own convictions and a humorous distrust of your own rhetoric, which can so easily carry you away. You should bear yourself as a member of humankind, knowing that we are all sinners, all redundant, and all too fond of big words. Here is an example from—I blush to admit—the pen of a professor:

> The general problem is perhaps correctly stated as inadequacy of nursing personnel to meet demands for nursing care and services. Inadequacy, it should be noted, is both a quantitative and qualitative term and thus it can be assumed that the problem as stated could indicate insufficient numbers of nursing personnel to meet existing demands for their services; deficiencies in the competencies of those who engage in the various fields of nursing; or both.

Too few good nurses, and a badly swollen author—that is the problem. "Nursing personnel" may mean nurses, but it also may mean "the nursing of employees," so that the author seems to say, for a wildly illogical moment, that someone is not properly pampering or suckling people for the necessary services. Notice the misfiring *it* (fourth line of quotation), which seems to refer to *term* but actually refers to nothing. And the ponderous jingle of "deficiencies in the competencies" would nearly do for a musical comedy. The author is taking herself too seriously and taking her readers almost nowhere.

Consider your readers.

If you are to take your subject with all the seriousness it deserves and yourself with as much skeptical humor as you can bear, how are you to take your readers? Who are they, anyway? Hypothetically, your vocabulary and your tone would vary all the way from Skid Row to Oxford as you turn from social work to Rhodes scholarship; and certainly the difference of audience would reflect itself somewhat in your language. Furthermore, you must indeed sense your audience's capacity, its susceptibilities and prejudices, if you are to win even a hearing. No doubt our language skids a bit when down on the Row, and we certainly speak different tongues with our friends, and with the friends of our parents.

But the notion of adjusting your writing to a whole scale of audiences, though attractive in theory, hardly works out in practice. You are *writing,*

and the written word presupposes a literate norm that immediately eliminates all the lower ranges of mere talk. Even when you speak, you do
not so lose your identity as to pass for a total illiterate. You stand on your
own linguistic feet, in your own linguistic personality, and the only adjustment you should assiduously practice in your writing, and in your
speaking as well, is the upward one toward verbal adulthood, a slight
grammatical tightening and rhetorical heightening to make your thoughts
clear, emphatic, and attractive.

Consider your audience a mixed group of intelligent and reasonable
adults. You want them to think of you as well informed and well educated.
You wish to explain what you know and what you believe. You wish to
persuade them pleasantly that what you know is important and what you
believe is right. Try to imagine what they might ask you, what they might
object to, what they might know already, what they might find interesting.
Be simple and clear, amusing and profound, using plenty of illustration
to show what you mean. *But do not talk down to them.* That is the great
flaw in the slumming theory of communication. Bowing to your readers'
supposed level, you insult them by assuming their inferiority. Thinking
yourself humble, you are actually haughty. The best solution is simply to
assume that your readers are as intelligent as you. Even if they are not,
they will be flattered by the assumption. Your written language, in short,
will be respectful toward your subject, considerate toward your readers,
and somehow amiable toward human failings.

THE WRITTEN VOICE

Make your writing talk.

That the silent page should seem to speak with the writer's voice is
remarkable. With all gestures gone, no eyes to twinkle, no notation at all
for the rise and fall of utterance, and only a handful of punctuation marks,
the level line of type can yet convey the writer's voice, the tone of his
personality.

To achieve this tone, to find your own voice and style, simply try
to write in the language of intelligent conversation, cleared of all the stum-
bles and weavings of talk. Indeed, our speech, like thought, is amazingly
circular. We can hardly think in a straight line if we try. We think by
questions and answers, repetitions and failures; and our speech, full of
you know's and *I mean*'s, follows the erratic ways of the mind, circling
around and around as we stitch the simplest of logical sequences. Your

writing will carry the stitches, not the loopings and pauses and rethreadings. It should be literate. It should be broad enough of vocabulary and rich enough of sentence to show that you have read a book. It should not be altogether unworthy to place you in the company of those who have written well in your native tongue. But it should nevertheless retain the tone of intelligent and agreeable conversation. It should be alive with a human personality—yours—which is probably the most persuasive rhetorical force on earth. Good writing should have a voice, and the voice should be unmistakably your own.

Suppose your spoken voice sounded something like this (I reconstruct an actual response in one of my classes):

> Well, I don't know, I like Shakespeare really, I guess—I mean, well, like when Lear divides up his kingdom like a fairy tale or something, I thought that was kind of silly, dividing his kingdom. Anyone could see that was silly if you wanted to keep your kingdom, why divide it? But then like, something begins to happen, like a real family, I mean. Cordelia really gets griped at her older sisters, I mean, like all older sisters, if you've ever had any. There's a kind of sibling rivalry, you know. Then she's kind of griped at her father, who she really loves, but she thinks, I mean, like saying it right out spoils it. You can't really speak right out, I mean, about love, well, except sometimes, I guess, without sounding corny.

Your written voice might then emerge from this with something of the same tone, but with everything straightened out, filled in, and polished up:

> The play begins like a fairy tale. It even seems at first a little abstract and silly. A king has three daughters. The two elder ones are bad; the youngest is good. The king wishes to keep his kingdom in peace, and keep his title as king, by dividing his kingdom in a senseless and almost empty ceremonial way. But very soon the play seems like real life. The family seems real, complete with sibling rivalry. It is the king, not the play, who is foolish and senile. The older daughters are hypocrites. Cordelia, the youngest, is irritated at them, and at her father's foolishness. As a result, she remains silent, not only because she is irritated at the flattering words of her sisters, but because anything she could say about her real love for her father would now sound false.

You might wish to polish that some more. You might indeed have said it another way, one more truly your own. The point, however, is to write in a tidy, economical way that wipes up the lapses of talk and fills in the gaps of thought, and yet keeps the tone and movement of good conversation, in your own voice.

EXERCISES

4. *To find your own modern voice, translate the following passage from Walton's* The Compleat Angler* *(1653) into modern English and your own idiom. Try to say as economically and accurately as possible what he is saying, as if you were talking to, or writing to, one of your own contemporaries.*

The Chub, though he eat well thus dressed, yet as he is usually dressed he does not: he is objected against, not only for being full of small forked bones, dispersed through all his body, but that he eats waterish, and that the flesh of him is not firm; but short and tasteless. The French esteem him so mean, as to call him *un Vilain;* nevertheless he may be so dressed as to make him very good meat: as, namely, if he be a large Chub, then dress him thus:—

First scale him, and then wash him clean, and then take out his guts; and to that end make the hole as little and near to his gills as you may conveniently, and especially make clean his throat from the grass and weeds that are usually in it, for if that be not very clean, it will make him to taste very sour. Having so done, put some sweet herbs into his belly; and then tie him with two or three splinters to a spit, and roast him, basted often with vinegar, or rather verjuice and butter, with good store of salt mixed with it.

Being thus dressed, you will find him a much better dish of meat than you, or most folk, even than Anglers themselves, do imagine; for this dries up the fluid watery humor with which all Chubs do abound.

But take this rule with you, that a Chub newly taken and newly dressed is so much better than a Chub of a day's keeping after he is dead, that I can compare him to nothing so fitly as to cherries newly gathered from a tree, and others that have been bruised and lain a day or two in water. But the Chub being thus used and dressed presently, and not washed after he is gutted,—for note, that, lying long in water, and washing the blood out of any

*Izaak Walton and Charles Cotton, *The Compleat Angler, or The Contemplative Man's Recreation,* ed. James Russell Lowell (Boston; Little, Brown, and Company, 1889), pp. 66–67.

fish after they be gutted, abates much of their sweetness,—you will find the Chub, being dressed in the blood and quickly, to be such meat as will recompense your labor and disabuse your opinion.

Don't apologize.

"In my opinion," the beginner will write repeatedly, until he seems to be saying "It is only *my* opinion, after all, so it can't be worth much." He has failed to realize that his whole essay represents his opinion—of what the truth of the matter is. Don't make your essay a personal letter to Diary, or to Mother, or to Teacher, a confidential report of what happened to you last night as you agonized upon a certain question. "*To me*, Robert Frost is a great poet"—this is really writing about yourself. You are only confessing private convictions. To find the "public reasons" often requires no more than a trick of grammar: a shift from "*To me*, Robert Frost is . . ." to "Robert Frost is . . .," from "*I thought* the book was good" to "The book is good," from you and your room last night to your subject and what it *is*. The grammatical shift represents a whole change of viewpoint, a shift from self to subject. You become the informed adult, showing the reader around firmly, politely, and persuasively.

Once you have effaced yourself from your thesis, once you have erased *to me* and *in my opinion* and all such signs of amateur terror, you may later let yourself back into the essay for emphasis or graciousness: "Mr. Watson errs, I think, precisely at this point." You can thus ease your most tentative or violent assertions, and show that you are polite and sensible, reasonably sure of your position but aware of the possibility of error. Again: the reasonable adult.

You go easy on the *I*, in short, to keep your reader focused on your subject. But you can use the *I* as much as you like to *illustrate* your thesis, once established, using a personal experience among several other pieces of evidence, or even all by itself. Take, for instance, the thesis "The thrilling high-speed ride, if survived, will probably open the teen-ager's eyes to the dynamics of the group." You could then write all the rest of your essay illustrating that thesis with a personal anecdote, beginning your second paragraph with "Once three friends and I borrowed my dad's car to go to a drive-in." This is the point: use the *I* to *illustrate,* or for rhetorical politeness, but not to apologize or to limit your subject to yourself alone. *Generalize* your opinions and emotions. Change "I cried" to "The book is very moving." But your personal happenings can nicely illustrate your thesis with an immediate and specific example.

Consider your pronouns.

Effacing the *I*, then letting it back in on occasion, fixes your point of view. But what about the other pronouns, *we, you, one*? *One* objectifies the personal *I*, properly generalizing the private into the public. But it can seem too formal, and get too thick:

> FAULTY: **One** finds **one's** opinion changing as **one** grows older.
> REVISED: **Opinions change with age.**
> REVISED: **Our** opinions change as **we** grow older.

That *we* is sometimes a useful generalizer, a convenient haven between the isolating *I* and the impersonal *one*. *We* can seem pompous, but not if it honestly handles those experiences we know we share, or can share. Suppose we wrote:

> **As I watched program after program, I got bored and began to wonder what values, if any, they represented.**

We can easily transpose this to:

> **As *we* watched program after program, *we* are progressively bored, and *we* begin to wonder what values, if any, they represent.**

Thus, *we* can generalize without going all the way to *one,* or to the fully objective:

> **Program after program. TV bores its audiences and leaves its sense of values questionable.**

We also quite naturally refers to earlier parts of your demonstration, through which you have led your reader: *as we have already seen.* But you will have noticed from the preceding examples that *we* tends slightly toward wordiness. Used sparingly, then, *we* can ease your formality and draw your reader in. Overused, it can seem too presumptuous or chummy. Try it out. See how it feels, and use it where it seems comfortable and right.

You raises two different problems. The first is the one we have been discussing: how to generalize that *I* effectively into something else, either *one* or *we* or full objectivity. The indefinite *you*, like the indefinite *they,* is usually too vague, and too adolescent.

> FAULTY: **You have your own opinion.**
> FAULTY: **They have their own opinion.**

REVISED: **Everyone has his own opinion.**
REVISED: **We all have our own opinions.**

You as direct address to the reader poses a different problem. I have consistently addressed this book to *you,* the reader. But this is a special case, the relationship of tutor to student projected onto the page. None of my essays, I think, contains any *you* at all. Our stance in an essay is a little more formal, a little more public. We are better holding our pronouns to *one* or *we,* an occasional *I,* or none at all, as we find a comfortable stance between our subject and audience, and find our written voice.

Plan to rewrite.

As you write your weekly assignments and find your voice, you will also be learning to groom your thoughts, to present them clearly and fully, to make sure you have said what you thought you said. Good writing comes only from *rewriting.* Even your happy thoughts will need resetting, as you join them to the frequently happier ones that a second look seems to call up. Even the letter-perfect paper will improve almost of itself if you simply sit down to type it through again. You will find, almost unbidden, sharper words, better phrases, new figures of speech, and new illustrations and ideas to replace the weedy patches not noticed before.

Allow yourself time for revision. After you have settled on something to write about, plan for at least three drafts—and try to manage four. Thinking of things to say is the hardest part at first. Even a short assignment of 500 words seems to stretch ahead like a Sahara. You have asserted your central idea in a sentence, and that leaves 490 words to go. But if you step off boldly, one foot after the other, you will make progress, find an oasis or two, and perhaps end at a run in green pastures. With longer papers, you will want some kind of outline to keep you from straying, but the principle is the same: step ahead and keep moving until you've arrived. That is the first draft.

The second draft is a penciled correction of the first. Of course, if the first has been really haphazard, you will probably want to type it again, rearranging, dropping a few things, adding others, before you can do much detailed work with a pencil. But the second, or penciled, draft is where you refine and polish, checking your dubious spellings in the dictionary, sharpening your punctuation, clarifying your meaning, pruning away the deadwood, adding a thought here, extending an illustration there—running in a whole new paragraph on an inserted page. You will also be tuning your sentences, carefully adjusting your tone until it is clearly that of an intelligent, reasonable person at ease with his knowledge and his audience.

Here is my penciled draft of the paragraph above, as it appeared on my first typescript:

```
                                  ed correction              Of course,
    The second is a penciling of the first.∧ if

the first has been really haphazard, you will prob-
                                                 a few
ably want to type it again, rearranging, dropping, or
things, adding others,
 filling out, before you can do much detailed work
                                                ed
with a pencil.  But the second, or pencil, draft is
                                    dubious      3 in a dictionary
where you refine and polish, checking your spelling,
                                   clarifying
sharpening your punctuation, clearing up your mean-
             pruning away
ing, clearing out the deadwood, adding a thought
             illustration            perhaps
here, extending an explanation there--you may need
       using
 arrows leading you to the back of the page to write a

whole new paragraph.  You will also be tuning your
              carefully adjusting        until it is clearly
sentences, sophisticating your tone into that of the

intelligent, reasonable person perfectly at ease with

his knowledge and his audience.
```

Your third draft is a smoothing of all this for public appearance. Still other illustrations and better phrases will suggest themselves as you get your penciled corrections into order. My penciled paragraph, above, stood up unusually well. I chose it as an example of revision, in fact, because most of my other paragraphs are so crisscrossed and scarred, draft after draft, that their evolution would be too complicated to represent in any practical way. For a classroom paper, three drafts, with several rereadings of the first and the second, are usually adequate. But, if you have time, a fourth draft will do no harm. Reading aloud will frequently pick up errors, lapses in punctuation, and infelicities of phrase. You may have to retype a page of your most polished draft, as a brilliant idea hits you at last, or a terrible sentence finally rears its fuzzy head.

Here is a passage from a student's paper that has gone the full course. First you see the student's initial draft, with his own corrections on it. Next you see the passage after a second typing (and some further changes), as it was returned by the instructor with his marks on it. Then you see the final revision, handed in again, as this particular assignment required:

FIRST DRAFT

In a college education, students should be al-
lowed to ~~make~~ *choose* their own course. ~~Too many~~ *All the* requirements*,* *they*
~~are discouraging to~~ *must take* *discourage* people's creativity*,* and they cannot learn anything ~~which is~~ *they are* not motivated ~~for him~~ to
learn. ~~With~~ *R* requirements*,* *restrict* their freedom to choose
and their eagerness to learn. They are *only discouraged*
~~what he is interested in is taken away~~ by having to
study dull subjects like German*,* *in which they can see no* ~~which he is not in-~~
relevance to their interests.
~~terested in.~~

THE PAPER, WITH INSTRUCTOR'S MARKINGS

In a college education, students <u>should be</u>
<u>allowed</u> to choose their own curricula and select   *can you get rid of the passive?*
redundant? their own courses. <u>All the requirements they must take</u>
relevant? stifle their <u>creativity</u>. Moreover, they <u>cannot learn</u>   *true?*
anything they are not motivated to learn. Require-
ments restrict their freedom to choose and their
eagerness to explore the subjects they are interested
activate in. <u>They are only discouraged by</u> having to study
dull subjects like German, in which they can see no
relevance.

REVISED PAPER

Students should choose their own education,
their own curricula, their own courses. Their education is really theirs alone. Every college re-
quirement threatens to stifle the very enthusiasms
upon which true education depends. Students learn
best when motivated by their own interests, but, in
the midst of a dozen complicated requirements, they
can hardly find time for the courses they long to
take. Requirements therefore not only restrict their

freedom to choose but destroy their eagerness to
explore. Dull subjects like German, in which they
can see no relevance anyway, take all their time and
discourage them completely.

A NOTE ON MECHANICS

Type, or write, on 8½-by-11-inch paper. Use one side only. Keep your type clean of fuzz and your handwriting neat. Unless otherwise instructed, follow the customs of publication by putting your name and identifications in the upper *right* corner:

    Charles Meckman
    English 123
    Paper No. 6
    October 12, 1984

Next, center your title about three inches from the top of your first page (not numbered). Put it in regular roman (*not* italics) or in capitals. Place no period after the title.

    Hooked on People Young
    HOOKED ON PEOPLE YOUNG

Put titles of books in italics by underlining them; put titles of poems and other "quoted" phrases in quotation marks:

    The Problem of Time in Faulkner's The Sound
                 and the Fury
    Heaven in Frost's "After Apple Picking"
         They All Said "Nuts"

Leave an inch and a half of margin on the left, and an inch on the right, to give your instructor some room for marks. Double-space your typewriting, and leave space in your handwriting: you and your instructor may want to put in a word above the line, with a caret (∧) to show where it goes. Start your paragraphs five letterspaces in from your margin. See Chapter 3, pp. 68–69, for details about how to space your long quotations. Also see the sample paper in Chapter 12 for other elements and numbering of pages.

A FIRST PAPER

Now you have surveyed the problem of how to get an essay started. You find a subject that interests you. You turn it into a thesis by affirming something about it. You evolve your written voice as you think up points and illustrations, discovering that revision is not only necessary and inevitable but positively creative as it brings your thoughts fully alive and makes them persuasive.

Now with the concepts and the style in hand, we need a framework, a structure, to put them in. This we shall look at in the next chapter. But let us close with a student's paper to illustrate the points of this chapter as it looks ahead to the structural points of the next. In it you can see the mechanics of typing, spacing, quoting, and so forth. The author has made a few small last-minute corrections in pencil, which are perfectly acceptable. Her writing is a little wordy and awkward. She is a little uncertain of her language. Her *one*'s, for instance, seem far too stiff and insistent. This is her first paper, and she has not yet fully discovered her own written voice. But it is an excellent beginning. It shows well how a personal experience produces a publicly valid thesis, then turns around to give that thesis its most lively and specific illustration. The assignment had asked for a paper of about five hundred words on some book (or movie, or TV program) that had proved personally meaningful. Even a memorable experience would do—fixing a car, or building a boat, or being arrested. The aim of the assignment was to generalize from a personally valuable experience and to explain to others how such an experience can be valuable to them.

Emily Maddox
English 123
Paper No. 1
September 15, 1981

ON FINDING ONESELF IN NEW GUINEA

Opposing
View

Reading for pleasure is not considered to be popular. Young adults prefer the "boob tube," the television set with which they have spent so many childhood hours. Too many attractions beckon them away from the books ~~which~~ *that* the teacher recommended to the class for summer reading. One's friends come by in their automobiles to drive down for a coke. The kids go to the moving pictures, or to the beach, and

the book one had intended to read remains on the shelf,
or pr*o*bably *in* the library, where one has not yet been
able to find the time to go. Nevertheless, a book
can furnish real enjoyment.

The reader enjoys the experience of being in
another world. While one reads, one forgets that one
is in one's own room. The book has served as a magic
carpet to *transport* take one to India, or Africa, or Sweden,
or even to the cities and areas of one's own country
where one has never been. It has also transported
one into the lives of people with different experiences and problems, from which one can learn to solve
one's own problems of the future. The young person,
in particular, can learn by the experience of reading
what it is like to be a complete adult.

A book is able to help the young person to mature even further, and change one's whole point of
view. Growing up in New Guinea by Margaret Mead is
a valuable experience for this reason. I found the
book on our shelf, after having seen Margaret Mead
on TV. I was interested in her because the teacher
had referred to her book entitled Coming of Age in
Samoa. I was surprised to find this one about New
Guinea. I thought it was a mistake. I opened it and
read the first sentence:

> The way in which each human infant is
> transformed into the finished adult, into the
> complicated individual version of his city and
> his century, is one of the most fascinating
> studies open to the curious minded.

The idea that the individual is a version of his city
and his century was fascinating. I started reading

and was surprised when I was called to dinner to learn that two hours had passed. I could hardly eat my dinner fast enough so that I could get back to New Guinea.

From this book I learned that different cultures have very different conceptions about what is right and wrong, in particular about the sex relations and the marriage ceremony, but that people have the same problems all over the world, namely the problem of finding one's place in society. I also learned that *Thesis* books can be more enjoyable than any form of plea-*Restated* sure. Books fascinate the reader because while one is learning about other people and their problems, particularly about the problem of becoming a full member of society, one is also learning about one's own problems.

EXERCISES

5. *Now expand one of your thesis-statements from the preceding exercises into a paper about the length of the preceding example. First, introduce your thesis with a few remarks to get your reader acquainted, then write your paper straight through to illustrate your thesis as fully as you can. Then go back over this draft and make it publicly presentable, revising until you know you have done your best.*

Chapter 2

BASIC STRUCTURE

BEGINNING, MIDDLE, END

As Aristotle long ago pointed out, works that spin their way through time need a beginning, a middle, and an end to give them the stability of spatial things like paintings and statues. You need a clear beginning to give your essay character and direction so the reader can tell where he is going and can look forward with expectation. Your beginning, of course, will set forth your thesis. You need a middle to amplify and fulfill. This will be the body of your argument, the bulk of your essay. You need an end to let readers know that they have arrived and where. This will be your final paragraph, a summation and reassertion of your theme.

Give your essay the three-part *feel* of beginning, middle, and end—the mind likes this triple order. Many a freshman's essay has no structure and leaves no impression. It is all chaotic middle. It has no beginning, it just starts; it has no end, it just stops, fagged out at two in the morning.

The beginning must feel like a beginning, not just like an accident. It should be at least a full paragraph that lets your reader gently into the subject and culminates with your thesis. The end, likewise, should be a full paragraph, one that drives the point home, pushes the implications wide, and brings the reader to rest, back on the fundamental thesis to give a sense of completion. When we consider paragraphing in the next chapter, we will look more closely at beginning paragraphs and end paragraphs. The "middle" of your essay, which constitutes its bulk, needs further structural consideration now.

MIDDLE TACTICS

Arrange your points in order of increasing interest.

Once your thesis has sounded the challenge, your reader's interest is probably at its highest pitch. He wants to see how you can prove so outrageous a thing, or to see what the arguments are for this thing he has always believed but never tested. Each step of the way into your demonstration, he is learning more of what you have to say. But, unfortunately, his interest may be relaxing as it becomes satisfied: the reader's normal line of attention is a progressive decline, arching down like a wintry graph. Against this decline you must oppose your forces, making each successive point more interesting. And save your best till last. It is as simple as that.

Here, for example, is the middle of a short, three-paragraph essay developing the thesis that "Working your way through college is valuable." The student has arranged his three points in an ascending order of interest:

> **The student who works finds that the experience is worth more than the money. First, he learns to budget his time. He now supports himself by using time he would otherwise waste, and he studies harder in the time he has left because he knows it is limited. Second, he makes real and lasting friends on the job, as compared to the other casual acquaintances around the campus. He has shared rush hours, and nighttime cleanups with the dishes piled high, and conversation and jokes when business is slow. Finally, he gains confidence in his ability to get along with all kinds of people, and to make his own way. He sees how businesses operate, and how waitresses, for instance, can work cheerfully at a really tiring job without much hope for the future. He gains an insight into the real world, which is a good contrast to the more intellectual and idealistic world of the college student.**

Again, each successive item of your presentation should be more interesting than the last, or you will suddenly seem anticlimactic. Actually, minor regressions of interest make no difference so long as the whole tendency is uphill and your last item clearly the best. Suppose, for example, you were to try a thesis about cats. You decide that four points would make up the case, and that you might arrange them in the following order of increasing interest: (1) cats are affectionate but make few demands; (2) cats actually look out for themselves; (3) cats have, in fact, proved extremely useful to society throughout history in controlling mice and other plaguy rodents; (4) cats satisfy some human need for a touch of the jungle, savagery in repose, ferocity in silk, and have been worshiped for the exotic power they still seem to represent. It may be, as you write, that you will find Number 1 developing attractive or amusing instances, and perhaps even virtually usurping the whole essay. Numbers 2, 3, and 4 should then be moved ahead as interesting but brief preliminaries. Your middle structure, thus, should range from least important to most important, from simple to complex, from narrow to broad, from pleasant to hilarious, from mundane to metaphysical—whatever "leasts" and "mosts" your subject suggests.

EXERCISES

1. *In the following exercise you will find groups of information and ideas haphazardly arranged. Rewrite the statements with the information arranged in an ascending order of interest and importance. Then, in a sentence or two, explain your reasons for using that order.*

1. We are now being made to realize the negative aspects of the technological "progress" of the twentieth century: 50,000 highway deaths per year, air and water pollution, the population explosion, nuclear warfare, loss of privacy.
2. Four different levels of government are investigating the effectiveness of the methadone treatment for heroin addiction. State, national, county, and city governments have all instituted research programs within the last year.
3. The psychological effects of the Depression are observable in an increase in the frequency of mental breakdown, an increase in the suicide rate, and a decrease in the birth rate.
4. Although most classrooms have tile floors, carpeting is actually better in several ways. First, if you figure maintenance into the total cost of floor covering, carpeting is cheaper than tile; second, carpeting is more aesthetically pleasing than tile; and third, carpeting serves a useful acoustical function, absorbing the noise of scuffing feet and scooting chairs.
5. This car not only looks sporty, but is also equipped for sporty performance. It has a turbo charger, five-speed gear box, heavy-duty springs and shocks,

high-back bucket seats, vinyl roof, a 3000cc engine, heavy-duty cooling system, power disc brakes, corduroy upholstery trim, rally accent stripes.

6. An all-volunteer army may be undesirable because it tends to draw from a limited segment of the population, to create an elitist military caste such as those in Hitler's Germany and in tsarist Russia, and to cost more. But it does away with the draft.

7. Marijuana should be legalized because people are going to use it whether it is legalized or not. Legalizing it would make a sensible distinction between hard and soft drugs, would allow authorities to control the quality of the drugs available for sale, would eliminate criminal profiteering, and would prevent numbers of people from becoming cynical violators of the law.

8. If you have gotten along without a credit card until now, applying for one is really a mistake. If you have one, you might lose it or have it stolen, and then you might be liable for the expenses run up by someone else using your card. Then there are the interest charges. Few people realize that the interest on most credit cards is 18 percent a year. And obviously, if you have a credit card, you are going to spend more than if you were using cash.

9. Talking about scientific knowledge today, she identified three of its characteristics. First, this knowledge is not within the reach of most of us. Second, this knowledge is mostly new. And, finally, this knowledge has become almost the exclusive property of a very small group of scientists and engineers.

Acknowledge and dispose of the opposition.

Your cat essay, because it is moderately playful, can proceed rather directly, throwing only an occasional bone of concession to the dogs, and perhaps most of your essays, as you discuss the Constitutional Convention or explain a poem, will have no opposition to worry about. But a serious controversial argument demands one organizational consideration beyond the simple structure of ascending interest. Although you have taken your stand firmly as a *pro,* you will have to allow scope to the *con's,* or you will seem not to have thought much about your subject. The more opposition you can manage as you carry your point, the more triumphant you will seem, like a high-wire artist daring the impossible.

This balancing of *pro's* against *con's* is one of the most fundamental orders of thought: the dialectic order, which is the order of argument, one side pitted against the other. Our minds naturally swing from side to side as we think. In dialectics, we simply give one side an argumentative edge, producing a thesis that cuts a clear line through any subject: "This is better than that." The basic organizing principle here is to get rid of the opposition first, and to end on your own side. Probably you will have already organized your thesis-sentence in a perfect pattern for your *con-pro* argument:

> **Despite their many advantages, welfare payments . . . .**
> **Although dogs are fine pets, cats . . . .**

The subordinate clause (*see* p. 141) states the subordinate part of your argument, which is your concession to the *con* viewpoint; your main clause states your main argument. As the subordinate clause comes first in your thesis sentence, so does the subordinate argument in your essay. Sentence and essay both reflect a natural psychological principle. You want, and the reader wants, to get the opposition out of the way. And you want to end on your best foot. (You might try putting the opposition last, just to see how peculiarly the last word insists on seeming best, and how, when stated last by you, the opposition's case seems to be your own.)

Get rid of the opposition first. This is the essential tactic of argumentation. You have introduced and stated your thesis in your beginning paragraph. Now start the middle with a paragraph of concession to the *con*'s:

> **Dog-lovers, of course, have tradition on their side. Dogs are indeed affectionate and faithful. . . .**

And with that paragraph out of the way, go to bat for the cats, showing their superiority to dogs in *every* point. In a very brief essay, you can use the opposition itself to introduce your thesis in the first paragraph, and dispose of your opponents at the same time:

> **Shakespeare begins *Romeo and Juliet* with ominous warnings about fate. His lovers are "star-crossed," he says: they are doomed from the first by their contrary stars, by the universe itself. They have sprung from "fatal loins." Fate has already determined their tragic end. The play then unfolds a succession of unlucky and presumably fated accidents. Nevertheless, we soon discover that Shakespeare really blames the tragedy not on fate but on human stupidity and error.**

But usually your beginning paragraph will lead up to your thesis more or less neutrally, and you will attack your opposition head-on in paragraph two, as you launch into the middle.

If the opposing arguments seem relatively slight and brief, you can get rid of them neatly all together in one paragraph before you get down to your case. Immediately after your beginning, which has stated your thesis, you write a paragraph of concession: "Of course, security is a good thing. No one wants people begging." And so on to the end of the paragraph, deflating *every* conceivable objection. Then back to the main line: "But the price in moral decay is too great." The structure of the essay, paragraph by paragraph, might be diagrammed something like the scheme shown in Diagram I:

Diagram I

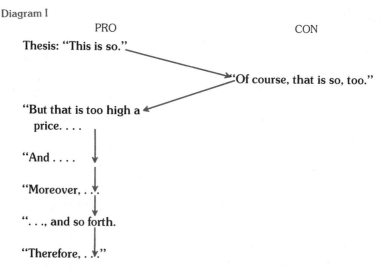

PRO   CON

Thesis: "This is so."

"Of course, that is so, too."

"But that is too high a price. . . .

"And . . . .

"Moreover, . . .

". . ., and so forth.

"Therefore, . . ."

If the opposition is more considerable, demolish it point by point, using a series of *con*'s and *pro*'s, in two or three paragraphs, before you steady down to your own side. Each paragraph can be a small argument that presents the opposition, then knocks it flat—a kind of Punch-and-Judy show: "We must admit that . . . . But . . . ." And down goes the poor old opposition again. Or you could swing your argument through a number of alternating paragraphs: first your beginning, the thesis, then a paragraph to the opposition (*con*), then one for your side (*pro*), then another paragraph of *con,* and so on. The main point, again, is this: *get rid of the opposition first.* One paragraph of concession right after your thesis will probably handle most of your adversaries, and the more complicated argumentative swingers, like the ones shown in Diagram II, will develop naturally as you need them.

You will notice that *but* and *however* are always guides for the *pro*'s, serving as switches back to the main line. Indeed, *but, however,* and *nevertheless* are the basic *pro*'s. *But* always heads its turning sentence (not followed by a comma); *Nevertheless* usually does (followed by a comma). I am sure, however, that *however* is always better buried in the sentence between commas. "However, . . ." at a sentence's beginning is the habit of heavy prose. *But* is for the quick turn; the inlaid *however* for the more elegant sweep.

The structural line of your arguments, then, might look like Diagram II, and an actual *pro-con* argument like Diagram III (p. 34).

Diagram II

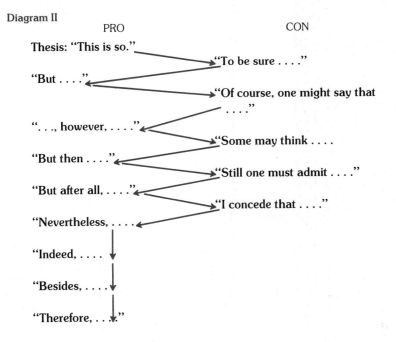

PRO   CON

Thesis: "This is so."

            "To be sure . . . ."

"But . . . ."

            "Of course, one might say that . . . ."

". . ., however, ..."

            "Some may think . . . .

"But then . . . ."

            "Still one must admit . . . ."

"But after all, ..."

            "I concede that . . . ."

"Nevertheless, ...

"Indeed, ...

"Besides, ...

"Therefore, ..."

EXERCISES

2. *To strengthen your feeling for argumentative opposition, write three con-and-pro thesis-sentences, beginning "Although . . . ."*

3. *In the exercise that follows, you will find a series of general assertions. Supply one argument against and one argument for each proposition. Then combine the statements into one thesis-sentence that includes not only the assertion, but also the reasons against and for it.*

EXAMPLE   Assertion: Movies should not be censored.

    Con: Children should not be exposed to obscene and explicitly sexual images on the screen. [*Example continued on p. 35.*]

Diagram III
(see p. 33)

LEGALIZATION OF MARIJUANA—PRO AND CON

PRO   CON

Thesis: "Marijuana should be
legalized."

To be sure, soft drugs can lead
to hard drugs. . . .

But most users of marijuana
seek only mild pleasures
among a group of friends.
. . .

Of course, one might argue
that marijuana only prolongs
the groupiness of
adolescence. . . .

People at every age, however,
seek support from their
peers. . . .

I concede that legalizing
marijuana invites certain
serious risks. . . .

Nevertheless, the present
punishment and its social
consequences far exceed
these risks. . . .

Indeed, the law could eliminate
many dangers by controlling
quality. . . .

Besides, legality would
eliminate the profiteers. . . .

Therefore, legalizing marijuana
would solve more problems
than its illegality now
creates. . . .

[Example continued from p. 33.]

    Pro: Obscenity is far too subjective a thing for any person to define for anyone else.

    Thesis-Statement: Although it is probably undesirable for young people to be exposed to scenes of explicit sex in films, movies still should not be censored because obscenity is so subjective a thing that no one can legitimately serve as censor for the rest of us.

1. Assertion: Discussion classes are superior to lectures.
2. Assertion: Rapid and convenient transit systems must be built in our cities.
3. Assertion: The federal government should subsidize large companies forced near bankruptcy.
4. Assertion: Medical schools should reduce the time required for a degree in general medicine from four years to two.
5. Assertion: States should prohibit the sale of beverages in nonreturnable containers.
6. Assertion: A guaranteed annual income would not wipe out poverty for all Americans.
7. Assertion: As exercise, golf is a waste of time.
8. Assertion: The law should require that all drivers and passengers in cars use seat belts.
9. Assertion: College students should study a foreign language.

Run comparisons point by point.

    After blasting the opposition first, only one argumentative principle remains: *run your comparisons point by point.* Don't write all about sheep for three pages, then all about goats. Every time you say something about a sheep, say something comparable about a goat, pelt for pelt, horn for horn, beard for beard. Otherwise your essay will fall in two, and you will need to repeat all your sheep points when you get down to goats, and at last begin the comparison. The tendency to organize comparisons by halves is so strong that you will probably find you have fallen into it unawares, and in rewriting you will have to reorganize everything point for point—still arranging your pairs of points from least important to most. Finally, the most interesting comparison aims to demonstrate a superiority—"Resolved: Sheep are more useful than goats."

    Of course, comparing and contrasting two poems, two stories, two ballplayers, is an essential process of thought, an essential way to understanding. You may wish simply to set two similars, or dissimilars, side by side to illustrate some larger point—that excellence may come in very different packages, for instance. Comparing and contrasting can illuminate the unfamiliar with the familiar, or it can help you discover and convey to your readers new perspectives on things well known—two popular singers, two of Shakespeare's sonnets, two nursery rhymes. But, whether or not you are presenting one side as superior to the other, the structural tactics are the same: illuminate by comparing point for point, as long as the comparison illuminates.

EXERCISES

4. *In the exercise that follows, you will find an essay in which the author advances his thesis point by point. First, state the thesis, then number and identify the arguments both for and against the thesis. Also identify as* con *or* pro *the words or phrases the author uses to mark the switch from one side of the argument to the other. List the arguments for and against the assertion, and make another double list, headed "Pro" and "Con," of the writer's transitional devices.*

I should start by admitting that as little as five years ago carpeted classrooms would rightly have seemed too fanciful and expensive. The carpeting then available would have been costly, difficult to maintain, and would have required frequent replacement. Now, however, because of improved materials, the arguments in favor of extensive carpeting seem a great deal more plausible. New indoor-outdoor synthetics—stain resistant, fade resistant, durable, and inexpensive—have made carpeting seem much less a luxury than a reasonable, even desirable, alternative to tile floors. Briefly, there seem to be three central arguments in favor of carpeting.

First, of course, carpeting is attractive. Now, admittedly, modern technology offers a great variety of attractively colored tiles, and the days of the drab, institutional grays, greens, and browns in tile are—happily—over. But, even though tile may approach carpeting in terms of color, it still has a hard and unattractive texture. Carpeting, on the other hand, is colorful, attractive to touch, and comfortable to walk on. It goes a long way toward creating a pleasant atmosphere all of us would like to work in, both in and out of class. Richly colored carpeting, such as the bold reds often used in banks, restaurants, department stores, and commercial offices, would make our facilities far less "institutional." Bright carpeting can easily make attractive an area that would otherwise seem Spartan and sterile. In short, carpeting seems desirable simply because it is more attractive to look at and walk on than tile.

The second argument in favor of carpeted classrooms is essentially pragmatic: carpeting serves a useful acoustical function. Of course, the flexible backing and roughened texture of modern tiles make them far less noisy than those of just a few years ago. Both tiles and carpets have improved significantly.

Carpeting, however, is a superior dampener of sound; it cuts noise from crowded hallways, absorbs annoying background noise in classrooms—scuffing feet, scooting chairs, coughs—and makes busy space less noisy and, therefore, much more practical. In industry, if not in schools, one frequently finds carpeting in busy areas because it reduces noise.

A final argument in favor of carpeting is that, over a period of time, carpeting is no more expensive than tile. Certainly, carpeting costs more than tile, and it does need eventual replacement. But carpeting costs much less to maintain than tile, which needs frequent washing, waxing, and dusting. The new synthetic carpets resist stains and fading. An ordinary vacuum cleaner will keep them in shape. But the tile floor, unfortunately, needs frequent scrubbing and waxing if it is not to look dull and yellow with accumulated wax. This process is laborious and slow, and, in large institutions, it requires expensive scrubbing machines. In short, tile costs less than carpeting to install. But count in the maintenance, and carpeting becomes a legitimate economic alternative to tile.

Were it not for the obvious advantages in appearance and acoustics of carpeting over tile, one could perhaps argue fairly in favor of conventional flooring. After all, the costs over a very long period, say twenty or thirty years, are genuinely unpredictable. We simply haven't yet accumulated enough experience with the new synthetics, and perhaps over a quarter of a century carpets will prove more expensive. Perhaps we will discover that, after a decade or so, the savings in maintaining carpets will evaporate. To this point, however, our experience with synthetic materials is essentially affirmative. And so, given the clear edge carpeting has over tile aesthetically and acoustically, and given its apparent economic justification, carpeting for classrooms seems completely sensible.

OUTLINING

In diagramming the *pro-con* structures, I have been outlining my argument, first only tactically, then, with marijuana, actually—jotting down the points of my argument. Outlining will start your thoughts moving, and start getting them in useful order, giving you something to lean on as you write.

The first thing to grasp about outlines is that they seldom work out to the letter. The second is that they always help. The third is that the headings do not represent equal space in the finished essay: one heading may become two paragraphs and the next only two sentences. The fluid pressure of writing will always force revision of your best-laid plans. An incidental sentence may swell into an entire section; a scheduled section may end up scrapped. But an outline helps you lay things straight, it helps you to spot gaps in your own argument and in the arguments of others, to test the relationships of parts, to certify a thesis, to validate an assertion. Outline your reading, and you will really grasp it. Outline the plan of your essay, and you straighten out your thinking for your reader to grasp.

We think and write largely by free association, but to explain these thoughts fully to our readers, and to ourselves, we need to discover and outline their logical pattern. With the logic down on paper, we can write from heading to heading, sure of our direction, with an order of ascending interest. We can push aside the good ideas constantly crowding in: our outline has already scheduled a place for them up ahead, each where it will be most logical and effective.

Begin your paper with a jotted outline.

With a firm thesis and a short paper, you may need no outline at all. But even with only three points to make, jotting them down will help you arrange them for ascending interest, and will probably turn up another point or two as well. Take a sheet of paper. Think up a good title. Put down your thesis. If it is firm and assertive, it will win much of your battle with logic at the very beginning. Jot down your points, rearranging as you go. And, lo and behold!, you almost have a completed essay. One tactical point: adjusting your headings to make them grammatically parallel will keep your reasoning running clearer as you write, all -*ing* phrases for instance: *Getting up, Going to class, Organizing free time;* or *Income, Expenses, Taxes, Savings.* Explanatory phrases after each of these headings, also grammatically parallel, make your jotting complete. Here is a jotted outline for a paper against smoking:

THE WICKED CIGARETTE

THESIS: **Despite certain hazy benefits, we must admit that cigarettes are bad for us.**

1. **Social benefits—put you "in," give you something to do and say, make you feel mature (in charge of your own life)**
2. **Economic benefits—support a tremendous industrial network, from farmer to company to advertising agency to magazines and newspapers, providing thousands of livelihoods**

   3. But moral hazards—become a habit controlling you, defeating
      your personal autonomy, making you "follow the pack"
   4. Physical hazards—pose an unnecessary risk to the only heart and
      lungs you have

Notice how easily you may now convert this outline into an essay. The
subordinate clause—"Despite certain hazy benefits"—in your thesis has
set aside the concessions you must make to the opposition, and the main
clause—"We must admit that cigarettes are bad for us"—has asserted the
main point. The jotted main headings fall neatly into place, each grammatically parallel, each a noun with its adjective ("social benefits"), each
structurally equal, and the four effectively balanced—two for opposition,
two for affirmation. The lesser elements of your explanation are also in
parallel—*put, give, make,* for example—to indicate equivalent treatment.
Your paper's structure firmly before you, now you are free to write it
out.

Outline your exam answers.

   The jotted outline helps immensely in answering essay questions,
particularly because it hangs on a thesis, which is the real secret of organizing any information whatever. Find your Big Idea, then jot down the
points you want to conver, quickly saving best for last—the one you know
best and can cover most fully.

   Here is the trick: MAKE YOURSELF ANSWER THE QUESTION IN ONE SENTENCE.
However well or poorly you are prepared, this forces all you know on the
subject to its widest dimension. If you start your answer with this sentence,
even desperately throwing in any old detail as it comes (as I used to do
until I hit on the one-sentence idea), every detail will seem to illustrate
your opening declaration, and your instructor will say, "Now *this* one is
organized—a real grasp of the subject." So, start your answer with your
seminal sentence, and your answer will sound like an essay. With a few
points jotted to attain an ascending order of importance, it will sound even
more so. It will indeed *be* an essay, in seminal form. Your instructor, after
all, needs no introduction.

   Next point: incorporate the language of the question in your
one-sentence opener. This works even with the broadest kind of question—those barn doors opened so wide you can drive in any kind of load:

   1. Discuss the fall of the Roman Empire.
   2. What is the most valuable thing you have learned in this course?
   3. Demonstrate your knowledge of the materials of this course.

Your one-sentence openers might go like this:

1. The Roman Empire fell because of decay from within and attack from without.
2. The most valuable thing I have learned this semester is that people usually conceal their true motivations from themselves.
3. The materials of this course illustrate biological evolution, particularly the role of mutation in the survival of the fittest.

Jot down your points, quickly arranging for ascending order, and you are off and running.

EXERCISES

5. *Write an essay from the outline on smoking on pp. 38–39, or, reversing the viewpoint, write one on the same pattern.*

6. *Make a comparable jotted outline on a subject you prefer, then write an essay from it, handing in both.*

Proceed to the topic outline.

The topic outline is the most common, an arranging of your jotted thoughts into heads and subheads, each rank in parallel phrasing. The major headings rise in ascending importance, but their minor headings descend in smaller and smaller components. You alternate numbers and letters, proceeding from Roman numeral *I* through capital *A* to Arabic *1* and little *a*, until you reach, if you need them, parenthesized (*1*) and (*a*). You indent equal heads equally, so that they fall in the same column, Roman under Roman, capital under capital, and so on:

I. _____

   A. _____

      1. _____

      2. _____

   B. _____

      1. _____

a. _____

   (1) _____

      (a) _____

      (b) _____

   (2) _____

b. _____

2. _____

II. _____

You will probably need no more than the Roman headings—*I, II, III*—with an *A, B,* and perhaps a *C* under each, but you arrange the *1*'s and *a*'s, the *(1)*'s and *(a)*'s on the same scheme if you need them.

Check your outline for balance.

Ideally, every *I* should have its *II,* every *A* its *B,* every *1* its *2,* since an unpaired heading suggests that it is a detail too small for separate treatment, really a part of the larger heading above. For instance:

POOR	GOOD
II. **Value of cats**	II. **Value of cats as pets**
A. **As pets**	
III. **Kinds of cats**	III. **Kinds of cats**
A._____	A._____
B._____	B._____

One of your first revisions should be to absorb any such unpaired heading into its related major heading. Then see that each heading is a noun (or noun phrase), with or without modifiers: "Benefits," for instance, or "Benefits to the individual." This will keep your outline parallel. You can signal your major turns by adding a *But* or *Nevertheless.*

Now for a topic outline of your projected essay on cigarettes. Suppose you have read Thackeray's *Vanity Fair* and remember that Dobbin took out a cigar "and amused himself for half an hour with the pernicious vegetable." The phrase suggests a title that catches the subject exactly as you mean to treat it, straightforwardly but humorously. You will work in Thackeray himself later on, letting your reader in on the secret of your title as you cite an eminent man who apparently liked a cigar himself but knew the awful truth.

THE PERNICIOUS VEGETABLE

THESIS: **Although cigarettes have brought certain benefits to society, we must ultimately judge them harmful.**

I. **Beneficial effects**
- A. **Benefits to society**
  - 1. **Income for the tobacco industry**
    - a. **Farmers**
    - b. **Wholesalers**
    - c. **Retailers**
  - 2. **Income for the communications industry**
    - a. **Advertising agencies**
    - b. **Advertising media**
  - 3. **Income for the government**
    - a. **National tax revenues**
    - b. **State and local tax revenues**
- B. **Benefits to the individual**
  - 1. **Feeling of social ease and acceptance**
  - 2. **Feeling of self-responsibility**
  - 3. **Feeling of maturity**

II. **But: harmful effects**
- A. **Income for criminal elements**
  - 1. **Vending-machine racketeers**
  - 2. **Narcotics and gambling racketeers**
- B. **Physical harm to the individual**
  - 1. **Historical opinions**
    - a. **James I's condemnation of tobacco**
    - b. **Thackeray's characterization of the cigar**
    - c. **Edison's refusal to hire smokers**
  - 2. **Modern findings**
    - a. **Impairment of physical stamina**
      - (1) **Views of athletes and coaches**
      - (2) **Personal experience in sports**
    - b. **Relation to heart disease**
    - c. **Relation to cancer**
      - (1) **Laboratory findings with animals**

Topic Outline

Logical Order
Chronological
Order

Order of
Ascending
Interest

(2) **Laboratory findings with human beings**
   (a) **Lip cancer**
   (b) **Laryngeal cancer**
   (c) **Lung cancer**
C. **Moral harm to the individual**
   1. **Surrender of one's individuality to the group**
   2. **Surrender of one's destiny to the habit**

Notice two things about this outline. First, section II.B on "physical harm to the individual," itself in *logical* order, can freely organize its subordinate parts in *chronological* order: historical opinions, then modern findings. Moreover, the historical opinions themselves fall into chronological order, but the subheads under "modern findings" then revert effectively to the order of ascending interest. The point is this: each heading and subheading is parallel to its co-equal—*A* matches *B*, *1* matches *2*, *a* matches *b*.

Second, notice that we have ended rather more with character than with cancer—an order opposite from that of our jotted outline back on pp. 38–39. Why? Strangely but inevitably, sheer length has changed the dynamics of our argument. For the shorter essay, "the only heart and lungs you have" seemed stronger than the equivalent business about losing individuality in habit. But in the plan for the longer essay, the laboratory details are now too extensive for a single climactic point. They have indeed moved to subordinate rank—*(1)*, not *1*, and not even *a*. Now the moral argument stands in higher rank, simpler and more lofty, a fitting climax before the concluding summation.

Refine with the sentence outline.

In the sentence outline, you phrase each heading as a complete sentence. Such an outline lays out the plan of your essay as no other can, giving the fullest statement of your ideas, and showing clearly and explicitly the logical relation of parts. Often a required procedure in the assigned research paper, the sentence outline is useful for leading you through organizational intricacies and saving you from logical snares. Because it forces you to think out your plan so thoroughly beforehand, a good sentence outline can speed the actual writing of any essay that depends greatly on logical structure. But outlining in sentences consumes your time—and therein lies the danger. The outlining may leave too little time for the writing. A few experiments in the form, however, should help you decide when to use it to your advantage. An initial topic outline is often helpful, though not always necessary.

A sentence outline for your cigarette essay would begin like this:

THE PERNICIOUS VEGETABLE

THESIS: **Although cigarettes have brought certain benefits to society, we must ultimately judge them harmful.**

  I. **These benefits are both social and personal.**

      A. **The most evident social benefit is the tremendous income generated from tobacco.**

          1. **A wide variety of people make a living in the tobacco industry.**

               a. **The growing, transplanting, and curing of tobacco supports thousands of farmers and farm workers in the United States alone.**

               b. **The wholesaling of tobacco is virtually an industry of its own.**

               c. **From cigarette stand to supermarket, money from cigarettes flows steadily into the cash register.**

Remember, each heading, whether in a jotted, topic, or sentence outline, will require widely differing amounts of space as you write out your essay. Heading *I* would probably also absorb heading *A,* as you started your paragraph:

> **These benefits are both social and personal, most evidently in the tremendous income generated from tobacco. Annual retail sales of cigarettes alone are estimated at . . . .**

Your next paragraph would probably use headings *1* and *a,* also consecutively:

> **A wide variety of people make a living in the tobacco industry. The growing, transplanting, and curing of tobacco . . . .**

And then your next paragraph would probably begin with the wholesaling, run on through its associated trucking and railroading, and end with sentence *c* and the cash register.

Observe the basic rules of outlining.

1. TITLE. Keep your title independent of the text of your outline. Do not number it in with the text; do not use it as a heading for subheads; do not refer to it by pronouns. Do *not* do this:

I. THE ADVANTAGES OF THE BIKINI

A. Its convenience in packing

2. THESIS. To keep your logical structure straight, make as explicit a thesis as you can.

3. CAPITALIZATION. Capitalize only the first word of each heading (and other words normally capitalized).

4. PUNCTUATION. Omit periods after your title and your headings, but put one after your thesis-sentence. If outlining in sentences, include periods, of course.

5. HEADINGS. For the topic outline especially, use all nouns (or noun phrases), with modifiers accompanying them, as needed. Do not mix kinds of headings: some single nouns, some sentences, some fragments. Keep headings equivalent:

A. **Benefits to society**
B. **Benefits to the individual**
   1. **Feeling of social ease**
   2. **Feeling of self-responsibility**
      . . .
      a. **James I's condemnation**
      b. **Thackeray's characterization**
      c. **Edison's refusal**

EXERCISES

7. *Outlining is useful in analyzing the logical structure of a printed essay and coming to understand it. To outline your reading, you first boil the essay down to its true thesis, in one sentence. Then, you go through the essay, typing out a series of topics that identify the key ideas as they come along. Finally, to make a full topic outline, you group your topics into what seem to be their major and minor hierarchies, probably recasting some A's for I's, some I's for A's, and so forth.*

Making a sentence outline really masters an essay for you. You discover the essay's parts; you summarize them into clear sentences; you work out their logical relations. You may even discover some logical lapses. But most important, you will have made the writer's thoughts and their relationships your own.

(a) *Read the following essay and then develop a topic outline for it, including, of course, a title.*

I had a job interview several weeks ago. Friends warned me not to be too aggressive. During the interview, I tried to present myself as a competent candidate, able to "think like a man" and yet not be a "masculine" female. After fielding several questions relevant to the job, I suddenly heard, "Miss Stern, are you in love?" Do you think they asked my competition—seven men—this same question? No, for a cultureful of reasons. Jacqueline Kennedy Onassis was once quoted as saying, "There are two kinds of women: those who want power in the world, and those who want power in bed." The majority seem to agree with Jackie that the latter is the more desirable and more socially acceptable. That's how most women in America have been taught to think.

Children are taught sexual stereotypes early, as well as the appropriate behavior for a sex-determined role in life. Asking a little boy, "What do you want to be when you grow up?" implies to him unlimited possibilities in his future. But most often we ask a little girl, "Where did you get that pretty dress?" suggesting that she has only one real option open to her. If we ask her what she wants to be, she's liable to give the conditioned female response: "A mother." Why? So she can replace her dolls with real babies. The inspiration for teaching girls to expect less than boys comes from a wide range of cultural sources: religious, literary, psychiatric and pop.

One may begin by observing that in the Bible the exceptional, independent women like Rebecca, Sarah, Deborah or Ruth are practically "unknowns" compared with the infamous Eve or Delilah. Eve was made from one of Adam's spare parts, almost as an afterthought, to help him out on earth: "And God said, 'It is not good that the man should be alone; I will make a helpmeet for him.' " Today, the heirs to the Bible in America (the Jews and Christians) have formalized biblical biases in laws and ceremonies and thereby elevated folklore to religious truths. Among the Orthodox Jews, for example, discrimination against women is so blatant that they are forced to sit segregated behind a curtain or in a balcony. The reasoning is that women will distract men from their prayers. It is no wonder that the men thank God every morning in their ritual prayer ". . . that Thou hast not made me a woman." The majority of Jews have modified most traditional formalities, but independent female expression is still discouraged if it is outside the confines of the home or not channeled through the husband and children.

A Jewish wife is less subservient to her husband than a gentile wife, so say comparative studies on the subject. That's somewhat understandable, since Christianity owes much to a prominent classical heritage that held the second sex even lower in esteem. Utopia, for the male chauvinist, is Demosthenes' description of the Greek male-female relationship: "We have hetairae for the pleasure of the spirit, concubines for sensual pleasure, and wives to bear our sons.'' Aristotle's definition of femininity was ''a certain lack of qualities; we should regard the female as afflicted with a natural defectiveness.'' And his disciple, Saint Thomas Aquinas, echoed him religiously, ''. . . a female is something deficient and by chance.'' Contempt for women explains why they can't become Catholic priests, and why theologians, religious education courses, and Catholic marriage manuals highlight the supposedly inferior and passive qualities of women, who ''naturally'' subordinate themselves to men.*

(b) *Develop a sentence outline for the following essay on limiting the Presidency of the United States to a single term (the Twenty-Second Amendment now limits the Presidency to two four-year terms). If it helps, develop a topic outline first.*

> *The Hon. Mike Mansfield*
> *United States Senator, Montana, Democrat*
> *Senate Majority Leader*
> *Testimony before the Senate Constitutional Amendments Subcommittee*
> *October 28, 1971.*

I welcome the chance to express my views pertaining to the proposed Constitutional Amendment that would limit the Presidency to a single term of six years. I am particularly proud and pleased to join with the distinguished Senator from Vermont[†] in this endeavor which I personally regard as one of the most important reforms that our system of government could undergo.

In recent years there have been a number of significant amendments to the Constitution of the United States. Correcting the matter of Presidential succession and particularly extending the franchise of the ballot to young adults 18, 19 and 20 years of age represent enormous steps forward: steps that protect and enhance immensely the Democratic processes of this Nation. In my judgment there is still another step that must be taken in this area of Constitutional evolution. It is only in providing a single Presidential term of six years, I believe, that this Nation will preserve for its highest office a sufficient degree of freedom and independence to function properly and adequately today and in the years ahead; years that will produce enormous trials and tensions on the national and global scale, some of which have yet to emerge.

By no means do I intend to imply that with this proposed amendment

---

*From Paula Stern, ''The Womanly Image, or Character Assassination Through the Ages,'' copyright © 1970 by Paula Stern. Reprinted by permission of The Atlantic Monthly Company and the author.

†The Hon. George D. Aiken.

new ground is being broken or that a topic of first impression is here being raised. Indeed, the suggestion of a single six-year term has been with us ever since the delegates to the Constitutional Convention of 1787 thrashed over the question of a President's term and his eligibility for re-election. It is interesting to note that popular election was not considered with any great favor at all during the proceedings of that convention. But proposals limiting the tenure of the President were put forth and discussed. Ultimately none were approved and the question then became moot when the suggestion for an electoral college system gained the widest support.

Since the Constitution was ratified hundreds of amendments have been introduced in the Senate and House of Representatives proposing a change in Presidential tenure. More than 130 of these recommended a single term of six years. Twice, the House reported legislation providing for the six-year term. And in 1913, the Senate passed S.J. Res. 78 calling for a term of six years, but no action was taken by the other body. Presidents themselves have been most active in their support for the concept. Nearly 150 years ago Andrew Jackson recommended that the electoral college be abolished—also a good suggestion—that the President be elected by direct vote, and that he be limited to a single term of either four or six years. Presidents Hayes and Cleveland and William Howard Taft also offered the proposal. In more recent years on this issue I have followed the lead of the able and distinguished Senator from Vermont, the dean of the Republicans and a wise and prudent judge on all matters and particularly on those affecting the needs of democratic institutions in a rapidly changing world. That brings us up to today, and I must say that the merits of the proposal dictate its need now as never before.

It is just intolerable that a President of the United States—any President, whatever his party—is compelled to devote his time, energy and talents to what can be termed only as purely political tasks. I do not refer solely to a President's own re-election campaign. To be sure a re-election effort and all it entails are burdens enough. But a President facing re-election faces as well a host of demands that range from attending to the needs of political office holders, office seekers, financial backers and all the rest, to riding herd on the day-to-day developments within the pedestrian partisan arena. Surely this amendment does not represent a panacea for these ills which have grown up with our system of democracy. But it would go far, I think, in unsaddling the Presidency from many of these unnecessary political burdens that an incumbent bears.

Clearly such a change to a very great extent would free the President to devote a far greater measure of his time to the enormous task of serving all of the people of this Nation as Chief Executive. More time would thus be provided for policy-making and policy-implementing, for program initiating and for shaping and directing the kind of Administration a President chooses. More time would be provided for the kind of experimentation that a successful Presidency requires; such experimentation has come too infrequently in recent years, and as a Nation we suffer from that inadequacy. . . .

To sum it up, what this amendment seeks is to place the office of the Presidency in a position that transcends as much as possible partisan political considerations of whatever nature and source. That it cannot do the job completely, I would agree. The man who achieves the office carries with him his full political heritage. But its adoption would do much, I think, to streamline the Presidency in a manner that ultimately will make the position more fully responsive to the concerns of all Americans.*

8. *Write an essay on stereotypes, the six-year Presidency, or some topic you prefer, beginning with a full topic outline, to be handed in with your paper.*
your paper.

*The Congressional Digest, March 1972, pp. 80–84.

Chapter 3

PARAGRAPHS: BEGINNING, MIDDLE, END

THE STANDARD PARAGRAPH

A paragraph is a structural convenience—a building block to get firmly in mind. I mean the standard, central paragraph, setting aside for the moment the peculiarly shaped beginning paragraph and ending paragraph. You build the bulk of your essay with standard paragraphs, with blocks of concrete ideas, and they must fit smoothly. But they must also remain as perceptible parts, to rest your reader's eye and mind. Indeed, the paragraph originated, among the Greeks, as a resting place and place-finder, being first a mere mark (*graphos*) in the margin alongside (*para*) an unbroken sheet of handwriting—the proofreader's familiar ¶. You have heard that a paragraph is a single idea, and this is true. But so is a word, usually; and so is a sentence, sometimes. It seems best, after all, to think of a paragraph as something you use for your reader's convenience, rather than as some granitic form laid down by molten logic.

The medium determines the size of the paragraph. Your average longhand paragraph may look the same size to you as a typewritten one, and both may seem the same size as a paragraph in a book. But the printed page might show your handwritten paragraph so short as to be embarrassing, and your typewritten paragraph barely long enough for decency. Handwriting plus typewriting plus insecurity equals inadequate paragraphs. Your first impulse may be to write little paragraphs, often only a sentence to each. If so, you are not yet writing in any medium at all.

Journalists, of course, are habitually one-sentence paragraphers. The narrowness of the newspaper column makes a sentence look like a paragraph, and narrow columns and short paragraphs serve the rapid transit for which newspapers are designed. A paragraph from a book might fill a whole newspaper column with solid lead. It would have to be broken—paragraphed—for the reader's convenience. On the other hand, a news story on the page of a book would look like a gap-toothed comb, and would have to be consolidated for the reader's comfort.

Plan for the big paragraph.

Imagine yourself writing for print, but in a book, not a newspaper. Force yourself to four or five sentences at least, visualizing your paragraphs as about all of a size. Think of them as identical rectangular frames to be filled. This will allow you to build with orderly blocks, to strengthen your feel for structure. Since the beginner's problem is usually one of thinking of things to say rather than of trimming the overgrowth, you can do your filling out a unit at a time, always thinking up one or two sentences more to fill the customary space. You will probably be repetitive and wordy at first—this is our universal failing—but you will soon learn to fill your paragraph with clean and interesting details. You will get to feel a kind of constructional rhythm as you find yourself coming to a resting place at the end of your customary paragraphic frame.

Once accustomed to a five-sentence frame, say, you can then begin to vary the length for emphasis, letting a good idea swell out beyond the norm, or bringing a particular point home in a paragraph short and sharp—even in one sentence, like this.

The paragraph's structure, then, has its own rhetorical message. It tells the reader visually whether or not you are in charge of your subject, and are leading him confidently to see what you already know. Tiny, ragged paragraphs display your hidden uncertainty, unless clearly placed among big ones for emphasis. Brief opening and closing paragraphs sometimes can emphasize your thesis effectively, but usually they make your beginning seem hasty and your ending perfunctory. So aim for the big paragraph all the way, and vary it only occasionally and knowingly, for rhetorical emphasis.

Find a topic sentence.

Looked at as a convenient structural frame, the paragraph reveals a further advantage. Like the essay itself, it has a beginning, a middle, and an end. The beginning and the end are usually each one sentence long, and the middle gets you smoothly from one to the other. Since, like the essay, the paragraph flows through time, its last sentence is the most emphatic. This is your home punch. The first sentence holds the next most emphatic place. It will normally be your *topic sentence,* stating the small thesis of a miniature essay, something like this:

> *Jefferson believed in democracy because he firmly believed in reason.* He knew that reason was far from perfect, but he also knew that it was the best faculty we have. He knew that it was better than all the frightened and angry intolerances with which we fence off our own back yards at the cost of injustice. Thought must be free. Discussion must be free. Reason must be free to range among the widest possibilities. Even the opinion we hate, and have reasons for believing wrong, we must leave free so that reason can operate on it, so that we advertise our belief in reason and demonstrate a faith unafraid of the consequences—because we know that the consequences will be right. Freedom is really not the aim and end of Jeffersonian democracy: freedom is the means by which democracy can rationally choose justice for all.

If your topic sentence covers everything within your paragraph, your paragraph is coherent, and you are using your paragraphs with maximum effect, leading your reader into your community block by block. If your end sentences bring him briefly to rest, he will know where he is and appreciate it.

BEGINNING PARAGRAPHS: THE FUNNEL

State your thesis at the END of your beginning paragraph.

Your beginning paragraph should contain your main idea, and present it to best advantage. Its topic sentence is also the *thesis sentence* of your entire essay. The clearest and most emphatic place for your thesis sentence is at the *end*—not at the beginning—of the beginning paragraph. If you put it first, you will have to repeat some version of it as you bring your beginning paragraph to a close. If you put it in the middle, the reader will very likely take something else as your main point, probably whatever the last sentence contains. The inevitable psychology of interest, as you move your reader through your first paragraph and into your essay, urges you to put your thesis last—in the last sentence of your beginning paragraph.

Think of your beginning paragraph, then, not as a frame to be filled, but as a funnel. Start wide and end narrow:

OPENING   INVITATION

THESIS

If, for instance, you wished to show that "Learning to play the guitar pays off in friendship"—your thesis—you would start somewhere back from that thesis-idea with something more general—about music, about learning, about the pleasures of achievement, about guitars: "Playing the guitar looks easy," "Music can speak more directly than words," "Learning anything is a course in frustration." You can even open with something quite specific, *as long as it is more general than your thesis:* "Pick up a guitar, and you bump into people." A handy way to find an opener is to take one word from your thesis—*learning, play,* or *guitar,* for instance—and make a sentence out of it. Say something about it, and you are well on your way to your thesis, three or four sentences later.* Your opening line, in other words, should look forward to your thesis, should be something to engage interest easily, something to which most readers would assent without a rise in blood pressure. (Antagonize and startle if you wish, but beware of having the door slammed before you have a chance and of making your thesis an anticlimax.) Therefore: broad and genial. From your opening geniality, you move progressively down to

*I am grateful to James C. Raymond, of the University of Alabama, for this helpful idea.

smaller particulars. You narrow down: from learning the guitar, to its musical and social complications, to its rewards in friendship (your thesis). Your paragraph might run, from broad to narrow, like this:

> Learning anything has unexpected rocks in its path, but the guitar seems particularly rocky. It looks so simple. A few chords, you think, and you are on your way. Then you discover not only the musical and technical difficulties, but a whole unexpected crowd of human complications. Your friends think you are showing off; the people you meet think you are a fake. Then the frustrations drive you to achievement. You learn to face the music and the people honestly. You finally learn to play a little, but you also discover something better. You have learned to make and keep some real friends, because you have discovered a kind of ultimate friendship with yourself.

Now, that paragraph turned out a little different from what I anticipated. I used the informal *you*, and it seemed to suit the subject. I also overshot my original thesis, discovering, as I wrote, a thesis one step farther—an underlying cause—about coming to friendly terms with oneself. But it illustrates the funnel, from the broad and general to the one particular point that will be your essay's main idea, your thesis. Here is another example:

> The environment is the world around us, and everyone agrees it needs a cleaning. Big corporations gobble up the countryside and disgorge what's left into the breeze and streams. Big trucks rumble by, trailing their fumes. A jet roars into the air, and its soot drifts over the trees. Everyone calls for massive action, and then tosses away his cigarette butt or gum wrapper. The world around us is also a sidewalk, a lawn, a lounge, a hallway, a room right here. Cleaning the environment can begin by reaching for the scrap of paper at your feet.

In a more argumentative paper, you can sometimes set up your thesis effectively by opening with the opposition, as we have already noted (p. 31):

> Science is the twentieth century's answer to everything. We want the facts. We conduct statistical poles to measure the President's monthly popularity. We send space ships to bring back pieces of the moon and send back data from the planets. We make babies in test tubes. We believe that eventually we will discover the chem-

ical formula for life itself, creating a human being from the basic elements. Nevertheless, one basic element, what has been called the soul, or spirit, may be beyond science and all human planning, as Gore Vidal's recent novel *Kalki* suggests.

EXERCISES

1. *Below is a list of thesis-sentences. Choose one (or its opposite), or make one of your own on the same pattern. Then back off from it at least four or five sentences, and write a funnel-like beginning paragraph leading your reader down to it: your thesis, the last sentence of your beginning funnel.*

EXAMPLE *with thesis italicized follows:*

The coal operators will tell you that stripping is cheaper and more efficient than conventional mining. Their 250-cubic-yard drag-lines, their 200-cubic-yard shovels, their 50-ton trucks, can rip the top off a mountain and expose a whole seam of coal in a fraction of the time it takes to sink a shaft. "It is cheaper," they will say, "to bring the surface to the coal than to bring the coal to the surface." And of course they are right; in a sense it is cheaper. But visit Eastern Kentucky and look at the real price we pay for stripped coal. Visit a stripped area and you will see that, no matter how low the price for a truckload of stripped coal, *the real price for strip-mining has to be reckoned in terms of blighted land, poisoned streams, and stunted human lives.*

1. Although motivated by proper concern for the public welfare, the FCC's ban of cigarette advertising on television is ineffective and discriminatory.
2. Although currently exempt, camper buses and vans should face the same federal safety requirements as automobiles.
3. Despite the evident advantages of artificial turf in football stadiums, it is dangerous and should, therefore, be banned.
4. Even though durable and convenient, tape cassettes reproduce sound with only mediocre fidelity.
5. Legalizing off-track betting may annoy some citizens, but, because it would weaken the underworld, we should support it.

MIDDLE PARAGRAPHS

Make your middle paragraphs full, and use transitions.

The middle paragraph is the standard paragraph, the little essay in itself, with its own little beginning and little end. But it must also declare its allegiance to the paragraphs immediately before and after it. Each topic sentence must somehow hook onto the paragraph above it, must include some word or phrase to ease the reader's path: a transition. You may simply repeat a word from the sentence that ended the paragraph just above. You may bring down a thought left slightly hanging in air: "Smith's idea is different" might be a tremendously economical topic sentence with automatic transition. Or you may get from one paragraph to the next by the usual steppingstones, like *but, however, nevertheless, therefore, indeed, of course.* One brief transitional touch in your topic sentence is usually sufficient.

The topic sentences in each of the following three paragraphs by James Baldwin contain neat transitions. I have just used an old standby myself: repeating the words *topic sentence* from the close of my preceding paragraph. Baldwin has just described the young people of Harlem who have given up, escaping into day-long TV, or the local bar, or drugs. He now begins his next paragraph with *And the others,* a strong and natural transition, referring back, reinforced with the further transitional reference *all of these deaths.* In the next paragraph, *them* does the trick; in the last, *other* again makes the transition and sets the contrast. The paragraphs are nearly the same length, all cogent, clear, and full. No one-sentence paragraphing here, no gaps, but all a vivid, orderly progression:

Topic
Sentence with
Transition

And the others, who have avoided **all of these deaths**, get up in the morning and go downtown to meet "the man." They work in the white man's world all day and come home in the evening to this fetid block. They struggle to instill in their children some private sense of honor or dignity which will help the child to survive. This means, of course, that they must struggle, stolidly, incessantly, to keep this sense alive in themselves, in spite of the insults, the indifference, and the cruelty they are certain to encounter in their working day. They patiently browbeat the landlord into fixing the heat, the plaster, the plumbing; this demands prodigious patience; nor is patience usually enough. In trying to make their hovels habitable, they are perpetually throwing good money after bad. Such

End Sentence:
The Point

frustration, so long endured, is driving many strong, admirable men and women whose only crime is color to the very gates of paranoia.

Topic
Sentence with
Transition

One remembers **them** from another time—playing handball in the playground, going to church, wondering if they were going to be promoted at school. One remembers them going off to war—gladly, to escape this block. One remembers their return. Perhaps

End Sentence:
The Point

one remembers their wedding day. And one sees where the girl is now—vainly looking for salvation from some other embittered, trussed, and struggling boy—and sees the all-but-abandoned children in the streets.

    Now I am perfectly aware that there are other slums in which white men are fighting for their lives, and mainly losing. I know that blood is also flowing through those streets and that the human damage there is incalcuable. People are continually pointing out to me the wretchedness of white people in order to console me for the wretchedness of blacks. But an itemized account of the American failure does not console me and it should not console anyone else. That hundreds of thousands of white people are living, in effect, no better than the "niggers" is not a fact to be regarded with complacency. The social and moral bankruptcy suggested by this fact is of the bitterest, most terrifying kind.*

Topic
Sentence with
Transition

End Sentence:
The Point

Check your paragraphs for clarity and coherence.

Baldwin's paragraphs run smoothly from first sentence to last. They are coherent. The *topic sentence* is the key. It assures that your subsequent sentences will fall into line, and it is the first point to check when you look back to see if they really do. Many a jumbled and misty paragraph can be unifed and cleared by writing a broader topic sentence. Consider this disjointed specimen:

> **Swimming is healthful. The first dive into the pool is always cold. Tennis takes a great deal of energy, especially under a hot sun. Team sports, like basketball, baseball, and volleyball, always make the awkward player miserable. Character and health go hand in hand.**

What is all that about? From the last sentence, we can surmise something of what the writer intended. But the first sentence about swimming in no way covers the paragraph, which treats several sports not in the least like swimming, and seems to be driving at something other than health. The primary remedy, as always, is to find the paragraph's thesis and to devise a topic sentence that will state it, thus covering everything in the paragraph. Think of your topic sentence as a roof—covering your paragraph and pulling its lines and contents together.

    *From "Fifth Avenue Uptown: A Letter from Harlem," in *Nobody Knows My Name* (New York: Dial Press, 1961), pp. 59–61. Copyright © 1960 by James Baldwin. Reprinted by permission of Dial Press. Originally published in *Esquire*.

POOR COVERAGE

GOOD COVERAGE

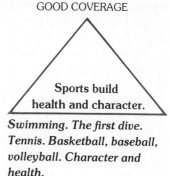

The first dive. Tennis. Basketball, baseball, volleyball. Character and health.

Swimming. The first dive. Tennis. Basketball, baseball, volleyball. Character and health.

Suppose we leave the paragraph unchanged for the moment, adding only a topic sentence suggested by our right-hand diagram. It will indeed pull things together:

Topic
Sentence

> *Sports demand an effort of will and muscle that is healthful for the soul as well as the body.* **Swimming is healthful. The first dive into the pool is always cold. Tennis takes a great deal of energy, especially under a hot sun. Team sports, like basketball, baseball, and volleyball, always make the awkward player miserable. Character and health go hand in hand.**

But the paragraph is still far from an agreeable coherence. The islands of thought still need some bridges. Gaining coherence is primarily a filling in, or a spelling out, of submerged connections. You may fill in with (1) thought and (2) specific illustrative detail; you may spell out by tying your sentences together with (3) transitional tags and (4) repeated words or syntactical patterns. Let us see what we can do with our sample paragraph.

From the first, you probably noticed that the writer was thinking in pairs: the pleasure of sports is balanced off against their difficulty; the difficulty is physical as well as moral; character and health go hand in hand. We have already indicated this doubleness of idea in our topic sentence. Now to fill out the thought, we need merely expand each sentence so as to give each half of the double idea its due expression. We need also to qualify the thought here and there with *perhaps, often, some, sometimes, frequently, all in all,* and the like. As we work through the possibilities, more specific detail will come to mind. We have already made the general ideas of *character* and *health* more specific with *will, muscle, soul,* and *body* in our topic sentence, and we shall add a touch or two more of illustration, almost automatically, as our imagination becomes more stimulated by the subject. We shall add a number of transitional ties like *but, and, of course, nevertheless,* and *similarly.* We shall look for chances to repeat key words, like *will,* if we can do so gracefully; and to repeat syntactical patterns, if we can emphasize similar thoughts by doing so, as with *no matter how patient his teammates . . . no matter how heavy his heart,* toward the end of our revision below (the original phrases are in italics):

Sports demand an effort of will and muscle that is healthful for the soul as well as the body. *Swimming* is physically *healthful,* of course, although it may seem undemanding and highly conducive to lying for hours inert on a deck chair in the sun. But *the first dive into the pool is always cold:* taking the plunge always requires some effort of will. And the swimmer soon summons his will to compete, against himself or others, for greater distances and greater speed, doing twenty laps where he used to do one. Similarly, *tennis takes* quantities *of energy,* physical and moral, *especially* when the competition stiffens *under a hot sun. Team sports, like basketball, baseball, and volleyball,* perhaps demand even more of the amateur. *The awkward player* is miserable when he strikes out, or misses an easy fly, or an easy basket, no matter how patient his teammates. He must drive himself to keep on trying, no matter how heavy his heart. Whatever the sport, a little determination can eventually conquer one's awkwardness and timidity, and the reward will be more than physical. *Character and health* frequently *go hand in hand.*	Topic Sentence

Illustrative Sentences with Transitions

End Sentence: The Point |

Accustom yourself to the transitional tags.

We have already looked at some of the transitional bridges, first those that take you from the *pro* side of your argument to the *con* and back, and then those that, paragraph by paragraph, connect the paths of your thought from start to finish. Now let us simply summarize, in the table on pp. 60–61, the common transitional possibilities, since beginners usually do not think of transitions, and since any and all transitions contribute importantly to the inner coherence of your paragraphs.

You should use such tags economically, of course. You should vary them, and avoid switching your argument back and forth so frequently that you spoil your paragraph's coherence. The more various the transitional tags at your command, the more flexible your resources. Keep an eye open for unusual ones. A rare *contrariwise, mind you, egad* or *alas* may give you just the right turn of humor or irony. But remember, these tags may easily become wordy. Make them work, or retire them with your revising pencil.

Lead your reader with specific details.

Transitional tags help the reader around the turns, but specific details give him solid footing. He needs to step from detail to detail, or his progress will not be coherent. Your topic sentences are generalizations. Your reader now needs to feel the support of facts, the specific items, numbers, quotations, men, and women, that illustrate your general points. Mr. George Ramsey of Sacramento, California, likes to give his classes his Ramsey Test of Specifics. "Look at your paragraph, class," he says,

TRANSITIONS		USES
1. and or, nor also moreover	furthermore indeed in fact first, second . . .	You are adding something. *And* can be a good sentence-opener, when used with care.
2. for instance for example for one thing	similarly likewise	Again you are adding, and illustrating or expanding your point.
3. therefore thus so and so hence consequently	finally on the whole all in all in other words in short	You are adding up consequences, summarizing minor points to emphasize a major point.
4. frequently occasionally in particular in general	specifically especially usually	You are adding a qualifying point or illustration.
5. of course no doubt doubtless	to be sure granted (that) certainly	You are conceding a point to the opposition, or recognizing a point just off your main line.

TRANSITIONS		USES
6. but however yet on the contrary	not at all surely no	You are reversing or deflecting the line of thought, usually back to your own side.
7. still nevertheless notwithstanding		You return the thought to your own side after a concession.
8. although though whereas		You are attaching a concession to one of your points. Do not use *while* for *whereas; while* means, basically, "during the time that," and is thus ambiguous unless restricted to time. (See *Whereas; While, Glossary of Usage.*)
9. because since for		You are connecting a *reason* to an assertion.
10. if provided in case	unless lest when	You are qualifying and restricting a more general idea.
11. as if as though even if		You are glancing at tentative or hypothetical conditions that strengthen and clarify your point.
12. this that these those who whom he she	it they all of them few many most several	These relative and demonstrative words (adjectives and pronouns) tie things together, pointing back as they carry the reference ahead. But be sure there can be no mistaking the specific word to which each refers.

"and score one point for each capital letter on a name of a person or place; score one point for each direct quotation; score one point for any numbers; and score one point for each example or illustration." Scores are frequently zero. All generalization. No specific details whatsoever. The reader has nothing under his feet at all.

The following paragraph by Loren Eiseley would score about 10 or so. He has been writing of Alfred Russel Wallace's and Charles Darwin's conflicting views as to the evolution of man's brain, and has just referred to the small-brained humanoid apes:

> **These apes are not all similar in type or appearance. They are men and yet not men. Some are frailer-bodied, some have great, bone-cracking jaws and massive gorilloid crests atop their skulls. This fact leads us to another of Wallace's remarkable perceptions of long ago. With the rise of the truly human brain, Wallace saw that man had transferred to his machines and tools many of the alterations of parts that in animals take place through evolution of the body. Unwittingly, man had assigned to his machines the selective evolution which in the animal changes the nature of its bodily structure through the ages. Man of today, the atomic manipulator, the aeronaut who flies faster than sound, has precisely the same brain and body as his ancestors of twenty thousand years ago who painted the last Ice Age mammoths on the walls of caves in France.***

To illustrate his opening generalization that "these apes are not similar," Eiseley adds the specific details of *frailer-bodied, great bone-cracking jaws,* and *massive gorilloid crests atop their skulls.* Rather than merely stating his general point about man and machines, he goes on to illustrate specifically with *the atomic manipulator* and *the aeronaut who flies faster than sound.* Notice that he does not say *manipulators* or *aeronauts,* plural, but takes *the* single and specific *aeronaut* and lets him illustrate the whole range of what man can do with machines. Notice especially how he extends his closing general idea into specific detail: not merely "ancestors," but ancestors of specifically *twenty thousand years ago;* not merely "lived," let us say, but *who painted,* and not merely "pictures," but *the last Ice Age mammoths,* and specifically on *walls* in specific *caves* in one specific country, *France.* The point is to try to extend each of your generalizations by adding some specific detail to illustrate it. Don't stop

---

*"The Real Secret of Piltdown," in *The Immense Journey* (New York: Random House, Inc., 1955). © Copyright 1955 by Loren C. Eiseley.

with *awkward player:* go on to *when he strikes out, or misses an easy fly, or an easy basket.*

Here are the four points to remember about middle paragraphs. First, think of the middle paragraph as a miniature essay, with a beginning, a middle, and an end. Its beginning will normally be its topic sentence, the thesis of this miniature essay. Its middle will develop, explain, and illustrate your topic sentence. Its last sentence will drive home the idea. Second, see that your paragraph is coherent, not only flowing smoothly but with nothing in it not covered by the topic sentence. Third, make your paragraphs full and well developed, with plenty of details, examples, and full explanations, or you will end up with a skeletal paper with very little meat on its bones. Fourth, remember transitions. Though each paragraph is a kind of miniature essay, it is also a part of a larger essay. Therefore, hook each paragraph smoothly to the paragraph preceding it, with some transitional touch in each topic sentence.

EXERCISES

2. *Read the following paragraph from W. E. B. DuBois's* The Souls of Black Folk, *in which he describes Georgia's "Black Belt" (a name referring to the soil, not the people) as he saw it in 1903, and then answer the following questions:*

It is a land of rapid contrasts and of curiously mingled hope and pain. Here sits a pretty blue-eyed quadroon hiding her bare feet; she was married only last week, and yonder in the field is her dark young husband, hoeing to support her, at thirty cents a day without board. Across the way is Gatesby, brown and tall, lord of two thousand acres shrewdly won and held. There is a store conducted by his black son, a blacksmith shop, and a ginnery. Five miles below here is a town owned and controlled by one white New Englander. He owns almost a Rhode Island county, with thousands of acres and hundreds of black laborers. Their cabins look better than most, and the farm, with machinery and fertilizers, is much more business-like than any in the county, although the manager drives hard bargains in wages. When now we turn and look five miles above, there on the edge of town are five houses of prostitutes,—two of blacks and three of whites; and in one of the houses of the whites a worthless black boy was harbored too openly two years ago; so he was hanged for rape. And here, too, is the high whitewashed fence of the "stockade," as the county prison is called; the white folks say it is ever full of black criminals,—the black folks say that only colored boys are sent to jail, and they not because they are guilty, but because the State needs criminals to eke out its income by their forced labor.*

1. What is most interesting about this paragraph?
2. What is the topic sentence of the paragraph?
3. How does DuBois use detail to support his topic sentence? Be specific.
4. Is there a consistent order of the details in the paragraph? Give examples to support your answer.
5. What transitional tags are there?
6. Does DuBois repeat key terms? If so, which and where?
7. Is the point of view consistent? If so, describe it.
8. Does the author interrupt his paragraph with parenthetical comments?
9. What do you think are the clearest evidences of coherence within this paragraph?

3. (a) *Pick a topic sentence from those following the example, or make a similar one and develop from it a full middle paragraph, remembering the four points: (1) the miniature essay, with beginning, middle, and end: (2) coherence; (3) fullness; (4) transition. Your paragraph should seem to be taken from the middle of a longer paper. You will have to imagine what comes before and after, supplying a transitional* But, Another aspect of, also, *and the like.*

EXAMPLE, *with transitional touch italicized:*

TOPIC SENTENCE: The fashions current in the late 1970's suggest an urge to get back to a simpler and more secure past.

The fashions current in the late 1970's suggest *the same* urge *we have already seen in films and music* to get back to a simpler and more secure past. For the more stylish dressers among us, the Sunday supplements and fashion magazines are featuring 1920's, 1930's, and 1940's styles in both men's and women's clothing. On the street, you can see fashionable women in broad-shouldered and boxy suits, middy blouses, or "sensible shoes" with ugly, clomping heels, all clearly echoing the past. Or you can see modish men wearing huge bow ties for the first time in thirty years. And you see them wearing the wide lapels, fitted waists, flared trousers, and patterned shirts of the 1920's and 1930's. Even for the remaining anti-Establishment or Bohemian dressers among us, the styles current in the early 1970's reflect the urge to get back to the past. Bibbed overalls, work shirts, clodhoppers, bandannas, wide belts, and Western hats, all conjure up images of a frontier past.

*W. E. B. DuBois, The Souls of Black Folk, Essays and Sketches (Chicago: A. C. McClurg & Co., 1903), pp. 125–126.

Undergraduates go to class dressed like "sod-busters," trappers, or miners fresh from the Virginia City of the 1880's. And in any city park you can still find a guitar player whose long hair, beard, and fringed leather jacket would make him appear completely at home in the turn-of-the-century West. It is as if all of us, from the solid Establishment to the Bohemian youth-culture, are seeking by our dress to recapture a more simple and secure past. It is as if we are trying to escape the complexity of the 1970's by costuming ourselves in the styles of the past. We are like children who escape by playing dress-up.

1. No matter what the advertisements promise, the X-rated movie usually turns out to be dull and wearisome; it turns out to be two hours of heavy breathing.
2. The computer has contributed to the modern sense of alienation.
3. If the filibuster is supposed to guarantee respect for minority opinion, it usually turns out to be a flagrant waste of time.
4. The new sense of black pride is our increasing awareness of black accomplishments in the past.
5. If women are discriminated against in schools and in industry, they are far more discriminated against in politics.

(b) *Now check the coherence of your paragraph by answering the following questions:*

1. What is most interesting about this paragraph?
2. What is the topic sentence of the paragraph?
3. How do you use details to support your topic sentence?
4. Is there a consistent order of the details in the paragraph?
5. What transitional tags are there?
6. Do you repeat key terms?
7. Is the point of view consistent?
8. Do you interrupt your paragraph with parenthetical comments.
9. What do you think are the clearest evidences of coherence within this paragraph?

END PARAGRAPHS: THE INVERTED FUNNEL

Reassert your thesis.

If the beginning paragraph is a funnel, the end paragraph is a funnel upside down: the thought starts moderately narrow—it is more or less the thesis you have had all the time—and then pours out broader and broader implications and finer emphases. The end paragraph reiterates, summarizes, and emphasizes with decorous fervor. This is your last chance.

This is what your reader will carry away—and if you can carry *him* away, so much the better. All within decent intellectual bounds, of course. You are the person of reason still, but the person of reason supercharged with conviction, sure of your idea and sure of its importance.

The final paragraph conveys a sense of assurance and repose, of business completed. Its topic sentence should be some version of your original thesis sentence, since the end paragraph is the exact structural opposite and complement of the beginning one. Its transitional word or phrase is often one of finality or summary—*then, finally, thus,* and *so:*

> **So, the guitar is a means to a finer end.**
> **The environment, then, is in our lungs and at our fingertips.**

The paragraph would then proceed to expand and elaborate this revived thesis. We would get a confident assertion that both the music and the friendships are really by-products of an inner alliance; we would get an urgent plea to clean up our personal environs and strengthen our convictions. One rule of thumb: the longer the paper, the more specific the summary of the points you have made. A short paper will need no specific summary of your points at all; the renewed thesis and its widening of implications are sufficient.

Here is an end paragraph by Sir James Jeans. His transitional phrase is *for a similar reason.* His thesis was that previous concepts of physical reality had mistaken surfaces for depths:

> **The purely mechanical picture of visible nature fails for a similar reason. It proclaims that the ripples themselves direct the workings of the universe instead of being mere symptoms of occurrences below; in brief, it makes the mistake of thinking that the weather-vane determines the direction from which the wind shall blow, or that the thermometer keeps the room hot.***

Here is an end paragraph by Charles Wyzanski, Jr. His transitional phrase is *Each generation,* since he has been talking of the perpetual gap. His thesis was that differences, including those between generations, have stimulated life to higher modes:

> **Each generation is faced with a challenge of making some kind of sense out of its existence. In advance, it knows from the Book of Job and the Book of Ecclesiastes and the Greek drama that there will be no right answer. But there will be forms of answer. There**

*The New Background of Science (Cambridge: Cambridge University Press, 1933), p. 261.

will be a style. As ancient Greece had the vision of *arete* (the noble warrior), as Dante and the Medievalists had the vision of the great and universal Catholic Church, even as the founding fathers of the American Republic had the vision of the new order which they began, so for the young the question is to devise a style—not one that will be good *semper et ubique,* but one for our place and our time, one that will be a challenge to the very best that is within our power of reach, and one that will make us realize, in Whitehead's immortal terms, that for us the only reality is the process.†

Here is an end paragraph of Professor Richard Hofstadter's. His transitional word is *intellectuals,* carried over from the preceding paragraphs. His thesis was that intellectuals should not abandon their defense of intellectual and spiritual freedom, as they have tended to do, under pressure to conform:

> This world will never be governed by intellectuals—it may rest assured. But *we* must be assured, too, that intellectuals will not be altogether governed by this world, that they maintain their piety, their longstanding allegiance to the world of spiritual values to which they should belong. Otherwise there will be no intellectuals, at least not above ground. And societies in which the intellectuals have been driven underground, as we have had occasion to see in our own time, are societies in which even the anti-intellectuals are unhappy.*

Remember this, when you have used up all your points and had your say. You and your argument are both exhausted. You will be tempted to stop, but don't stop. You need an end, or the whole thing will unravel in your reader's mind. You need to buttonhole him in a final paragraph, to imply "I told you so" without saying it, to hint at the whole round experience he has just had, and to leave him convinced, satisfied, and admiring. One more paragraph will do it: beginning, middle, *and* end.

EXERCISES

4. *Now try the inverted funnel, in which your topic sentence is some version of the thesis with which you began and your final paragraph broadens its impli-*

---

†"A Federal Judge Digs the Young," *Saturday Review,* July 20, 1968, p. 62.
*Democracy and Anti-intellectualism in America," *Michigan Quarterly Review,* 59 (1953), 295.

cations outward to leave the reader fully convinced and satisfied. Using the the-sis-sentences in Exercise 1, write two ending paragraphs for imaginary papers.

EXAMPLE with the rephrased thesis (its topic sentence) italicized, and some of the evidence from the paper's middle summarized for emphasis:

So, at last, we should add up the real costs of strip-mining; we should admit that the ultimate price of coal is far too high if we must rape the land, poison the streams, and wreck human lives to mine it. For after the drag-lines have gone, even after the coal itself has been burned, the bills for strip-mining will keep coming in. So far, following the expedient path, we have laid bare more than 2,600 square miles of our land, and we show no signs of stopping. Every year we strip an additional 50,000 acres. Just as we cut down our forests in the nineteenth century and fouled our air in the twentieth, we still blunder along toward ecological and social disaster. Isn't it time to stop?

MORE ON MECHANICS:
PARAGRAPHS AND LONG QUOTATIONS

You indent your topic sentence, of course, to signal your paragraph's beginning—usually five letterspaces from your margin. When you want to illustrate a point with a sizable quotation, you indent it twice your original amount from the margin, omitting quotation marks and single-spacing your quotation to simulate insets in smaller print. Also give an extra line of space above and below your quotation, to distinguish it even more clearly from your own text. (See Chapter 12, the sample term paper, for good examples.) With short-lined poetry, you will probably need to indent even more, to center it attractively within the frame of your paragraph. To keep your paragraph clear as a whole, try to conclude, after the inset quotation, by coming back out to the margin with a sentence or two of your own. With a very long quotation, however, which may take up a full block of paragraphing, and more, you had best let the paragraph go at that, and start again with your own text in a new paragraph.

For clear paragraphing with long quotations, which you may want to introduce with no more than a single topic sentence of your own, try to make that introductory sentence long enough to come back out to the margin, making the opening notch of your paragraph clearly visible to your reader. If your quotation itself begins as a paragraph, indent it *one more* full indentation (five, in all, from your margin), to show your reader just how it stands in *its* original text (see p. 293 for an example). A glance at the paragraphs I have seen quoting in these pages in both the text discussions and exercises will also show approximately how this looks.

THE WHOLE ESSAY **69**

One more point: if you are quoting and insetting blocks of poetry, you may need "hanging indentation" for the longer lines, indenting their endings three or four letter spaces under the line-head to keep the line standing clear—perhaps even several times, as you would in quoting Walt Whitman's "There Was a Child Went Forth":

```
There was a child went forth every day,          Indented
And the first object he looked upon he became,   Quotation
And that object became part of him for the
    day or a certain part of the day,            Hanging
Or for many years or stretching cycles of        Indentation
    years.
The early lilacs became part of this child,
And grass and white and red morning glories,
    and white and red clover, and the song       Hanging
    of the phoebe-bird,                          Indentation
And the third-month lambs. . . .
```

When quoting poetry in your running text, however, you enclose it in quotation marks, and indicate the line-end with a virgule (slant): "That is no country for old men, the young / In one another's arms . . . ."

THE WHOLE ESSAY

You have now discovered the main ingredients of a good essay. You have learned to find and to sharpen your thesis in one sentence, to give your essay that all-important argumentative edge. You have learned to arrange your points in order of increasing interest, and you have practiced disposing of the opposition in a *pro-con* structure. You have seen that your beginning paragraph should seem like a funnel, working from broad generalization to thesis. You have tried your hand at middle paragraphs, which are almost like little essays with their own beginnings and ends. And finally, you have learned that your last paragraph should work like an inverted funnel, broadening and embellishing your thesis.

Some students have pictured the essay as a Greek column, with a narrowing beginning paragraph as its top, or capital, and a broadening end paragraph as its base. Others have seen it as a keyhole,* (see the

---

*Mrs. Fran Measley of Santa Barbara, California, has devised for her students a mimeographed sheet to accompany my discussion of structure and paragraphing—to help them to visualize my points, through a keyhole, as it were. I am grateful to Mrs. Measley to be able to include it here.

THE KEYHOLE

TITLE

OPENING INVITATION

BEGINNING PARAGRAPH

THESIS
(Last Sentence)

MIDDLE PARAGRAPHS

*Standard Paragraphs, Each
with Topic Sentence*

Present your weakest argument first.

Lead up to the strongest, which is the last in the
body of your essay, whether your points are sentences
or paragraphs.

Illustrate with facts and examples, in vivid
and lively language.

THESIS REWORDED

Generalize again.

END PARAGRAPH

CLINCHER
(Your Final Sentence and Last Word)

* Focal Points

diagram opposite). But either way, you should see a structure, with solid beginning and end, supported by a well-shaped middle. The student's essay that follows illustrates this structure. The assignment, early in the semester, had been to find something in a newspaper or magazine from which to develop a thesis, and then to illustrate that thesis with (1) the newspaper or magazine item and (2) a personal experience. Again, the writer's language has not fully ripened,but he has grasped the basic ideas of structure: a thesis well set, and a good sense of Beginning, Middle, and End.

THE VALUE OF WORK

America is materialistic. Newspapers and magazines are full of articles about the way greedy American materialism is burning up the world's supply of fuel, eating great quantities of food while others starve, and polluting the rivers and the atmosphere. The "Protestant Work Ethic," inherited from our Pilgrim forefathers, is supposed to be driving us to materialistic ruin.

Broad Subject, Opposition

Nevertheless, the Pilgrims had a point. Work is not only essential to modern society but beneficial to the individual in nonmaterialistic ways.

Thesis

An article in The Milhaven Daily last summer outlined the difficulty teenagers and

Topic Sentence

college students were having in finding work,
and it showed pictures of teenagers painting
a mural on the side of a large brick building,

Middle:
General
Evidence
under the supervision of an artist. The
project was funded by the government, and it
was frankly intended to give the teenagers
something constructive to do, improving
property instead of destroying it through
vandalism because they had nothing else to
do. Money and materialistic gain were not
the purpose of the project, although the
workers were paid and probably enjoyed
getting their paychecks.

Topic
Sentence
Work can in this way satisfy a person's
need to feel useful, to do something
constructive, which other people will

Middle:
Personal
Evidence
respect. I discovered this last year during
my final year in high school. Like many
others, I had completed most of my college
requirements and was feeling restless and
discontented. I answered an ad for a
dishwasher in one of our town's popular steak

houses. I did not need the money. I had an allowance, and there was no problem about sending me to college. For some reason, I wanted to work for the sake of work. Like the teenagers painting the brick wall, I had almost no materialistic motivation.

My first clear motivation was just not to give up. My parents thought that working on school nights, sometimes until midnight, was a poor idea, both because of grades and health. The dishwashing, even with a monster garbage disposal and dishwashing machine, was hard and almost revolting, like stirring around for hours in hot liquid garbage. But I kept up with the load, and I satisfied myself that it would not beat me.

Topic Sentence

Personal Evidence

Then my satisfactions changed from negative to positive. In two weeks, after several other dishwashers had quit, I was promoted to assistant cook, or "pit man." I was teamed with a chef, and taught to set up the different orders on plates, with just

Topic Sentence

Personal Evidence

the right amount of parsley in just the right place, and to cook certain parts of certain orders. In another three weeks, I was training for chef, with pay raises at each step. When summer came, I was a full-time chef, with a pit man of my own. I could work quickly handling the different orders as they came in. I once turned out a banquet for seventy with steaks cooked to order from rare to well done. I liked the job so much that I hated to give it up for a short vacation before entering college this fall.

Topic Sentence: The Opposition I admit some of the charges against the work ethic as materialistic. I bought some expensive new stereo equipment. I bought a new ten-speed bicycle, and I put $1,000 into a time-certificate at the bank. The ability to do these things on my own decision with my own money was very satisfying. But I do not believe that this is really materialism.

Thesis Restated The wish to work, and the satisfaction, are actually psychological, not material. I

once said to my dad, when he congratulated me
on my paycheck, "But I'm really not doing
this for the money—I really don't know why
I'm doing it." He said, "You're doing it to
prove to yourself that you can do a job in
the world, and do it well, that you can make
it on your own if you have to." That really
is the psychological satisfaction in work.
You demonstrate to yourself that you are
useful and able in the adult world. The
paychecks and the raises, although they are
materialistic in themselves, are symbols of
your ability to please others in a useful
way, to be respected for your ability, and to
stand on your own feet.

The Clincher

EXERCISES

5. *Now work your beginning, middle, and end paragraphs into a coherent essay, adding a coherent paragraph or two, with good transitions.*

Chapter 4

PARAGRAPHS: DESCRIPTIVE, NARRATIVE, EXPOSITORY

Descriptive and narrative paragraphs—showing and telling—are essential parts of argument as we display our evidence. Expository paragraphs, the usual laying out and explaining of the idea in our topic sentences, are more factual, but they often contain bits of description and narration too. In fact, describing a process, probably the commonest of expository forms, is description narrated. All three are ways of illustrating our ideas for the reader.

DESCRIPTIVE PARAGRAPHS

Put your perceptions into words.

Description is essentially *spatial*. When your subject concerns a campus, or a failing business district, you may want to write your middle as some orderly progress through space, and your paragraphs virtually as units of space: one paragraph for the intersection, one for the first building, one for the second, one for the tattered drug store at the end of the block. Within a paragraph, you simply take your reader from one detail to the next in order. Your topic sentence summarizes the total effect: "The Whistler Building was once elegant, three stories of brick with carved stone pediments." Then your paragraph proceeds with noteworthy details in any convenient spatial order: first the sagging front door, then the windows to the left, then those to the right, then the second floor's windows, with their suggestion of dingy apartments, then those of the third, which suggest only emptiness.

The best spatial description follows the perceptions of a person entering or looking at the space described, as with the imaginary visitor in this description by R. Prawer Jhabvala of a modern house in India:

> Our foreign visitor stands agape at the wonderful residence his second host has built for himself. No expense has been spared here, no decoration suggested by a vivid taste omitted. There are little Moorish balconies and Indian domes and squiggly lattice work and an air-conditioner in every window. Inside, all is marble flooring, and in the entrance hall there is a fountain lit up with green, yellow, and red bulbs. The curtains on the windows and in the doorways are of silk, the vast sofa-suites are upholstered in velvet, the telephone is red, and huge vases are filled with plastic flowers.*

This procedure may be seen in elaborate extension, paragraph after paragraph, at the beginning of Thomas Hardy's *The Return of the Native* in which we are moved into the setting from a great distance, as if, years before moving pictures, we are riding a cameraman's dolly.

Guide some descriptions through time.

Description frequently blends space and time, with the observer's perceptions unifying the two as he moves through them, and takes his readers with him. You pick out the striking features, showing the reader what would strike him first, as it did you, then proceeding to more minute but no less significant details. This is the usual way of describing people, as in this paragraph (by the anonymous reporter for the *New Yorker's* "Talk of the Town") about an actual Englishman, whose odd occupation is mending the broken eggs brought to him by bird's-egg collectors:

> Colonel Prynne, who is sixty-seven, lives and carries on his singular pursuit in a rambling, thatch-roofed, five-hundred-year-old cottage in the tiny village of Spaxton, Somerset, and there, on a

*Encounter, May 1964, pp. 42–43.

recent sunny afternoon, he received us. A man of medium build who retains a military carriage, he was sprucely turned out in a brown suit, a tan jersey vest, a green shirt and tie, and tan oxfords. He has a bald, distinctly egg-shaped head, wears a close-cropped mustache and black shell-rimmed glasses, and seems always to have his nose tilted slightly upward and the nostrils faintly distended, as if he were sniffing the air. After taking us on a rather cursory tour of his garden, which is as neat and well tended as its owner, he remarked crisply that it was time to get cracking, and we followed him indoors, past an enormous fireplace, which burns five-foot logs, and up a flight of stairs to a room that he calls his studio.*

Here is a remarkable passage from the concluding chapter of D. H. Lawrence's *The Plumed Serpent,* in which you may profitably observe space and time blended to perfection. Lawrence first describes his dream-like Mexican scene in spatial terms, as if it were a spacious and timeless Grecian frieze. Then he moves through time, bringing us to see and feel its stately process. Notice how the implied *now,* the *then,* and the *and at last* fall into natural sequence in the second paragraph, the "timed" paragraph:

Space   A black boat with a red-painted roof and a tall mast was moored to the low breakwater-wall, which rose about a yard high, from the shallow water. <u>On the wall</u> stood loose little groups of white-clad men, looking into the black belly of the ship. And perched immobile in silhouette <u>against the lake,</u> was a black-and-white cow, and a huge monolithic black-and-white bull. The whole silhouette frieze motionless, <u>against the far water</u> that was coloured brown like turtle doves.

Time   It was near, yet seemed strange and remote. Two peons fixed a plank gangway up to the side of the boat. <u>Then</u> they began to shove the cow towards it. She pawed the new broad planks tentatively, <u>then,</u> with that slow Mexican indifference, she lumbered unwillingly on to the gangway. They edged her slowly to the end, where she looked down into the boat. <u>And at last,</u> she dropped neatly into the hold.†

The New Yorker, May 23, 1964, p. 37.
†Copyright 1926 by Alfred A. Knopf, Inc., and renewed in 1954 by Frieda Lawrence Ravagli.

This passage continues with undiminished magic for several pages, until the enchanted boat moves slowly off across the lake—''across the waters, with her massive, star-spangled cargo of life invisible.'' And Lawrence has in fact organized his entire chapter on a span of spaciously slackened time, entitling it ''Here!'' and implying the somehow static ''and now'' of deep experience.

Like space, time is a natural organizer, ancient and simple. Hour follows hour, day follows day, year follows year, life follows life. Again, you simply take your reader along the natural sequence of what happens— to us, or to nations, or to any items in experience or experiment. We understand *processes* (see pp. 101–103) most clearly by tracking the way they move through time, even processes complicated by other, simultaneous events. Underscores mark the temporal signposts serving as guides to the reader.

> And <u>when</u> this wheel turns, that lever tips the food into the trough.
>
> <u>While</u> this conveyor moves into the oven, the other one is bringing the chassis to point B.
>
> And <u>all the time</u> he talked, his hands were moving the shells and flicking the invisible pea.

Other temporal signposts of a similar function are *at the same time, now, soon, then, before, after, next, during, as soon as.*

John James Audubon, the nineteenth-century naturalist, describes in his *Ornithological Biography* the passenger pigeon and its astounding flights in masses a mile wide and one hundred and eighty miles long; he naturally presents his observations as they occurred in time. I have underlined the temporal words in one of his paragraphs:

> <u>As soon as</u> the pigeons discover a sufficiency of food to entice them to alight, they fly around in circles, reviewing the country below. <u>During</u> their evolutions, <u>on such occasions</u>, the dense mass which they form exhibits a beautiful appearance, as it changes direction, <u>now</u> displaying a glistening sheet of azure, <u>when</u> the backs of the birds come <u>simultaneously</u> into view, <u>and anon</u>, <u>suddenly</u> presenting a mass of rich deep purple. They <u>then</u> pass lower, over the woods, and <u>for a moment</u> are lost among the foliage, <u>but again</u> emerge, and are seen gliding aloft. They <u>now</u> alight, but the <u>next moment</u>, as if <u>suddenly</u> alarmed, they take to wing, producing by the flappings of their wings a noise like the roar of distant thunder,

> and sweep through the forests to see if danger is near. Hunger, however, <u>soon</u> brings them to the ground. <u>When</u> alighted, they are seen industriously throwing up the withered leaves. . . .

You can most clearly explain any kind of development or decline—the civil rights movement, the decay of a neighborhood—by taking your reader up or down the path of time. You can sometimes gain dramatic effect, for example, by beginning with the present and moving back to former insignificance or splendor, as in describing a battered tenement that was once the mayor's mansion. But you will do your reader a favor by keeping to a consistent order, whether forward or backward, and not reversing it inadvertently somewhere along the way.

Whether purely spatial, or a blend of space and time, a descriptive paragraph enlivens almost any kind of essay with a detailed picture—the face of a town, the face of a drifter—the physical grounds for your convictions. For this, the paragraph makes an extremely convenient and coherent unit.

EXERCISES

1. *Write a paragraph describing a unit of space, taking your reader from the outside to the inside of your own home, for instance, or dealing with some interesting spatial unit as in the following paragraph from a student's paper.*

> The courtyard of the hotel at Uxmal was a wonderfully cool and welcome surprise after the sweaty bus trip out from Mérida. Surrounding the whole yard was a large *galería,* its ceiling blocking out the few rays of the sun that managed to filter through the heavy plantings that filled the yard. Overhead, along the *galería,* ceiling fans quietly turned, and underfoot the glazed tile floors felt smooth and delightfully cool even though the temperature on the road had pushed up past 100 degrees. Airy wicker chairs lined the railing, and just a few feet away, flowering jungle plants rose almost to the top of the stone arches on the second floor. Under the branches of a tall tree in the middle of the courtyard, out beyond the rail and the thick plantings, raised tile walkways crisscrossed the yard, bordered all along by neatly cultivated jungle flowers. And right in the middle of the yard, at the base of the big tree, a small waterfall splashed down over mossy rocks into a tiny bathing pool. The splashing water, the shade, the cool tile, all made the road outside seem very far off indeed.

2. *Write a one-paragraph description of a person, blending space and time,* as in the paragraph on Colonel Prynne (pp. 77–78), including details of appearance, as well as surroundings.

3. Turn a fixed description into process, as in the Lawrence or Audubon passages, through two or more paragraphs. Try a scene such as, for example, a part of your campus with a solitary figure—a professor of distinct appearance—or a group moving across it.

NARRATIVE PARAGRAPHS

Narrate to illustrate.

As we have seen, even the most stationary description is a kind of *narrative*, since it takes time. Time is the essence of narrative. The narrative paragraph merely exploits convenient temporal units. Narrative is the primary business of fiction, of course, but occasionally an expository essay will give over its entire middle to a narrative account of some event that illustrates its thesis. Of this kind is George Orwell's great essay "Shooting an Elephant." Orwell's thesis is that imperialism tyrannizes over the rulers as well as the ruled. To illustrate it, he tells of an incident during his career as a young police officer in Burma, when he was compelled, by the expectations of the watching crowd, to shoot a renegade elephant. Here is a narrative paragraph in which Orwell reports a crucial moment; notice how he mixes external events and snippets of conversation with his inner thoughts, pegging all perfectly with a topic sentence:

> **But I did not want to shoot the elephant. I watched him beating his bunch of grass against his knees, with that preoccupied grandmotherly air that elephants have. It seemed to me that it would be murder to shoot him. At that age I was not squeamish about killing animals, but I had never shot an elephant and never wanted to. (Somehow it always seems worse to kill a *large* animal.) Besides, there was the beast's owner to be considered. Alive, the elephant was worth at least a hundred pounds; dead, he would only be worth the value of his tusks, five pounds, possibly. But I had got to act quickly. I turned to some experienced-looking Burmans who had been there when we arrived, and asked them how the elephant had been behaving. They all said the same thing: he took no notice of you if you left him alone, but he might charge if you went too close to him.***

*From "Shooting an Elephant," in *Shooting an Elephant and Other Essays* by George Orwell, copyright 1945, 1946, 1949, 1950 by Sonia Brownell Orwell. Reprinted by permission of Harcourt Brace Jovanovich, Inc., and Martin Secker & Warburg Limited.

Orwell is simply giving us an account of events, and of his inner thoughts, as they happened, one after the other. Almost any kind of essay could use a similar paragraph of narrative to illustrate a point.

But to select details and get them in order is not so simple as it may seem. Here are four of the most common flaws in narrative paragraphs, against which you may check your own first drafts:

I. INSUFFICIENT DETAIL. A few words, of course, can tell what happened: "I saw an accident." But if the reader is to feel the whole sequence of the experience, he needs details, and many of them. He also needs in the first sentence or two some orientation to the general scene—a topic sentence of setting and mood. The following is the opening of a narrative paragraph from an essay that has already logically discussed its thesis that "haste makes waste." It is not a bad beginning, but a few more details, as we shall see in a moment, would help us know where we are, and at what time of day or night:

> **The sky was very dark. People were walking quickly in all directions. . . .**

II. DETAILS OUT OF ORDER. The writer of the dark-sky paragraph went on in her next two sentences with additional detail:

> **The sky was very dark. People were walking quickly in all directions. The trees were tossing and swaying about. The air felt heavy, and lightning flickered here and there behind the gray sky.**

But, clearly, the further details are out of order. Although she has said the trees were moving, the air seems to have remained still. She eventually rearranged these details, but not before committing another error.

III. COMMENTS BREAKING INTO THE NARRATIVE FLOW. Our dark-sky student went on to intrude an editorializing comment, and a clever one at that. But she would have been better off letting her details *imply* the moral of the story. Here is her paragraph, revised after conference, with the opening details of setting filled and rearranged, but with the intruding comment, which she actually deleted, left in italics to illustrate the fault:

> **One day, going home from school, I came to understand for the first time how costly haste can be. The sky was very dark, and people were walking quickly across the streets through the afternoon traffic. The air was heavy, and lightning flickered here and there behind the overcast. Suddenly, a soft wind moved through the trees,**

setting them tossing and swaying; and then came a great gust, sending leaves and papers scurrying, and rattling shop signs. Wet splotches the size of quarters began to dapple the sidewalk; and then it started to pour. Everyone began to run in a frenzied scramble for shelter. *People should not lose their heads at the very time they need them most.* At the street corner ahead of me, two girls, running from different directions, crashed together. A boy riding a bicycle slammed on his brakes to avoid them, and he went skidding, out of control, into the middle of the street. A car caught him squarely. Next day, still stunned, I read in the paper that he had died on the way to the hospital.

IV. SHIFTING VIEWPOINT. The effect of a shift of viewpoint is about the same as that of the intruding comment. The narrative flow is broken. The author seems to have jumped out of his original assumptions, from one location to another, as the italicized sentence shows:

My boys of Tent Five were suddenly all piling on top of me on the shaky bunk. I didn't feel much like a counselor, but at least I was keeping them amused. The giggling heap on top of me seemed happy enough. It was organized recreation time, and they seemed pretty well organized. *The Chief hurried across the camp ground, wondering what was going on over there, and issuing a silent death warrant for the counselor of Five.* I looked out through a wiggly chink in the heap and saw the Chief in the doorway, with his face growing redder and redder.

The writer of this paragraph has let his imagination shift from his recollected location on the bunk, beneath the heap of boys, to his reconstruction of what must have been going on in the Chief's head, out on the campground. Similar unwarranted shifts occur when you have been writing *he,* and suddenly shift to *they,* or when you unwittingly shift your tenses from present to past, or past to present.

EXERCISES

4. *Make a running list of the specific words or phrases that signal movement through time in the extended passage that follows—at the same time, when, then, after, and so forth—and then follow that list with a brief comment on the effectiveness of the temporal arrangement. Does the author need few or many such signals? How else does he guide us through the flow of time? (Hanson W. Baldwin* *is describing the Battle of Jutland, in the North Sea near Denmark, of May 31–June 1, 1916.)*

The battle was joined at 3:48 P.M. in a sullen afternoon. Steaming hard, the two battle cruiser forces made contact off the Skagerrak. Hipper immediately reversed course to draw Beatty back upon the main body of the [German] High Seas Fleet. Beatty, always aggressive, followed hard, despite the fact that four fast battleships of his command were well out of range astern. The battle opened at ranges varying from 10,000 to 17,000 yards, with the British ships clear against the western skyline, the German ships dull shapes in the mist to the east. Superior German gunnery and defects in the designs of the British battle cruisers quickly told.

By 4 P.M. *Tiger* had been hit, and *Lion*, Beatty's Flagship, had received its fourth hit from *Lützow*. Q. Turret blew up. Major F. J. W. Harvey of the Royal Marines—both legs severed—ordered the handling room crew to flood the magazines and saved the ship with his dying words. At 4:30 *Indefatigable* disappeared in a terrible sheet of flame and smoke; only two of her crew survived. At 4:06 Sir Hugh Evan-Thomas, with Beatty's four fast battleships, got into the fight at 19,000 yards range, and a 15-inch shell from *Barham* cut through *Von der Tann's* armor and 600 tons of water flooded into the German ship.

The running fight stood on to the south at twenty-three knots as Hipper led Beatty toward the High Seas Fleet. The *Queen Mary* died at 4:26; a column of smoke mushroomed a thousand feet high and great fluttering clouds of paper, bodies, limbs, turret armor, and a lifeboat were hurled high into the air. Nine men out of 1,275 survived.

Princess Royal took a German salvo and a signalman on *Lion's* flag bridge mistakenly reported her blown up.

Beatty, imperturbable, turned to his flag captain: "Chatfield, there seems to be something wrong with our bloody ships today. Turn two points to port [toward the Germans]."

At 4:50, as the dusk was coming down soon after Scheer's main battle fleet had been sighted, Beatty reversed course to the north, falling back upon Jellicoe in a running fight. Evan-Thomas's tough battleships brought up the rear and gave as good as they received. By 6 P.M. all of *Von der Tann's* guns were out of action, her decks a shambles; *Seydlitz* was afire; *Lützow* and *Derfflinger* seriously damaged.

The sun was low before the main fleets met at last about 6:15 P.M. Squarely across Scheer's course, capping the T of his column, lay the might and majesty of England—*King George V* and *Ajax; Iron Duke* and *St. Vincent;*

Tremeraire and *Marlborough; Agincourt* and *Collingwood;* and a host of others bearing proud and ancient names and flying the cross of St. George.

The range was shortened now to 11,000 to 16,000 yards and the British had the advantage of the fading light. At 6:36 Scheer simultaneously reversed the course of his entire fleet—turning southward away from the gaping jaws of the British crescent. But not before he drew blood again; *Invincible,* British battle cruiser, joined the growing company of the departed. Scheer turned north again to the assault at 6:55, partly to try to succor the sinking light cruiser *Wiesbaden* and to aid the crippled *Lützow.* But not for long. His van was the focus for the broadsides of no fewer than thirty-three major British ships. It was too much. Scheer turned again to southward, covering his retirement with a torpedo attack upon the British battleships. Jellicoe, the cautious, turned his battleships *away* from the torpedoes of the retreating Germans and the main fight was over.*

5. *Write a paragraph in which you blend the incidents and thoughts of a crucial moment, as in Orwell's paragraph on p. 81.*

6. *Write two paragraphs that would be part of a longer essay, using the following excerpt from Alfred Kazin's* Starting Out in the Thirties *as a model (notice the effective topic sentence in both paragraphs).*

The dinner was not a success. I kept trying to see everything through Ferguson's eyes, and I felt that everything looked very strange to him. For the first time, I had brought into our home someone from "outside," from the great literary world, and as Ferguson patiently smiled away, interrupted only by my mother's bringing in more and more platters and pleading with him to *eat something,* I tried to imagine his reactions. We all sat around him at the old round table in the dining room—my father, my little sister, and myself—and there poor Ferguson, his eyes bulging with the strain and the harsh bright lights from the overhead lamp, his cheeks red with effort, kept getting shoveled into him cabbage and meatballs, chicken, meat loaf, endless helpings of seltzer and cherry soda; and all the while I desperately kept up a line of chatter to show him that he was not completely isolated, our cousin Sophie sat at the table silently staring at him, taking him in. In our boxlike rooms, where you could hear *every* creak, *every* cough, *every* whisper, while the Brooklyn street boiled outside, there was a strangled human emotion that seemed to me unworthy of Ferguson's sophistication, his jazz, his sardonic perch on Union

*__*World War I: An Outline History__ (New York: Harper & Row, Publishers, 1962), pp. 89–92. Copyright © 1962 by Hanson W. Baldwin. Reprinted by permission of Harper & Row, Publishers, Inc.

Square. But as Sophie sat at the table in her withdrawn silence, my sister stared wide-eyed at the visitor, my mother bustlingly brought in more platters, and my father explained that he had always followed and admired the *New Republic*—oh, ever since the days of Walter Lippmann and Herbert Croly!—I felt, through Ferguson's razor-sharp eyes, how dreary everything was. My father kept slurping the soup and reaching out for the meat with his own fork; since I had warned him that Ferguson would expect a drink, he self-consciously left the bottle of whiskey on the table and kept urging our visitor all through the meal to take another drink. My mother, who did not have even her personal appreciation of the *New Republic* to regale Ferguson with, had nothing to do but bring food in, and after a while Sophie took to her room and barricaded herself in.

So the meal which I had so much advertised in advance—which I had allowed Ferguson to believe would be exotic, mysterious, vaguely Levantine—passed at last, and after he had charmingly said good-by to my parents and I walked him back to the subway at Rockaway Avenue, he studied me quietly for a moment and said, "What the hell was so exotic about that?" . . .*

EXPOSITORY PARAGRAPHS

Develop most paragraphs by examples.

We naturally illustrate our general ideas with specific examples. To explain beauty, we hold up a rose. Most expository paragraphs follow this natural pattern. You begin with your topical assertion. You follow with three or four sentences of illustration. You round off with some concluding sentence or phrase. After your topic sentence, you may well fill your whole paragraph with a single narrative illustration, as does Albert Schweitzer in this paragraph from his "The Evolution of Ethics":

> For the primitive man the circle of solidarity is limited to those whom he can look upon as his blood relatives—that is to say, the members of his tribe, who are to him his family. I am speaking from experience. In my hospital I have primitives. When I happen to ask a hospitalized tribesman, who is not himself bedridden, to render little services to a bedridden patient, he will consent only if the latter belongs to his tribe. If not, he will answer me candidly: "This, no

*Boston: Little, Brown and Company, 1965, pp. 45–57. Copyright © 1962, 1965 by Alfred Kazin. By permission of Little, Brown and Co. in association with The Atlantic Monthly Press.

brother for me," and neither attempts to persuade him nor threats will make him do this favor for a stranger.*

Or you may illustrate your topical assertion with several parallel examples:

> The undercurrent of admiration in hatred manifests itself in the inclination to imitate those we hate. Thus every mass movement shapes itself after its specific devil. Christianity at its height realized the image of the antichrist. The Jacobins practiced all the evils of the tyranny they had risen against. Soviet Russia is realizing the purest and most colossal example of monopolistic capitalism. Hitler took the Protocols of the Wise Men of Zion for his guide and textbook; he followed them "down to the veriest detail."†

Your illustration may also be hypothetical, as it frequently is in scientific explanation. "Suppose you are riding along in a car," the scientist will say, as he tries to convey the idea of relative motion. "You drop a baseball straight down from your hand to the floor between your feet." And he continues by explaining that this vertical drop describes a long line slanting downward in relation to the line of the rapidly receding highway beneath the car. After this paragraph, he might have an additional one for each new aspect of relativity, illustrating each by the same dropped ball in its relation to curves in the road, the earth itself, the sun, and to whatever hypothetical platforms he may wish to put into orbit.

EXERCISES

7. *Write two illustrative paragraphs, using the same topic sentence for both. In the first paragraph, illustrate by one extended example, as in the paragraph from a student's paper below. In the second paragraph, illustrate the same point by several different examples. This student would have shortened his illustration from Marlowe, then added similar examples from Shakespeare, Jonson, Kyd, and so forth.*

> But if the Elizabethan playwright had to be anything, he had to be a **Topic** showman who could entertain and delight his audiences with the kinds of **Sentence** spectacle they loved so well. Witness, for example, Christopher Marlowe, whose play *The Tragical History of Doctor Faustus* was one of the most popular

*The Atlantic Monthly, November 1958, p. 69. Copyright © 1958 by The Atlantic Monthly Company, Boston, Mass. Reprinted with permission.

†Eric Hoffer, *The True Believer* (New York: Harper & Row, Publishers, 1951), pp. 94–95.

Illustration

plays ever presented upon the Elizabethan stage. The play begins with the protagonist, Dr. Faustus, acquiring supernatural powers by signing a pact with the devil, Mephostopheles, who first appears before the audience "in the shape of a dragon." From that point on, as Faustus exercises his magical power, the stage is filled with showy and miraculous scenes, one after the other. Elaborately costumed angels, clowns, and devils appear. A Pope, Helen of Troy, an Emperor, and The Seven Deadly Sins, all troop across Marlowe's stage. The ghost of Alexander the Great shows up. There are pantomimes, dances, and songs in quick succession. And the sound effects must be exciting too, for fireworks are exploded on stage several times during the play. But, best of all, from the Elizabethan point of view, there is a good lot of violence and vulgar sexual humor sprinkled throughout. Oh, of course, the play ends piously enough: Faustus loses his soul for having bargained with the devil. But for two hours, at least, Marlowe gave Faustus—and his Elizabethan audience— a heady excursion through all the pleasures of this world. The fact that the play was enormously popular and frequently revived on the Elizabethan stage is good evidence that Marlowe knew what his audiences wanted and gave it to them.

Cause and effect: trace back or look ahead.

Because is the impulse of your thinking here: "Such and such is so *because. . . .*" You think back through a train of causes, each one the effect of something prior; or you think your way into the future, speculating about the possible effects of some present cause. In other words, you organize your paragraph in one of two ways:

I. You state a general effect, then deal with its several causes.

II. You state a general cause, then deal with its possible effects.

In Arrangement I, you know the effect (a lost football game, or the solar system, let us say), and you speculate as to causes. In Arrangement II, you know the cause (a new restriction, or abolishing nuclear weapons, let us say), and you speculate as to the effects.

ARRANGEMENT I: EFFECT FOLLOWED BY CAUSES.

An unusual cluster of bad luck lost the game. Many blamed Fraser's failure to block the tackler who caused the fumble that produced the winning touchdown. But even here, bad weather and bad luck shared the blame. Both teams faced a slippery field, of course. But Fraser was standing in a virtual bog when he lunged for the block and slipped. Moreover, the storm had delayed the bus for hours, tiring and frustrating the team, leaving them short of sleep and with no chance to practice. Furthermore, Hunter's throwing arm was still not back in shape from his early injury. Finally, one must admit, the Acorns were simply heavier and stronger, which is the real luck of the game.

You will probably notice, as you try to explain causes and effects, that they do not always run in a simple linear sequence, one thing following another, like a row of falling dominoes. Indeed, mere sequence is so famously untrustworthy in tracing causes that one of the classical errors of thought has been named *post hoc, ergo propter hoc* ("after this, therefore because of this"). It is wrong, in other words, to suppose that A caused B because A preceded B. The two may have been entirely unrelated. But the greatest danger in identifying causes is to fasten upon a single cause while ignoring others of equal significance. Both your paragraph and your persuasiveness will be better if you do not insist, as some did, that only Fraser's failure to block the tackler lost the game.

In the lost ball game, you were interested in explaining causes, but sometimes your interest will lie with effects. When describing a slum problem, for instance, your topic sentence might be *The downtown slum is a screaming disgrace* (the effect), and you might then in a single sentence set aside the causes as irrelevant, as water over the dam, as so much spilt milk: "perhaps caused by inefficiency, perhaps by avarice, perhaps by the indifference of Mayor Richman." Your interests will dictate your proportions of cause and effect. You might well write an entire essay that balances the slum's causes and effects in equal proportions: a paragraph each on inefficiency, avarice, and the mayor's indifference, then a paragraph each on ill health, poor education, and hopelessness.

Here is how a brief essay, in three paragraphs, can work out in dealing with cause and effect alone. I have begun and ended with the *effect* (the peculiar layout of a town). First, I located the *immediate cause* (cattle) as my thesis, and then, in the middle paragraph, I moved through the cause and its *conditions* up to the *effect* again—the town as it stands today:

NORTH OF THE TRACKS

If you drive out west from Chicago, you will notice something happening to the towns. After the country levels into Nebraska, the smaller towns are built only on one side of the road. When you stop
    Effect

Cause

for a rest, and look south across the broad main street, you will see the railroad immediately beyond. All of these towns spread northward from the tracks. Why? As you munch your hamburger and look at the restaurant's murals, you will realize that the answer is cattle.

Conditions

These towns were the destinations of the great cattle drives from Texas. They probably had begun at the scattered watering places in the dry land. Then the wagon trails and, finally, the transcontinental railroad had strung them together. Once the railroad came, the whole southwest could raise cattle for the slaughterhouses of Chicago. The droves of cattle came up from the south, and all of these towns reflect the traffic: corrals beside the tracks to the south, the road for passengers and wagons paralleling the tracks on the northern side, then, along the road, the row of hotels, saloons, and businesses, with the town spreading northward behind the businesses.

Cause

The cattle-business itself shaped these one-sided Nebraska towns. The conditions in which this immediate cause took root were the growing population in the East and the railroad that connected the plains of the West, and Southwest, with the tables of New York. The towns took their hopeful being north of the rails, on the leeward side of the vast cattle drives from the south. The trade in cattle has now changed, all the way from Miami to Sacramento. But the great herds of the old Southwest, together with the transcontinental railroad and man's need to make a living, plotted these

Effect

Western towns north of the tracks.

ARRANGEMENT II: CAUSE FOLLOWED BY PROBABLE EFFECTS.

Arrangement II is rarer, and more conjectural. Your order of presenting cause and effect is reversed. You are looking to the future. You state a known cause (a new restriction on dormitory hours) or a hypothetical cause ("If this restriction is passed"), and then you speculate about the possible, or probable, effects. Your procedure will then be much the same as before. But for maximum persuasiveness, try to keep your supposed effects, which no one can really foresee, as nearly probable as you can. Occasionally, of course, you may put an improbable hypothetical cause to good use in a satiric essay, reducing some proposal to absurdity: "If all restrictions were abolished. . . ." "If no one wore clothes. . . ." Or the improbable *if* may even help clarify a straightforward explanation of real relationships, as in the following excerpt from *Time* magazine's report on Fred Hoyle, the British astronomer and mathematician who has been modifying Newton's gravity and Einstein's relativity. The paragraph states the general condition, proposes its hypothetical cause with an *if*, then moves to the effects, first in temporal order and then in order of human interest:

> **The masses, and therefore the gravity, of the sun and the earth are partly due to each other, partly to more distant objects such as the stars and galaxies. According to Hoyle, if the universe were to be cut in half, local solar-system gravitation would double, drawing the earth closer to the sun. The pressure in the sun's center would increase, thus raising its temperature, its generation of energy, and its brightness. Before being seared into a lump of charcoal, a man on earth would find his weight increasing from 150 to 300 lbs.**

EXERCISES

8. *Below is a list of statements about the population of the United States, some general, some particular. First arrange them in a suitable order for Arrangement I (pp. 89–90), then arrange them again in a suitable order for Arrangement II. Remember that subordinate points should also follow the order of ascending importance.*

1. An expanding population quickly expends resources and energy for new housing, and often neglects existing housing.
2. The annual death rate has declined slightly since 1960 (a decrease of slightly over one death per thousand of population).
3. Rapidly increasing population over-strains the classrooms in public schools, and has forced enlarged classes and, in some instances, half-day sessions.
4. The birth rate, which had declined from 1965 to 1976 (19.4 to 14.7), began to rise again in 1977 (15.1).
5. Despite our more recent concern and awareness, the total population in the United States has continued to increase alarmingly since the 1960's.
6. The annual birth rate per thousand of population has declined (15.1 in 1977 compared with the 1960 rate of 23.7). Nevertheless, 3.2 million babies were born in 1977, almost exactly the same number as thirty years previously.
7. An increasing population strains college facilities; the number of college students doubled between 1960 and 1970 and may be half again as large by 1980.
8. Immigration has gradually increased in recent years (399,000 in 1976 compared with 323,000 in 1966).

9. An expanding population forces cities to fill land once used for recreation and crops with shopping centers, streets, and houses.

10. A rapidly expanding population eventually crowds more people into less space, increasing their vulnerability to disease, to squalor, and to strife.

9. *Write a paragraph following Arrangement I, with* effect *as the topic sentence, followed by causes.*

10. *Write a paragraph following Arrangement I that sets causes aside in a sentence or phrase and concentrates on effects.*

11. *Write a paragraph following Arrangement II, with* some *cause followed by its probable effects. Work in a hypothetical effect if you can.*

12. *Work up any one of these into a three- or four-paragraph essay, handing in your original paragraph as well.*

Problem and solution: follow the natural order.

As with cause and effect, this expository mode exploits a natural order. Your topic sentence sets the problem; the rest of your paragraph gives the solution. It may state the problem—what to do about a run-down park; how to arouse interest in student government—and suggest solutions yet to come, steps to be taken. It may reverse the direction, as in looking for causes, speculating on such problems as how humans learned speech, or how they domesticated cats. Or it may outline how problems have been solved. In each case, the problem gives you a natural topic sentence organizing the solutions that fill your paragraph.

Building the Panama Canal, for instance, posed problems of politics, geology, and human survival. After you had picked up the information, your paragraph would fall naturally into place:

	Building the Panama Canal posed problems of politics, geol-
Problem 1	**ogy, and human survival from the beginning. A French company,** **organized in 1880 to dig the canal, repeatedly had to extend its** **treaties at higher and higher prices as the work dragged on. Uneasy**
Solution to 1	**about the French, the United States made treaties with Nicaragua** **and Costa Rica to dig along the other most feasible route. This** **political threat, together with the failure of the French and the revolt** **of Panama from Colombia, finally enabled the United States to buy** **the French rights and negotiate new treaties, which, nevertheless,**
Problem(s) 2	**continue to cause political trouble to this day. Geology also posed** **its ancient problems: how to manage torrential rivers and inland**
Solutions to 2	**lakes; whether to build a longer but more enduring canal at sea**

level, or a shorter, cheaper, and safer canal with locks. Economy eventually won, but the problem of yellow fever and malaria, which had plagued the French, remained. By detecting and combating the fever-carrying mosquito, William Gorgas solved these ancient tropical problems. Without him, the political and geological solutions would have come to nothing.

Problem 3

Solution to 3

You could easily organize this into three paragraphs of problem and solution, with topic sentences like these:

The Panama Canal posed three major problems, the first of which was political.

The second problem was geological, a massive problem of engineering.

The third problem, that of human survival, proved the most stubborn of all.

Any problem and its solution can produce a neatly ordered paragraph— or essay, for that matter: choosing a college, or something to wear (if you want to be light-hearted), making an apartment or a commune work, building the Eiffel Tower or the pyramids.

EXERCISES

13. *Write a paragraph of problem and solution, following the suggestions and hints in this section.*

14. *Using the order of problem and solution, write a three- or four-paragraph paper in which you describe some particularly interesting architectural or engineering accomplishment. Choose any topic you wish. For example, how did architects design the high-rise buildings in San Francisco so that they would withstand the shock of the severe earthquakes of 1971? Or how did medieval man make a suit of armor? Or how do you plan to convert your VW bus into a camper that will sleep four people? In the first paragraph, state the problem as your thesis sentence. Then go on to describe how the problem could be, or was, solved. Here, for example, is one student's paper:*

NOTHING PRIMITIVE ABOUT IT

Stonehenge, the gigantic prehistoric construction on Salisbury Plain in England, cannot fail to fascinate us with a number of nearly unanswerable questions. How long has it been there? Who built it? Why? But of the questions

Thesis

Problem 1

Problem 2

Solutions to 1

Solutions to 2

Stonehenge raises, none is more intriguing than "*How* was it built?" How did these primitive people, whose only tools were rock, bone, or crudely fashioned sticks, who had not yet even discovered the wheel, manage to transport the huge rocks, most of them more than twenty feet in length and weighing over thirty tons, more than twenty miles overland? And by what ingenuity did they manage, having transported the rocks, to stand them on end and support them so that now, thousands of years later, most of them still stand? What primitive engineering geniuses were these?

Transporting the stones from their original site at Marlborough Downs, some twenty miles to the north of Stonehenge, must have been, by any of the possible means, a very slow process. One possibility is that hundreds of men, some pulling on the rock, some cutting down trees and filling in holes as they went, simply dragged the stones over the bare ground. Or perhaps they used snow or mud to "grease" the path. Foot by foot, and day by day, they may have dragged the rocks all the way from Marlborough Downs to Stonehenge. Another guess is that these primitive men, even though they had not yet invented the wheel, knew about using logs as rollers. If so, perhaps they mounted each stone on a sledge, and rolled the sledge slowly forward, workmen placing logs in its path as it moved. Such a method, while a good deal easier than dragging the rock along the ground, would still have required as many as seven or eight hundred men, and perhaps as much as a decade to move all the stones. A third possibility is that the stones were moved along riverbeds, the shallow water helping to buoy the weight, and the muddy banks helping to slide the weight along. Though much less direct than the overland route, the riverbed route would have provided these primitive men with a relatively clear path that ran approximately halfway from the stones' point of origin to their final location. Of course, the point is that any of these three means of transporting the stones must have been an incredibly laborious task, occupying as many as a thousand men, year after year after year.

Lifting the stones into an upright position, once they had been transported, was another triumph of ingenuity and brute strength. Apparently, the workmen dug closely fitted holes where they wanted the stones eventually to stand. Probably they cut away one side of the hole, the side nearest the stone, to form a ramp. Perhaps they also lined the hole with wooden skids. Then gradually they eased the stone down the ramp until it rested in a tilted position at the bottom of the hole. Next, they used brute strength, some men pushing, some pulling on primitive ropes, to raise the rock into a vertical position. If we suppose each man lifted only his own weight, say 150 pounds, it might have taken as many as 400 men to stand the stones upright. Finally, while some workers held the rock in position, others quickly filled in the excavation left by the ramp. For many months afterward they probably refilled and pounded the dirt until it was completely firm. They probably placed the huge transverse pieces across the tops of columns by similarly dragging them up long earthern ramps. The fact that most of the rocks are still standing after thousands of years is testimony of their planning and workmanship.

We may never know quite why these primitive men chose to build Stonehenge, or who the men were. We may never know where they came from, or where they went. In Stonehenge, however, they have left a testament to their perserverance and their ingenuity. Clearly, they rivaled any of the builders of the ancient world. Thesis Restated

Comparison and contrast: run similarities side by side.

Comparison and contrast is another basic order of thought, another natural means of organizing a paragraph—or an entire essay. The process is indeed recurrent. It may be the very basis of thought itself, or at least one of the primary elements. All knowledge involves comparing things for their similarities and noticing their contrasting differences. We group all people together as People, and then tell them apart as individuals.

We instinctively know our friends in this way, for instance. Two of them drift side by side in our thoughts. We are comparing them. They are both boys; they are the same age and stature; we like them both. But one bubbles up like a mountain spring, and the other runs deep. Their appearances, mannerisms, and tastes match their contrasting personalities. One's room is messy; the other's is neat. One races his car; the other collects stamps. We compare the similar categories—looks, habits, hobbies, goals—and contrast the differences. In the process, we have come to know both friends more completely.

Your topic sentence sets the comparison and makes the contrast:

> **Opposites seem to attract. My father is tall, blond, and out-** Analogy
> **going. My mother is small, and even her dark brown hair, which**
> **is naturally wavy, has a certain quiet repose about it. My dad does**
> **everything at a cheerful run, whether he is off to a sales conference**
> **or off to the golf course with his foursome on Saturday mornings.**
> **My mother never seems to hurry. She hums at her work, and the**
> **house seems to slip into order without effort. She plays bridge with**
> **a few friends, and belongs to a number of organizations, but she is**
> **just as happy with a book. When dad bursts in at the end of the**
> **day, her face lights up. They grin at each other. They obviously still**
> **find each other attractive.**

With an analogy, you help your reader grasp your subject by showing how it is like something familiar. Your topic sentence asserts the comparison, and then your paragraph unfolds the comparison in detail:

> **School spirit is like patriotism. Students take their school's fortunes as their own, defending and promoting them against those of another school, as citizens champion their country, right or wrong. Their school is not only their alma mater but their fatherland as well. Like soldiers, they will give their utmost strength in field games and intellectual contests for both personal glory and the greater glory of the domain they represent. And, in defeat, they will mourn as if dragged in chains through the streets of Rome.**

Here is E. B. White describing Thoreau's *Walden* by analogy, a form of comparison that is really an extended metaphor:

Analogy

Topic
Sentence

> **Thoreau's assault on the Concord society of the mid-nineteenth century has the quality of a modern Western: he rides into the subject at top speed, shooting in all directions. Many of his shots ricochet and nick him on the rebound, and throughout the melee there is a horrendous cloud of inconsistencies and contradictions, and when the shooting dies down and the air clears, one is impressed chiefly by the courage of the rider and by how splendid it was that somebody should have ridden in there and raised all that ruckus.***

That is probably as long as an analogy can effectively run. One paragraph is about the limit. Beyond that, the reader may tire of it.

EXERCISES

15. *Write a paragraph comparing two people—like the one on p. 95.*

16. *Develop a paragraph by some humorous but apt comparison like E. B. White's above. You might find a helpful model in Mark Twain's two extended analogies—comparisons that clarify the unfamiliar by bringing the familiar alongside:*

Topic
Sentence

> But I am wandering from what I was intending to do, that is, make plainer than perhaps appears in the previous chapters some of the peculiar requirements of the science of piloting [a Mississippi steamboat]. First of all, there is one faculty which a pilot must incessantly cultivate until he has brought it

*"A Slight Sound at Evening," in *The Points of My Compass* (New York: Harper & Row, Publishers, 1962), p. 17.

to absolute perfection. Nothing short of perfection will do. The faculty is memory. He cannot stop with merely thinking a thing is so and so, he must *know* it, for this is eminently one of the "exact" sciences. With what scorn a pilot was looked upon in the old times, if he ever ventured to deal in that feeble phrase "I think," instead of the vigorous one, "I know!" One cannot easily realize what a tremendous thing it is to know every trivial detail of twelve hundred miles of river and know it with absolute exactness. If you will take the longest street in New York and travel up and down it, conning its features **Comparison** patiently until you know every house and window and lamppost and big and little sign by heart, and know them so accurately that you can instantly name the one you are abreast of when you are set down at random in that street in the middle of an inky black night, you will then have a tolerable notion of the amount and the exactness of a pilot's knowledge who carries the Mississippi River in his head. And then, if you will go on until you know every street-crossing, the character, size, and position of the crossing-stones, and the varying depth of mud in each of these numberless places, you will have some idea of what the pilot must know in order to keep a Mississippi steamer out of trouble. Next, if you will take half of the signs in that long street and *change their places* once a month, and still manage to know their new positions accurately on dark nights, and keep up with these repeated changes without making any mistakes, you will understand what is required of a pilot's peerless memory by the fickle Mississippi.

I think a pilot's memory is about the most wonderful thing in the world. To know the Old and New Testaments by heart and be able to recite them **Comparison** glibly, forward or backward, or begin at random anywhere in the book and recite both ways and never trip or make a mistake, is no extravagant mass of knowledge and no marvelous facility, compared to a pilot's massed knowledge of the Mississippi and his marvelous facility in the handling of it. I make this comparison deliberately, and believe I am not expanding the truth when I do it. Many will think my figure too strong but pilots will not.*

Comparison and contrast: develop differences point by point.

Your comparisons present helpful illustrations of your subject by emphasizing similarities. Contrasts, on the other hand, compare similar things to emphasize their differences—West Germany as against East Germany, for example—usually to persuade your reader that one is in some or most ways better than the other.

*Mark Twain, *Life on the Mississippi,* in *The Portable Mark Twain,* ed. Bernard De Voto (New York: Viking Press, Inc., 1956), pp. 109–111.

The problem in paragraphing such "comparative contrasts" is exactly what we have already seen with the sheep and goats in Chapter 2 and in the paragraph comparing the outgoing father and quiet mother: the problem of keeping both sides before the reader, of not talking so long about West Germany that your reader forgets all about East Germany. Again, the rule is to run your contrasts point by point, and this you may do in one of two ways: (1) by making a topic sentence to cover one point—agriculture, let us say—and then continuing your paragraph in paired sentences, one for the West, one for the East, another for the West, another for the East, and so on; or (2) by writing your paragraphs in pairs, one paragraph for the West, one for the East, using the topic sentence of the first paragraph to govern the second, something like this:

Topic Sentence

West

> **West Germany's agriculture is far ahead of the East's. Everywhere about the countryside, one sees signs of prosperity. Trucks and tractors are shiny. Fences are mended and in order. Buildings all seem newly painted, as if on exhibit for a fair. New Volkswagens buzz along the country roads. The annual statistics spell out the prosperous details . . . .**

Contrast

> **East Germany, on the other hand, seems to be dropping progressively behind. The countryside is drab and empty. On one huge commune, everything from buildings to equipment seems to be creaking from rusty hinges . . . . The annual statistics are equally depressing . . . .**

In an extended contrast, you will probably want to contrast some things sentence against sentence, within single paragraphs, and to contrast others by giving a paragraph to each. Remember only to keep your reader sufficiently in touch with both sides.

Here is a paragraph in which the writer illustrates his point (a seaman's sense of the weather) by contrasting it to something more familiar (the landsman's inattention to the weather):

Contrast

> **This was a sullen, dripping morning with wet, woolly clouds smothering the land and sea. Every few minutes, Mike or I would go up on deck and peer at the sky, wondering whether it would clear later and give us a decent day. In New York, I am like most people, only marginally aware of the weather. Before going out of my apartment, I want to know what the temperature is and whether it is raining, but I don't experience weather in any real sense; it is only an interim sensation, a transient state, known briefly between the enduring reality of interiors—living room, subway, stores, offices,**

the library. On the Sound, the situation is reversed; the sky and the air and the things they contain are the real world, and the interiors of boats and buildings are only burrows that one crawls into for brief periods to comfort oneself. The sailor is forever intensely aware of the sky, immense and enveloping. On the Sound, as on the open sea, one is in, under, and of the sky; one's eyes constantly search its vastness to know whether it means well or ill. When the sky changes, the man under it finds that his mood changes accordingly. Yet the moment he steps ashore, he becomes detached. The sky is now a thing apart.*

EXERCISES

17. (a) *Write a paragraph developed by contrasts, running them point by point, as "students" are contrasted with "athletes" in this paragraph:*

> The most essential distinction between athletics and education lies in the institution's own interest in the athlete as distinguished from its interest in its other students. Universities attract students in order to teach them what they do not already know; they recruit athletes only when they are already proficient. Students are educated for something which will be useful to them and to society after graduation; athletes are required to spend their time on activities the usefulness of which disappears upon graduation or soon thereafter. Universities exist to do what they can for students; athletes are recruited for what they can do for the universities. This makes the operation of the athletic program in which recruited players are used basically different from any *educational interest of colleges and universities.†*

(**b**) *Write two paragraphs contrasting something like high school and college, small town and city, football and baseball, men and women—the first paragraph describing one, the second the other, and the two using parallel contrasting terms, as in the example contrasting the two Germanys on p. 98. If your subject does not readily provide parallel contrasting terms, you might follow the lead of the freer contrast from a student's paper below.*

> In fact, in some respects the commercials are really better than the shows they sponsor. The commercials are carefully rehearsed, expertly photographed,

*Morton M. Hunt, "The Inland Sea," *The New Yorker*, September 5, 1964, pp. 57–58.

† Harold W. Stoke, "College Athletics, Education or Show Business?" *Atlantic Monthly*, March 1954, pp. 46–50. Copyright© 1954 by Harold W. Stoke. Reprinted by permission.

First Subject

highly edited and polished. They are made with absolute attention to detail and to the clock. One split-second over time, one bad note, one slightly wrinkled dress and they are done over again. Weeks, even months, go into the production of a single sixty-second commercial.

The Contrast

The shows, on the other hand, are slapped together hastily by writers and performers who have less than a week to put together an hour show. Actors have little time to rehearse, and often the pieces of a show are put together for the first time in front of the camera. Lighting, sound reproduction, and editing are workmanlike, but unpolished; a shadow from an overhead microphone on an actor's face causes no real concern in the control room. A blown line or a muffed cue is "just one of those things that happen." In all, it often takes less time and money to do an hour show than to do the four sixty-second commercials that sponsor it.

18. *Here are two famous poetic birds, Shelley's skylark ("To a Skylark") and Yeats's bird of hammered gold ("Sailing to Byzantium"). Write a paragraph comparing and contrasting the two, point for point, beginning with a topic sentence that covers your comparative or contrastive aim (something like "Both . . . are really imaginary" or "X's bird is more——than Z's"):*

> Hail to thee, blithe spirit!
> Bird thou never wert,
> That from Heaven, or near it,
> Pourest thy full heart
> In profuse strains of unpremeditated art.
> *Shelley*

> . . . such a form as Grecian goldsmiths make
> Of hammered gold and gold enameling
> To keep a drowsy emperor awake,
> Or set upon a golden bough to sing
> To lords and ladies of Byzantium
> Of what is past, or passing, or to come.*
> *Yeats*

Natural divisions: use the natural joints.

Many subjects fall into natural or customary partitions, which supply you with a kind of dialectic contrast not necessarily hostile, and even

*From Collected Poems (New York: Macmillan Publishing Co.). Copyright 1928 by Macmillan Publishing Co., Inc., renewed 1956 by Georgie Yeats. Reprinted by permission of Mr. M. B. Yeats, Miss Anne Yeats, and Macmillan, London & Basingstoke.

blandly jointed, like a good roast of pork, ready for carving: freshman, sophomore, junior, senior; Republicans, Democrats; right, middle, left; legislative, executive, judicial. You can easily follow these divisions in organizing a paragraph, or you can write one paragraph for each division, and attain a nicely coherent essay. Similarly, any manufacturing process, or any machine, will already have distinct steps and parts. These customary divisions will help your reader, since he knows something of them already. Describe the Democratic position on inflation, and he will naturally expect your description of the Republican position to follow. If no other divisions suggest themselves, you can often organize your paragraph—or your essay—into a consistent series of parallel answers, or "reasons for," or "reasons against," something like this:

> **A broad liberal education is best:**
> **I. It prepares you for a world of changing employment.**
> **II. It enables you to function well as a citizen.**
> **III. It enables you to make the most of your life.**

EXERCISES

19. *Here are a number of topics that fall conveniently into natural divisions. For each topic, list the divisions that occur to you.*

1. Causes affecting the rate at which a population grows.
2. Levels of government.
3. The "lunatic-fringe."
4. The early stages of space technology.
5. Undersea exploration.
6. Geological eras.
7. Mathematics in public schools.
8. Governmental response to the Depression.
9. Defrauding insurance companies.
10. Inequities in the tax structure.

20. *Write a paragraph using one of the topics and the divisions you have worked out in Exercise 19.*

Describing a process: follow the natural steps.

Again, your paragraph follows a natural sequence. This is probably exposition at its most basic intent: explaining how to assemble the Christmas toy, the hibachi, the bicycle. As always, you find a topic sentence to govern the job. Then you proceed through those steps that will most clearly help your reader to do the job:

> Growing iris, the poor man's orchid, is easy. Iris grow almost like weeds in well drained soil, but a little care pays glorious dividends. Plant your rhizomes—the iris root—in early fall. First, enrich your soil with an organic fertilizer low in nitrogen, at about one ounce to the square foot, three weeks before planting. Then plant the rhizomes almost even with the surface. Spruce up each plant in the spring with a quarter of a cup of superphosphate. In the fourth or fifth year, dig them up in late July or early September. Cut off the old tubers with a sharp knife. Let the hardy tubers harden in the sun for a day. Then replant them. They bloom long in the spring, and their attractive fans of leaves stand green until fall.

Here is a partial essay describing a more complicated process, manufacturing papyrus:

> . . . The account given by Pliny (*Natural History*, xiii, 11–13) of the manufacture of paper from the papyrus plant should be taken strictly to refer to the process followed in his own time; but, with some differences in details, the same general method of treatment had doubtlessly been practised from time immemorial. His text, however, is so confused, both from obscurity of style and from corruptions in the manuscripts, that there is much difference of opinion as to the meaning of many words and phrases employed in his narrative, and to their application in particular points of detail.
>
> In one important particular, however, affecting the primary construction of the material, there can be no doubt. The stem was cut into longitudinal strips, those from the centre of the plant being the broadest and most valuable. The strips were laid side by side to the required width, thus forming a layer across which another layer of shorter strips was laid at right angles. The two layers thus "woven" formed a sheet, which was then soaked in water of the Nile. The mention of a particular water has caused trouble to the commentators. Some have supposed that certain chemical properties of Nile water acted as a glue or cement to cause the two layers to adhere; others, with more reason, that glutinous matter contained in the material itself was dissolved by the action of water, whether from the Nile or any other source; and still others read in Pliny's words an implication that a paste was actually used.

The sheet was finally hammered and dried in the sun. Any roughness was leveled by polishing with ivory or a smooth shell. But the material was also subject to other defects, such as moisture lurking between the layers, which might be detected by strokes of the mallet; spots or stains; and spongy strips, in which the ink would run and spoil the sheet. When such faults occurred, the papyrus had to be remade.

To form a roll the several sheets were joined together with paste (glue being too hard), not more than 20 sheets to a roll. (There are, however, still extant rolls consisting of more than the prescribed number of sheets; perhaps the number was not constant in all times.) The roll (*scapus*) seems to have been a standard length of papyrus, as sold by the stationers. The best sheet formed the first or outside sheet of the roll, and the others were joined on in order of quality, so that the worst sheets were in the centre of the roll. This arrangement was adopted, not for the purpose of fraudulently selling bad material under cover of the better exterior, but in order that the outside of the roll should be composed of that which would best stand wear and tear. Besides, in case of the entire roll not being filled with the text, the unused and inferior sheets at the end could be better spared, and so might be cut off.*

Another fine passage describing a process is one we looked at in the first chapter: Sir Isaak Walton's own dressing the chub (p. 17).

EXERCISES

21. *Write a paragraph describing a process you well know—how to make a bracelet, a candle, a belt, a cake, how an internal combustion engine works.*

22. *Now find a thesis that will change this description into an argument making some statement about the subject: making a cake is no child's play; what's under the hood is really no mystery. Rewrite your descriptive paragraph into a brief three-paragraph essay, using everything you said before and expanding your points with comments rising from your thesis. Hand in your original paragraph with your essay.*

---

*Reprinted with permission from "Papyrus" in *Encyclopedia Britannica*, 14th edition; © 1967 by Encyclopedia Britannica, Inc. Prepared by Sir Edward Maunde Thompson and the Editors.

Chapter 5

STRAIGHT AND CROOKED THINKING: HANDLING THE EVIDENCE

All along, you have been bringing in evidence to support your thesis or your topic sentence. Evidence is simply an example. Your thesis has emerged from the specific things you have seen, in person, in print, or on TV. To illustrate your thesis, you simply turn the process around and bring in these specific things as your evidence. Make them brief, but sufficient. Three, proverbially, is an ideal number. But remember also that one extended description—a lonely old neighbor, an abandoned building, a high-speed scrape with automotive death—gives extremely interesting and persuasive evidence, especially when introduced with two or three brief examples, a statistic from the paper, a quotation from *Time*. These pieces of evidence, however, are liable to certain logical fallacies and unexamined assumptions that may defeat their persuasiveness.

FACTS, AND DEGREES OF BELIEF

Write as close to the facts as possible.

The nature of *fact*, and of *belief*, *opinion*, and *preference* poses some problems for the writer. You cannot really present the "hard facts" themselves. You cannot reach through the page to hand out actual lumps of coal and bags of wheat. You can only tell *about* these things, and then persuade the reader to see them as you believe they should be seen. Facts are the firmest kind of thought, but they are *thoughts* nevertheless— verifiable thoughts about the coal and wheat and other entities of our experience. The whole question of fact comes down to verifiability: things not susceptible of verification leave the realm of factuality. Fact is limited, therefore, to the kinds of things that can be tested by the senses (verified empirically, as the philosophers say) or by inferences from physical data so strong as to allow no other explanation. "Statements of fact" are assertions of a kind provable by referring to experience. The simplest physical facts—that a stone is a stone and that it exists—are so bound into our elementary perceptions of the world that we never think to verify them, and indeed could not verify them beyond gathering testimonials from the group. With less simple and tangible facts, verification is simply doing enough to persuade any reasonable person that the assertion of fact is true, beginning with what our senses can in some way check.

Measuring, weighing, and counting are the strongest empirical verifiers; assertions capable of such verification are the most firmly and quickly demonstrated as factual:

> **Smith is five feet high and four feet wide.**
> **The car weighs 2,300 pounds.**
> **Three members voted for beer.**

In the last assertion, we have moved from what we call physical fact to historical fact—that which can be verified by its signs: we have the ballots. Events in history are verified in the same way, although the evidence is scarcer the farther back we go.

Facts, then, are those things, states, or events of a kind susceptible of verification. Notice: *of a kind* susceptible of verification. Some perfectly solid facts we may never be able to verify. The place, date, and manner of Catullus's death; whether a person is guilty as accused or innocent as claimed—these may never be known to us, may never be established as "facts," because we lack the evidence to verify them. But we would not want to remove them from the realm of factuality; they are the *kind* of thing that *could* be verified, if only we could get at the evidence.

Believe what you write—but learn the nature of belief.

Facts, then, are things susceptible of verification. Belief presents an entirely different kind of knowledge: things believed true but yet beyond the reach of sensory verification—a belief in God, for instance. We may infer a Creator from the creation, a Beginning from the beginnings we see around us in the natural world. But a doubting Thomas will have nothing to touch or see; judging our inferences wrongly drawn, he may prefer to believe in a physical accident, or in a flux with neither beginning nor end. The point is that although beliefs are unprovable, they are not necessarily untrue, and they are not unusable as you discourse with your reader. You can certainly assert beliefs in your writing, establishing their validity in a tentative and probable way, so long as you do not assume you have *proved* them. State your convictions; support them with the best reasons you can find; and don't apologize. But, for both politeness and persuasion, you may wish to qualify your least demonstrable convictions with "I believe," "we may reasonably suppose," "perhaps," "from one point of view," and the like—unless the power of your conviction moves you beyond the gentilities, and you are writing heart to heart.

Don't mistake opinion for fact.

Halfway between fact and belief is *opinion*. An opinion is a candidate for fact, something you believe true but about whose verification you are still uncertain. All the facts are not in, you are not sure of the tests, and you may not be sure that there are tests; but you can at least present tentative verification. The difference between fact and opinion, then, is simply a difference in verifiableness. One opinion may eventually prove true, and another false; an opinion may strengthen, through verifying tests, into accepted fact, as with Galileo's opinion that the earth moved.

The testing of opinions to discover the facts is, indeed, the central business of argumentation. When you assert something as fact, you indicate (1) that you assume it true and easily verified, and (2) that its truth is generally acknowledged. When you assert something as opinion, you imply some uncertainty about both these things. Here are two common opinions that will probably remain opinions exactly because of such uncertainty:

> **Girls are brighter than boys.**
> **Men are superior to women.**

Although these statements are in *kind* susceptible of verification, we know we will probably never verify them satisfactorily. We know that the necessary tests are difficult, not merely to administer and control, but to agree upon, and we know that the terms *brighter* and *superior* have a range of meaning hard to pin down. Even when agreeing upon the tests for numerical and verbal abilities, and for memory and ingenuity, we

cannot be sure that we will not miss other kinds of brightness and superiority, or that our tests will measure these things in any thorough way.
The range of meaning in our four other terms, moreover, is so wide as
virtually to defy verification. We need only ask "At what age?" to illustrate how broad and slippery the terms *girls, boys, men,* and *women* really
are.

Dispute your preferences with care.

Preferences are something else again. They are farther from proof
than opinions—indeed, beyond the pale of proof. And yet they are more
firmly held than opinions, because they are primarily subjective, sweet-
ening our palates and warming our hearts. *De gustibus non est disputan-
dum:* tastes are not to be disputed. So goes the medieval epigram, from
the age that refined the arts of logic. You can't argue successfully about
tastes, empirical though they be, because they are beyond empirical demonstration. Are peaches better than pears? Whichever you choose, your
choice is probably neither logically defensible nor logically vulnerable. The
writer's responsibility is to recognize the logical immunity of preferences,
and to qualify them politely with "I think," "many believe," "some may
prefer," and so forth.

But that preferences are subjective does not eliminate their general
interest, nor remove them from discussion. Because they are immune,
because they are strong, and because everyone has them, preferences
have a certain validity that repays investigation. The medieval logicians
notwithstanding, tastes are indeed worth disputing, because discussing
them may lead to assertions demonstrable enough to be, in some measure,
persuasive. You will probably never convince a pear person, but you may
make a fairly sound case for peaches. I would guess that the annual
consumption of peaches exceeds that of pears three to one. And in a
best-selling cookbook, recipes for peaches outnumber those for pears three
to one. Of course, popularity is no criterion for quality; but a continued
preference by large numbers of people, if you can establish that as fact,
shows that what had seemed a private preference actually has a public
acceptance worth analyzing. Your private taste for peaches may then
translate into a perfectly demonstrable thesis: "People seem to prefer
peaches to pears." You could probably make even a qualitative judgment
stand up, with a thesis something like: "Although chilled pears are delicious, Americans seem to consider peaches more satisfying, as the annual
sales figures would indicate."

So go ahead, dispute over tastes, and you may find some solid grounds for them. Shakespeare *is* greater than Ben Jonson, his friend and greatest competitor. Subjective tastes have moved all the way up beside fact: the grounds for Shakespeare's margin of greatness have been exhibited, argued, and explored over the centuries, until we accept his superiority, as if empirically verified. Actually, the questions that most commonly concern us are beyond scientific verification. But you can frequently establish your preferences as testable opinions by asserting them reasonably and without unwholesome prejudice, and by using the secondary evidence that other reasonable people agree with you in persuasive strength and number.

ASSUMPTIONS AND IMPLICATIONS

Check your statements, root and branch.

Your statements spring from assumptions below the surface and sprout all kinds of unwritten sprigs. These latter, the implications, you can more readily control. Actually, language is at its best when implying more than it says. Irony, for instance, is a constant shadow-play of implication. When you say, "As an officer, he certainly had command of his tailor," you clearly imply that he could command little else. The danger in implications is in not seeing them yourself. If you say "The demonstration was unfair to the management," you must face your implication that the management has been fair to the customers and the help. Keep your eyes open for where your words are pointing, and either trim the pointers or follow them out.

Language naturally looks ahead, so we look for our implications almost by second nature. But we do not naturally check our assumptions, because our whole lives rest on acquired assumptions we hardly think to question: love is better than hate; life is better than death; self-preservation is primary; giving your life for others is good; security is good; success is good; and so on and on. Many of our assumptions conflict, as when our approvals of selfless dedication and of self-sufficiency clash. Sacrifice can be truly selfless, or morbidly self-serving; and selfishness can have a certain forthright honesty that works not too badly in the social mix. As when you first shaped your thesis in Chapter 1, you should continue to check your assumptions to see what your readers, or your opponents, will take for granted, and what they will not grant until proved. If you assume, simply, that football builds character or that socialism ruins it, that some races are inferior or all men equal, you may find your platform shot from under you as the opposition hits the narrowness of your assumptions.

Assumptions and implications can be seen as different ends of the same idea. By assuming that football builds character, you may overlook your implications that other things do not and that "character" means, for you, only a healthy competitive tenacity and a measure of physical courage. Overlooking the full width of the term, you may assume its meaning too narrowly; "character" also means a sense of responsibility, honesty, and humanity, which, along with tenacity and courage, may come readily from other sources. If you acknowledge this breadth of assumption behind your term, you can very well go ahead with the case, arguing that football does indeed build character in certain ways. Perhaps you need merely change your thesis to something like: "Although no magical guarantee, football contributes certain valuable disciplines toward the development of character." You immediately show that you are neither claiming nor assuming more than the reasonable truth. You have found a solid premise.

Assumptions and implications have to do with your thesis, or with any subordinate assertion you make in demonstrating it. Your proof is what makes your assertions stick. Proof is just enough of evidence and reasoning to persuade your readers that what you are saying is true. Usually, as I have already said, all you need is common sense and enough delicacy not to shout "proved" too loudly. Anything within reason goes; but keep in mind the kinds of proving within reason, and the traps beyond reason.

EXERCISES

1. *After each of the following assertions, write two or three short questions that will challenge its assumptions, questions like "Good for what? Throwing? Fertilizer?" For example: Girls are brighter than boys. "At what age? In chess? In physics?" In the questions, probe and distinguish among your facts, opinions, beliefs, and preferences.*

1. Men are superior to women.
2. The backfield made some mistakes.
3. Communism means violent repression.
4. Don't trust anyone over thirty.
5. All men are equal.
6. The big companies are ruining the environment.
7. Travel is educational.
8. Our brand is free of tar.

9. The right will prevail.
10. A long run is good for you.

DEFINITION

Clear up your terms.

Definition is a way to clear up those hidden or unwanted assumptions and implications. What the Russians and Chinese call a People's Democracy is the very opposite of what the Americans and British call democracy, assumed also to be of and for and by the people. Ideally, your running prose should make your terms clear to your reader, avoiding those definitions that can seem too stiff and stuffy. Nevertheless, what we mean by *egotism, superiority, education,* or *character* may need laying on the table.

Richard Hofstadter, for instance, found it necessary in his essay "Democracy and Anti-intellectualism in America" to devote a number of paragraphs to defining both *democracy* and *intellectual,* each paragraph clarifying one aspect of his term. Coming early in his essay, after he has set his thesis and surveyed his subject, his section of definition begins with the following paragraph:

> But what is an intellectual, really? This is a problem of definition that I found, when I came to it, far more elusive than I had anticipated. A great deal of what might be called the journeyman's work of our culture—the work of engineers, physicians, newspapermen, and indeed of most professors—does not strike me as distinctively intellectual, although it is certainly work based in an important sense on ideas. The distinction that we must recognize, then, is one originally made by Max Weber between living *for* ideas and living *off* ideas. The intellectual lives for ideas; the journeyman lives off them. The engineer or the physician—I don't mean here to be invidious—needs to have a pretty considerable capital stock in frozen ideas to do his work; but they serve for him a purely instrumental purpose: he lives off them, not for them. Of course he may also be, in his private role and his personal ways of thought, an intellectual, but it is not necessary for him to be one in order to work at his profession. There is in fact no profession which demands that one be an intellectual. There do seem to be vocations, however, which almost demand that one be an anti-intellectual, in which those who

live off ideas seem to have an implacable hatred for those who live for them. The marginal intellectual workers and the unfrocked intellectuals who work in journalism, advertising, and mass communication are the bitterest and most powerful among those who work at such vocations.*

Try different kinds of definition.

Your subject will prompt you in one of two ways, toward inclusiveness or toward exclusiveness. Hofstadter found that he needed to be inclusive about the several essentials in *democracy* and *intellectual*—terms used commonly, and often loosely. Inclusiveness is the usual need, as you will find in trying to define *love* or *loyalty* or *education*. But you may sometimes need to move in the opposite direction, toward exclusiveness, as in sociological, philosophical, or scientific discussion, when you need to nail your terms firmly to single meanings: "By *reality*, I mean only that which exists in the physical world, excluding our ideas about it."

Such exclusive defining is called *stipulative*, since you stipulate the precise meaning you want. But you should avoid the danger of trying to exclude more than the word will allow. If you try to limit the meaning of the term *course* to "three hours a week a semester," your discussion will soon encounter courses with different hours; or you may find yourself inadvertently drifting to another meaning, as you mention something about graduating from an "engineering course." At any rate, if you can avoid the sound of dogmatism in your stipulation, so much the better. You may well practice some disguise, as with *properly speaking* and *only* in the following stipulative definition: "Properly speaking, the *structure* of any literary work is only that framelike quality we can picture in two, or three, dimensions."

Definitions frequently seem to develop into paragraphs, almost by second nature. A sentence of definition is usually short and crisp, seeming to demand some explanation, some illustration and sociability. The definition, in other words, is a natural topic sentence. Here are three classic single-sentence kinds of definition that will serve well as topics for your paragraphs:

I. DEFINITION BY SYNONYM. A quick way to stipulate the single meaning you want: "Virtue means moral rectitude."

---

*The Michigan Quarterly Review, 59 (1953), p. 282. Copyright © 1953 by the University of Michigan.

II. DEFINITION BY FUNCTION. "A barometer measures atmospheric pressure"—"A social barometer measures human pressures"—"A good quarterback calls the signals and sparks the spirits of the whole team."

III. DEFINITION BY SYNTHESIS. A placing of your term in striking (and not necessarily logical) relationship to its whole class, usually for the purposes of wit: "The fox is the craftiest of beasts"—"A sheep is a friendlier form of goat"—"A lexicographer is a harmless drudge"—"A sophomore is a sophisticated moron."

Here are three more of the classic kinds of definition, of broader dimensions than the single-sentence kinds above, but also ready-made for a paragraph apiece, or for several. Actually, in making paragraphs from your single-sentence definitions, you have undoubtedly used at least one of these three kinds, or a mixture of them all. They are no more than the natural ways we define our meanings.

IV. DEFINITION BY EXAMPLE. The opposite of *definition by synthesis*. You start with the class ("crafty beasts") and then give an example of a member or two ("fox"—plus monkey and raccoon). But of course you would go on to give further examples or illustrations—accounts of how the bacon was snitched through the screen—that broaden your definition beyond the mere naming of class and members.

V. DEFINITION BY COMPARISON. You just use a paragraph of comparison to expand and explain your definition. Begin with a topic sentence something like: "Love is like the sun." Then extend your comparison on to the end of the paragraph (or even separate it, if your cup runneth over, into several paragraphs), as you develop the idea: love is like the sun because it too gives out warmth, makes everything bright, shines even when it is not seen, and is indeed the center of our lives.

VI. DEFINITION BY ANALYSIS. This is Hofstadter's way, a searching out and explaining of the essentials in terms used generally, loosely (and often in ways that emphasize incidentals for biased reasons), as when it is said that an *intellectual* is a manipulator of ideas.

Cover all the angles.

You may find that in a defining paragraph—or a defining essay—you have said all you wish to say as you clarified what a thing *is*. Nevertheless, in your preliminary sketching, try jotting down also what it *is not*. You can indeed build some good paragraphs (or parts of paragraphs, or parts of essays) by spelling out the *not*'s, especially if you can thus set aside or qualify (as Hofstadter does) such popular misconceptions as "the intellectual is a manipulator of ideas." You might come up with something like:

> **Love is not greed. It is no mere lust for gold or beefsteak or people of the opposite sex, although some component of greed has caused the popular misconception. We all declare, on occasion, that we love a good steak, and we mean it. But certainly this usage is only incidental to the real meaning of love as most of us understand it, fundamentally and seriously.**

Here are four good steps to take in reaching a thorough definition of something, assuring that you have covered all the angles. Consider:

1. What it *is not like.*

2. What it *is like.*

3. What it *is not.*

4. What it *is.*

This program can produce a good paragraph of definition:

> **Love may be many things to many people, but, all in all, we agree on its essentials. Love is not like a rummage sale, in which everyone tries to grab what he wants. It is more like a Christmas, in which gifts and thoughtfulness come just a little unexpectedly, even from routine directions. Love, in short, is not a matter of seeking self-satisfaction; it is first a matter of giving and then discovering, as an unexpected gift, the deepest satisfaction one can know.**

The four steps above can also furnish four separate and effective paragraphs, which you would present in the same order of ascending interest and climax.

Beware of cracks in your logic.

Defining is, of course, a way of classifying your concepts and of keeping your headings straight. Elucidation is your major concern; rigorous logical precision is not always necessary. Nevertheless, you should be aware of some pitfalls, and some standard precautions:

1. Avoid echoing the term you are defining. Do not write "Courtesy is being courteous" or "Freedom is feeling free." Look around for syn-

onyms: "Courtesy is being polite, being attentive to others' needs, making them feel at ease, using what society accepts as good manners." You can go against this rule to great advantage, however, if you repeat the *root* of the word meaningfully: "Courtesy is treating your girl like a princess in her *court.*"

2. Don't make your definitions too narrow—except for humor ("Professors are only disappointed students"). Do not write: "Communism is subversive totalitarianism." Obviously, your definition needs more breadth, something about sharing property, and so forth.

3. Don't make your definition too broad. Do not go uphill in your terms, as in "Vanity is pride" or "Affection is love." Bring the definers down to the same level: "Vanity is a kind of frivolous personal pride"—"Affection is a mild and chronic case of love."

EXERCISES

2. *Write a paragraph defining something by telling: (1) what it is not like, (2) what it is like, (3) what it is not, and, finally, (4) what it is. See p. 113.*

3. *Write two independent paragraphs, each defining some term. Use a single-sentence definition (synonym, function, or synthesis) as the topic sentence of the first (see pp. 111–112). Use a broader definition (example, comparison, or analysis) in your second paragraph (see p. 112). Here are two examples:*

(1) As the sun was going down, we saw the first specimen of an animal known familiarly over two thousand miles of mountain and desert—from Kansas clear to the Pacific Ocean—as the "jackass rabbit." He is well named. He is just like any other rabbit, except that he is from one third to twice as large, has longer legs in proportion to his size, and has the most preposterous ears that ever were mounted on any creature *but* a jackass. When he is sitting quiet, thinking about his sins, or is absent-minded or unapprehensive of danger, his majestic ears project above him conspicuously; but the breaking of a twig will scare him nearly to death, and then he tilts his ears back gently and starts for home. All you can see, then, for the next minute, is his long gray form stretched out straight and "streaking it" through the low sage-brush, head erect, eyes right, and ears just canted a little to the rear, but showing you where the animal is, all the time, the same as if he carried a jib. Now and then he makes a marvelous spring with his long legs, high over the stunted sage-brush, and scores a leap that would make a horse envious. Presently he comes down to a long, graceful "lope," and shortly he mysteriously disappears. He has crouched behind a sage-bush, and will sit there and listen and tremble

Margin labels:
Term
Definition by Synthesis

Function

until you get within six feet of him, when he will get under way again. But one must shoot at this creature once, if he wishes to see him throw his heart into his heels, and do the best he knows how. He is frightened clear through, now, and he lays his long ears down on his back, straightens himself out like a **Comparison** yard-stick every spring he makes, and scatters miles behind him, with an easy indifference that is enchanting.*

(2) Black Power means, for example, that in Lowndes County, Alabama, a **Term** black sheriff can end police brutality. A black tax assessor and tax collector and county board of revenue can lay, collect, and channel tax monies for the **Example** building of better roads and schools serving black people. In such areas as Lowndes, where black people have a majority, they will attempt to use power to exercise control. This is what they seek: control. When black people lack **Definition by** a majority, Black Power means proper representation and sharing of control. **Analysis** It means the creation of power bases, of strength, from which black people can press to change local or nation-wide patterns of oppression—instead of from weakness.

It does not mean *merely* putting black faces into office. Black visibility **What It *Is*** is not Black Power. Most of the black politicians around the country today are ***Not*** not examples of Black Power. The power must be that of a community, and **What It *Is*** emanate from there. The black politicians must start from there. The black politicians must stop being representatives of "downtown" machines, whatever the cost might be in terms of lost patronage and holiday handouts.†

LOGICAL FALLACIES

Trust your common sense.

From the first, in talking about a valid thesis, about proof, about assumptions and implications and definition, we have been facing logical fallacies—that is, flaws in thought, things that do not add up. Evidence itself raises the biggest question of logic. Presenting any evidence at all faces a logical fallacy that can never be surmounted: no amount of evidence can *logically* prove an assertion because *one* and *some* can never equal *all*. Because the sun has gotten up on time every morning so far

---

*Mark Twain, *Roughing It* (New York: Holt, Rinehart and Winston, 1964), pp. 12–13.
†Stokely Carmichael and Charles V. Hamilton, *Black Power, the Politics of Liberation in America* (New York: Random House, 1967), p. 15.

is—the logicians tell us—no logical assurance that it will do so tomorrow morning. Actually, we can take comfort in that fallacy. Since we can never *logically* produce enough evidence for certitude, we càn settle for a reasonable amount and call it quits. One piece of evidence all by itself tempts us to cry, "Fallacy! *One* isn't *all* or *every.*" But three or four pieces will probably suit our common sense and calm us into agreement.

Cite authorities reasonably.

An appeal to some authority to prove your point is really an appeal beyond logic, but not necessarily beyond reason. "Einstein said . . ." can silence many an objection, since we believe Einstein knew more about physical fact than anyone. "According to Freud" may win your point on human personality, as may an appeal to Winston Churchill or Matthew Arnold or H. W. Fowler on English usage. Shakespeare, the Bible, and Samuel Johnson can authenticate your claims about the ways of the world and the spirit.

Since authority has long since proved itself right, appeals to authority are not beyond reason. But they are beyond logic, because the logical proof that first established the authority has long since retired to the bookshelves. What Einstein said, we tend to take on faith, without demanding proof, which may well be beyond us. The greatest men in the field have accepted Einstein's logic and acknowledged his achievement. Who are we to question that? In this apparent infallibility, of course, reside the hazards of relying upon authority.

Appeals to authority risk four common fallacies. The first is in appealing to the authority outside of his field, even if his field is the universe. Although Einstein had a powerful intellect, we should not assume he knew all about economics too. Even if a chance remark of Einstein's sounds like the quantum theory of banking, you will do best to quote it only for its own rational merits, using Einstein's having said it only as a bonus of persuasive interest; otherwise, your appeal to his authority will seem naïve in the extreme. The good doctor, of the wispy hair and frayed sweater, was little known for understanding money.

The second fallacy is in misunderstanding or misrepresenting what the authority really says. Sir Arthur Eddington, if I may appeal to an authority myself, puts the case: "It is a common mistake to suppose that Einstein's theory of relativity asserts that everything is relative. Actually it says, 'There are absolute things in the world but you must look deeply for them. The things that first present themselves to your notice are for the most part relative.' ''* If you appeal loosely to Einstein to authenticate an assertion that everything is "relative," you may appeal in vain—since *relative* means relative *to* something else, eventually to some absolute.

The third fallacy is in assuming that one instance from an authority represents him accurately. Arguments for admitting the split infinitive (see pp. 470–472) to equal status with the unsplit, for instance, often present split constructions from prominent writers. But they do not tell us how many splits a writer avoided, or how he himself feels about the construction. A friend once showed me a split infinitive in the late Walter Lippmann's column after I had boldly asserted that careful writers like Lippmann never split their infinitives. Out of curiosity, I wrote Mr. Lippmann; after all, he might have changed his tune. He wrote back that the split had been simply a slip, that he disliked the thing and tried to revise it out whenever it crept in.

The fourth fallacy is deepest: the authority may have faded. New facts have generated new ideas. Einstein has limited Newton's authority. Geology and radioactive carbon have challenged the literal authority of Genesis. Jung has challenged Freud; and Keynes, Marx.

The more eminent the authority, the easier the fallacy. Ask these four questions:

1. Am I citing him outside his field?
2. Am I presenting him accurately?
3. Is this instance really representative?
4. Is he still fully authoritative?

Do not claim too much for your authority, and add other kinds of proof, or other authorities. In short, don't put all your eggs in one basket; write as if you knew the market and the risks. Every appeal to authority is open to logical challenge.

EXERCISES

4. *Each of the following statements contains at least one fallacious citation of authority. Identify it, and explain how it involves one or several of these reasons: "Outside Field," "Not Accurately Presented," "Not Representative," "Out of Date."*

The Nature of the Physical World (Ann Arbor: University of Michigan Press, 1958), p. 23.

1. According to Charles Morton, a distinguished eighteenth-century theologian and schoolmaster, the swallows of England disappear to the dark side of the moon in winter.
2. Einstein states that everything is relative.
3. "Nucular" is an acceptable pronunciation of "nuclear." President Eisenhower himself pronounced it this way.
4. War between capitalists and communists is inevitable, as Karl Marx shows.
5. Giving LSD to everyone, including children, as Timothy Leary says, will greatly improve modern society.
6. The American economy should be controlled in every detail; after all, economist John Kenneth Galbraith comes out for control.
7. "Smooths are America's finest cigarette," says Jimmy Connors.

Handle persistences as you would authorities.

That an idea's persistence constitutes a kind of unwritten or cumulative authority is also open to logical challenge. Because a belief has persisted, the appeal goes, it must be true. Since earliest times, for example, man has believed in some kind of supernatural beings or Being. Something must be there, the persistance seems to suggest. But the appeal is not logical; the belief could have persisted from causes other than the actuality of divine existence, perhaps only from man's psychological need. As with authority, new facts may vanquish persistent beliefs. The belief that the world was a pancake, persistent though it had been, simply had to give way to Columbus and Magellan. For all this, however, persistance does have considerable validating strength. Shakespeare's supremacy, upheld now for three centuries, and by people of many nations, has considerable force in upholding the assertion that he is, so far, supreme. As with appeals to authority, appeals to persistance are most effective when acknowledged as *indications* of validity rather than as logical proofs and validities themselves.

Inspect your documentary evidence before using.

Documents are both authoritative and persistent. They provide the only evidence, aside from oral testimony, for all that we know beyond the immediate presence of our physical universe, with its physical remains of the past. Documents point to what has happened, as long ago as Nineveh and Egypt and as recently as the tracings on last hour's blackboard. But documents are only records or traces, not events themselves, and you must be wary of presenting them at face value. Documents vary in reliability. The inscription on tombstone and monument would seem a firmer testimonial than the name in a legend; the diplomat's dairy firmer than the public announcement; the eyewitness's description firmer than the historian's summary. You must consider a document's historical context, since factuality may have been of little concern, as with stories of heroes and saints. You must allow, as with newspapers, for the effects of haste and limited facts. You should consider a document's author, his background, his range of knowledge and belief, his assumptions, his prejudices, his probable motives, his possible tendencies to suppress or distort the facts.

Finally, you should consider the document's data. Are the facts of a kind easily verifiable or easily collected? Indeed, can you present other verification? For example, numerical reports of population can be no more than approximations, and they are hazier the farther back you go in history, as statistical methods slacken. Since the data must have been selected from almost infinite possibilities, does the selection seem reasonably representative? Are your source's conclusions right for the data? Might not the data produce other conclusions? Your own data and conclusions, of course, must also face questioning.

Statistics are particularly persuasive evidence, and because of their psychological appeal, they can be devilishly misleading. To reduce things to numbers seems scientific, incontrovertible, final. But each "1" represents a slightly different quantity, as one glance around a class of 20 students will make clear. Each student is the same, yet entirely different. The "20" is a broad generalization convenient for certain kinds of information: how many seats the instructor will need, how many people are absent, how much the instruction costs per head, and so forth. But clearly the "20" will tell nothing about the varying characteristics of the students or the education. So present your statistics with some caution so that they will honestly show what you want them to show, and will not mislead your readers.

Averages and percentages can be especially misleading, carrying the numerical generalization one step farther from the physical facts. The truth behind a statement that the average student earns $10 a week could be that nine students earn nothing and one earns $100. A statement in an eminent professional journal that 73 percent of the "cultivated informants" in the North Central States say "ain't I" is actually reporting on a group of only 31 cultivated informants, a mere 11 of whom answered the question about "ain't I"—and only 8 of these used "ain't I." Dividing 8 by 11 does give .73. But put "73 percent" in print, and you seem to have scientific proof that 73 of every 100 cultivated persons say "ain't I," whereas the figure represents merely 8 people in a population of some 35 million. How many of 35 million persons are cultivated, and how we test for cultivation, are questions not easily answered. The statistic also ignores how often the "ain't I" people said "ain't" as against other possibilities, and whether humorously, or accidentally, and so forth. Be wary in presenting your statistics, especially when each number, so firm and final, can conceal variations beyond the reach of calipers and scales.

EXERCISES

5. *Each of the following statistical statements is fallacious in one or several ways, either omitting something necessary for full understanding or generalizing in unsupported ways. Identify and explain the statistical fallacies.*

1. This car gets twenty-five miles per gallon.
2. Fifty percent of his snapshots are poor.
3. Twenty-nine persons were injured when a local bus skidded on an icy road near Weston and overturned. Two were hospitalized. Twenty-seven were treated and released.
4. Women support this book one hundred percent, but fifty percent of American males are still antifeminist. (In a class of five girls and ten boys, all the girls and five of the boys vote to write about a book entitled *The Stereotyped Female.*)

6. *If baseball is in season, go to the sports page and write a brief explanation of the statistics on batting averages, RBI's, and so forth. Can you find any fallacies— things the statistics do not tell? Or do the same with another sport or subject where statistics are common.*

INDUCTIVE FALLACIES

Keep your hypothesis hypothetical.

Induction and deduction are the two paths of reasoning. Induction is "leading into" (*in ducere,* "to lead"), thinking through the evidence to some general conclusion. *Deduction* is "leading away from" some general precept to its particular parts and consequences. Both modes have their uses, and their fallacies.

Induction is the way of science: one collects the facts and sees what they come to. Sir Francis Bacon laid down in 1620 the inductive program in his famous *Novum Organum, sive indicia vera de interpretatione naturae* ("The New Instrument, or true evidence concerning the interpretation of nature"). Bacon was at war with the syllogism; its abstract deductions seemed too rigid to measure nature's subtlety. His new instrument changed the entire course of thought. Before Bacon, the world had deduced the consequences of its general ideas; after Bacon, the world looked around and induced new generalizations from what it saw. Observed facts called the old ideas into question, and theories replaced "truths." As you may know, Bacon died from a cold caught while stuffing a chicken's carcass with snow for an inductive test of refrigeration.

Induction has great strength, but it also has a basic fallacy. The strength is in taking nothing on faith, in having no ideas at all until the facts have suggested them. The fallacy is in assuming that the mind can start blank, with no prior ideas. Theoretically, Bacon had no previous ideas about refrigeration. Theoretically, he would experiment aimlessly until he noticed consistencies that would lead to the icebox. Actually, from experience, one would already have a hunch, a half-formed theory, that would suggest the experimental tests. Induction, in other words, is always well mixed with deduction. The major difference is in the tentative frame of mind: in making a hypothesis instead of merely borrowing an honored assumption, and in keeping the hypothesis hypothetical, even after the facts seem to have supported it.

Use analogies to clarify, not to prove.

The simplest kind of induction is analogy: because this tree is much like that oak, it too must be some kind of oak. You identify the unknown by its analogy to the known. You inductively look over the similarities until you conclude that the trees are very similar, and therefore the same kind. Analogies are tremendously useful indications of likeness; analogy is virtually our only means of classification, our means of putting things into groups and handling them by naming them. Analogy also illustrates the logical weakness of induction: assuming that *all* characteristics are analogous after finding one or two analogous. We check a few symptoms against what we know of colds and flu, and conclude that we have a cold and flu; but the doctor will add to these a few more symptoms and conclude that we have a virulent pneumonia.

Similarity does not mean total identity, and analogies must always make that shaky assumption, or clearly demonstrate that the mismatching details are unimportant. In your writing, you may use analogy with tremendous effect, since it is almost the very basis of knowledge. But watch out for the logical gap between *some* and *all*. Make sure that:

1. A reasonably large number of details agree.
2. These details are salient and typical.
3. The misfitting details are insignificant and not typical.

If the brain seems in some ways like a computer, be careful not to assume it is in all ways like a computer. Keep the analogy figurative: it can serve you well, as any metaphor serves, to illustrate the unknown with the known.

Look before you leap.

The hypothetical frame of mind is the essence of the inductive method, because it acknowledges the logical flaw of induction, namely, the *inductive leap*. No matter how many the facts, or how carefully weighed, a time comes when thought must abandon the details and leap to the conclusion. We leap from the knowledge that *some* apples are good to the conclusion: "[All] apples are good." This leap, say the logicians, crosses an abyss no logic can bridge, because *some* can never guarantee *all*—except as a general *probability*. The major lesson of induction is that *nothing* can be proved, except as a probability. The best we can manage is a *hypothesis*, while maintaining a perpetual hospitality to new facts that might change our theory. This is the scientific frame of mind; it gets as close to substantive truth as we can come, and it keeps us healthily humble before the facts.

Probability is the great limit and guarantee of the generalizations to which we must eventually leap. You know that bad apples are neither so numerous nor so strongly typical that you must conclude: "Apples are unfit for human consumption." You also know what causes the bad ones. Therefore, to justify your leap and certify your generalization, you base your induction on the following three conditions:

1. Your samples are reasonably numerous.
2. Your samples are truly typical.
3. Your exceptions are explainable, and demonstrably not typical.

The inductive leap is always risky because all the data cannot be known. The leap might also be in the wrong direction: more than one conclusion may be drawn from the same evidence. Here, then, is where the inductive frame of mind can help you. It can teach you always to check your conclusions by asking if another answer might not do just as well. Some linguists have concluded that speech is superior to writing because speech has many more "signals" than writing. But from the same facts one might declare writing superior: it conveys the same message with fewer signals.

The shortcomings of induction are many. The very data of sensory observation may be indistinct. Ask any three people to tell how an accident happened, and the feebleness of human observation becomes painfully apparent. If the facts are slippery, the final leap is uncertain. Furthermore, your hypothesis, which must come early to give your investigation some purpose, immediately becomes a *deductive* proposition that not only will guide your selection of facts, but may well distort slightly the facts you select. Finally, as we have seen with statistics and averages, scientific induction relies heavily on mathematics, which requires that qualities be translated into quantities. Neither numbers nor words, those two essential generalizers of our experience, can adequately grasp all our particular diversities. The lesson of induction, therefore, is the lesson of caution. Logically, induction is shot full of holes. But it makes as firm a statement as we can expect about the physical universe and our experience in it. It keeps our feet on the ground, while it makes remarkable sense of our evidence. The ultimate beauty of science is perhaps not that it is efficient (and it is), but that it is hypothetical. It keeps our minds open for new hypotheses. The danger lies in thinking it absolute.

EXERCISES

7. *Explain the following fallacious analogies and inductive leaps.*

1. The brain is like a computer. Scientists have demonstrated that it, like the computer, works through electrical impulses.
2. This girl has ten sweaters; that girl has ten sweaters. They are equally rich in sweaters.
3. At sixty, Kirk retires with investments and savings worth more than $500,000. He has nothing to worry about for the rest of his life.
4. Every time the Boilers play a post-season game, they lose. They will lose this one.

5. English majors are poor mathematicians.

6. I studied hard. I answered every question. None of my answers was wrong. I have read my exam over again and again and can still see no reason for getting only a C.

DEDUCTIVE FALLACIES

Establish your premise.

Deductive reasoning characteristically operates in those areas of *values* and *qualities* where factual induction finds little to grasp. Induction starts with the particulars and sees what general proposition they make. Deduction, the only other possible way to reason, starts with the general proposition and sees what it implies for the particulars: granted that such and such is true, then these things also must be true. Both methods can fall down when the numbers or words they employ generalize too far from the skin of physical and mental actuality—which we can scarcely reach without them. Like induction, deduction can make some notorious mistakes. The greatest mistake may be in the premise itself. Since deductive reasoning *depends* on your premise—literally "hangs from" it—you must bolt your premise to solid assumptions, or your whole chain of logic will fall in a heap. First check your assumptions with an eye for termites; then attend to the logical linkage.

Check for the classic fallacies.

1. EITHER-OR. You assume only two opposing possibilities: "Either we abolish requirements or education is finished." Education will probably amble on, somehwere in between. Similarly, IF-THEN: "If I work harder on the next paper, then I'll get a better grade." You have overlooked differences in subject, knowledge, involvement, inspiration.

2. OVERSIMPLIFICATION. As with *either-or,* you ignore alternatives. "A student learns only what he wants to learn" ignores all the pressures from parents and society, which in fact account for a good deal of learning.

3. BEGGING THE QUESTION. A somewhat unhandy term: you assume as proved something that really needs proving. "Free all political prisoners" assumes that none of those concerned has committed an actual crime.

4. IGNORING THE QUESTION. The question of whether it is right for a neighborhood to organize against a newcomer shifts to prices of property and taxes.

5. NON SEQUITUR ("It does not follow"). "He's certainly sincere; he must be right." "He's the most popular; he should be president." The conclusions do not reasonably follow from sincerity and popularity.

6. POST HOC, ERGO PROPTER HOC. ("After this, therefore because of this.") The non sequitur of events: "He stayed up late and therefore won the race." He probably won in spite of late hours, and for other reasons.

EXERCISES

8. *Name and explain the fallacy in each of the following:*

1. Jones is rich. He must be dishonest.
2. He either worked hard for his money, or he is just plain lucky.
3. The best things in life are free, like free love.
4. Sunshine breeds flies, because when the sun shines the flies come out.
5. If they have no bread, let them eat cake. Cake is both tastier and richer in calories.
6. This is another example of American imperialism.
7. Smith's canned-soup empire reaches farther than the Roman empire.
8. *Chips* is America's most popular soap. It is clearly the best.
9. The draft is illegal. It takes young men away from their education and careers at the most crucial period of their lives. They lose thousands of dollars' worth of their time.
10. Women are the most exploited people in the history of the world.
11. Two minutes after the accused left the building, the bomb exploded.

THE INDUCTIVE ESSAY

Try some reverse English.

You can occasionally organize your essay on the inductive pattern, leading your reader into, or up to, your thesis, reversing the usual order. You simply lead your reader in—by successive questions and their dismissal, or partial answers—to your main and conclusive point. "Is it this? Well, no." "Then may it be this? No, not exactly this either." "Then how about this? Ah, yes, this seems to be it." The deductive order, beginning with your thesis and then explaining it, is much more usual, and usually clearer. But the inductive order has suspense, a kind of intellectual excitement, if you can keep your answer from slipping out.

Inductive order probably works best for short essays, since you must keep the cat in the bag, and you can't keep him in too long. You simply use a question for your thesis-sentence and then simulate for your reader the train of thought by which you arrived at a conclusion, as I did in the following passage:

Thesis Question

... **What does Walt Whitman mean when he says "I celebrate myself "?**

Possible Answer Rejected

Can he be simply an egotist? The pronoun "I" dominates his writing. "I will effuse egotism, and show it underlying all," he writes. He speaks of generations of Americans passing with "faces turned sideways or backward toward me to listen, / With eyes retrospective toward me." He loves to see the smoke of his own breath, and to hear the beating of his own heart. Yet this egotism is somehow not offensive. He is something more than a simple egotist.

Partial Answer

Perhaps he takes himself as the common man, since his "I" represents others as well as himself: "I am of old and young, of the foolish as much as the wise, / ... Maternal as well as paternal, a child as well as a man." All men and women are his equals, his brothers and sisters, and he says a great deal about democracy. We soon realize that Whitman could not have done many of the things the "I" claims to have done. The "I" has been at sea with John Paul Jones; he is an artillery man in a bombarded fort; he has been a trapper, a fisherman off Newfoundland. The "I," then, is both the actual Whitman and his imaginative identification of himself with all walks of American life.

Complete Answer

But the "I" seems even more than this. The "I" has slept for ages, has evolved upward through the eons, has been carried in a dinosaur's mouth. He has subsumed in himself all the ideas of God: "Taking myself the exact dimensions of Jehovah, / Lithographing Kronos, Zeus his son, and Hercules his grandson. ..." Like the hawk, he sounds his "barbaric yawp over the roofs of the world." He dissolves into the next fold of the future, and waits for us somewhere up ahead. The "I" is now the spirit of life itself. So when Whitman celebrates himself, he is also celebrating the spirit of democracy and the Life Force, which are evident to him no less in geological history than in the men and women and blades of grass around him, and in his own present breathing and heartbeat.

This will give you an idea of inductive order. You may well use a short inductive section in a longer essay, especially for dismissing the opposition's arguments by putting them as questions ("Do we want unlimited freedom?") and then reducing them to absurdities. But, as I say, a wholly inductive essay is usually short, and you won't even find many of these, because your answer, your thesis, tends to keep slipping out of the bag and spoiling your surprise.

EXERCISES

9. *Write a paragraph in which you start with a question, and then, dismissing partial answers, lead your reader to your main and conclusive point. ("What is A? It might be B, and I know a lot of people think it is C, but I think it is really D.") Here is an example taken from an interview with a man reminiscing about his experiences during the Depression:*

What was the worst thing about the Depression? Well, I don't know. I **Topical** guess for some folks it was losing their savings. For us that wasn't so bad. I **Question** only had about $400 in the McLain County Bank when it closed and I got **Answer 1** some of that back later, about 10 cents on the dollar. Then too, being out of **Answer 2** work was rough for a lot of people. But even that wasn't so bad for me. I lost my job with the coal company in 1931, but we lived on a farm. And with that and some odd jobs I picked up, I managed to keep pretty busy until I got a steady job again. Of course, I know a lot of people didn't have enough to eat **Answer 3** or enough to wear during the Depression. For us that wasn't too bad. We grew most of our own food, and my wife is pretty handy at sewing, so we got by. Nothing very fancy, you understand, but we managed. No, I guess for us the worst thing about the Depression was we got to feeling after a while that times **Main Answer** just weren't ever going to get better. It just went on too long. For us, things **(Thesis)** got a little rough in 1931 and they stayed pretty rough until I got a job with the Highway Commission in 1938. Seven years is a long time to keep hoping. It just went on so long.

THE DEDUCTIVE ESSAY

Hang your essay from your Big Idea.

This is the arrangement we have been working on from the start. It is much more widely used, and useful, than the inductive one, because it can sustain itself page after page, even through chapters in a whole book. You set down your thesis, your general proposition, then *explain* it in detail and at length. The mode of induction is question and partial answer; the mode of deduction is assertion and explanation. As we have seen, however, the usual deductive order does not simply begin with your Big Idea and then dwindle down to nothing. You match some of the inductive's suspense by saving your best for last. You can even include a short inductive paragraph or two for more suspense and variety. You start with your thesis, then jump down to your smallest small and work progressively uphill until you again reach your thesis, which is now restated as your conclusion and rounded off in a concluding paragraph.

In short, the deductive order of presentation is the normal one we have been talking about all along. To change your little inductive essay on Whitman into a deductive one, you would simply make your thesis an assertion to be demonstrated rather than a question to be answered: "Whitman's 'I' represents not only Whitman himself, but also the spirit of democracy and the Life Force." You would then expand your three paragraphs into three or four pages, following the same general order, adding more evidence, quoting and explaining more fully, from actual Whitman, through democracy, to the great force of life itself. Rather than the question that opened your second paragraph, you would assert: "At first, Whitman may strike the reader as a simple egotist." Rather than the tentative "Perhaps" that opened your third paragraph, you would assert: "We soon discover that Whitman's 'I' represents others, as well as himself."

EXERCISES

10. *Take your inductive paragraph from the previous exercise, turn the order around, and expand your paragraph into a brief deductive essay, with thesis to be demonstrated rather than question to be answered. You will probably find that in switching from induction to deduction your paper will expand almost by itself, as you fill out your thoughts and explanations for your reader. Notice how you use the direct first-person statement from the preceding interview—which happened to fall into inductive order—as a piece of evidence in your larger deductive essay, still giving the facts as Mr. Harris stated them:*

Topic   For most Americans, the stock market crash was not the worst thing about the Depression. True, it carried away billions of dollars of investors' money, but relatively few of us felt directly affected. Few of us owned stock, and for most of us the market collapse was something that happened to other people, not to us. Of course, as we found out, the stock-market collapse was only the trigger, and soon more and more Americans found their lives directly affected. By 1932, twenty-five percent of the workers had no jobs. Yet, for many Americans, the worst thing about the Depression was not the bank closures, or being out of work, or even shortages of food and clothing. For many of us,

Thesis   the worst thing about the Depression was that it lasted so long we almost gave up hoping that times would ever get better. George Harris of Wellsburg, West Virginia, is a good example of how the Depression hit most of us.

Demonstration

In 1931, Mr. Harris had a job with the Green Coal Company as a tender on a boat that pushed coal barges up and down the Ohio River. His income was generally pretty good, and Mr. Harris had managed to buy a small farm just outside town. But cutbacks in industrial production, particularly in the production of steel, soon forced cutbacks in coal mining as well. And in August of 1931, Mr. Harris was laid off. The next year, in 1932, the McLain County Bank closed, and with it went the only savings the Harrises had, $400, although later he did manage to collect ten percent of his lost savings. And so for the next seven years Mr. Harris bounced from job to job, whatever he could get: a few days here, a few days there. He was thus able to hold onto his small farm, and on it he raised most of the food for the Harris family for the next seven years. Mrs. Harris, too, helped to cut corners by making most of the family's clothes, and by repairing things when they wore out. In this way, taking it one day at a time, and living as simply and as frugally as possible, the Harrises managed to get by until, in 1938, Mr. Harris once again got a secure and well-paying job with the County Road Commission.

Restatement

So the Harrises are a good example of how the Depression hit many Americans. They lost some savings, they lost their jobs, they had to tighten their belts, but they managed to get by. For them, the worst thing about the Depression was not the deprivation; it was simply that the Depression went on year after year. As Mr. Harris says, "Seven years is a long time to keep hoping. It just went on so long."

THE DEDUCTIVE-INDUCTIVE ESSAY

Try a question for a thesis.

Actually, you can write a good essay about halfway between the inductive and deductive modes. The basic framework is deductive, a general thesis followed by its successive explanations in ascending order of interest and importance. But the inner movement is mostly inductive, a fairly large number of questions replacing the assertions that would otherwise guide the progress, section by section. You may set the mode very easily by putting your thesis as a broadly general question.

The more direct the question, the more purely inductive the essay. You launch a completely inductive essay when your questioning thesis asks for one specific answer among the several possibilities you will entertain and reject before letting the reader know your answer: "Is Whitman an egotist?" ("Not really"); "Should we make welfare payments?" ("Yes"). The more your question suggests your answer, the more deductive you become: "Is Whitman something more universal than a mere egotist?"; "Are welfare payments really the socialistic and bureaucratic evil they are so often said to be?"

Virginia Woolf's famous essay "How Should One Read a Book?"* is an almost perfect example of the deductive-inductive mode, as both her title and her thesis suggest. Even her questioning title implies an unstated deductive assertion: "One should read a book, and read it the right way." Her thesis, also a question, likewise implies an unstated deductive assertion, which her essay proceeds to illustrate: "How are we to bring order into this multitudinous chaos and so get the deepest and widest pleasure from what we read?" Her thesis-question does not say exactly *how*—her essay proceeds to fill in the answer somewhat inductively—but the question clearly suggests that we must bring order from chaos to achieve the deep and wide pleasure she sees as the purpose of reading. A thesis-question similar to Woolf's may get you a very nice deductive-inductive essay:

> **How should one plan a vacation?**
> **What is the greatest reward in sports?**
> **What makes an effective teacher?**

You may also set the deductive-inductive mode by trimming a fully explicit thesis to get something of the open-endedness of a question. You simply trim the full-blown thesis at both ends, cutting away from the beginning the concessive "Although . . ." and from the end the explanatory "because. . . ." Your most completely stated thesis might be:

> **Although welfare payments may offend the rugged individualist, we should nevertheless have a system of welfare payments because they relieve much want and anxiety, and they enable many a fatherless family to maintain its integrity.**

To remake this a thesis for a partially inductive essay, you simply trim it to something like: "All in all, we need some system to help those in need." You then proceed with a series of questions, or open-ended assertions, supplying the answers and *because*'s as you go:

*From *The Second Common Reader* (New York: Harcourt Brace Jovanovich, 1932).

1. But what about the threat to our ideal of self-sufficiency?

2. Private organizations already provide a number of charitable services.

3. But what about the actual needs of fatherless, poor families?

4. Surely our affluent society can care for its less fortunate members.

And so on, until you have reached and dealt with the want, anxiety, and frustration that are the center of your submerged but emerging thesis.

EXERCISES

11. *Here are two essays in which the internal movement is essentially inductive That is, the stress tends to fall at the end of the essay rather than at the beginning. In one of the two essays, however, an initial deductive framework helps to clarify the writer's central proposition, to give us a preview of the thesis before the paper's conclusion drives home his main idea. Read the two essays—the first is by Jean-Jacques Rosseau (1712–1778); the second, by Niccolo Machiavelli (1469–1527)—and then answer the questions that follow.*

THE SIGNS OF A GOOD GOVERNMENT

When, therefore, one asks what in absolute terms is the best government, one is asking a question which is unanswerable because it is indeterminate; or alternatively one might say that there are as many good answers as there are possible combinations in the absolute and relative positions of peoples.

But if it is asked by what signs one can tell whether a given people is well or badly governed, that is another matter; and the question of fact can be answered.

Even so, it is not really answered, because everyone will want to answer it in his own way. Subjects prize public tranquillity; citizens the freedom of the individual—the former prefer security of possessions, the latter security of person; subjects think the best government is the most severe, citizens that it is the mildest; the former want crimes to be punished, the latter want them prevented; subjects think it is a good thing to be feared by their neighbors, citizens prefer to be ignored by them; the former are satisfied so long as money circulates, the latter demand that the people shall have bread. But even if there were agreement on these and suchlike points, should we be any more advanced? Moral dimensions have no precise standard of measurement; even if we could agree about signs, how should we agree in appraisal?

For myself, I am always astonished that people should fail to recognize so simple a sign, or be so insincere as not to agree about it. What is the object of any political association? It is the protection and the prosperity of its members. And what is the surest evidence that they are so protected and prosperous? The numbers of their population. Then do not look beyond this much debated evidence. All other things being equal, the government under which, without external aids like naturalization and immigration, the citizens increase and multiply most, is infallibly the best government. That under which the people diminishes and wastes away is the worst. Statisticians, this is your problem: count, measure, compare.*

HOW CITIES OR STATES PREVIOUSLY INDEPENDENT MUST BE GOVERNED AFTER OCCUPATION

When those states which have been accustomed to live in freedom under their own laws are acquired, there are three ways of trying to keep them. The first is to destroy them, the second to go and live therein, and the third to allow them to continue to live under their own laws, taking a tribute from them and creating within them a new government of a few which will keep the state friendly to you. For since such a government is the creature of the prince it will know that it cannot exist without his friendship and authority and is thus certain to do its best to support him, and a city accustomed to freedom can be more easily held through its citizens than in any other way if it is desired to preserve it. Here we have the examples of the Spartans and the Romans. The Spartans held Athens and Thebes and created in both a government of a few; nonetheless they lost them. The Romans, in order to hold Capua, Carthage, and Numantia, razed them and did not lose them. They tried to keep Greece in the same way the Spartans had, permitting the country to be free under its own laws, but in this they were not successful inasmuch as they were compelled to destroy many cities of that province in order to hold it, for in truth there is no sure way of holding them other than by their ruin. And whoever becomes master of a city accustomed to living in freedom and does not destroy it may expect to be destroyed by it himself, for it has always as an incentive ·to rebellion the name of liberty and its own ancient laws which neither time nor favors received can cause the citizens to forget. And whatever action be taken or provision be made, as long as the inhabitants are not

---

*Jean-Jacques Rousseau, *The Social Contract*, translated by Maurice Cranston (Baltimore, Penguin Books, Inc., 1968), pp. 129–130. Reprinted by permission of A D Peters and Co Ltd., London.

separated or dispersed, that name and those laws are never forgotten but provide a rallying point in every emergency, as is shown by the case of Pisa after many years of subjection to the Florentines. Cities or provinces used to living under a prince are accustomed to obedience, and when the ruling house becomes extinct they are unable to agree on a successor and, having no experience of self-government, they are slow in taking up arms and so with greater ease a prince may overcome them and feel secure in his possession of them. In republics there is greater life, greater hatred, more desire of vengeance, and the memory of their ancient liberty gives them no rest; so the safest way is either to extinguish them or go and live in them.*

1. What is Rousseau's thesis?
2. Do you find any anticipations of the thesis in the paper's opening section? If so, what are they?
3. What is Machiavelli's thesis?
4. What anticipations of his thesis do you find in his opening section?
5. Which of these two seems to be the deductive-inductive essay?

*Niccolo Machiavelli, *The Prince*, translated and edited by Thomas G. Bergin (Arlington Heights, Ill.: AHM Publishing Corporation, 1947), pp. 12–13. Copyright ' 1947 by AHM Publishing Corporation. Reprinted by permission of AHM Publishing Corporation.

Chapter 6

WRITING GOOD SENTENCES

All this time you have been writing sentences, as naturally as breathing, and perhaps with as little variation. Now for a close look at the varieties of the sentence. Some varieties can be shaggy and tangled indeed. But they are all offshoots of the simple active sentence, the basic English genus *John hits Joe*, with action moving straight from subject through verb to object.

This subject-verb-object sentence can be infinitely grafted and contorted, but it really has only two general varieties: (1) the "loose, or strung-along," in Aristotle's phrase, and (2) the periodic. English naturally runs "loose." Our thoughts are by nature strung along from subject through verb to object, with whatever comes to mind simply added as it comes—a word order happily acquired from French as a result of the Norman Conquest. The loose sentence puts its subject and verb early. But we can also use the periodic sentence characteristic of our German and Latin ancestry, where ideas hang in the air like girders until all interconnections are locked by the final word, at the period: *John, the best student in the class, the tallest and most handsome, hits Joe.* A periodic sentence, in other words, is one that suspends its meaning until the end, usually with subject and verb widely separated, and the verb as near the end as possible.

So we have two varieties of the English sentence, partly because its old Germanic oak was first limbered by French and then cured by Latin, but mostly because (as Aristotle observed of Greek) the piece-by-piece and the periodic species simply represent two ways of thought: the first, the natural stringing of thoughts as they come; the second, the more careful contrivance of emphasis and suspense.

THE SIMPLE SENTENCE

Use the simple active sentence, loosely periodic.

Your best sentences will be hybrids of the loose and the periodic. First, learn to use active verbs (*John* HITS *Joe*), which will keep you within the simple active pattern with all parts showing (subject-verb-object), as opposed to verbs in the passive voice (*Joe* IS HIT *by John*), which put everything backwards and use more words: IS HIT *by John* is "passive voice" because it makes the real doer, John, seem to be inactive, or "passive," resting at the end of the sentence instead of starting the action, right at the beginning. So, keep active. Then learn to give your native strung-along sentence a touch of periodicity and suspense.

Any change in normal order can give you unusual emphasis, as when you move the object ahead of the subject:

> **That I like.**
> **The house itself she hated, but the yard was grand.**
> **Nature I loved; and next to Nature, Art.**
> **The manuscript, especially, he treasured.**

You can vary the subject-verb-object pattern more gently by interruptive words and phrases, so that the meaning gathers excitement from the delay. The *especially* does more for the manuscript than the words themselves could manage: the phrase postpones the already postponed subject and predicate. Put the phrase last, and the emphasis fades considerably; the speaker grows a little remote: "The manuscript he treasured, especially." Put the sentence in normal order—"He especially treasured the manuscript"—and we are, in fact, back to normal.

We expect our ideas one at a time, in normal succession—*John hits Joe*—and with anything further added, in proper sequence, at the end—

a real haymaker. Change this fixed way of thinking, and you immediately put your reader on the alert for something unusual. Consequently, some of your best sentences will be simple active ones sprung wide with phrases coloring subject, verb, object, or all three, in various ways. You may, for instance, effectively complicate the subject:

> King Lear, proud, old, and childish, probably aware that his grip on the kingdom is beginning to slip, devises a foolish plan.
> To come all this way, to arrive after dark, and then to find the place locked and black as ink was almost unbearable.

Or the verb:

> She made her way, carefully at first, then confidently, then with reckless steps, along the peak of the smoldering roof.
> A good speech usually begins quietly, proceeds sensibly, gathers momentum, and finally moves even the most indifferent audience.

Or the object:

> He finally wrote the paper, a long desperate perambulation, without beginning or end, without any guiding idea—without, in fact, much of an idea at all.
> Her notebooks contain marvelous comments on the turtle in the back yard, the flowers and weeds, the great elm by the drive, the road, the earth, the stars, and the men and women of the village.

These are some of the infinite possibilities in the simple active sentence as it delays and stretches and heightens the ordinary expectations of subject-verb-object.

EXERCISES

1. *Give each of the following sentences a touch of periodicity by changing the normal word order, by adding interruptive words or phrases, or by complicating one of the three principal elements of the sentence: the subject, the verb, the object.*

EXAMPLE She made her way along the smoldering roof. She made her way, carefully at first, then confidently, then with reckless steps, along the peak of the smoldering roof.

1. Commune residents are often escapees from solidly middle-class families.
2. Former friends are often embarrassed when they meet and find they have little in common.
3. Some firemen began carrying guns when they were frightened by the chaos of the riots.
4. The bottleneck in education is that the teacher can listen and respond to no more than one student at a time.
5. The car wheezed to a stop.
6. The editorial in the *New York Times* suggested that tight control of governmental spending might check inflation.
7. It was wholly unlike his father to give up without trying.
8. The inspector discovered a window that had been forced open.
9. We certainly remember that first night in the new house!
10. The escaped convict offered only token resistance when a private citizen captured and disarmed him after a short chase.
11. William Faulkner died of a heart attack on July 6, 1962.
12. The *Scientific American* customarily devotes its September issue to a single, unified topic.
13. We must note that some parents have misgivings about the schools.
14. The house sits at the edge of town in the middle of large grounds.

2. *Cull through your papers and find five of your own simple sentences. Revise them as in Exercise 1, handing in your original sentences paired with their revisions.*

COMPOUND AND COMPLEX SENTENCES

Learn the difference between compound and complex sentences.

You make a compound sentence by linking together simple sentences with a coordinating conjunction *(and, but, or, nor, yet)* or with a colon or a semicolon. You make a complex one by hooking lesser sentences onto the main sentence with *that, which, who,* or one of the many other subordinating connectives like *although, because, where, when, after, if.* The compound sentence *coordinates,* treating everything on the same level; the complex *subordinates,* putting everything else somewhere below one main self-sufficient idea. The compound links ideas one after the other, as in the basic simple sentence; the complex is a simple sentence elaborated by clauses instead of merely by phrases. The compound represents the strung-along way of thinking; the complex frequently represents the periodic.

Avoid simple-minded compounds.

Essentially the compound sentence *is* simple-minded, a set of clauses on a string—a child's description of a birthday party, for instance: "We got paper hats and we pinned the tail on the donkey and we had chocolate ice cream and Randy sat on a piece of cake and I won third prize." *And . . . and . . . and.*

But this way of thinking is necessary, even in postgraduate regions. It is always useful simply for pacing off related thoughts, and for breaking the staccato of simple statement. It often briskly connects cause and effect: "The clock struck one, and down he run." "The solipsist relates all knowledge to his own being, and the demonstrable commonwealth of human nature dissolves before his dogged timidity." The *and* can link causes with all sorts of different effect and speed, can bring in the next clause as a happy afterthought or a momentous consequence. Since the compound sentence follows the most enduring of colloquial patterns—the simple sequence of things said as they occur to the mind—it has the pace, the immediacy, and the dramatic effect of talk. Hemingway, for instance, often gets all the numb tension of a shell-shocked mind by reducing his character's thoughts all to one level, in sentences something like this: "It was a good night and I sat at a table and . . . and . . . and. . . ."

With *but* and *or,* the compound sentence becomes more thoughtful. The mind is at work, turning its thought first one way then another, meeting the reader's objections by stating them. With semicolon and colon (or, if the clauses are very short, with comma), the compound grows more sophisticated still:

> **John demands the most from himself; Pete demands.**
> **I came, I saw, I conquered.**
> **Economic theorists assume a common man: he commonly wants**
>   **more than he can supply.**

Think of the compound sentence in terms of its conjunctions—the words that yoke its clauses—and of the accompanying punctuation. Here are three basic groups of conjunctions that will help you sort out and punctuate your compound thoughts.

GROUP I. *The three common coordinating conjunctions:* and, but, *and* or (nor). *Put a comma before each.*

I like her, and I don't mind saying so.
Art is long, but life is short.
Win this point, or the game is lost.
We will not be coerced, nor will we be bought.

GROUP II. *Conjunctive adverbs:* therefore, moreover, however, nevertheless, consequently, furthermore. *Put a semicolon before, a comma after, each.*

Nations indeed seem to have a kind of biological span like human life, from rebellious youth, through caution, to decay; consequently, predictions of doom are not uncommon.

GROUP III. *Some in-betweeners—yet, still, so—which sometimes take a comma, sometimes a semicolon, depending on your pace and emphasis.*

We long for the good old days, yet we never include the disadvantages.
People long for the good old days; yet they rarely take into account
the inaccuracy of human memory.
The preparation had been halfhearted and hasty, so the meeting
was wretched.
Rome declined into the pleasures of its circuses and couches; so the
tough barbarians conquered.

Try compounding with semicolon and colon.

Though the conjunction usually governs the compound sentence, two powerful coordinators remain—the semicolon and the colon. These strong punctuations can replace both the , and and the period. The semicolon most effectively coordinates by *contrasts;* the colon, by *amplification.* You will notice in the preceding sentence how the semicolon pulls the contrasting clauses together for close inspection, so closely, in fact, that we can drop the verb in the second clause, substituting a comma, and so tighten the contrast still further. For contrasts, the semicolon is the prince of coordinators:

The dress accents the feminine; the pants suit speaks for freedom.   Contrast
Golf demands the best of time and space; tennis, the best of personal
energy.
The government tries to get the most out of taxes; the individual
tries to get out of the most taxes.

The colon similarly pulls two ''sentences'' together without blessing of conjunction, period, or capital. But it signals amplification, not contrast: the second clause explains the first.

Amplification

> **A house with an aging furnace costs more than the asking price suggests: ten dollars more a month in fuel means about eighty dollars more a year.**
>
> **A growing population means more business: more business will exhaust our supply of ores in less than half a century.**
>
> **Sports at any age are beneficial: they keep your pulses hopping.**

As a corollary to its role as amplifier, the colon also introduces lists:

> **The following players will start: Corelli, Smith, Jones, Baughman, and Stein.**

EXERCISES

3. *Convert the following pairs of sentences into compound sentences with the coordinator you think most appropriate to the sense and style of the sentences.*

1. He couldn't go on. He was just too tired.
2. The crime commission recommended a number of such programs. Federal funds have been made available for putting them into operation.
3. The governor told the President that the state could not cope with the disaster. The President dispatched federal troops.
4. The first plant generating electricity by reactor began operating in 1956. Nuclear technology has been growing rather slowly since then.
5. We can probably never perfect the process beyond its present state. We should still try.
6. In some instances, the seminar for freshman courses would be extremely helpful. In other instances, it might be of little value.
7. The thought of quitting his job excited him. The idea had been in the back of his mind for a long time.
8. Most schools are just now starting courses in computers for freshmen. To evaluate those programs will take several years.
9. In his manuscripts, F. Scott Fitzgerald's sentences are often haphazard and careless. His spelling is often atrocious.
10. On small farms, labor was not specialized. On medium farms, labor was partially specialized. But large farms carefully divided their workers into teams of specialists.
11. Few recipients of Social Security benefits can actually live on that income

alone. Most supplement their incomes with savings or by selling the possessions of a lifetime.

12. Mark Twain's book *The Gilded Age* attempts too much. It attempts to satirize an age.

13. Within the past few years, many kinds of jobs open to recent graduates have steadily shrunk. As a result, students are increasingly challenging the curriculum to provide them marketable skills.

14. We have made some progress in controlling exhaust. We still have a long way to go.

15. Statistically, your chances of being killed or injured in an airplane are lower than in an automobile. Most of us, however, are more nervous in planes than in cars.

Learn to subordinate.

You probably write compound sentences almost without thinking. But the subordinations of the complex usually require some thought. Indeed, you are ranking closely related thoughts, arranging the lesser ones so that they bear effectively on your main thought. You must first pick your most important idea. You must then change mere sequence into subordination—ordering your lesser thoughts "sub," or below, the main idea. The childish birthday sentence, then, might come out something like this:

> **After paper hats and chocolate ice cream, after Randy's sitting on a piece of cake and everyone's pinning the tail on the donkey, I WON THIRD PRIZE.**
>
> Subordinating by Adverbs "After"

You do the trick with connectives—with any word, like *after* in the preceding sentence, indicating time, place, cause, or other qualification:

> *If* they try, *if* they fail, THEY ARE STILL GREAT *because* their spirit is unbeaten.

You daily achieve subtler levels of subordination with the three relative pronouns *that, which, who,* and with the conjunction *that. That, which,* and *who* connect thoughts so closely related as to seem almost equal, but actually each tucks a clause (subject-and-verb) into some larger idea:

> **The car, *which* runs perfectly, is not worth selling.**
> **The car *that* runs perfectly is worth keeping.**
> **He thought *that* the car would run forever.**
>
> Relative Pronouns
>
> Conjunction

> **He thought [*that* omitted but understood] the car would run forever.**

But the subordinating conjunctions and adverbs (*although, if, because, since, until, where, when, as if, so that*) really put subordinates in their places. Look at *when* in this sentence of E. B. White's from *Charlotte's Web:*

Adverbs
> **Next morning *when* the first light came into the sky and the sparrows stirred in the trees, *when* the cows rattled their chains and the rooster crowed and the early automobiles went whispering along the road, Wilbur awoke and looked for Charlotte.**

Here the simple *when,* used only twice, has regimented five subordinate clauses, all of equal rank, into their proper station below that of the main clause, "Wilbur awoke and looked for Charlotte." You can vary the ranking intricately and still keep it straight:

Conjunctions
> **Although some claim *that* time is an illusion, *because* we have no absolute chronometer, *although* the mind cannot effectively grasp time, *because* the mind itself is a kind of timeless presence almost oblivious to seconds and hours, *although* the time of our solar system may be only an instant in the universe at large, WE STILL CANNOT QUITE DENY *that* some progression of universal time is passing over us, *if* only we could measure it.**

Complex sentences are, at their best, really simple sentences gloriously delayed and elaborated with subordinate thoughts. The following beautiful and elaborate sentence from the Book of Common Prayer is all built on the simple sentence "draw near":

> **Ye who do truly and earnestly repent you of your sins, and are in love and charity with your neighbors, and intend to lead a new life, following the commandments of God, and walking from henceforth in his holy ways, draw near with faith, and take this holy sacrament to your comfort, and make your humble confession to Almighty God, devoutly kneeling.**

Even a short sentence may be complex, attaining a remarkably varied suspense. Notice how the simple statement "I allowed myself" is skillfully elaborated in this sentence by the late Wolcott Gibbs of the *New Yorker:*

> Twice in my life, for reasons that escape me now, though I'm sure they were discreditable, I allowed myself to be persuaded that I ought to take a hand in turning out a musical comedy.

Once you glimpse the complex choreography possible within the dimensions of the simple sentence, you are on your way to developing a prose capable of turns and graceful leaps, one with a kind of intellectual health that, no matter what the subject or mood, is always on its toes.

EXERCISES

4. *Here are some pairs of sentences, some of them the same pairs you converted to compound sentences in the previous exercise. This time, convert them into complex sentences, trying to use a variety of subordinators.*

1. He couldn't go on. He was just too tired.
2. The crime commission recommended a number of such programs. Federal funds have been made available for putting them into operation.
3. We can probably never perfect the process beyond its present state. We should still try.
4. Many schools are just now starting courses in computers for freshmen. To evaluate those programs will take several years.
5. On small farms, labor was not specialized. On medium farms, labor was partially specialized. But large farms carefully divided their workers into teams of specialists.
6. Few recipients of Social Security benefits can actually live on that income alone. Most supplement their incomes with savings or by selling the possessions of a lifetime.
7. We desperately need more judges and more staff. Courts are as much as twenty-six months behind schedule, with little hope of catching up.
8. A large reduction in the prime interest rate is not likely. House seekers, therefore, must choose either mortgages with interests as high as nine percent, or no purchases.
9. Within the past few years, many kinds of jobs open to recent graduates have steadily shrunk. As a result, students are increasingly challenging the curriculum to provide them marketable skills.
10. An independent candidate for President has little chance of becoming a serious contender. He cannot rely upon large party machinery, and he has little money for advertising.

11. Two motorists were killed last night when their car hit a guard rail, overturned, and caught fire. Police were unable to determine the cause of the accident.

12. Plants can obtain the elements necessary for photosynthesis from water in the soil and from carbon dioxide in the air. Nevertheless, they need many other elements.

13. Federal control of prices could have encouraged a switch to coal. The government could have let the price of oil and gas soar with the market while monitoring pollution.

14. You may be familiar with our facilities and resources already. If not, simply fill out the enclosed form and return it to us, and we will send you a free brochure.

15. True scientific knowledge is no longer accessible to the majority of us. We wish it were, but it just isn't. It's too complicated for most of us.

5. *Supply five pairs of simple sentences from your previous papers, and subordinate one to the other so as to revise the pairs into complex sentences.*

6. *Write a one-hundred-word sentence with only one independent clause and with everything else subordinated. You can get started with a string of parallel clauses: "When I get up in the morning, when I look at my bleary eyes in the mirror, when I think of the paper still to be done . . .," or "After . . ., after . . ., after . . . ." See how far you can run on before you must bring in your main subject and verb.*

Try for still closer connections: modify.

Your subordinating *if*'s and *when*'s have really been modifying—that is, limiting—the things you have attached them to. But there is a smoother way. It is an adjectival sort of thing, a shoulder-to-shoulder operation, a neat trick with no need for shouting, a stone to a stone with no need for mortar. You simply put clauses and phrases up against a noun, instead of attaching them with a subordinator. This sort of modification includes the following constructions, all using the same close masonry: (1) appositives, (2) relatives understood, (3) adjectives-with-phrase, (4) participles, (5) absolutes.

APPOSITIVES. Those phrases about shoulders and tricks and stones, above, are all in apposition with *sort of thing,* and they are grammatically subordinate to it. The phrases are nevertheless nearly coordinate and interchangeable. They are compressions of a series of sentences ("It is an adjectival sort of thing. It is a neat trick . . .," and so forth) set side by side, "stone to stone." Mere contact does the work of the verb *is* and its subject *it.* English often does the same with subordinate clauses, omitting the *who is* or *which is* and putting the rest directly into apposition. "The William who is the Conqueror" becomes "William the Conqueror." "The Jack who is the heavy hitter" becomes "Jack the heavy hitter." These, incidentally, are called "restrictive" appositions, because they restrict to a particular designation the nouns they modify, setting this William and this Jack apart from all others (with no separating commas). Similarly, you can make nonrestrictive appositives from nonrestrictive clauses, clauses that simply add information (between commas). "Smith, who is a man to be reckoned with, . . ." becomes "Smith, a man to be reckoned with, ..." "Jones, who is our man in Liverpool, . . ." becomes "Jones, our man in Liverpool, ..." Restrictive or nonrestrictive, close contact makes your point with economy and fitness.

RELATIVES UNDERSTOOD. You can often achieve the same economy, as I have already hinted, by omitting any kind of relative and its verb, thus gaining a compression both colloquial and classic:

> **A compression [that is] both colloquial and classic. . . .**
> **The specimens [that] he had collected. . . .**
> **The girl [whom] he [had] left behind. . . .**

But be careful after verbs that easily take direct objects. Omitting *that* may lead to confusion:

> **She felt his ears were too big.**
> **He saw her nose was too small.**
> **This does not deny his daily habits and thoughts are his own.**

ADJECTIVES-WITH-PHRASE. This construction is also appositive and adjectival. It is neat and useful:

> **The law was passed, *thick with provisions and codicils, heavy with implications.***
> **There was the lake, *smooth in the early air.***

EXERCISES

   7. *Streamline the following sentences by using appositives wherever you can.*

1. The security guard, who must have been a very frightened man, fired point-blank into the crowd.

2. Professor Stanley, who is now associate vice-president and director of business operations, has been named a vice-president at the University of Nebraska.
3. The book, which has been a best seller for several months, will be made into a movie.
4. American social mores have undergone staggering changes since the early 1950's. These changes are so great in quality and number as to constitute a virtual revolution.
5. The Globe Theatre, which was immediately acclaimed the best designed and appointed playhouse in London, was completed in 1599.

8. *Eliminate relatives and their accompanying verbs from the following sentences:*

1. The freeze on wages and prices that was announced by the President shocked European investors.
2. *Pygmalion,* which had first been popular as a play, and which had later been rewritten as a popular musical comedy, was finally done as a movie.
3. Although Picasso executed the original design, he had nothing to do with erecting the sculpture which is now standing in front of the Hancock Building in Chicago.
4. The studded tire, which has long been popular for winter driving in some states, is now being outlawed in many states because of damage to roads.
5. Because of the recession, the renovation that we had all hoped for has been postponed.
6. Students who are now being admitted to the master's program will not have to pass the foreign language proficiency test that has always been required in the past.

9. *In the following sentences, insert the adjectival phrases ("pure terror in her eyes") next to the nouns they modify, within appropriate commas.*

1. The young girl cowered in the corner. There was pure terror in her eyes.
2. This construction is also appositional and adjectival. It is a neat trick for the beginning writer to remember.
3. Its deck was splintered and peeling. Its rigging was nearly all frayed and rotted. The boat obviously hadn't been cared for at all.
4. Griswell had neither eaten nor slept, and when he stumbled into the bar he was trembling with fatigue.
5. The ladder was sagging with his weight, and at last it collapsed.

6. The commission's final report will probably not be ready for Friday's meeting. After all, the report is over three hundred pages long and has more than seventy charts.
7. The street in Lawrence was completely familiar to Andrews. It was firmly rooted in his memory even after three years in the Army.
8. The narrator in *Autobiography of an Ex-Colored Man* was so lightskinned that he could easily pass for white, and when he finally decided to give up his black identity, he found it easy to do. Still, the choice left him bitter and embarrassed.

PARTICIPLES. Participles—verbs acting as adjectives—are extremely supple subordinators. Consider this sequence of six simple sentences:

He had been thrown.
He had accepted.
He felt a need.
He demanded money.
He failed.
He chose not to struggle.

Now see how Richard Wright, in *Native Son*, subordinates with participles the first five of these to the sixth. He elaborates the complete thought into a forceful sentence that runs for eighty-nine words with perfect clarity:

Having been thrown by an accidental murder into a position where he had sensed a possible order and meaning in his relations with the people about him; *having accepted* the moral guilt and responsibility for that murder because it had made him feel free for the first time in his life; *having felt* in his heart some obscure need to be at home with people and *having demanded* ransom money to enable him to do it—*having* done all this and *failed,* he chose not to struggle any more.

The following participles have the same adjectival force:

Dead to the world, *wrapped* in sweet dreams, *untroubled* by bills, he slept till noon.

Notice that the participles operate exactly as the adjective *dead* does.
    Beware of dangling participles. They may trip you, as they have

tripped others. The participle, with its adjectival urge, may grab the first noun that comes along, with shocking results.

Dangling
Participles

> Bowing to the crowd, the bull caught him unawares.
> Observing quietly from the bank, the beavers committed several errors in judgment.
> Squandering everything at the track, the money was never paid.
> By bending low, the snipers could not see the retreating squad.
> Tired and discouraged, half the lawn was still uncut.
> What we need is a list of teachers broken down alphabetically.

Move the participle next to its intended noun or pronoun. You will have to supply this word if inadvertence or the passive voice has omitted it entirely. Recast the sentence for good alignment when necessary. You may also save the day by changing a present participle to a past, as in the third example.

> The bull caught him unawares as he bowed to the crowd.
> Observing quietly from the bank, they saw the beavers make several errors in judgment.
> Squandered at the track, the money was never repaid.
> Because the retreating squad bent low, the snipers could not see them.
> Tired and discouraged, she had cut only half the lawn.
> What we need is an alphabetical list of teachers.

Here is a sentence from Jane Austen's *Persuasion* that illustrates the adjectival and subordinating power of the participle—*delighted* twice modifying *She* and subordinating everything to the one basic four-word clause that begins the sentence:

> She always watched them as long as she could, delighted to fancy she understood what they might be talking of, as they walked along in happy independence, or equally delighted to see the Admiral's hearty shake of the hand when he encountered an old friend, and observe their eagerness of conversation when occasionally forming into a little knot of the navy, Mrs. Croft looking as intelligent and keen as any of the officers around her.

This sentence ends so gracefully because, with the phrase *Mrs. Croft looking*, it achieves the ultimate in participial perfection—the ablative absolute, which we will consider in the next section.

EXERCISES

10. *Keeping an eye out for dangling participles, revise the following sentences by transforming as many verbs as reasonably possible into participles.*

1. Apparently the boxer thought the bell had sounded. He dropped his guard, and he was immediately knocked out.
2. He settled into a Bohemian life in the French Quarter. He started publishing in all the appropriate little magazines. And at last he found himself presiding over a colony of artists and writers.
3. The prisoners were obviously angered by the news that no guards were fired. They felt cheated and betrayed. And so on August 4, they seized three guards as hostages to force the warden to reconsider.
4. Trumbo was blacklisted in Hollywood; he was vilified in the press; and he was forced to write scripts under an assumed name until nearly 1960.
5. The student-designed rocket functioned perfectly. It rose one hundred miles above the earth, flew for ten minutes, traveled some fifty miles down range, and splashed down precisely on target.
6. After 100 miles, Hunt showed his winning style. He came out of each turn at 6000 rpm, accelerated to 8000 rpm on the following straight, then braked and shifted down for the next turn.
7. Nineteenth-century women were isolated and unenfranchised; they were sexually "used" and relegated to the kitchen and the nursery; in essence, society regarded them as brainless decorations.
8. He didn't check the charts for the water's depth and consequently ran aground thirty minutes after the race started.
9. The assembly line was invented by Ford. It was institutionalized by the UAW. It is now extensively automated. It produces many components that are untouched by human hands.
10. It depends on the smoothness and porosity of the surface. It will also vary with the kind of wood. You should test the color of this stain on a small inconspicuous area and then thin it to the shade you desire.

ABSOLUTES. The absolute phrase has a great potential of polished economy. Many an absolute is simply a prepositional phrase with the preposition dropped:

> **He ran up the stairs, [with] *a bouquet of roses under his arm,* and rang the bell.**
> **She walked slowly, [with] *her camera ready.***

But the ablative absolute (*ablative* means "removed") is absolutely removed from grammatical connection with the main clause, modifying only by proximity. If you have had some Latin, you will probably remember this construction as some kind of brusque condensation, something like *The road completed,* Caesar moved his camp." But it survives in the best of circles. Somewhere E. B. White admits to feeling particularly good one morning, just having brought off an especially fine ablative absolute. And it is actually more common than you may suppose. A recent newspaper article stated that "the Prince has fled the country, *his hopes of a negotiated peace shattered."* The *hopes shattered* pattern (noun plus participle) marks the ablative absolute (also called, because of the noun, a "nominative absolute"). The idea might have been more conventionally subordinated: "since his hopes were shattered" or "with his hopes shattered." But the ablative absolute accomplishes the subordination with economy and style.

Take a regular subordinate clause: "*When* the road *was* completed." Cut the subordinator and the finite verb. You now have an ablative absolute, a phrase that stands absolutely alone, shorn of both its connective *when* and its full predication *was:* "*The road completed,* Caesar moved his camp." Basically a noun and a participle, or noun and adjective, it is a kind of grammatical shorthand, a telegram: *ROAD COMPLETED CAESAR MOVED*—most said in fewest words, speed with high compression: this is its appeal and its power. Here are further examples:

> The cat stopped, its *back arched,* its *eyes frantic.*
> The whole company, *God willing,* soon will return to normal.
> *All things considered,* the plan would work.
> The *dishes washed,* the *baby bathed* and *asleep,* the last *ashtray emptied,* they could at last relax.

It is certainly a construction you should use with caution. It can sound exactly like a bad translation. But able writers come to it sooner or later, whether knowingly or through discovering for themselves the horsepower in a subordinate clause milled down to its absolute minimum of noun and participle, or noun and adjective, or even noun and noun. Hemingway uses it frequently. Here is one of the noun-noun variety at the end of a sentence about pistols in *To Have and Have Not:* ". . . their only *drawback the mess* they leave for relatives to clean up." And here are two noun-participle ones (*he playing* and *the death administered*), in a passage that will serve as a closing illustration of how a complex sentence can subordinate as many as 164 words to the 7 of its one main clause ("They will put up with mediocre work"):

> **If** the spectators know the matador is capable of executing a complete, consecutive series of passes with the muleta in which there will be valor, art, understanding and, above all, beauty and great emotion, THEY WILL PUT UP WITH MEDIOCRE WORK, cowardly work, disastrous work *because* they have the hope sooner or later of seeing the complete faena; the faena that takes a man out of himself and makes him feel immortal while it is proceeding, that gives him an ecstacy, that is, while momentary, as profound as any religious ecstasy; moving all the people in the ring together and increasing in emotional intensity as it proceeds, carrying the bullfighter with it, he playing on the crowd through the bull and being moved as it responds in a growing ecstasy of ordered, formal, passionate, increasing disregard for death that leaves you, when it is over, and the death administered to the animal that has made it possible, as empty, as changed, and as sad as any major emotion will leave you.*

Subordinating Conjunction

Main Clause

Sub. Conj.

Relatives

Participles

Absolutes

EXERCISES

11. *Try turning prepositional phrases and subordinate clauses in the following sentences into absolutes.*

1. With examinations coming and with the temperature dropping, students are beginning to show up at the health service with all sorts of nebulous ailments, most of them purely imagined.
2. Ted left the room, where his things were still scattered over the floor.
3. Even though the tank was filled with gas and the ignition was working perfectly, the engine still wouldn't start.
4. Even though the stock market had collapsed, and fifteen percent of the workers were jobless, Hoover nonetheless felt the economy would eventually right itself without tinkering.
5. With mud splattered all over her stockings, she looked as if she had been out playing in puddles.
6. When his three minutes were up, he deposited another quarter.

*Reprinted by permission of Charles Scribner's Sons from *Death in the Afternoon*, pp. 206–207. Copyright 1932 Charles Scribner's Sons; renewal copyright © 1960 Ernest Hemingway.

PARALLEL CONSTRUCTION

Use parallels to strengthen equivalent ideas.

Hemingway's 171-word sentence could not have held together without parallel construction. No complex sentence can hold up very long without it. Actually, Hemingway's "that is" after "ecstasy" makes a false parallel, throwing his sentence briefly out of line (he should have used "which is" or something like "an ecstasy as profound, though momentary, as any . . ."). You have also seen examples of parallel ranking in White's *when* sentence (p. 142) and in the sentence that followed, dealing with time. The sentence about the cat and the one about the relaxing couple (p. 150) have shown you ablative absolutes laid parallel.

Paralleling can be very simple. Any word will seek its own kind, noun to noun, adjective to adjective, infinitive to infinitive. The simplest series of things automatically runs parallel:

> **shoes and ships and sealing wax**
> **I came, I saw, I conquered**
> **to be or not to be**
> **a dull, dark, and soundless day**
> **mediocre work, cowardly work, disastrous work**

But they very easily run out of parallel too, and this you must learn to prevent. The last item especially may slip out of line, as in this series: "friendly, kind, unobtrusive, and *a bore*" (boring). The noun *bore* has jumped off the track laid by the preceding parallel adjectives. Your train of equivalent ideas should all be of the same grammatical kind to carry their equivalence clearly—to strengthen it: either parallel adjectives, *friendly, kind, unobtrusive,* and *boring,* or all nouns, *a friend, a saint, a diplomat,* and *a bore.* Your paralleling articles and prepositions should govern a series as a whole, or should accompany *every* item:

> **a hat, cane, pair of gloves, and mustache**
> **a hat, a cane, a pair of gloves, and a mustache**
> **by land, sea, or air**
> **by land, by sea, or by air**

Verbs also frequently intrude to throw a series of adjectives (or nouns) out of parallel:

> **He thought the girl was *attractive, intelligent,* and *knew* how to make him feel needed.**

> He thought the girl was *attractive, intelligent,* and *sympathetic,* knowing how to make him feel needed.

Here is an example from one of my students that illustrates how faulty paralleling obscures equivalent ideas:

> He stated two ways in which man could hope to continue survival. (1) World citizenship, or 2) destroying most of the inventions that man is uncertain of and go back to where we can understand ourselves and progress.

The most glaring error is the period in the second line and the capitalized *World.* This not only seems to start a new sentence, leaving the reader hanging in air at the end, still waiting for a verb to complete the thought, but also breaks the two parallel solutions away from the *two ways* that have set them up. A colon and small *w* will pull the sentence together, and a full parenthesis at "(2)" will make the parallel visibly equivalent. Next, we must bring the ideas themselves to the surface as equals by putting them into the same kind of grammatical slot, using either two nouns, as in the first solution below, or two participles, as in the second:

> (1) world citizenship, or (2) destruction . . .
> (1) seeking world citizenship, or (2) destroying . . .

But the sentence goes farther out of parallel still: *go back* needs to be parallel with *destroying* (or *destruction,* if you choose the noun). And what are we to make of that blurred parallel at the end? Are we to understand *ourselves* and the nature of *progress* (two nouns)? Or are we to *go back* and then begin to *progress* all over again (two verbs)? We do not know to which of the two choices *progress* is parallel, nor whether to accent it as a verb or a noun. Parallel construction would have told us. I found out by asking the student. The solution we worked out, with parallel ideas underlined, was this:

> He stated two ways in which man could hope to survive: (1) <u>creating</u> some kind of world government, or (2) <u>destroying</u> most of our inventions, <u>going back</u> to where we can understand ourselves as simple human beings, and <u>beginning</u> the painful history of progress all over again.

The speaker, of course, was arguing for world government (not *citizenship*), and he saw the present nuclear predicament as so threatening that the only parallel alternative to world government was scrapping *everything* and beginning again. We discovered that *creating* was the thought really parallel to *destroying*. By searching out the parallel ideas and putting them into grammatically equivalent structures, we brought the writer's idea clearly up to visibility where both he and I could understand it fully for the first time. Actually, only by first reaching for the grammatical parallels did we discover the really crucial parallel between *creating* and *destroying*.

Repeat your paralleling connectives.

When your series consists of phrases or of clauses, you should repeat the preposition or conjunction introducing them, to ensure clarity:

> *By* weeks of careful planning, *by* intelligence, *by* thorough training, and *by* a great deal of luck. . . . .
>
> *Since* all things are not equal, *since* consequences cannot be fore-seen, *since* we live but a moment. . . .
>
> He looked *for* clean fingernails and polished shoes, *for* an air of composure and a quick wit.

Watch the paralleling of pairs.

Pairs should be pairs, not odds and ends. Notice how the faulty pairs in these sentences have been corrected:

> She liked *the lawn and gardening* (the lawn and the garden).
>
> They were *all athletic or big men on campus* (athletes or big men on campus).
>
> They wanted *peace without being disgraced* (peace without dishonor).
>
> She liked *to play well and winning before a crowd* (to play well and to win; playing well and winning).
>
> He was *shy but a creative boy* (shy but creative).

Check your terms on both sides of your coordinating conjunctions (*and*, *but*, *or*) and see that they match:

> Orientation week seems both worthwhile [adjective] and
> necessary
> ~~a necessity~~ [noun].
>
>   that
> He prayed that they would leave and ∧ the telephone would not
> ring.

Learn to use paralleling coordinators.

The sentence above about "Orientation week" has used one of a number of useful (and tricky) parallel constructions: *Both/and; either/or;*

not only/but also; not/but; first/second/third; as well as. This last one is similar to *and,* a simple link between two equivalents, but it often causes trouble:

> **One should take care of one's physical self [noun]** *as well as* **being [participle] able to read and write.**

Again, the pair should be matched: "one's *physical self* as well as one's *intellectual self,*" or "one's physical *self* as well as one's *ability* to read and write"—though this second is still slightly unbalanced, in concept if not in grammar. The best cure would probably extend the underlying antithesis, the basic parallel:

> **One should take care of one's physical self as well as one's intellectual self, of one's ability to survive as well as to read and write.**

With the *either/or*'s and the *not only/but also*'s you continue the principle of pairing. The *either* and the *not only* are merely signposts of what is coming: two equivalents linked by a coordinating conjunction (*or* or *but*). Beware of putting the signs in the wrong place—too soon for the turn.

> Either he is an absolute piker or a fool.

> Neither in time nor space. . . .

> He not only likes the girl, but the family, too.

In these examples, the thought got ahead of itself, as in talk. Just make sure that the word following each of the two coordinators is of the same kind, preposition for preposition, article for article, adjective for adjective—for even with signs well placed, the parallel can skid:

> **The students are not only organizing [present participle] social ac-**
> **   discussing**
> **tivities, but also are** ~~interested~~ **[passive construction]** ~~in~~ **political questions.**

Put identical parts in parallel places; fill in the blanks with the same parts of speech: "not only ———, but also ———." You similarly parallel the words following numerical coordinators:

> **However variously he expressed himself, he unquestionably thought, first, *that* everyone could get ahead; second, *that* workers gen-**

Numerical
Coordinators

erally were paid more than they earned; and, third, *that* laws enforcing a minimum wage were positively undemocratic.

For a number of reasons he decided (1) that he did not like it, (2) that she would not like it, (3) that they would be better off without it. [Note that the parentheses around the numbers operate exactly as any parentheses, and need no additional punctuation.]

My objections are obvious: (1) it is unnecessary, (2) it costs too much, and (3) it won't work.

In parallels of this kind, *that* is usually the problem, since you may easily, and properly, omit it when there is only one clause and no confusion:

. . . he unquestionably thought everyone could get ahead.

If second and third clauses occur, as your thought moves along, you may have to go back and put up the first signpost:

that

. . . he unquestionably thought ∧ everyone could get ahead, that workers . . ., and that laws. . . .

Enough of *that.* Remember simply that equivalent thoughts demand parallel constructions. Notice the clear and massive strategy in the following sentence from the concluding chapter of Freud's last book, *An Outline of Psychoanalysis.* Freud is not only summing up the previous discussion, but also expressing the quintessence of his life's work. He is pulling everything together in a single sentence. Each of the parallel *which* clauses gathers up, in proper order, an entire chapter of his book (notice the parallel force in repeating *picture,* and the summarizing dash):

The picture of an ego which mediates between the id and the external world, which takes over the instinctual demands of the former in order to bring them to satisfaction, which perceives things in the latter and uses them as memories, which, intent upon its self-preservation, is on guard against excessive claims from both directions, and which is governed in all its decisions by the injunctions of a modified pleasure principle—this picture actually applies to the ego only up to the end of the first period of childhood, till about the age of five.

Such precision is hard to match. This is what parallel thinking brings—balance and control and an eye for sentences that seem intellectual totalities, as if struck out all at once from the uncut rock. Francis Bacon also can seem like this (notice how he drops the verb after establishing his pattern):

> For a crowd is not company, and faces are but a gallery of pictures,
> and talk but a tinkling cymbal, where there is no love.
> Reading maketh a full man; conference a ready man; and writing
> an exact man.

And the balance can run from sentence to sentence through an entire passage, controlled not only by connectives repeated in parallel, but by whole phrases and sentences so repeated, as in this passage by the Victorian historian T. B. Macaulay:

> To sum up the whole: we should say that the aim of the Platonic philosophy was to exalt man into a god. The aim of the Baconian philosophy was to provide man with what he requires while he continues to be man. The aim of the Platonic philosophy was to raise us far above vulgar wants. The aim of the Baconian philosophy was to supply our vulgar wants. The former aim was noble; but the latter was attainable.

EXERCISES

12. *Review the discussion of parallel coordinators on pages 154–156. Then write two sentences apiece for each of the following sets of coordinators. Try different parts of speech, but keep your parallels true by filling the blanks in any one sentence with the same parts of speech.*

> both _____ and _____
> either _____ or _____
> not only _____ but also _____
> (1) _____, (2) _____, (3) _____
> _____ as well as _____

13. *Correct the faulty parallelism in the following sentences from students' papers, and clean up any wordiness you find.*

1. Twain seems eventually to become completely cynical, seemed to doubt even that any human life could be happy.
2. The Hemingway hero is a man who moves from one affair to another, who seeks adventure, enjoys bullfights, did a great deal of drinking, who was involved in activities we all wish we could try at least once.

3. In this way not only the teacher needs to be concerned with the poorest student, but every class member helped.

4. A student follows not only a special course of training, but among his studies and social activities finds a liberal education.

5. Either the critics attacked the book for its triteness, or it was criticized for its lack of organization.

6. By driving carefully, by making sure the engine was tuned, keeping the tires carefully filled, we were able to increase the gas mileage by about 18 percent.

7. When they go to church, it is only because they have to go and not of their own desire.

8. Many people argue that the so-called virtues of man belong to the age of chivalry, and they do not apply to the present.

9. This is not only the case with the young voters of the United States but also of the adult ones.

10. Certain things are not actually taught in the classroom. They are learning how to get along with others, to depend on oneself, and managing one's own affairs.

11. Not only did he delight in youth, but he had an almost pathological fear of growing old.

12. Knowing Greek and Roman antiquity is not just learning to speak their language but also their culture.

13. I think fraternities are sociable as well as the dormitories.

14. We have seen that Wright was always fascinated by violence, that he had often seen violence first-hand, and he was himself a potentially violent person.

14. (a) *In the following famous sentence of Bacon's, straighten the faulty parallels and fill out all the phrasing implied by them:*

Histories make men wise; poets witty; the mathematics subtle; natural philosophy deep; moral grave; logic and rhetoric able to contend.

(b) *Now write three sentences on the Baconian pattern: "Jack would eat no fat; his wife no lean; the old dog only soup . . .; the young. . . ."*

15. *To discover how far parallelism might take you, write a parody of the following passage from Samuel Johnson, matching him phrase for phrase and sentence for sentence. Pick out two ball players, two TV actresses, two rock stars, or the like, and have some fun. You simply substitute your terms for Johnson's, leaving everything else as it is, where it fits ("Of genius, that power that constitutes a ball player, that quality without which fielding is cold and batting is inert. . . ." "Of glamour, that power which constitutes an actress. . . .")*

Of genius, that power which constitutes a poet; that quality without which judgement is cold and knowledge is inert; that energy which collects, combines, amplifies, and animates—the superiority must, with some hesitation, be allowed to Dryden. It is not to be inferred that of this poetical vigour Pope had only a little, because Dryden had more, for every other writer since Milton must give place to Pope; and even of Dryden it must be said that if he has brighter paragraphs, he has not better poems. Dryden's performances were always hasty, either excited by some external occasion, or extorted by domestick necessity; he composed without consideration, and published without correction. What his mind could supply at call, or gather in one excursion, was all that he sought, and all that he gave. The dilatory caution of Pope enabled him to condense his sentiments, to multiply his images, and to accumulate all that study might produce, or chance might supply. If the flights of Dryden therefore are higher, Pope continues longer on the wing. If of Dryden's fire the blaze is brighter, of Pope's the heat is more regular and constant. Dryden often surpasses expectation, and Pope never falls below it. Dryden is read with frequent astonishment, and Pope with perpetual delight.

THE LONG AND SHORT OF IT

Your style will emerge once you can manage some length of sentence, some intricacy of subordination, some vigor of parallel, and some play of long against short, of amplitude against brevity. Try the very long sentence, and the very short. The best short sentences are meatiest:

> **Money talks.**
> **A stitch in time saves nine.**
> **The mass of men lead lives of quiet desperation.**
> **The more selfish the man, the more anguished the failure.**

Experiment with the fragment.

The fragment is close to conversation. It is the laconic reply, the pointed afterthought, the quiet exclamation, the telling question. Try to cut and place it clearly (usually at beginnings and ends of paragraphs) so as not to lead your reader to expect a full sentence, or to suspect a poor writer:

> **Not at all.**
> **First, a look behind the scenes.**
> **Expert within limits, that is.**
> **Enough of that.**

The fragment, of course, usually counts as an error. The reader expects a sentence and gets only a fragment of one: you leave him hanging in air, waiting for the second shoe to fall, or the voice to drop, with the thought completed, at the period. The *rhetorical* fragment—the effective and persuasive one—leaves him satisfied: *Of course.* The *grammatical* fragment leaves him unsatisfied: *When the vote was counted.* A question hangs in the air: *what* happened? who won? who got mad? Each of the following typical grammatical fragments—italicized—could be cured by attaching it, with a comma, to its governing sentence:

> He dropped his teeth. *Which had cost five hundred dollars.*
> A good example is Hawthorne. *A writer who could dramatize abstract moral theories.*
> Cleopatra is the stronger. *Trying to create Antony in her own Egyptian image.*

The grammatical, or *accidental,* fragment usually follows its governing sentence, as in the examples above.

Here is a paragraph with rhetorical fragments placed at the surest and most emphatic places, beginning and end, with a faulty grammatical fragment, to illustrate the difference, still wandering in the middle (all fragments in italics):

> *Not quite.* **The battle, as it proved, still had two bloody hours to run. B Company, presumed lost by allies and enemy alike, had finally worked through the jungle and flanking outposts, virtually intact.** *Tired but fully equipped.* **They now brought the full force of surprise and weaponry to bear on the attackers' weakened right flank. The attack turned to meet the surprise. The defenders, heartened, increased their pressure. Reinforcements by helicopter completed the flaming drama.** *Curtains for the assault on Won Thang.*

That floating fragment in the middle needs to be attached to the sentence of which it is really a part, either the one before or the one following.

> EITHER: **B Company, presumed lost by allies and enemy alike, had finally worked through the jungle and flanking outposts, virtually intact, tired but fully equipped.**
> OR: **Tired but fully equipped, they now brought the full force . . .**

But the point here about rhetorical fragments is to use their short, conversational staccato as one of your means to vary the rhythm of your long and longer sentences, playing long against short.

Develop a rhythm of long and short.

The conversational flow between long and short makes a passage move. Study the subordinations, the parallels, and the play of short and long in this elegant passage of Virginia Woolf's—after you have read it once for sheer enjoyment. She is writing of Lord Chesterfield's famous letters to Philip Stanhope, his illegitimate son:

But while we amuse ourselves with this brilliant nobleman and his	Subordinate
views on life we are aware, and the letters owe much of their fas-	Long
cination to this consciousness, of a dumb yet substantial figure on	
the farther side of the page. Philip Stanhope is always there. It is	Short
true that he says nothing, but we feel his presence in Dresden, in	Long
Berlin, in Paris, opening the letters and poring over them and looking	
dolefully at the thick packets which have been accumulating year	
after year since he was a child of seven. He had grown into a rather	Short
serious, rather stout, rather short young man. He had a taste for	Shorter
foreign politics. A little serious reading was rather to his liking. And	Longer
by every post the letters came—urbane, polished, brilliant, imploring	Long
and commanding him to learn to dance, to learn to carve, to consider	
the management of his legs, and to seduce a lady of fashion. He	Short
did his best. He worked very hard in the school of the Graces, but	Longer
their service was too exacting. He sat down halfway up the steep	
stairs which lead to the glittering hall with all the mirrors. He could	Short
not do it. He failed in the House of Commons; he subsided into some	Parallel
small post in Ratisbon; he died untimely. He left it to his widow to	Long
break the news which he had lacked the heart or the courage to	
tell his father—that he had been married all these years to a lady	
of low birth, who had borne him children.	
The Earl took the blow like a gentleman. His letter to his	Short
daughter-in-law is a model of urbanity. He began the education of	Longer
his grandsons. . . .*	

Those are some sentences to copy. We immediately feel the rhythmic play

*The Second Common Reader, p. 81. Copyright, 1932, by Harcourt Brace Jovanovich, Inc.; renewed, 1960, by Leonard Woolf. Reprinted by permission of Harcourt Brace Jovanovich, Inc., the Author's Literary Estate and The Hogarth Press, Ltd.

of periodic and loose, parallel and simple, long and short. Such orchestration takes years of practice, but you can always begin.

EXERCISES

16. *Write a paragraph beginning and ending with a deliberate rhetorical fragment, and containing one or two clearly faulty grammatical ones, on the model of the paragraph on page 160. Then show how you would correct the faulty fragments.*

17. *Write an imitation of the passage (just preceding) from Virginia Woolf, choosing your own subject but matching the patterns, lengths, and rhythms of her sentences, sentence for sentence, if you can. At any rate, aim toward effective rhythms of long and short.*

18. *Below is an awkward and monotonous passage. One after another, the sentences march along for nearly the same number of words. Rewrite the passage, giving its sentences variety in both pattern and length.*

In 1911, Cal Rodgers was the first American pilot to attempt a successful coast-to-coast flight across the United States. He was tempted by the $50,000 prize offered by the Hearst papers to the first man to fly coast-to-coast in under 30 days. But as it turned out, poor Rodgers had to endure a lot of trouble and hardship and still did not win any of the prize money. First, he had to pay all of his own expenses for the trip, and that included the very high cost of having a train follow his route with spare parts. Admittedly, he was able to sell some advertising space on the side of his plane to a beer manufacturer, but he still finished the trip deeply in debt. Next, he had to travel an especially long and zigzag route because his tiny plane was not powerful enough to fly directly over the mountains. And to top it off, he had to put up with long delays for repairs both to his plane and to himself. He had 68 stops and 19 crashes and incurred a broken ankle as well as numerous cuts and bruises. When he arrived in California the plane he was flying was almost entirely different from the plane he had started with. In all, the trip took him 49 days and Rodgers covered the 3,390-mile distance in 82 hours of flying. His average speed was 40 miles per hour and his longest hop was 133 miles. And in the end, the Hearst papers did not award him the prize because he was 19 days over the stipulated time.

Chapter 7

CORRECTING WORDY SENTENCES

Now let us contemplate evil—or at least the innocently awful, the bad habits that waste our words, fog our thoughts, and wreck our delivery. Our thoughts are naturally roundabout, our phrases naturally secondhand. Our satisfaction in merely getting something down on paper naturally blinds us to our errors and ineptitudes. It hypnotizes us into believing we have said what we meant, when our words actually say something else: "Every seat in the house was filled to capacity." Two ways of expressing your thought, two clichés, have collided: *every seat was taken* and *the house was filled to capacity.* Cut the excess wordage, and the absurd accident vanishes: "Every seat was taken." Good sentences come from constant practice in correcting the bad.

Count your words.

Writing is devilish; the general sin is wordiness. We put down the first thought that comes, we miss the best order, and we then need lengths of *is*'s, *of*'s, *by*'s and *which*'s—words virtually meaningless in themselves— to wire our meaningful words together again. Look for the two or three words that carry your meaning; then see if you can rearrange them to speak for themselves, cutting out all the little useless wirings:

163

> **This is the young man who was elected to be president by the class.**
> [This is the young man the class elected president. *Or:* The class
> elected this young man president. *9 words, or 7 words, for 14*]

See if you can't promote a noun into a verb; and cut overlaps in meaning:

> **Last week, the gold stampede in Europe reached near panic pro-
> portions.** [Last week, Europe's gold speculators almost *stampeded.*
> *7 words for 11*]

When you convert the noun, *stampede,* into a verb, *stampeded,* you
suddenly discover that you have already said "near panic proportions"
and you can drop it entirely: stampedes *are* panics. The ungrammatical
near (which, incidentally, should be either *nearly* or *almost*) is usually a
symptom of wordiness, probably because it reveals a general inattention
to meanings: the writer is not, as his word seems to say, visualizing a hand
reaching near something called "panic." Frequently you can reduce tautologies (see p. 473):

advance notice	**notice**
each separate incident	**each incident**
many different ways	**many ways**
dash quickly	**dash**

As these examples show, the basic cure for wordiness is to count the
words in any suspected phrase or sentence—and to make each word
count. If you can rephrase to save even one word, your sentence will be
clearer. And seek the active verb: *John* HITS *Joe.*

EXERCISES

1. *Clear up the blurred ideas, and grammar, in these sentences from students'
papers and official prose, making each word say what it means, and counting your
words to make sure your version has fewer.*

1. Tree pruning may be done in any season of the year. [11 words]
2. After reading a dozen books, the subject is still as puzzling as ever. [13]
3. The secret teller vote used in the past was this time a recorded teller vote. [15]
4. I awoke at midnight, my bones aching and my back felt as if it were being pricked with electric needles. [20]
5. The courses listed herein are those which meet the college level requirements which were stated above. [16]
6. Summer is a time in which more engines overheat than any other. [12]

7. Records can be used in the Audio Room by individual students for their suggested listening assignments. [16]
8. My counter was for refunds for which the customer had already paid for. [13]
9. Entrance was gained by means of skylight. [8]
10. The reason we give this test is because we are anxious to know whether or not you have reflexes that are sufficiently fast to allow you to be a safe worker. [31]
11. The final upshot is whether or not the students have actually grasped the basic essentials, or just merely bare facts. [20]
12. What we have recently called early beginnings is now past history. [11]

   2. *From magazines, newspapers, or your own papers, collect ten sentences you can improve. Cut excess words, promote nouns to verbs, convert to active voice, and generally economize by attending to what the words say. Hand in the wordy sentences with your revisions, indicating the number of words saved.*

Shun the passive voice.

The passive voice is more wordy and deadly than most people imagine, or it would not be so persistent.

> **It was voted that there would be a drive for the cleaning up of the people's park.** [*passive voice—17 words*]
> **We [the town, the council] voted a drive to clean up the people's park.** [*active voice—10 or 11 words, depending on subject*]

The passive voice puts the cart before the horse: the object of the action first, then the harnessing verb, running backwards, then the driver forgotten, and the whole contraption at a standstill. The passive voice is simply "passive" action, the normal action backwards: object-verb-subject (with the true subject usually forgotten) instead of subject-verb-object— *Joe was hit by John* instead of *John hit Joe.*

   The passive voice liquidates and buries the active individual, along with most of the awful truth. Our massed, scientific, and bureaucratic society is so addicted to it that you must constantly alert yourself against its drowsy, impersonal pomp. The simple English sentence is active; it *moves* from subject through verb to object: "The dean's office has turned down your proposal." But the impersonal bureau usually emits instead a passive smoke screen, and the student sees no one at all to help him:

> **It has been decided that your proposal for independent study is not sufficiently in line with the prescribed qualifications as outlined by the college in the catalog.**

Committees always write this way, and the effect on academic writing, as the professor goes from committee to desk to classroom, is astounding. "It was moved that a meeting would be held," the secretary writes, to avoid pinning the rap on anybody. So writes the professor, so writes the student.

I reluctantly admit that the passive voice has certain uses. It can, in a string of active sentences, give more variety, although phrasal and clausal variations are better. It can also vary the emphasis, and the interest, by inverting normal order. *Joe was hit by John* throws selective light on Joe, by inverting regular consequences and distinguishing him from all other unfortunates, and it gives John a certain dubious distinction too. The passive voice can, indeed, eliminate the doer with meaningful effect. *Joe was hit.* ("I was sunk." "It was done.")

In fact, your meaning sometimes demands the passive voice: the agent may be better under cover—insignificant, or unknown, or mysterious. The active "Shrapnel hit him" seems to belie the uncanny impersonality of "He was hit by shrapnel." The broad forces of history similarly demand the passive: "The West was opened in 1848." Moreover, you may sometimes need the passive voice to place your true subject, the hero of the piece, where you can modify him conveniently: *Joe was hit by John, who, in spite of all. . . .* And sometimes it simply is more convenient: "This subject-verb-object sentence can be infinitely contorted." You can, of course, find a number of passive constructions in this book, which preaches against them, because they can also space out a thought that comes too fast and thick. In trying to describe periodic sentences, for instance (p. 134), I changed "until all interconnections lock in the final word" (active) to ". . . are locked by the final word" (passive). The *lock* seemed too tight, especially with *in*, and the locking seemed contrary to the way buildings *are built.* Yes, the passive has its uses.

But most of the time, it is simply wordy. It puts useless words in a sentence. Its dullness derives as much from its extra wordage as from its impersonality. *Joe was hit by John* says no more than *John hit Joe,* but takes 66 percent more words! The passive's inevitable *was* and *by* do nothing but connect; worse, all the *was*'s and *by*'s and *has been*'s actually get in the way of the words carrying the meaning, like underbrush slowing you down and hiding what you want to see.

The best way to prune is with the active voice, cutting the passive and its fungus as you go. Notice the effect on the following typical, and actual, samples:

PASSIVE: **Public concern *has* also *been given* a tremendous impetus *by* the findings of the Hoover Commission on the federal government, and "little Hoover" commissions to survey the organizational structure and functions of many state governments *have been established*.**

ACTIVE: **The findings of the Hoover Commission on federal government *have* also greatly stimulated public concern, and many states *have established* "little Hoover" commissions to survey their governments. [*27 words for 38*]**

PASSIVE: **The algal mats *are made up of* the interwoven filaments of several genera.**

ACTIVE: **The interwoven filaments of several genera *make up* the algal mats. [*11 words for 13*]**

PASSIVE: **Many of the remedies *would* probably *be shown to be* faith cures.**

ACTIVE: **Many of the remedies *are* probably faith cures. [*8 words for 12*]**

PASSIVE: **Anxiety and emotional conflict *are lessened* when latency sets in. The total personality *is oriented* in a repressive, inhibitory fashion so as to maintain the barriers, and what Freud has called "psychic dams," against psychosexual impulses.**

ACTIVE: **When latency sets in, anxiety and emotional conflict *subside*. The personality *inhibits* itself, maintaining its barriers—Freud's "psychic dams"—against psychosexual impulses. [*22 words for 36*]**

The passive voice, in its wordiness alone, is always a bit unclear even on the surface; but, if it eliminates the real subject of the verb, as it usually does, it is intrinsically unclear as well. "This passage has been selected because . . . ," the student will write, and the reader cannot tell who did the selecting. Does he mean that he, the writer, has picked it, or does he describe some process of natural or popular selection? We surmise he means himself, of course; but why doesn't he say so, and save a word, and avoid confusion? "I selected this passage because . . . . "

Any form of the verb *is* may reveal a passive construction. Our language must use some form of *is* so frequently in stating that things *are* and in forming its compound verbs (*is falling, were playing*) that you should drop as many *is*'s and *was*'s as possible, simply to avoid monotony. But when they are—as they often are—signs of the passive voice, you can also avoid rigor mortis by replacing your *is*'s with active verbs, along with their true subjects, the real doers of the action.

EXERCISES

3. *Write five sentences in the passive voice, and change each to its active equivalent.*

4. *Recast these sentences in the active voice, clearing out all passive constructions, saving as many words as you can, and indicating the number saved:*

1. The particular topic chosen by the instructor for study in his section of English 2 must be approved by the Steering Committee. [Start with "The Steering Committee," and don't forget the economy of an apostrophe-*s*. I managed 14 words for 22.]

2. Avoidance of such blunders should not be considered a virtue for which the student is to be commended, any more than he would be praised for not wiping his hands on the tablecloth or polishing his shoes with the guest towels. [Begin "We should not"; try *avoiding* for *avoidance*, and *virtuous* for *virtue*. I managed to score 27 for 41.]

3. The first respect in which too much variation seems to exist is in the care with which writing assignments are made. ["First, care in assigning"—8 for 21.]

4. The remaining variations that will be mentioned are concerned not with the assignment of papers but with the marking and grading of them. ["Finally, I shall mention"—14 for 23.]

5. The difference between restrictives and nonrestrictives can also be better approached through a study of the different contours that mark the utterance of the two kinds of element than through confusing attempts to differentiate the two by meaning. ["One can differentiate restrictives"—I managed 13 for 38.]

6. Individuals whose income is insufficient to lift them above poverty must be provided with assistance from public sources. [Start active, and try "supplement"—11 for 18.]

7. In the next thirty-five years it is expected that there will be more engineering work to be done than has been done in all of recorded history. [Make "The next thirty-five years" the subject—14 for 27.]

8. If expansion is not accomplished, then two less-efficient alternatives must be acted upon: either the book sales will have to be in separate quarters or else the whole enterprise will have to be moved to a new location. [Try "we"—18 for 38.]

9. Trees on average sites are expected to be about twenty inches in diameter when they are eighty years old if they are managed properly since youth. [Start "Managed properly"—16 for 26.]

10. Any amended declaration should be filed with the Internal Revenue Office with whom the original declaration was filed even if you move to another district. [Keep it clear, but repeat no words—19 for 25.]

5. *Pick three obese and passive passages from your textbooks (including this one, if I have slipped). Change them to clean active sentences, indicating the number of words saved in each passage.*

Check the stretchers.

To be, itself, frequently ought not to be:

He seems [to be] upset about something.
She considered him [to be] perfect.
This appears [to be] difficult.

Above all, keep your sentences awake by not putting them into those favorite stretchers of the passivists, *There is . . . which, It is . . . that,* and the like:

Moreover, [there is] one segment of the population [which] never
 seeks employment.
[There are] many women [who] never marry.
[There] is nothing wrong with it. [Nothing is . . .]
[It is] his last book [that] shows his genius best.
[It is] this [that] is important.

The bracketed words can disappear without a ripple. Furthermore, *It is* frequently misleads your reader by seeming to mean something specific (*beer*, in the following example):

Several members voted for beer. *It is* hard to get *it* through some
 people's heads that minors can't buy it.
 REVISED: **Some people never learn that minors can't buy it.**

Cut *every it* not referring to something. Next to activating your passive verbs, and cutting the passive *there is*'s and *it is*'s, perhaps nothing so improves your prose as to go through it systematically also deleting *every to be,* every *which, that, who,* and *whom* not needed for utter clarity or for spacing out a thought. All your sentences will feel better.

Beware the of-and-which disease.

The passive sentence also breaks out in a rash of *of* 's and *which's*, and even the active sentence may suffer. Diagnosis: something like sleeping sickness. *With*'s, *in*'s, *to*'s, and *by*'s also inflamed. Surgery imperative. Here is a typical, and actual, case:

> Many biological journals, especially those *which* regularly publish new scientific names, now state *in* each issue the exact date *of* publication *of* the preceding issue. *In* dealing *with* journals *which* do not follow this practice, or *with* volumes *which* are issued individually, the biologist often needs *to* resort *to* indexes . . . *in order to* determine the actual date *of* publication *of* a particular name.

Note *of publication of* twice over, and the three *which's*. The passage is a sleeping beauty. The longer you look at it the more useless little attendants you see. Note the inevitable passive voice (*which are issued*) in spite of the author's active efforts. The *of* 's accompany extra nouns, *publication* repeating *publish,* for instance. Remedy: (1) eliminate *of's* and their nouns, (2) change *which* clauses into participles, (3) change nouns into verbs. You can cut more than a third of this passage without touching the sense (using 39 words for 63):

> Many biological journals, especially those regularly *publishing* new scientific names, now give the date of each preceding issue. With journals not *following* this practice, and with some books, the biologist must turn to indexes . . . *to date* a particular name.

I repeat: you can cut most *which's*, one way or another, with no loss of blood. Participles can modify their antecedents directly, since they are verbal adjectives, without an intervening *which*: "a car *which was* going south" is "a car going south"; "a train *which is* moving" is "a moving train." Similarly with the adjective itself: "a song *which was* popular last year" is "a song popular last year"; "a person *who is* attractive" is "an attractive person." Beware of this whole crowd: *who are, that was, which are.*

If you need a relative clause, remember *that. Which* has almost completely displaced it in labored writing. *That* is still best for restrictive clauses, those necessary to definition: "A house that faces north is cool" (a participle would save a word: "A house facing north is cool"). *That* is tolerable; *which* is downright oppressive. *Which* should signal the nonrestrictive clause (the afterthought): "The house, which faces north, is a good buy." Here you need *which.* Even restrictive clauses must turn to *which* when complicated parallels arise. "He preaches the brotherhood of man *that* everyone affirms" elaborates like this: "He preaches the brotherhood of man *which* everyone affirms, *which* all the great philosophies support, but *for which* few can make any immediate concession." Nevertheless, if you need relatives, a *that* will often ease your sentences and save you from the *which*'s.

Verbs and their derivatives, especially present participles and gerunds, can also help to cure a string of *of*'s. Alfred North Whitehead, usually of clear mind, once produced this linked sausage: "Education is the acquisition *of* the art *of* the utilization *of* knowledge." Anything to get around the three *of*'s and the three heavy nouns would have been better: "Education instills the art of using knowledge"—"Education teaches us to use knowledge well." Find an active verb for *is the acquisition of,* and shift *the utilization of* into some verbal form: the gerund *using,* or the infinitive *to use.* Shun the *-tion*'s! Simply change your surplus *-tion*'s and *of*'s— along with your *which* phrases—into verbs, or verbals (*to use, learning*). You will save words, and activate your sentences.

EXERCISES

6. *Eliminate the italicized words in the following passages, together with all their accompanying wordiness, indicating the number or words saved (my figures again are merely guides; other solutions are equally good, or better).*

1. *There is* a certain tendency to defend one's own position *which* will cause the opponent's argument to be ignored. [13 for 19.]
2. *It is* the other requirements *that* present obstacles, some *of which* may prove insurmountable in the teaching of certain subjects. [11 for 20]
3. In the sort of literature-centered course being discussed here, *there is* usually a general understanding *that* themes will be based on the various literary works *that* are studied, the theory being *that* both the instruction in literature and *that* in writing will be made more effective by this interrelationship. [21 for 49]
4. The person *whom* he met was an expert *who was* able to teach the fundamentals quickly. [13 for 16]
5. They will take a pride *which is* wholly justifiable in being able to command a prose style *that is* lucid and supple. [13 for 22]
6. This is a book on social status in America *that* has the benefit of sure insight into the revolutionary changes *that* have taken place in the political and economic structure since the New Deal. [18 for 34]

7. *It is* expected *that* the new schedule will be announced by the bus company on Monday morning. [11 for 17]

8. In our company *there are* wide-open opportunities for professional growth with a company *that* enjoys an enviable record for stability in the dynamic atmosphere of aerospace technology. [21 for 27]

9. A minority finds it difficult to progress in such a society due to the fact *that* a majority can perpetuate inequality by simply insuring *that* the vast majority of its members acquire the positions *that* pay the greater amounts of money and carry the greatest authority. [23 for 41]

10. It is not really any act *which* Julian commits *which* turns all his friends against him, but the fact *that* his sins are exposed publicly *that* makes him unforgiveable. [17 for 29]

   7. *To cap your editorial skills, here are two of my favorites, two official statements, one from an eminent linguist, one from an eminent publisher. Clear up the wordiness, especially the italicized patches.*

1. The work *which is* reported *in this* study *is* an investigation *of* language *within* the social context *of* the community *in which it is* spoken. *It is* a study *of* a ilnguistic structure *which is* unusually complex, but no more than the social structure of the city in which it functions. [22 for 52]

2. Methods *which are* unique to the historian *are illustrated* throughout the volume *in order to* show how history *is written* and how historians work. The historian's approach to his subject, *which* leads to the asking of provocative questions and to a new understanding of complex events, situations, and personalities *is probed.* The manner *in which* the historian reduces masses of chaotic fact—and occasional fancy—to reliable meaning, and the way *in which* he formulates explanations and tests them *is examined and clarified* for the student. *It is its* emphasis on historical method *which* distinguishes this book from other source readings in western civilization. The problems *which are examined* concern *themselves with* subjects *which* are *dealt with by* most courses in western civilization [66 for 123. The all-time winner from a student is 45 words.]

Beware "the use of."

   In fact, both *use,* as a noun, and *use,* as a verb, are dangerously wordy words. Since *using* is one of our most basic concepts, other words in your sentence will already contain it:

He uses rationalization. [He rationalizes.]
He uses the device of foreshadowing. [He foreshadows.]
Through [the use of] logic, he persuades.
His [use of] dialogue is effective.

The utilization of and *utilize* are only horrendous extremes of the same pestilence, to be stamped out completely.

Break the noun habit.

Passive writing adores the noun, modifying nouns with nouns in pairs, and even in denser clusters—which then become official jargon. Break up these logjams, let the language flow, make one noun of the pair an adjective:

> *Teacher militancy* **is not as marked in Pittsburgh.** [*Teachers* **are not so** *militant* **in Pittsburgh.** *7 words for 8*]

Or convert one noun to a verb:

> *Consumer demand* **is falling in the area of services.** [Consumers *are* **demanding** fewer services. *5 words for 9*]

Of course, nouns have long served English as adjectives, as in "*rail*road," "*railroad* station," "*court*house," and "*noun* habit." But modern prose has aggravated the tendency beyond belief; and we get such monstrosities as *child sex education course* and *child sex education curriculum publication deadline reminder*—whole strings of nothing but nouns. Education, sociology, and psychology produce the worst noun-stringers, the hardest for you not to copy if you take these courses. But we have all caught the habit. The nouns *level* and *quality,* used as adjectives, have produced a rash of redundancies. A meeting of "high officials" has now unfortunately become a meeting of "high-*level* officials." The "finest cloth" these days is always "finest *quality* cloth." Drop those two redundant nouns and you will make a good start, and will sound surprisingly original. In fact, using the noun *quality* as an adjective has become almost obssessive—*quality food, quality wine, quality service, quality entertainment, high-quality drilling equipment*—blurring all distinctions of *good, fine, excellent, superb, superior,* in one dull and inaccurate cliché. A good rule: DON'T USE NOUNS AS ADJECTIVES. You can drop many an excess noun:

WORDY	DIRECT
advance notice	notice
long in size	long
puzzling in nature	puzzling
of an indefinite nature	indefinite
of a peculiar kind	peculiar
in order to	to
by means of	by
in relation to	with
in connection with	with
1981-model car	1981 car

Wherever possible, find the equivalent adjective:

of great importance	important
highest significance level	highest significant level
government spending	governmental spending
teaching excellence	excellent teaching
encourage teaching quality	encourage good teaching

Or change the noun to its related participle:

advance placement	advanced placement
charter flight	chartered flight
uniform police	uniformed police
poison arrow	poisoned arrow

Or make the noun possessive:

reader interest	reader's interest
factory worker wage	factory worker's wage
veterans insurance	veterans' insurance

Or try a cautious *of:*

STACKED NOUNS	IMPROVED
color lipstick	color of lipstick
teaching science	science of teaching
production quality	quality of production
high quality program	program of high quality
significance level	level of significance

Of all our misused nouns, *type* has become peculiarly pestilential and trite. Advertisers talk of *detergent-type cleansers* instead of *detergents;* educators, of *apprentice-type situations* instead of *apprenticeships;* newspapermen, of *Marxist-type organizations* instead of *Marxist organizations.* Don't copy your seniors; write boldly. We have become a nation of hairsplitters, afraid of saying *Czechoslovakia's Russian tanks* for fear that the reader will think they really belong to Russia. So the reporter writes *Russian-type tanks,* making an unnecessary distinction, and cluttering the page with one more *type-type* expression. We have forgotten that making the individual stand for the type is the simplest and oldest of metaphors: "Give us this day our daily bread." A twentieth-century supplicant might have written "bread-type food."

The simple active sentence transmits the message by putting each word unmistakably in its place, a noun as a noun, an adjective as an adjective, with the verb—no stationary *is*—really carrying the mail. Recently, after a flood, a newspaper produced this apparently succinct and dramatic sentence: **Dead animals cause water pollution.** (The word *cause,* incidentally, indicates wasted words.) That noun *water* as an adjective throws the meaning off and takes 25 percent more words than the essential active message: **Dead animals pollute water.** As you read your way into the sentence, it seems to say *dead animals cause water* (which is true enough), and then you must readjust your thoughts to accommodate *pollution.* The simplest change is from *water pollution* (noun-noun) to *polluted water* (adjective-noun), clarifying each word's function. But the supreme solution is to make *pollute* the verb it is, and the sentence a simply active message in which no word misspeaks itself. Here are the possibilities, in a scale from most active and clearest to most passive and wordiest, which may serve to chart your troubles if you get tangled in causes and nouns:

Dead animals pollute water.
Dead animals cause polluted water.
Dead animals cause water pollution.
Dead animals are a factor in causing the pollution of water.
Dead animals are a serious factor in causing the water pollution situation.
Dead farm-type animals are a danger factor in causing the post-flood clearance and water pollution situation.

So the message should now be clear. Write simple active sentences, outmaneuvering all passive eddies, all shallow *is*'s, *of*'s, *which*'s, and *that*'s, all overlappings, all rocky clusters of nouns: they take you off your course, delay your delivery, and wreck many a straight and gallant thought.

EXERCISES

8. *Clear these passages of passives, "the use of," noun-nouns, and any other congestions that may block the reader's understanding.*

1. Actually, "thinking" was included in the later treatments of the communications arts and the language arts because of the eventual realization by both communicationists and language arts educationists of the merely mechanical interpretation which could be and was given to a pure "arts" orientation. The segregation of thought from expression by the exile of logic, dialiectic, and rhetoric from the field of English is probably the most serious defect of the present composition situation in both college and high school. [44 for 80]

2. Still another problem concerns the comprehensiveness of exercise content in the several assessments. As noted from the outset, the exercises actually used in any one assessment constitute only a sample of those required to exhaustively measure attainment of assessment objectives, which are global in scope. No claims for comprehensive representativeness of the exercise samples can be made. In fact, there is no way to decide the question of comprehensiveness except by reference to particular instructional models designed by individual schools or teachers to implement given sets of objectives. [49 for 88]

3. Economic policy-making with respect to persons earning low incomes must center around making such individuals more productive. Particularly, it should work toward removing impediments to geographic and to upward mobility. This is, of course, the aim of much recent antipoverty legislation. As impediments are removed, the price system should become more effective in performing its reallocation functions. [33 for 57]

4. The purpose of every control system is to maintain a certain "desired value" (also known as the "reference value" or "index value") of the controlled condition. This is very clearly exemplified by the thermostat, a device for the regulation of temperature. Thermostats are extensively used in connection with present-day heating appliances, refrigerators, and so on. In most cases, the actual temperature-sensing element is a bimetallic strip, a composite strip which is formed when two metals, having different coefficients of thermal expansion, are bonded together. [44 for 84]

Give your writing warmth.

I have been urging condensation, to get rid of useless and obstructive phrases, especially those that, along with the passive voice, harden into habitual jargon in almost every profession. But your sentences can be *too* short and dense. Many thoughts *need* explanation and an example or two. Many *need* the airing of *and's and of's*. Many simply need some loosening of phrase. In fact, colloquial phrasing, which is as clear and unnoticed as a clean window, is usually longer than its formal equivalent: *something to eat* as compared to *dinner.* By all counts, *dinner* should be better. It is shorter. It is more precise. Yet "Let's have something to eat" is friendlier than the more economical "Let's have dinner." We don't want to push our friends around with precise and economical suggestions. We want them at their *ease*, with the choices slightly vague. Consequently, when we write *what we are after* for *object* and *how it is done* for *method,* we give our all-too-chilly prose some social warmth. These colloquial phrases use more words, but they are not wordy if they pull with the rest of the sentence. It all comes down to redundancy, the clutter of useless words and tangential ideas—"the accumulation of words that add nothing to the sense and cloud up what clarity there is," as Aristotle says. What we write should be *easy* to read.

Avoid excessive distinctions and definitions.

Too many distinctions, too many nouns, and too much Latin makes pea soup:

> **Reading is a processing skill of symbolic reasoning sustained by the interfacilitation of an intricate hierarchy of substrata factors that have been mobilized as a psychological working system and pressed into service in accordance with the purpose of the reader.**

This comes from an educator, with the wrong kind of education. He is saying:

> **Reading is a process of symbolic reasoning aided by an intricate network of ideas and motives. [16 words for 40]**

Except with crucial assumptions and implications (see pp. 108–109), try *not* to define your terms. If you do, you are probably either evading the toil of finding the right word, or defining the obvious:

> **Let us agree to use the word signal as an abbreviation for the phrase "the simplest kind of sign." (This agrees fairly well with the customary meaning of the word "signal.")**

That came from a renowned semanticist, an authority on the meanings of words. The customary meaning of a word *is* its meaning, and uncustomary meanings come only from careful punning. Don't underestimate your readers, as this semanticist did.

The definer of words is usually a bad writer. Our semanticist continues, trying to get his signals straight and grinding out about three parts sawdust to every one of meat. In the following excerpt, I have bracketed his sawdust. Read the sentence first as it was written; then read it again, omitting the bracketed words:

> **The moral of such examples is that all intelligent criticism [of any instance] of language [in use] must begin with understanding [of] the motives [and purposes] of the speaker [in that situation].**

Here, each of the bracketed phrases is already implied in the others. Attempting to be precise, the writer has beclouded himself. Naturally, the speaker would be "in that situation"; naturally, a sampling of language would be "an instance" of language "in use." *Motives* may not be *purposes*, but the difference here is insignificant. Our semanticist's next sentence deserves some kind of immortality. He means "Muddy language makes trouble":

> **Unfortunately, the type of case that causes trouble in practice is that in which the kind of use made of language is not transparently clear. . . .**

Clearly, transparency is hard. Writing is hard. It requires constant attention to meanings, and constant pruning. Count your words, and make your words count.

EXERCISES

9. *Here are some wordy, awkward, and flat passages from students' papers, with their wordage indicated in parentheses. Improve their diction by making their meaningful words count, cutting all the waste, and indicating your own wordage. Make it less, and grow rich with economy.*

1. Machines are merely amplifiers of the abilities of workmen, and exist only as they can do man's bidding effectively. (19)
2. Clearly, the only way to deal with machines is to neither flee from them nor surrender to them, but to use them as means to ends appointed not by them but by ourselves. (33)
3. The question is pertinent today, and painfully practical, as people examine the premises of their personal morality. (17)
4. Civil disobedience, then, is not the product of a recalcitrant minority intent on abolishing law and order, but exists in consequence of and as an important

integral part of the give-and-take in democratic adjustment. It serves as a kick in the pants for legislators and the unconcerned majority, making them aware of faults in the democratic system. (57, *give-and-take* counted as one word)

5. The criticism of the military in connection with the draft needs not be of only its character, which overshadowed the draft machinery, but also of its direct involvement with the selective service system. The draft, an institution created by Congress with the intention that it might be civilian-operated, administered by civilians for civilians, became what it was through the gradual infusion of the military. (64)

6. The ability to rapidly handle enormous amounts of data and make rapid decisions often enables the computer to do control applications, such as the generation of power at an electrical power plant. (32)

7. It is wrong to assume, although many criticisms are being raised against technology as it affects human values, that the author does not appreciate its great capacity for good. (29)

8. As the establishment filled with people, an air of stuffiness and a feeling of being uncomfortable permeated the room. (19)

9. This reviewer, after reading about a dozen reviews of the book, was struck by the lack of perception and openmindedness that the critics showed. (24)

10. With all the loud activity in the next apartment, the thinness of the walls became painfully apparent, and sleeping became impossible. (21)

11. The most essential prerequisite that any student group must have in order to be recognized as a power is a leader that acts both as a mouthpiece of the students' ideas and as an originator of students' strategy in their war against the administrators. (44)

12. When a student becomes a member of the Student Government Council, it is expected that he give up much of his spare time for the council. However, it is not, or at least should not, be expected that he quit school to take on the responsibility of a council member. (50)

13. Another fact which is revealed by the census statistics is that 72.4 percent of the total nonwhite population lives in urban areas. (22)

14. A minority finds it difficult to progress in such a society due to the fact that a majority can perpetuate inequality by simply insuring that the vast majority of its members acquire the positions that pay the greater amounts of money and carry the greatest authority. (46)

15. There are two major results of the increasing mechanization of industry. One is a great reduction in the number of simple, repetitive jobs where all you need is your five senses and an untrained mind. The other result is a great increase in the number of jobs involved in designing, engineering, programming, and administering these automatic production systems. (58)

10. *To culminate this chapter on wordiness, write a* TERRIBLE ESSAY. *Have some fun with this perennial favorite, in which you reinforce your sense of clear, figurative, and meaningful language by writing the muddiest and wordiest essay you can invent, gloriously working out all the bad habits. Make it a parody of the worst kind of sociological and bureaucratic prose—the kind you have been editing in the previous exercises. Pick some trivial subject, like dripping faucets, and then write, in good essay form but with terribly abstract and jargonish language,* A Report of a Study of the Person Sociology and Night Loss Cost Economics of the Faucets Which Drip in the Second Floor North Corner Woman Dormitory Lavatory, *or some similarly inflated piece of nonsense. Here are the rules:*

1. Put EVERYTHING in the passive voice.
2. Modify nouns *only* with nouns, preferably in strings of two or three, never with adjectives: *governmental spending* becomes *government level spending;* an *excellent idea* becomes *the excellence of conception of program.*
3. Use only big abstract nouns—as many *-tion*'s as possible.
4. Use no participles: not *dripping faucets* but *faucets which drip,* and use as many *which*'s as possible.
5. Use as many words as possible to say the least.
6. Work in as many trite and wordy expressions as possible: *needless to say, all things being equal, due to the fact that, in terms of, as far as that is concerned.*
7. Sprinkle heavily with *-wise*-type and *type*-type expressions, say *hopefully* every three or four sentences, make *quality* your only commendatory adjective (remember each time that it's really a noun).
8. Compile and use a basic terrible vocabulary: *situation, aspect, function, factor, phase, utilize, the use of,* and so on. The class may well cooperate in this.

   One class has had great success with a three-paragraph terrible essay, incorporating each terrible error only once, and then having everyone rewrite the winning worst essay into the best prose possible.

Chapter 8

WORDS

Here is the word. Thesis, structure, paragraph, sentence, thought—our thoughts live in words. Our concepts are words. Sesquipedalian or short, magniloquent or low, Latin or Anglo-Saxon, Celtic, Danish, French, Spanish, Indian, Hindustani, Dutch, Italian, Portuguese, Choctaw, Swahili, Chinese, Hebrew, Turkish, Greek—English contains them all, a million words at our disposal, if we are disposed to use them. No language is richer than English. But our expository vocabularies average probably fewer than eight thousand words. We all have a way to go to possess our heritage.

We can realize that heritage only through reading and writing—discovering the words for what we have in mind to know, writing them out to express our thoughts, enriching our concepts as we enrich our vocabulary. Our written words uncoil the data of our perceptions and lay them out reasonably straight on paper so we can see them.

So we can see them—here is the key to the power of written words. We want to see them as well as hear them; we want Space to collaborate with Time—so we may have time and space to think. The ancient world designated sight as the chief of the five senses—superior to hearing, smell, taste, and touch. And certainly most of us would still agree. We would probably rather be deaf than blind, and *light* is our commanding metaphor for intelligence (*illumination, enlightenment, throw light on the subject*). Because the spoken word, or the mind's idea, spins away as soon as it comes, we want to get it down on paper where it will stay put, where, by seeing it, we come to understand. Writing, then, both records and straightens our thoughts.

WORDS AND THINGS

Learn the multiple meanings of words.

Speech, in a sense, is virtually "wordless," since our meaningful utterances are words blended together in a fluid sweep of sound, with their meanings selected for us by their position and emphasis and pitch. You have probably heard about the difference between "HEza-LIGHThousekeeper" and "HEzalightHOUSEkeeper," and about the subtle differences in stress, pitch, and pause by which we select from a word's several meanings the one we want. When conversing, we enjoy a total context of understanding, complete with shrugs and *you know*'s, that makes individual words and sentences of minimal importance. We actually speak as much in fragments as in sentences, and we constantly repeat and circle, even after we know we have been understood. In a sense, the other person doesn't hear a word we say: he gets the meaning without necessarily noticing the words at all.

But on the silent printed page, you must place your words with care: the pitch, the stress, the general context of understanding—all the elements that free our speech from care—are gone. And the visible presence of words heightens our awareness of them *as* words. So much so, indeed, that we sometimes think them physical things, confusing them with the actual sticks and stones of this world.

Words are not things, nor are they symbols of things: words are symbols of our *ideas* of things. The primary fact about words is that they are the abstractions or generalizations by which we pick up the particular sticks of this world. A word is a symbol for a generalization in our heads. Since we like our words to be as concrete as possible, the idea of generalization may bother us. But a word's function is to name a general class of things, or states, or thoughts, or whatever, and we want a word's limits no narrower. When I say *bed*, I mean the general idea of "bed." The physical bed you may picture will be different from mine, but we will understand each other sufficiently. You will get the general idea, and you will also know that I do not specifically mean your little bunk at the dorm, though I mean something like it.

So: words are symbols for our general ideas of things. They are classifiers not only of the sticks and stones of the physical world, but of all the qualities, movements, functions, and conditions we know—*cold, grateful, walk, marry, mother, president, slow, exactly.* Many words refer to nothing in the physical world, though we may infer the entity by its effects—*anger, confidence, peace,* for example; and many words seem to symbolize a kind of mental gesture, the grammar with which we connect our thoughts or describe the connections of the physical world, as with *of, by, in, with, when.*

Words, like other symbols, usually represent a multiplicity of things, not all closely related to each other. A *log* is something for cabins or hearths, a gadget towed behind a ship, or a book on its bridge. A *bridge* may be not only on a ship, but in someone's mouth, or across the Golden Gate (which has neither gold nor hinges). The skipper could take out his bridge while sailing under the bridge and playing bridge on the bridge. Context is usually sufficient to select the wanted meanings automatically from the unwanted. That words have varieties of meanings bothers no one but the theoreticians—or your readers, if you are careless.

Try a little punning.

To master words you must keep alert to all their possibilities of meaning. Hence the punster usually makes the good writer: he forestalls any diabolical misreading because he has already seen the possibility himself. He would never accidentally write: "The situation was explosive, and he was no match for it." Nor: "The girls were barely attractive." A certain devilish eye for meanings will keep your words straight, and save you from innocent damnation.

Words are full of deviltry. *Pale* means bloodless of complexion (from Latin *pallidus*); and *pale* means a region staked out for one's reign (from Latin *palus*, or stake). Add such homophones ("same-sounders") as *rain* and *reign* to *pail* (bucket) and *pale* (bloodless; region), and you can see what Shakespeare, that prince of punsters and master of meanings, could do when full of springtime, as in this, the best of all his songs, from *The Winter's Tale:*

> When daffodils begin to peer,
> With heigh! the doxie over the dale—
> Why, then comes in the sweet o' the year,
> For the red blood reigns in the winter's pale.

A good writer revels in multiple meanings, letting the ones he doesn't want just linger around the edge of the fun, to show that he knows them but decrees them temporarily insignificant.

A word acquires multiple meanings as it drifts into a new general usage and its specific meaning fades. A circle is a circle, but in expressions like *well known in artistic circles* the word has faded until it means no more than "group." It is a dead metaphor, ready for the touch of the good writer's pencil. The first user was making a metaphor (a *metonymy,* in fact), in which he pictured admirers literally standing around an artist in a ring; he called them not people but a *circle,* naming them by something logically similar. In ordinary thoughtless parlance, we certainly do not see the circle; the physical, literal origin has faded. But the good writer will turn up the color a little, will bring the physical origin back for the reader to see: "The artist found in his circle a charmed protection from the world." Or he will at least prevent any unwanted physical or literal meanings, never writing, for instance, "The artist painted his circle." The writer's best control of a word's multiple meanings lies in respecting the essentially physical thing it says, and in keeping an impudent eye open for all transferred and metaphorical meanings.

EXERCISES

1. *Find as many meanings as you can, in your head and dictionary, for each of the following words.* **EXAMPLE:** *bridge—a structure over a river; false teeth; a card game; the navigating platform on a ship.*

> hatch, hitch, runs, fair, case, draft, lock, down, prove, club, grave, fashion, light, medium, joint, sole, cross, term, check

VOCABULARY

Build your vocabulary.

As you build your sense of multiple meanings, build your vocabulary. If you can increase your hoard, you increase your chances of finding the right word when you need it. Read as widely as you can, and look words up the second or third time you meet them. I once knew a man who swore he learned three new words a day from his reading by using each at least once in conversation. I didn't ask him about *polyphiloprogenitive* or *antidisestablishmentarianism.* It depends a little on the crowd. But the idea is sound. Keeping the commerce flowing through your reading, your speech, and your writing not only builds your vocabulary but develops your style, with your speech and writing working together in a kind of mutual body building. The bigger the vocabulary, the more various the ideas one can get across with it—the more the shades and intensities of meaning.

The big vocabulary also needs the little word. The vocabularian often stands himself on a Latin cloud and forgets the Anglo-Saxon ground—the common ground between him and his audience. So do not forget the little things, the *stuff, lint, get, twig, snap, go, mud, coax.* Hundreds of small words not in immediate vogue can refresh your vocabulary. The Norse and Anglo-Saxon adjectives in *-y (muggy, scrawny, drowsy)*, for instance, rarely appear in sober print.* The minute the beginner tries to sound dignified, in comes a misty layer of words a few feet off the ground and nowhere near heaven, the same two dozen or so, most of them verbs. One or two will do no harm, but any accumulation is fatal—words like *depart* instead of *go:*

accompany—go with	place—put
appeared—looked *or* seemed	possess—have
arrive—come	prepare—get ready
attempt—try	questioned—asked
become—get	receive—get
cause—make	relate—tell
cease—stop	remain—stay
complete—finish	remove—take off
continue—keep on	retire—go to bed
delve—dig	return—go back
discover—find	secure—get
locate—find	transform—change

I add one treasured noun: *manner* for *way.* The question, as always, is one of meaning. *Manner* is something with a flourish; *way* is the usual way. But the beginner makes no distinction, losing the normal *way,* and meaning, in a false flourish of *manners.* Similarly, "she *placed* her cigarettes on the table" is usually not what the writer means (*place* connotes *arrange*). *Delve* is something that happens only when students begin to meditate. *Get* and *got* may be too colloquial for constant use in writing, but a discreet one or two can limber many a stiff sentence. Therefore, use the elegant Latin and the commonplace Anglo-Saxon, tastefully fitted;

*See pp. 310–318, Section A, "The English Language," for the early background of English.

but shun the frayed gentility of *secure* and *place* and *remain,* whose shades of meaning you can find in your dictionary.

Abraham Lincoln read the dictionary from cover to cover, and you really can browse it with pleasure, looking at the pictures and finding out about aardvarks and axolotls, jerboas and jerkins. You can amaze yourself at the number of things *set* can mean. Best of all, you can look at a word's derivation and get a quick sense of our linguistic history, of families of words and ideas, of how some meanings have changed and some others have persisted through centuries and across continents. *Mid,* for instance, is still what it has been for the last five thousand years, persisting in most of the Indo-European languages all the way from Sanskrit to Old Norse and giving English a whole family of words from *middle* to *Mediterranean* to *intermezzo.* Acquaintance with a family can make you feel at home. You can know and use a *ramp,* or a *rampage,* or a lion *rampant* familiarly, once you see the Old French for *climb* in all three. You can cut your meaning close to the old root, as in "He was *enduring* and *hard* as nails," where the Latin *durus* ("hard") has suggested its Anglo-Saxon synonym and given you a phrase your readers will like, though most of them won't know why.

Through the centuries, English has added Latin derivatives alongside the Anglo-Saxon words already there, keeping the old with the new: after the Anglo-Saxon *deor* (now *deer*) came the *beast* and then the *brute,* both from Latin through French, and the *animal* straight from Rome. Although we use more Anglo-Saxon in assembling our sentences (*to, by, with, but, is*), well over half our total vocabulary comes one way or another from Latin. The things of this world tend to be Anglo-Saxon (*man, house, stone, wind, rain*): the abstract qualities, Latin and French (*value, duty, contemplation*).

Our big words are Latin and Greek. Your reading acquaints you with them; your dictionary will show you their prefixes and roots. Learn the common prefixes and roots (see Exercises 2, 3, and 4 at the end of this section), and you can handle all kinds of foreigners at first encounter: *con-cession* (going along with), *ex-clude* (lock out), *pre-fer* (carry before), *sub-version* (turning under), *trans-late* (carry across), *claustro-phobia* (dread of being locked in), *hydro-phobia* (dread of water), *ailuro-philia* (love of cats), *megalo-cephalic* (big-headed), *micro-meter* (little-measurer). You can even, for fun, coin a word to suit the occasion: *megalopede* (big-footed). You can remember that *intramural* means "within the (college) walls," and that "intermural sports," which is the frequent mispronunciation and misspelling, would mean something like "wall battling wall," a physical absurdity.

Besides owning a good dictionary, you should refer, with caution, to a thesaurus, a treasury of synonyms (''together-names''), in which you can find the word you couldn't think of. The danger lies in raiding this treasury too enthusiastically. Checking for meaning in a dictionary will assure that you have expanded, not distorted, your vocabulary.

EXERCISES

2. *Browse your dictionary and find three families of words, like* ramp-rampage-rampant. *Give the root-idea of each family, and a word or two in definition of each word.*

3. *Make a permanent reference list by looking up in your dictionary each of the Latin and Greek prefixes and constituents listed below. Illustrate each with several English derivatives, and put in parentheses after each derivative its close literal English translation, as in these two examples:*

> *con-* (with): convince (conquer with), conclude (shut with) concur (run with)
>
> *chron-* (time): chronic (lasting a long time), chronicle (a record of the time), chronometer (time-measurer)

LATIN: *a- (ab-), ad-, ante-, bene-, bi-, circum-, con-, contra-, di- (dis), e- (ex-), in- (two meanings), inter-, intra-, mal-, multi-, ob-, per-, post-, pre-, pro-, retro-, semi-, sub- (sur-), super-, trans-, ultra-*

GREEK: *a- (an-), -agogue, allo-, anthropo-, anti-, apo-, arch-, auto-, batho-, bio-, cata-, cephalo-, chron-, -cracy, demo-, dia-, dyna-, dys-, ecto-, epi-, eu-, -gen, geo-, -gon, -gony, graph-, gyn-, hemi-, hepta-, hetero-, hexa-, homo-, hydr-, hyper-, hypo-, log-, mega-, -meter, micro-, mono-, morph-, -nomy, -nym, -pathy, penta-, -phag, phil-, -phobe (ia), -phone, poly-, pseudo-, psyche-, -scope, soph-, stero-, sym- (syn-), tele-, tetra-, theo-, thermo-, tri-, zoo-*

4. *Think up and look up seven or eight more words, or as many as you can (omitting mere parts of speech, like* acts, acted, acting*) to add to the list of derivations already started after each of the following Latin verbs and their past participles. Add a note to explain any particularly interesting one, like* actuary *(an insurance expert), that turns up in your own list.*

> *agere, actus* (do)—agent, act . . .
> *audire, auditus* (hear)—audit . . .
> *capere, captus* (seize)—capable . . .
> *cedere, cessus* (go)—concede . . .

claudere, clausus (shut)—close, include . . .

currere, cursus (run)—recur, course . . .

dicere, dictus (say)—dictate . . .

ducere, ductus (lead)—produce . . .

facere, factus (make)—infect . . .

ferre, latus (carry)—infer, relate . . .

fidere, fisus (trust)—confide, Fido . . .

fundere, fusus (pour)—refuse, refund . . .

gradi, gressus (step)—grade, digressions . . .

ire, itus (go)—exit, tradition . . .

jacere, jactus (throw)—reject . . .

legere, lectus (choose, read)—legible, elect . . .

loqui, locutus (speak)—circumlocution . . .

mittere, missus (send)—permit, mission . . .

pellere, pulsus (drive)—impel, repulse . . .

pendere, pensus (hang)—depend, pension . . .

plicare, plicatus (fold)—implication, complex . . .

ponere, positus (put)—response, position . . .

portare, portatus (carry)—import . . .

rumpere, ruptus (break)—rumpus, erupt . . .

scribere, scriptus (write)—scribble, script . . .

sedere, sessus (sit)—sedentary, assess . . .

sentire, sensus (feel)—sense . . .

specere, spectus (look)—speculate . . .

tendere, tensus (stretch)—tend, tense . . .

tenere, tentus (hold)—content . . .

trahere, tractus (drag)—tractor . . .

venire, ventus (come)—convene, invent . . .

vertere, versus (turn)—diverting, verse . . .

videre, visus (see)—divide, visible . . .

vocare, vocatus (call)—vocation . . .

ABSTRACT AND CONCRETE

Every good stylist has perceived, in one way or another, the distinction between the abstract and the concrete. Tangible things—things we can touch—are "concrete"; their qualities, along with all our emotional, intellectual, and spiritual states, are "abstract." The rule for a good style is to be as concrete as we can, to illustrate tangibly our general propositions, to use *shoes* and *ships* and *sealing wax* instead of *commercial concomitants.* But this requires constant effort: our minds so crave abstraction we can hardly pin them down to specifics.

Abstraction, a "drawing out from," is the very nature of thought. Thought moves from concrete to abstract. In the strictest sense, *all* words are abstractions. *Stick* is a generalization of all sticks, the crooked and the straight, the long and the short, the peeled and the shaggy. No word fits its object like a glove, because words are not things: words represent ideas of things. They are the means by which we class eggs and tents and trees so that we can handle them as ideas—not as actual things but as *kinds* of things. A person can hold an egg in his hand, but cannot think about it, or talk about it, unless he has some larger idea with which his mind, too, can grasp it, some idea like *thing,* or *throwing thing,* or *egg*—which classes this one white ellipsoid with all the eggs he has known, from ostrich to hummingbird, with the *idea* of egg. One word per item would be useless; it would be no idea at all, since ideas represent not items, but *classes* of items.

But what we call abstract words—*virtue, abstract, concrete*—can attain a power of their own, as the rhetorician heightens attention to their meanings. This ability, of course, does not come easily or soon. First, and for the present, I repeat, you need to be as concrete as you can, to illustrate tangibly, to pin your abstractions down to specifics. But once you have learned this, you can move on to the rhetoric of abstraction, which is, indeed, a kind of squeezing of abstract words for their specific juice.

Lincoln does exactly this when he concentrates on *dedication* six times within ten sentences—in his dedication at Gettysburg. Similarly, Eliot refers to "faces/Distracted from distraction by distraction" (*Four Quartets*). Abstractions can, in fact, operate beautifully as specifics: "As a knight, Richard the Lion-Hearted was a *triumph*; as a king, he was a *disaster.*" Many rhetorical patterns likewise concentrate on abstract essences:

> . . . **tribulation works patience, and patience experience, and experience hope. (Rom. v.3–4)**
> **The humble are proud of their humility.**
> **Care in your youth so you may live without care.**

An able writer like Samuel Johnson can make a virtual poetry of abstractions, as he alliterates and balances them against each other (I have capitalized the alliterations and italicized the balances):

> **Dryden's performances were always hasty, either *Excited* by some *External occasion,* or *Extorted* by some *domestic necessity;* he**

ComPosed without Consideration, and Published without Correction.

Notice especially how *excited* ("called forth") and *extorted* ("twisted out"), so alike in sound and form, so alike in making Dryden write, nevertheless contrast their opposite essential meanings. Johnson thus *extorts* the specific juice of each abstract word.

So before we disparage abstraction, we should acknowledge its rhetorical power; and we should understand that it is an essential distillation, a primary and natural and continual mental process. Without it, we could not make four of two and two. So we make abstractions of abstractions to handle bigger and bigger groups of ideas. *Egg* becomes *food*, and *food* becomes *nourishment*. We also classify all the psychic and physical qualities we can recognize: *candor, truth, anger, beauty, negligence, temperament*. But because our thoughts drift upward, we need always to look for the word that will bring them nearer earth, that will make our abstractions seem visible and tangible, that will make them graspable—mentioning a *handle*, or a *pin*, or an *egg*, alongside our abstraction, for instance. We have to pull our abstractions down within reach of our reader's own busily abstracting headpiece. In short, we must pin our abstractions down with constant comparisons to the concrete eggs from which they sprang.

The writer's ultimate skill perhaps lies in making a single object represent its whole abstract class. I have paired each abstraction below with its concrete translation:

> *Friendliness* is the salesman's best asset.
> A *smile* is the salesman's best asset.
>
> *Administration of proper proteins* might have saved John Keats.
> A *good steak* might have saved John Keats.
>
> To *understand* the world by *observing all of its geological details*. . . .
> To *see* the world in *a grain of sand*. . . .

EXERCISES

5. *Write three sentences using abstractions concretely, as in "As a knight, Richard was a triumph; as a king, he was a disaster."*

6. *Write three sentences in which a single concrete item represents its whole abstract class, as in "A good steak might have saved John Keats."*

7. *Revise the following sentences to make them more vivid and distinct by replacing as many of the abstract terms as possible with concrete terms.*

1. Unhappy because of their lack of recognition, the Wright brothers temporarily quit flying in October, 1905.
2. For the better part of the year, he was without gainful employment.
3. Of the students who go to college outside their own state, seventy percent do not go back after completing their studies.
4. A sizable proportion of those people who use long-distance movers are large corporation employees whose moving expenses are entirely underwritten by their companies.
5. His great-grandfather once ran successfully for high public office, but he never served because his opponent mortally wounded him in a gunfight.
6. There was a severe disturbance in Jackson prison one day in the spring of 1952.
7. Convicts, armed with makeshift weapons, took some of the prison personnel hostage.
8. Her husband had one extramarital relationship after another and finally disappeared with a hotel dining room employee in one of our larger midwestern cities.
9. The lava issued slowly from the openings in the ground along the side of the trail.
10. Rejected by the military because of an impairment of his vision, Ernest became a journalist with a midwestern newspaper.
11. Hemingway was gravely injured when a trench mortar shell exploded directly behind him.
12. Several prominent labor leaders were entertained at the White House today.
13. Disadvantaged people are often maltreated by the very social-service agencies ostensibly designed to help them.
14. The newspaper reported that a small foreign car had overturned on the expressway just north of town.
15. The new contract offers almost no change in the fringe-benefit package.

METAPHOR

As you have probably noticed, I frequently use metaphors—the most useful way of making our abstractions concrete. The word is Greek for "transfer" (*meta* equals *trans* equals *across; phor* equals *fer* equals *ferry*). A metaphor treats something as if it were something else, ideas as if all of them were eggs, abstractions as if they were chickens that are also vaguely like flowers springing, thought as if it were rising steam. Metaphors illustrate, in a word, our general ideas. I might have written at length about how an idea is like an egg. I did, in fact, follow each declaration with an example, and I illustrated the point with a person holding an egg (p. 189). But the metaphor makes the comparison at a stroke. I used our common word *grasp* for "understanding," comparing the mind to something with hand, *transferring* the physical picture of the clutching hand to the invisible mental act.

Almost all our words are metaphors, usually with the physical picture faded. *Transfer* itself pictures a physical portage. When the company *transfers* its men, it is sending them about the country as if by piggyback, or raft, or whatever. But mercifully the physical facts have faded—*transfer* has become a "dead metaphor"—and we can use the word in comfortable abstraction. Now, precisely because we are constantly abstracting, constantly letting the picture fade, you can use metaphor to great advantage—or disastrously, if your eyes aren't sharp. With metaphors, you overcome the nonpictorial quality of most of our writing; you make your writing both vivid and unique. As Aristotle said, the metaphor is clear, agreeable, and strange; like a solved riddle, it is the most delightful of teachers.

Metaphor seems to work at about four levels, each with a different clarity and force. Suppose you wrote "he swelled and displayed his finery." You have transferred to a man the qualities of a peacock to make his appearance and personality vivid. You have chosen one of the four ways to make this transfer.

I. SIMILE: **He was like a peacock.**
He displayed himself like a peacock.
He displayed himself as if he were a peacock.
II. PLAIN METAPHOR: **He was a peacock.**
III. IMPLIED METAPHOR: **He swelled and displayed his finery.**
He swelled and ruffled his plumage.
He swelled, ruffling his plumage.
IV. DEAD METAPHOR: **He strutted.**

I. SIMILE. The simile is the most obvious form the metaphor can take, and hence would seem elementary. But it has powers of its own, particularly where the writer seems to be trying urgently to express the inexpressible, comparing his subject to several different possibilities, no one wholly adequate. In *The Sound and the Fury*, Faulkner thus describes two jaybirds (my italics):

[they] whirled up on the blast *like gaudy scraps of cloth or paper*
and lodged in the mulberries, ... screaming into the wind that
ripped their harsh cries onward and away *like scraps of paper or
of cloth* in turn.

The simile has a high poetic energy. D. H. Lawrence uses it frequently,
as here in *The Plumed Serpent* (my italics):

The lake was quite black, *like a great pit.* The wind suddenly blew
with violence, with a strange ripping sound in the mango trees, *as
if some membrane in the air were being ripped.*

II. PLAIN METAPHOR. The plain metaphor makes its comparison in one
imaginative leap. It is shorthand for "as if he were a peacock." It pretends,
by exaggeration *(hyperbole),* that he *is* a peacock. We move instinctively
to this kind of exaggerated comparison as we try to convey our impressions
with all their emotional impact. "He was a maniac at Frisbee," we might
say, or "a dynamo." The metaphor is probably our most common figure
of speech: *the pigs, the swine, a plum, a gem, a phantom of delight, a
shot in the arm.* It may be humorous or bitter; it may be simply and aptly
visual: "The road was a ribbon of silver." Thoreau extends a metaphor
through several sentences in one of his most famous passages:

Time is but the stream I go a-fishing in. I drink at it; but while I
drink I see the sandy bottom and detect how shallow it is. Its thin
current slides away, but eternity remains. I would drink deeper; fish
in the sky, whose bottom is pebbly with stars.

III. IMPLIED METAPHOR. The implied metaphor is even more widely
useful. It operates most often among the verbs, as in *swelled, displayed,*
and *ruffled,* the cocky verbs suggesting "peacock." Most ideas can suggest
analogues of physical processes or natural history. Give your television
system *tentacles* reaching into every home, and you have compared TV
to an octopus, with all its lethal and wiry suggestions. You can have your
school spirit *fall below zero,* and you have implied that your school spirit
is like temperature, registered on a thermometer in a sudden chill. In the
following passage about Hawthorne's style, Malcolm Cowley develops his
explicit analogy first into a direct simile *(like a footprint)* and then into
the metaphor implying that phrases are people walking at different speeds:

He dreamed in words, while walking along the seashore or under
the pines, till the words fitted themselves to his stride. The result
was that his eighteenth-century English developed into a natural,

> a *walked,* style, with a phrase for *every* step and a comma after
> every phrase like a footprint in the sand. Sometimes the phrases
> hurry, sometimes they loiter, sometimes they march to drums.*

Cowley's implied metaphor about hurrying and loitering phrases is in fact
a kind of extended pun, to illustrate the *walked* style he italicizes. You can
even pun on the physical Latin components in our abstract words, turning
them back into their original suggestions of physical acts, as in "The
enterprise grabbed everything" (some beast or army is rushing in), for
enterprise means in Latin something like "to rush in and grab." Too
subtle? No, the contrast between *enterprise* and *grabbed* will please anyone, and the few who see it all will be delighted.

IV. DEAD METAPHOR. *Enterprise* is really a dead metaphor, and the art
of resuscitation is the metaphorist's finest skill. It comes from liking words
and paying attention to what they say. The punster makes the writer, if
he can restrain himself. Simply add onto the dead metaphor enough
implied metaphors to get the circulation going again: "He strutted, *swelling and ruffling his plumage.*" He *strutted* means by itself "walked in a
pompous manner." By bringing the metaphor back to life, we keep the
general meaning but also restore the physical picture of a peacock puffing
up and spreading his feathers. We recognize *strut* concretely and truly for
the first time. We know the word, and we know the man. We have an
image of him, a posture strongly suggestive of a peacock.

Perhaps the best dead metaphors to revive are those in proverbial
clichés. See what Thoreau does (in his *Journal*) with *spur of the moment:*

> **I feel the spur of the moment thrust deep into my side. The present
> is an inexorable rider.**

Or again, when in *Walden* he speaks of wanting "to improve *the nick
of time,* and notch it on my stick too," and of not being *thrown off the
track* "by every nutshell and mosquito's wing that falls on the rails." In
each case, he takes the proverbial phrase literally and physically, adding
an attribute or two to bring the old metaphor back alive.

You can go too far, of course. Your metaphors can be too thick and
vivid, and the obvious pun brings a howl of protest. Jane Austen disliked
metaphors, as Mary Laselles notes (*Jane Austen and Her Art,* pp. 111–
112), and reserved them for her hollow characters. I have myself some-

---

***The Portable Hawthorne* (New York: The Viking Press, 1948).

times advised scholars not to use them because they are so often over-worked and so often tangled in physical impossibilities. "The violent population explosion has paved the way for new intellectual growth" looks pretty good—until you realize that explosions do not pave, and that new vegetation does not grow up through solid pavement. The metaphor, then, is your most potent device. It makes your thought concrete and your writing vivid. It tells in an instant how your subject looks to you. But it is dangerous. It should be quiet, almost unnoticed, with all details agreeing, and all absolutely consistent with the natural universe.

EXERCISES

8. *Write two sentences illustrating each of the following (six sentences in all): (1) the simile, (2) the metaphor, (3) the implied metaphor.*

9. *Write a sentence for each of the following dead metaphors, bringing it to life by adding implied metaphorical detail, as in "She bridled, snorting and tossing her mane," or by adding a simile, as in "He was dead wrong, laid out like a corpse on a slab."*

dead center, pinned down, sharp as a tack, stick to, whined, purr, reflected, run for office, yawn, take a course, pull up stakes

10. *Revise the following sentences so as to clear up the illogical or unnatural connections in their metaphors and similes.*

1. The violent population explosion has paved the way for new intellectual growth.
2. The book causes a shock, like a bucket of icy water suddenly thrown on a fire.
3. The whole social fabric will become unstuck.
4. The tangled web of Jack's business crumbled under its own weight.
5. His last week had mirrored his future, like a hand writing on the wall.
6. The recent economic picture, which seemed to spell prosperity, has wilted beyond repair.
7. They were tickled to death by the thunderous applause.
8. Stream-of-consciousness fiction has gone out of phase with the new castles in the air of fantasy.
9. The murmured protests drifted from the convention floor to the podium, cracking the facade of his imperturbability.
10. Richard was ecstatic with his success. He had scaled the mountain of difficulties and from here on out he could sail with the breeze.

ALLUSION

Allusions illustrate your general idea by referring it to something else, making it take your reader as Grant took Richmond, making you the Mickey Mantle of the essay, or the Mickey Mouse. Allusions depend on common knowledge. Like the metaphor, they illustrate the remote with the familiar—a familiar place, or event, or personage. "He looked . . . like a Japanese Humphrey Bogart," writes William Bittner of French author Albert Camus, and we instantly see a face like the one we know so well (a glance at Camus' picture confirms how accurate this unusual allusion is). Perhaps the most effective allusions depend on a knowledge of literature. When Thoreau writes that "the winter of man's discontent was thawing as well as the earth," we get a secret pleasure from recognizing this as an allusive borrowing from the opening lines of Shakespeare's *Richard III:* "Now is the winter of our discontent/Made glorious summer by this sun of York." Thoreau flatters us by assuming we are as well read as he. We need not catch the allusion to enjoy his point, but, if we catch it, we feel a sudden fellowship of knowledge with him. We now see the full metaphorical force, Thoreau's and Shakespeare's both, heightened as it is by our remembrance of Richard Crookback's twisted discontent, an allusive illustration of all our pitiful resentments now thawing with the spring.

Allusion can also be humorous. For instance, the hero of Peter De Vrie's "The Vale of Laughter"* (an allusion to the biblical "vale of tears") contemplates adultery but decides for home and honor:

> **If you look back, you turn into a pillar of salt. If you look ahead, you turn into a pillar of society.**

He alludes, of course, to Lot's wife, who looked back on the adulterous city of Sodom, against orders, and was turned into a pillar of salt (Gen. xix.26). De Vries begins his book with a wildly amusing allusion to Melville's already allusive beginning of *Moby Dick,* the archetypal whale hunt. Melville's narrator says to call him "Ishmael," the biblical outcast (Gen. xvi.11–12). De Vries throws a devilish comma into Melville's opening sentence, then turns allusion into metaphor:

> **Call me, Ishmael. Feel absolutely free to. Call me any hour of the day or night at the office or at home, and I'll be glad to give**

*From Blood of the Lamb (Boston: Little, Brown and Co.) Copyright 1953© 1962, 1964, 1967 by Peter De Vries. The two excerpts are reprinted by permission of Little, Brown and Co.

you the latest quotation with price-earnings ratio and estimated dividend of any security traded in those tirelessly tossing, deceptively shaded waters in which we pursue the elusive whale of Wealth, but from which we come away at last content to have hooked the twitching bluegill, solvency. And having got me, call me anything you want, Ish baby. Tickled to death to be of service.

EXERCISES

11. *Write a sentence for each of the following, in which you allude either humorously or seriously to:*

1. A famous—or infamous—person (Caesar, Napoleon, Barnum, Lincoln, Stalin, Picasso, Bogart)
2. A famous event (the Declaration of Independence, the Battle of Waterloo, the landing on Plymouth Rock, the Battle of the Bulge, the signing of the Magna Carta, Custer's Last Stand, Watergate)
3. A notable place (Athens, Rome, Paris, London Bridge, Jerusalem, the Vatican)
4. This famous passage from Shakespeare, by quietly borrowing some of its phrases:

> To be, or not to be—that is the question:
> Whether 'tis nobler in the mind to suffer
> The slings and arrows of outrageous fortune,
> Or to take arms against a sea of troubles,
> And by opposing end them.

DICTION

"What we need is a mixed diction," said Aristotle, and his point remains true twenty-three centuries and several languages later. The aim of style, he says, is to be clear but distinguished. For clarity, we need common, current words; but, used alone, these are commonplace, and as ephemeral as everyday talk. For distinction, we need words not heard every minute, unusual words, large words, foreign words, metaphors; but, used alone, these become bogs, vapors, or at worst, gibberish. What we need is a diction that weds the popular with the dignified, the clear current with the sedgy margins of language and thought.

Not too low, not too high; not too simple, not too hard—an easy breadth of idea and vocabulary. English is peculiarly well endowed for this Aristotelian mixture, with the long abstract Latin words played against the short concrete Anglo-Saxon. Most of our ideas have Latin and Anglo-Saxon partners. In fact, many have a whole spectrum of synonyms from Latin through French to Anglo-Saxon, from general to specific—from *intrepidity* to *fortitude* to *valor* to *courage* to *bravery* to *pluck* to *guts*. You can choose the high word for high effect, or you can get tough with Anglo-Saxon specifics. But, again, you do not want all Anglo-Saxon, and you must especially guard against sobriety's luring you into all Latin. Tune your diction agreeably between the two extremes.

Indeed, the two extremes generate incomparable zip when tumbled side by side, as in *incomparable zip, inconsequential snip, megalomaniacal creep,* and the like. Rhythm and surprise conspire to set up the huge adjective first, then to add the small noun, like a monumental kick. Here is a passage from Edward Dahlberg's *Can These Bones Live,* which I opened completely at random to see how the large fell with the small (my italics):

> Christ walks on a *visionary sea;* Myshkin . . . has his ecstatic premonition of infinity when he has an *epileptic fit.* We know the inward size of an artist by his *dimensional thirsts. . . .**

This mixing of large Latin and small Anglo-Saxon, as John Crowe Ransom has noted, is what gives Shakespeare much of his power:

> This my hand will rather
> The multitudinous seas incarnadine,
> Making the green one red.

The short Anglo-Saxon *seas* works sharply between the two magnificent Latin words, as do the three short Anglo-Saxons that bring the big passage to rest, contrasting the Anglo-Saxon *red* with its big Latin kin, *incarnadine.* William Faulkner, who soaked himself in Shakespeare, gets much the same power from the same mixture. He is describing a very old Negro woman in *The Sound and the Fury* (the title itself comes from Shakespeare's *Macbeth,* the source of the *multitudinous seas* passage). She has been fat, but now she is wrinkled and completely shrunken except for her stomach:

> . . . a paunch almost dropsical, as though muscle and tissue had been courage or fortitude which the days or the years had consumed until only the indomitable skeleton was left rising like a ruin or a landmark above the somnolent and impervious guts. . . .

*Ann Arbor: University of Michigan Press, Ann Arbor Paperbacks, 1967.

The impact of that short, ugly Anglo-Saxon word *guts,* with its slang metaphorical pun, is almost unbearably moving. And the impact would be nothing, the effect slurring, without the grand Latin preparation.

A fully worded sentence, each word in place and pulling its weight, is a joy to see. But a sentence full of words is not. Words should count, I say again. And again, the best way to make them count is to count the words in each suspicious case. Suspect every *by,* every *of,* every *which,* every *is,* and especially that impersonal passive voice. Any shorter version will be clearer. I once counted the words, sentence by sentence, in a thirty-page manuscript rejected as "too loose." In some sentences, I cut no more than one or two words. I rephrased many, but I think I cut no entire sentence. In fact, I added a considerable paragraph; and I still had five pages fewer, and a better essay. If you cut only one word from every sentence, you will in ten pages (if you average ten words a sentence) save your reader one whole page of uselessness and obstruction and wasted time.

A good diction takes work. It exploits the natural, but does not come naturally. It demands a wary eye for the way meanings sprout, and the courage to prune. It has the warmth of human concern. It is a cut above the commonplace, a cut above the inaccuracies and circumlocutions of speech, yet within easy reach. Clarity is the first aim; economy, the second; grace, the third; dignity, the fourth. Our writing should be a little strange, a little out of the ordinary, a little beautiful, with words and phrases not met every day but seeming as right and natural as grass. A good diction takes care and cultivation.

It can be overcultivated. It may seem to call attention to itself rather than to its subject. Suddenly we are aware of the writer at work, and a little too pleased with himself, reaching for the elegant cliché and the showy phrase. Some readers find this very fault with my own writing, though I do really try to saddle my maverick love of metaphor. If I strike you in this way, you can use me profitably as a bad example along with the following passage. I have italicized elements that individually may have a certain effectiveness, but that cumulatively become mannerism, as if the writer were watching himself gesture in a mirror. Some of his phrases are redundant; some are trite. Everything is somehow cozy and grandiose, and a little too nautical:

> **There's** little excitement *ashore* when merchant ships from *faraway* India, Nationalist China, or Egypt *knife through* the *gentle swells* of Virginia's Hampton Roads. This *unconcern* may simply reflect the *nonchalance* of people who live by *one of the world's*

great seaports. Or perhaps *it's just* that *folk* who *dwell* in the *home towns* of atomic submarines and Mercury astronauts are not likely to be impressed by a visiting freighter, *from however distant a realm.* . . . *Upstream a bit* and also *to port,* the mouth of the Elizabeth River leads to Portsmouth and a major naval shipyard. *To starboard lies* Hampton, where at Langley Air Force Base the National Aeronautics and Space Administration prepares to send a man *into the heavens.*

EXERCISES

12. (a) *As a warmup, clear the preceding example of its overdone phrases. Then* (b) *look for similar passages in your own papers written thus far for this course, and do the same for several of your most overblown paragraphs.*

13. *Write a paragraph in which you mix your diction as effectively as you can, with the big Latin word and the little Anglo-Saxon, the formal word and just the right touch of slang, working in at least two combinations of the extremes, on the pattern of* multitudinous seas, diversionary thrust, incomparable zip, *underlining these for your instructor's convenience.*

Chapter 9

WRITING ABOUT LITERATURE

Writing about literature (or film or music or painting) is really no different from writing about life—though literature and life are distinctly different. Writing about either art or life is a way to discover meanings and then to deepen them for ourselves as we try to make them clear and meaningful to others. The significant difference lies not between literature and life, but between expository argument and literature, between the essay you write and the story, between the essay you write and the poem.

An essay states its point; literature implies its point. Poem, short story, novel, play, or motion picture, each acts out in its particular way some underlying idea that probably remains unstated. Even the brief lyric poem is really a dramatized moment, a voice speaking intensely and beautifully from some larger drama, which is probably life itself. So, poem or novel, each enacts and demonstrates—each *presents,* or represents—something about life, but usually does not tell exactly what. These are the *mimetic* arts—actions imitating life, grand mimickings of the human predicament.

So, to write about literature, you must first discover, and decide for yourself, what *it* is about. What point, or points, *does* it imply, or act out? Poems make statements, of course, and characters in plays, novels, or films also make statements. A poem or a character may even state the author's thesis explicitly. Even so, you must select the stated thesis from all the other things said, and then interpret it in the light of all the other statements, or of the entire action. When Hamlet says "the readiness is all," we know we have a thesis. Hamlet has found an important answer to both his brooding inaction and his impetuosity. Yet, is it *the* thesis? Perhaps—but certainly we need to qualify it with something about murderous ambitions, about thinking too little and too much, about appearance and reality, about the strange, dark web of thought and circumstance in which all life in this play seems caught beyond control.

Your first step, then, is to find the action's thesis, even though—and precisely because—the writer may have bent his best efforts to avoid stating a thesis or seeming to have one. The writer has wanted to *dramatize* his problem, or his mood, not to state it flatly, to display it in action, not merely to describe it. He has not wanted to tack a moral to his tale. That is the reader's job: to find the one idea toward which all these statements, all these moral and immoral actions, point.

To write an essay about literature, then, you first try to discover its point—or the significance of some part or feature—and assert something *about* it, probably that this *is* the point, that this feature *is* significant. *Your* thesis is an *aboutness* asserted.

EXPLICATION

Explication is an unfolding of meanings (from *ex*, "out", and *plicare*, "to fold")—detail by detail, pleat by pleat. You unfold for your reader what this play, or novel, or poem, is about. Your *aboutness* may be simply that the unfolding is necessary for full understanding, or it may find some commanding detail or pattern or metaphor and assert its preeminence, showing how all the others fit under it. Poetry, intense and compressed, metaphoric and symbolic, especially invites explication, invites an explanation and demonstration of what it is all about. But a scene or a passage in a novel or play also may evoke a valuable explication as you argue for its importance to the work as a whole in all its details and levels of suggestion. You may not wish to, or need to, unfold everything.

Now let me try my hand at explicating a conveniently short and justly famous little poem, so you can see something of the range of possibilities—of the questions you might ask and write about. Robert Herrick wrote it in 1648, and it has remained popular ever since.

UPON JULIA'S CLOTHES

Whenas in silks my *Julia* goes,
Then, then (me thinks) how sweetly flowes
That liquefaction of her clothes.

Next, when I cast mine eyes and see
That brave Vibration each way free;
O how that glittering taketh me!

Perhaps the first thing that strikes us, before we take in the two statements very fully, is the smoothness of Herrick's meter and rhymes. He is fitting his two sentences into a metrical frame as if with no effort at all, talking in a perfectly easy way within a set of artificial conditions few of us can manage without awkwardness, like the person who walks a high-wire in a way the rest of us walk a street. His skill furnishes part of our wonder and delight.

You will probably notice that Herrick's meter is iambic, far and away the most usual of the meters, though modern poetry goes predominantly for free verse, with no metrical pattern nor rhyme (for more on meter, see pp. 215–217). In explicating poetry, you usually need to say very little, if anything, about meter. But certainly Herrick's unusual smoothness calls for some comment on his metrical pattern and his handling of it. He here writes two brief stanzas of three iambic tetrameter (four-beat) lines each, rhymed as triplets, or triads. His iambic feet are unusually regular. The poem has only two inverted feet (trochees), which, as line-beginners, are so common to iambic writing as to be what we might call a regular variation. And both of these (*Next, when* and *O how*) come in the second stanza as the excitement rises. Another interesting variation is *Then, then,* which we would presumably read as two heavies /— —/, a spondee, slowed even further by the comma. What looks like a redundancy, a mere line-filler (and it probably was), Herrick has made into a dramatic measuring out of expectation, or an emphasis on the very moment of the thrill. We will notice two other pleasing variations in pace: how Herrick's sentence twice "runs on" to the next line without stopping at the line-end, at *flowes/That liquefaction* and at *see/That brave Vibration.* These are his two key phrases similarly patterned, similarly set up with a rush of expectation. And we will notice how the last line of each stanza carries the punch.

Next, we will have enjoyed that unusual word, which has probably caught every reader's eye from 1648 to the present, *liquefaction.* Part of our pleasure comes from seeing how naturally Herrick has fitted a big, four-syllable, unpoetic word, directly from Latin, into his regular meter, and has made it poetry. And it is poetry because it climaxes those liquid s-sounds with which Herrick has prepared us: *Whenas, silks, goes, thinks, sweetly flowes.* Then the idea hits us: silks rubbing softly against each other would indeed rustle with a liquid sound, which the very name, *silks,* also suggests in its sound. Finally, Herrick may have intended that *liquefaction* would also bring the word *satisfaction* to mind by their similarity, an idea that has struck more than one of my students, since the sound itself is satisfying, and satisfaction is certainly what the young man wants, though he dare not say so, or even think so. *Liquefaction,* "turning something into water," completes the metaphor that Julia's silken clothes, from their sound as she moves, seem as if they were water. Her movement turns them into water, and their *liquefaction* suggests that the clothes might indeed sweetly flow away, leaving the imagination filled with actuality.

When we come to the second stanza, we realize something further. The first stanza concerns sounds only. Julia is apparently approaching her admirer from behind, coming up a hall, let us say. He hears her. He knows it is she. She is dressed elegantly, perhaps for some gathering at court. The sound of her silks, flowing as she flows, epitomizes his thrill at her presence. And certainly she must be beautiful to look at. *Next,* he says, after savoring the sound of her approach, he must turn to look at her, almost as with an effort to face a brilliant light (*cast mine eyes*).

But what is a *brave Vibration* that is *each way free?* Well, we certainly know what a vibration is. Again the big Latin word is neatly fitted to the meter among its short Anglo-Saxon companions, and with an inner rhyming, or alliteration, of *brave* and *brations* (for a discussion of sounds, see page 215), and we know it is significant. And we certainly know what parts of a woman are apt to vibrate. *Brave* we must look up in the dictionary to discover a seventeenth-century meaning, still occasionally in use, which has nothing to do with courage. *Brave,* here, primarily means "splendid," suggesting both "excellence" and "resplendence," value and brightness. Yet the vibration is a little bold, too, a little courageous, to display such hidden beauty. *Vibration,* which Herrick capitalizes, apparently for emphasis, is also, in Latin, not only a quick shaking back and forth, but such a motion of human limbs, trembling in excitement, and of flames, lightning, or, especially significant here, the sea or other waters glittering with lights, as are Julia's silks, sparkling outward.

But exactly what is producing those brave vibrations? Julia could be walking past her admirer, going away, and a rear view might certainly provide him with a brave vibration each way free. But again our explication needs history. Seventeenth-century portraits will show us that skirts were very full. We must further assure ourselves that *goes* in the first line meant "walks" not "departs." Julia is certainly *approaching,* as her admirer's first hearing, then seeing, clearly indicates. Julia's breasts, then, free under the silk in an age before the bra, must be furnishing the vibration, though her admirer—at least for the moment—is too much the gentleman (and too much the poet) to say so. Of course, her entire dress is "vibrating" to and fro with light, so we need not be anatomically specific. Nevertheless, the bright sheen of the silk, glittering as she moves, takes her admirer so powerfully precisely because it represents, as had the liquefaction earlier, the desired beauty beneath.*

*I append this detailed footnote to show what others have thought on some points, indeed to show how their thoughts have stimulated mine, and to credit these several authors properly so that readers can pursue these matters as they desire. I also want to present a paradigm for the problems of footnoting (see pp. 273–279). I reproduce the text of Herrick's first edition as edited by J. Max Patrick, *The Complete Poetry of Robert Herrick,* The Stuart Editions (New York: New York University Press, 1963), p. 344.

Herrick did write a poem "Upon Julia's Breasts," which has nothing of the clothed ambiguity of "brave Vibration," a phrase that has raised much controversy. Elisabeth Schneider argues that the first stanza has Julia dressed; and the second, Julia undressed. Jeremy Bentham, an eighteenth-century English jurist, referred to taking a walk as "vibrating," and, in the seventeenth century, vibration was generally connected with the slow swing of a pendulum. Hence, Schneider believes, Herrick pictures "the rhythmical motion back and forth, 'each way free,' of [Julia's] unencumbered naked limbs" (*Explicator,* 13 [March 1955], item 30). Michael J. Preston backs her up, by pointing to Ovid's *Amores* I.5, about his Corinna (a name Herrick used in several distinctive poems), who many think is Augustus's daughter Julia, coming to his apartment one afternoon dressed, and then undressing, and both Herrick and his readers were full of classical knowledge (*Explicator,* 30 [May 1972], item 82). Lewis E. Weeks, Jr., unaware of Schneider's suggestions, also opts for nudity ("Julia Unveiled: A Note on Herrick's 'Upon Julia's Clothes,' " *CEA Critic,* 25 [June, 1963], 8).

But most commentators agree that Julia keeps her clothes on, many, however, preferring the rear view. The poem is, after all, about Julia's clothes, not her limbs. William O. Harris points out the significant distinction between sound in the first stanza and sight in the second, as he answers Schneider's complaint that nothing new would happen in the second stanza, leaving it repetitive and redundant, unless Julia had undressed between stanzas (*Explicator,* 21 [December 1962], item 29). The only other significant point, which I have omitted, is the "submerged metaphor" about fishing—Julia in the liquid element, then *cast,* then something glittering, like both a fish and a fisherman's lure, then *takes,* in which the fisherman finds himself caught, in the typical wiles of love: first pointed out by Louis H. Leiter (*Modern Language Notes 73* [1958], 331; *Explicator,* 25 [January 1967], item 41; see also J. D. Shuchter (*Explicator* 25 [November 1966], item 27), and Roger B. Rollin, *Robert Herrick* (New York: Twayne, 1966), pp. 86–87. Schneider, however, well states the inescapable point, which all the poem's admirers have registered in one way or another, that the poem's power and charm lie it its "neatness and symmetry." Earl Daniels finds an interesting smoothness in the "Julia" lines (I.1 and 3; II.2) and an excited unevenness in the "observer" lines (I.2 and II.1 and 3) (*Explicator,* 1 [March 1943], item 35).

Now we have just about explicated everything, down to the bare facts, as it were, except why this poem is so good. Why has it stood out, as a favorite, these three centuries, among all the changes of costume and changing customs of frankness and reticence? It says nothing profound. It is a tiny little thing, really. A young man liked to look at the girl he loved ("*my* Julia" tells us that). Men, young and old, still can hardly keep their eyes off shapely women, loved or not. So what is so great about it? Well, my own explication would start with the audacious thesis that no other piece of literature conveys so beautifully, vividly, and succinctly a young man's pleasure in looking at the woman he loves, making this particular moment of emotional intensity both explicit and universal. Can you find six lines anywhere that do as much on this most central human emotion? I know I cannot. But this is probably farther than you will want to go. Your own explication would feature one salient point—the *liquefaction–brave Vibration* bit, perhaps. The point about explication is to find some thesis that justifies all its searching-out of detail and local meaning, and then simply to ask yourself questions and find answers wherever they are, in dictionaries, mythologies, histories, portraits, the author's other works, or whatever—anywhere that will yield answers and illumination.

EXERCISES

1. *Here is another love poem, this one modern and from the woman's viewpoint:*

KIDNAP POEM

ever been kidnapped
by a poet
if i were a poet
i'd kidnap you
put you in my phrases and meter
you to jones beach
or maybe coney island
or maybe just to my house
lyric you in lylacs
dash you in the rain
blend into the beach
to complement my see
play the lyre for you
ode you with my love song

anything to win you
wrap you in the red Black green
show you off to mama
yeah if i were a poet i'd kid
nap you

Nikki Giovanni*

*From *Re:Creation*. Copyright © 1970 by Nikki Giovanni; Broadside/Crummell Press, Detroit, Michigan.

Write a comparison, on any point you wish, between Herrick's poem and Giovanni's. Here are some questions to ponder. In what way does any poet kidnap the beloved in a love poem? What image of the poet emerges from Giovanni's lower-case letters—i, jones beach, coney island—and her omission of punctuation? Why is Black the only capitalized word? (The poet is black.) What is her pun on meter? On see? On lyre? Perhaps on ode? Who blends into the beach? What is the implication behind wrap, show you off to mama, kid, *and* nap? *Do the two poems show anything typical about the male and female attitudes?*

2. *Explicate the following poem by Emily Dickinson, considering the following questions. What is the* it *the poem talks about? What advantage is there, if any, in setting the poem up as a riddle? Why not come right out and say what the answer to the riddle is, what the* it *represents? What are the metaphors—what is being compared to what? What is the main metaphor? What words convey it? Are there other metaphors?*

Consider lap. *What are the possible metaphors that* lap *implies? Which one, if any, is most appropriate to the subject being described? Likewise consider* lick, peer, pare, crawl, stanza, chase itself, star. *Explain* Boanerges *(you will need a dictionary for this one). Is this an effective allusion? What do meter and rhyme contribute to this poem? Is there a pattern in stanzas? If so, how does it vary? Does this patterning or lack of it contribute anything to what the poem is saying? What is notable about the rhyming, or lack of it? Is this a good poem? Why? (Incidentally, what do you think of that* it's *in line nine?)*

*Emily
Dickinson*

I LIKE TO SEE IT LAP THE MILES

*a train
to a horse*

I like to see it lap the Miles—
And lick the Valleys up—
And stop to feed itself at Tanks—
And then—prodigious step

Around a Pile of Mountains—
And supercilious peer
In Shanties—by the sides of Roads—
And then a Quarry pare

To fit it's sides
And crawl between
Complaining all the while
In horrid—hooting stanza—
Then chase itself down Hill—

And neigh like Boanerges—
Then—prompter than a Star
Stop—docile and omnipotent
At its own stable door—*

STEPS AND QUESTIONS

Each work stirs its own interest, and, as with Julia and her clothes, presents us with questions, and more questions, as we become more interested. These questions are what you write about. We want ultimately to possess what the author wanted us to possess, since each literary work is, after all, a communication from author to reader. A writer may wish only to express himself, yes, but he expects us to understand and value that self-expression as he does. So, as with Herrick, the questions will arise, almost of themselves, from each different work. But in writing, and explaining, a questioning mind will help. Why does the author do this? Why that? What does he intend that vase on the mantle to signify?

This first natural onrush of questions can perhaps be controlled so as to provide us with a kind of system for our explication. How can we formulate questions whose answers will indeed help our reader's understanding? What particularities of a work will most likely provoke the questions you will want to answer in your essay?

To summarize, paraphrase.

The simplest way to start the questions and find the answers is to summarize, letting the process of writing do its fundamental job of discovering our ideas for us. A paraphrase is the closest kind of summary.

*Reprinted by permission of the publishers and the Trustees of Amherst College from *The Poems of Emily Dickinson,* edited by Thomas H. Johnson, Cambridge, Mass.: The Belknap Press of Harvard University Press, Copyright © 1951, 1955 by the President and Fellows of Harvard College.

Paraphrasing a poem—translating it into clear English prose in your own words—is an excellent way to come to grips, in your own mind, with exactly what it says, raising the primary questions as to which of the possible meanings the author seems to intend. Shakespeare writes (Sonnet 116):

> O, no; [love] is an ever-fixed mark
> That looks on tempests and is never shaken;
> It is a star to every wandering bark,
> Whose worth's unknown, although his height be taken.

One student paraphrases like this:

> O, no; love is an object that always needs fixing, that looks on
> storms and is never shaken; it is a moon barked at by every
> wandering dog, who is probably worthless and homeless,
> although his height is taken into account.

In class, he defends his paraphrase by saying that the moon is a kind of star, and Shakespeare is saying that love is like the moon, which wears away and fixes itself up each month. Love is also always in need of repair. The moon looks down on storms untouched; dogs always bark at the moon. Other students argue that *bark* means a ship, and that love is like an actual star, fixed and stationary above storms, which a wandering ship would use in navigating, taking its height with a sextant but never knowing its actual physical nature or worth. The first student says, "Well, I guess *bark* threw me off." The practice of paraphrasing has pinpointed the ambiguous words, and has made them yield the meaning the author probably intended, since it fits better, as we put aside the less probable meanings.

A summary of a poem, a novel, or a play will yield much the same kind of clarification; we might summarize a hypothetical story like this:

> The story opens with an unnamed "he" alone in a dingy room.
> One door of a cabinet is hanging from a single hinge. A spring and
> some stuffing stick up through a sofa cushion. We soon learn that
> his wife has just left him. He is angry and bitter. Piece by piece,
> from his thoughts, we learn what has happened—their high-school
> romance, their fashionable wedding, his "bad luck," as he calls it,
> losing one job after another only because he likes "to have a little
> fun." In the end, he finishes wrecking the cabinet, his wife's special
> treasure, and stamps off to the local bar, never learning what a
> hopeless fool he is, and will continue to be.

Such a summary has crystallized the story clearly and whole. Use such a summary in your own essay, to help your readers see the story as you see it. Some thesis about the story in general, or particular, a little more detail and illustration, and you would have a complete essay.

To search out style, imitate with parody.

Parody is a kind of burlesque paraphrase that alerts one especially to style, though it will also get well into what the author is saying. It is most effective with short passages, since a joke can go on too long. If you imitate a paragraph of James Joyce, Donald Barthelme, William Faulkner, or Dashiell Hammett, let us say, you will learn something about his style that may open the way to an essay about how it works, what patterns are characteristic, what words and kinds of phrasing are favorites. This is only an exercise to strengthen your own style as you discover possibilities in his—as you discover what, in his, needs explaining to your readers. The game is to match the sentences exactly, borrowing especially characteristic words, but with a totally different subject. Here is a brief passage from Faulkner's *Sanctuary,* followed by a parody:

> He dozed. The train clicked on, stopped, jolted. He waked and dozed again. Someone shook him out of sleep into a primrose dawn. Among unshaven puffy faces washed lightly over as though with the paling ultimate stain of holocaust, blinking at one another with dead eyes into which personality returned in secret opaque waves.*

> She hosed. The shower poured on, stopped, squirted. She scrubbed and hosed again. Someone beckoned her out of the shower into the primrose dressing room. Among sagging puffy faces washed lightly over then smeared with face cream as though with the paling ultimate frost of the final freeze, blinking in the mirror at dead eyes into which she hoped some personality would return before her secret opaque class.

With poems, parody is a pleasant way to find out how meter works, as again you attend to what the poet is saying. Shakespeare's Sonnet 30 begins:

> When to the sessions of sweet silent thought
> I summon up remembrance of things past,
> I sigh the lack of many a thing I sought,
> And with old woes new wail my dear time's waste:

*New York: The Modern Library (Random House, Inc.), 1932, pp. 201–202.

Then can I drown an eye, unused to flow,
For precious friends hid in death's dateless night
And weep afresh love's long since cancel'd woe,
And moan the expense of many a vanished sight . . . .

An anonymous parody:

When to the sessions of sweet midnight talk
I summon up my roommate, Mildred Bod,
I sigh the lack of many a moonlight walk
And with old beaus new wail my present clod:
Then can I drown an eye, unused to flow,
For Charlie, and another dateless night,
And weep afresh love's never cancel'd woe,
And moan the expense of everything in sight . . . .

EXERCISES

3. *Pick one of your favorite authors and attempt a parody of one or two
paragraphs from a novel or short story with which you are especially familiar. This
should deepen your insight and your feeling for style—whether "lean" (Hemingway), comparatively "lush" (Faulkner), or even profuse (Henry James). If you feel
really ambitious, try a parody on one of your favorite poems.*

Explain the metaphors.

Metaphor is the heart of poetry—and that is a metaphor, as if poetry
were a living being with a heart for vital life and feeling. All poems, even
the most starkly pictorial, present their meanings in some kind of metaphorical *as if.* Ted Hughes, for instance, begins a poem about a dead pig
in straight description:

VIEW OF A PIG

The pig lay on a barrow dead.
It weighed, they said, as much as three men.
Its eyes closed, pink white eyelashes.
Its trotters stuck straight out.*

But very soon Hughes's description reaches for a metaphorical analogy.
In fact, he has already moved toward metaphor in his second line: *as*

*From *Selected Poems* (1972) by Ted Hughes. Copyright © 1960 by Ted Hughes.
By permission of Harper & Row, Publishers, Inc., and Faber and Faber Ltd.

much as three men. Already the dead pig represents more than itself. And soon comes a full simile: *like a sack of wheat.* Others come, as Hughes tries to convey the pig's startling deadness, so dead as to arouse neither guilt nor pity, as the butchers prepare to *Scald it and scour it like a doorstep*—the simile with which he ends his poem. He has not only found several metaphorical *as if's*, but entailed a vaster one, *as if* this one pig represents the total enigma of lifelessness.

This metaphorical process is everywhere in poetry. Herrick hears Julia's silks rustling *as if* they were turning to water. Nikki Giovanni would like to possess someone *as if* in a kind of verbal and cuddly kidnapping. Emily Dickinson sees a train *as if* it were a horse. For Shakespeare, love is a star, firm above tempests and wandering ships, and thought is a courtroom summoning up past deeds and debts. Whether in direct similes (*like a sack of wheat*), or in plain metaphor (*love is a star*), or implied metaphor (*the sessions of sweet silent thought*), the metaphorical process needs to be spelled out for your readers, as you explain your poem's spell. (See pp. 191–195 in "Words" for fuller discussion of these terms.)

Because they need spelling out for full understanding and appreciation, metaphors probably give you more to write about than anything else in a poem. You can write a good paper comparing how two poets, or several, spin their metaphors from the same thing—love, death, or the same physical object, as in these two examples:

> Slowly, silently, now the moon
> Walks the night in her silver shoon.
>
> > *Walter de la Mare, from "Silver"**

> Greatly shining,
> The Autumn moon floats in the thin sky;
> And the fish-ponds shake their backs and flash their
> > dragon scales
> As she passes over them.
>
> > *Amy Lowell, "Wind and Silver"†*

In De la Mare's metaphor the moon is a woman, mysterious because she walks slowly and silently through the night, majestic and magical because of her archaic "shoon" of silver. Amy Lowell's moon is also mysterious, rendered medieval and magical by the dragons, also with something of

---

*Reprinted by permission of The Literary Trustees of Walter de la Mare and The Society of Authors (London).

†From The Complete Poetical Works of Amy Lowell. Copyright 1955 by Houghton Mifflin Company. Reprinted by permission of the publisher.

the mysterious East as fish-ponds become dragons. De la Mare's passive and silent lady goes on to turn windows, doves, and fish to silver with her beams. But Lowell's moon radiates a magical power. It shines "greatly," and the ponds respond in mysterious obedience, as if they were fish-scaled dragons arching their backs at the water's surface, flashing back their respect for the moon's sovereignty. Lowell's moon, like De la Mare's, is a "she." But is it also a woman? Probably not, since we already see that "floats in the thin sky," like an airy ship in a very thin kind of water, of which the ponds are a denser kind at the bottom of the sky. Ships, we know, are traditionally *she*. "Autumn" also gives Lowell's moon a more somber and shivery presence than De la Mare's, since autumn suggests winter and a change for the worse, and the dragons suggest dire things in the offing. Finally, Lowell's title fills out her metaphorical picture in a way De la Mare's does not. His "Silver" appears again in his verses. Lowell's "Wind and Silver" are not repeated, and by that very economy they underline her metaphor-making. Wind has actually rippled the fish poinds. The moonlight has actually caught the ripples in little silver points, making the water momentarily look like fish-scales, or dragon-scales. Out of this actual sight, evidently Lowell has made her metaphor and her poem, creating her autumnal moon-ship with its mysterious influence that reaches down through its thin sea to its depths in this world with its denser waters. Clearly, Lowell's metaphor is more imaginative and exciting than De la Mare's. But the smooth meter and attractive sound of his language have carried his couplet, with its attractive metaphor, into dictionaries of familiar quotations, where we do not find Amy Lowell's lines.

EXERCISES

4. *Explain the metaphors in the following two poems by Carl Sandburg,* and compare their effectiveness.*

FOG

The fog comes
on little cat feet.
It sits looking
over harbor and city
on silent haunches
and then moves on.

personification
comparing fog
to a cat!

*From *Chicago Poems* by Carl Sandburg, copyright 1916 by Holt, Rinehart and Winston, Inc.; copyright 1944 by Carl Sandburg. Reprinted by permission of Harcourt Brace Jovanovich, Inc.

LOST

Desolate and alone
All night long on the lake
Where fog trails and mist creeps,
The whistle of a boat
Calls and cries unendingly,
Like some lost child
In tears and trouble
Hunting the harbor's breast
And the harbor's eyes.

In which poem is the metaphor most concentrated? Which of these words work metaphorically, which not?—trails, creeps, whistle, Hunting. If you were Sandburg's editor, would you have suggested changes in either poem? If so, what?

5. *Explain the contrasting metaphors in these two poems:*

THE BATH TUB

As a bathtub lined with white porcelain,
When the hot water gives out or goes tepid,
So is the slow cooling of our chivalrous passion,
O my much praised but-not-altogether-satisfactory lady.*

Ezra Pound

Comparing lady to cold water

*From Personae, *copyright 1926 by Ezra Pound. Reprinted by permission of New Directions.*

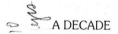

A DECADE

When you came, you were like red wine and honey,
And the taste of you burnt my mouth with its sweetness.
Now you are like morning bread,
Smooth and pleasant.
I hardly taste you at all for I know your savor,
But I am completely nourished.*

Amy Lowell

*From The Complete Poetical Works of Amy Lowell. *Copyright © 1955 by Houghton Mifflin Company. Reprinted by permission of the publisher.*

VERSIFICATION

Find the sound in poetry.

Poetry heightens the sounds of language in six major ways, each depending on some kind of repetition-with-variation.

1. *Meter*—the regular measure, as varied by the language flowing over it. See METER, below.

2. *Rhyme*—line-ends the same, with a necessary difference: *bird/ third.*

3. *Reiteration*—the same word repeated, often with different force: "Of hammered *gold* and *gold* enameling" (Yeats).

4. *Alliteration*—first sounds of words or first accented syllables the same: "*a little lost alliteration.*"

5. *Assonance*—middle vowel-sounds the same: smoky loam, glad rag, hot rod.

6. *Consonance*—middle- or end-consonant sounds the same, but vowels different (also called "slant rhyme" at line-ends): *abhorred/third, supple/apple, cried/bleed, love/over.*

METER. English has one dominant meter—iambic—and three others that lend iambic an occasional foot, for variety, and produce a few poems. (Modern verse is predominantly "free," with no regular pattern.)

RISING METERS
Iambic: ⏑ —
Anapestic: ⏑ ⏑ —

FALLING METERS
Trochaic: — ⏑
Dactylic: — ⏑ ⏑

The number of these metrical units, or feet, in a line also gives the verse a name:

1 foot: monometer
2 feet: dimeter
3 feet: trimeter
4 feet: tetrameter

5 feet: pentameter
6 feet: hexameter
7 feet: heptameter (rare)

All meters will show some variations, and substitutions of other kinds of feet, but three variations in iambic writing are virtually standard:

Inverted foot: — ∪ (a trochee)
Spondee: — —
Ionic double foot: ∪ ∪ | — —

Examples of scansion:

IAMBIC TETRAMETER

∪ —| ∪ —| ∪ —| ∪ — |
An-ni-hil-a-ting all that's made
∪ ∪|— — |∪ ∪|— — |
To a green thought in a green shade.

Andrew Marvell, "The Garden"

IAMBIC TETRAMETER
(with two inverted feet)

— ∪ |— ∪|∪ — | ∪ — |
Slowly, silent- ly, now the moon
— ∪| — ∪|∪ —| ∪ — |
Walks the night in her sil- ver shoon.

Walter de la Mare, "Silver"

IAMBIC PENTAMETER

— —| — —| ∪ —|∪—| ∪ — |
Love's not Time's fool, though ros -y lips and cheeks
∪ —| ∪ —| ∪ —| ∪ —| ∪ — |
Within his bend -ing sick -le's com -pass come

Shakespeare, Sonnet 116

— ∪|∪ — | ∪ —| ∪ —| ∪ — |
When to the ses -sions of sweet si -lent thought
[or]

```
 —  ∪|∪ —|  ∪   ∪|— —|  ∪   —  |
When to the ses -sions of sweet si -lent thought
```

Shakespeare, Sonnet 30

ANAPESTIC TETRAMETER

```
  ∪  —|  ∪   ∪   —  |∪   —|∪  ∪   —  |
The pop -lars are felled; farewell to the shade
  ∪  ∪    —|  ∪  ∪    —  |∪  ∪   —|∪  ∪  —|
And the whis -pering sound of the cool colonnade
```

William Cowper, "The Popular Field"

TROCHAIC TETRAMETER

```
 —  ∪|— ∪|  —  ∪|  —   ∪ |
Tell me not in mournful numbers
```
Longfellow, "A Psalm of Life"

DACTYLIC HEXAMETER

```
 —  ∪  ∪ |— ∪   ∪ | —∪    ∪|  —   ∪  ∪|  —     ∪  ∪ |—   ∪ |
This is the forest prim -eval. The murmuring pines and the hemlocks
 —  ∪  ∪ | —
Bearded with moss . . . .
```
Longfellow, "Evangeline"

A *caesura* ("siZHURa") is a frequent and attractive variation, in which punctuation suspends the meter for a moment as a phrase ends. A *masculine caesura* suspends the meter at the end of a foot, as after *felled* in Cowper's lines above. A *feminine caesura* suspends the meter mid-foot, as in De la Mare's *-ly, now* (second example), and as after Longfellow's *primeval* in the last example.

These are the major sounds of poetry, which you can appreciate, and can describe for your readers, as they contribute to the poem's pleasures and emphasize its meanings.

EXERCISES

6. *See what meter and other sound-effects contribute to the following poem, "Eve," by Ralph Hodgson. What is Hodgson's metrical pattern and rhyme scheme? Note that his short lines scan* | —∪| ∪ — |, *an iambic dimeter with* *inverted foot, as they bring his metrical run and his phrasing to rest. But what is his dominant meter? Note where he varies his pattern. Is there a reason? What does he achieve by turning the Garden of Eden into an orchard? What by omitting Adam? What by having the snake in the grass "successful and/Taking his leave" as the evidently female birds scold? Why does Hodgson have Eve eating, rather than just strolling, or lying around? Who is toasting Eve tonight, and why? What does Hodgson seem to mean by* bells? *What is the force of* motherless? *What are his slant rhymes? (Each of the first seven verses has eight lines; the last verse has ten lines.)*

EVE

Eve, with her basket, was
Deep in the bells and grass
Wading in bells and grass
Up to her knees,
Picking a dish of sweet
Berries and plums to eat,
Down in the bells and grass
Under the trees.

Mute as a mouse in a
Corner the cobra lay,
Curled round a bough of the
Cinnamon tall . . .
Now to get even and
Humble proud heaven and
Now was the moment or
Never at all.

"Eva!" Each syllable
Light as a flower fell,
"Eva!" he whispered the
Wondering maid,
Soft as a bubble sung
Out of a linnet's lung,
Soft and most silvery
"Eva!" he said.

Picture that orchard sprite,
Eve, with her body white,
Supple and smooth to her
Slim finger tips,

Wondering, listening,
Listening, wondering,
Eve with a berry
Half-way to her lips.

Oh had our simple Eve
Seen through the make-believe!
Had she but known the
Pretender he was!
Out of the boughs he came,
Whispering still her name,
Tumbling in twenty rings
Into the grass.

Here was the strangest pair
In the world anywhere,
Eve in the bells and grass
Kneeling, and he
Telling his story low . . .
Singing birds saw them go
Down the dark path to
The Blasphemous Tree.

Oh, what a clatter when
Titmouse and Jenny Wren
Saw him successful and
Taking his leave!
How the birds rated him,
How they all hated him!
How they all pitied
Poor motherless Eve!

Picture her crying
Outside in the lane,
Eve, with no dish of sweet
Berries and plums to eat,
Haunting the gate of the

Orchard in vain . . .
Picture the lewd delight
Under the hill tonight—
"Eva!" the toast goes round,
"Eva!" again.*

*From *Collected Poems* (1961) by Ralph Hodgson. Reprinted by permission of Mrs. Ralph Hodgson, and the publisher, Macmillan, London and Basingstoke.

Determine the genre.

A sonnet is a sonnet. It belongs to the *genre,* or class, we recognize as "sonnet"—fourteen lines of iambic pentameter rhymed in certain ways (see next exercises). Recognizing the genre and its conventions will help you understand how well a writer exploits or varies the conventional pattern, especially with such unconventional sonnets as a number of E. E. Cummings's fourteen-liners, which he seems to carve from the conventional sonnet-block. So—if you write about a sonnet, explain how well it employs the conventional form to express its thought, or how it varies the conventional form to express its freedom (and its thought).

Tragedy and comedy are the largest genres. Recognizing to which one a story, novel, or play belongs, or where it lies between, will help you to describe it. Romance is a special genre on the comic side, ending happily, like comedy, but without the laughs and comic foolery and with a high coloration of the wishful and the far away in time and place. Satire, again on the comic side, though more cruel, pokes fun at some social absurdity, allegedly to cure it by laughing it out of countenance. Fantasy is unreality made real, with perhaps a touch of comic fear, as when *Alice in Wonderland* engages our psychic misgivings, or of grim humor, as when Vonnegut's *The Cat's Cradle* freezes to death man's scientific irresponsibility. Fantasy, indeed, may be the predominant characteristic of contemporary literature, as writer after writer projects our overreachings and shortcomings into some horrifying future. Placing any work in its genre will help your reader to understand it.

EXERCISES

7. *Here is Shakespeare's Sonnet 18, built on the pattern he and others derived from the Italians: fourteen lines of iambic pentameter (five beats, ten syllables, alternating light-heavy), organized by alternate rhymes into three groups of four lines (quatrains) with a concluding couplet (two lines rhymed). His rhyme*

scheme is a,b,a,b, c,d,c,d, e,f,e,f, g,g. The Italian is a,b,b,a, a,b,b,a, c,d,e,c,d,e,
with the last six lines often arranged c,d,d,c,e,e, or otherwise varied. Shakespeare,
like the Italians, also organized his rhetoric into an octave (eight lines), which states
the problem, or poses the question, and a sestet (six lines), which concludes the
problem, or answers the question.

> Shall I compare thee to a summer's day?
> Thou art more lovely and more temperate:
> Rough winds do shake the darling buds of May,
> And summer's lease hath all too short a date:
> Sometime too hot the eye of heaven shines,
> And often is his gold complexion dimm'd;
> And every fair from fair sometime declines,
> By chance or nature's changing course untrimm'd;
> But thy eternal summer shall not fade,
> Nor lose possession of that fair thou owest;
> Nor shall Death brag thou wander'st in his shade,
> When in eternal lines to time thou grow'st:
>> So long as men can breathe, or eyes can see,
>> So long lives this, and this gives life to thee.

First, scan the poem into its iambic feet and stresses, as follows:

Shall I / compare / thee to / a sum / -mer's day! /

Does the poem seem mostly regular or irregular?

Are there more inverted feet (–ᴗ)? Are there any, or many, spondees (– –)?

Does Shakespeare use the sonnet's conventional structure to organize his
  statements?

Do his sentences and phrases end with the line-end or run on?

What effect does this have?

  Now, consider meaning: Why will the person's "eternal summer"
never fade?

What does this in the last line refer to?

What significance have breathe and eyes?

What is the essential metaphor, or comparison?

What metaphor do lease and date suggest?

What is wrong with the metaphor concerning the eye of heaven and his gold
  complexion?

Explain fair from fair.

What is the metaphor in nature's changing course untrimm'd?

Explain When in eternal lines to time thou grow'st.

Write a brief essay of explication, using your findings and organized by some thesis about the poem, perhaps that it has remained a favorite because many readers probably do not understand what it says.

8. *Here are two versions of a sonnet by* Robert Frost, *the first sent in a letter, the second as Frost finally entitled and published it. Write out as full a prose paraphrase as you can of the published version, adding explanatory phrases as needed. Then see what you can do to explicate his changes in a brief essay.*

IN WHITE

A dented spider like a snowdrop white
On a white Heal-all, holding up a moth
Like a white peace of lifeless satin cloth—
Saw ever curious eye so strange a sight?
Portent in little, assorted death and blight
Like the ingredients of a witches' broth?
The beady spider, the flower like a froth,
And the moth carried like a paper kite.
What had that flower to do with being white,
The blue Brunella every child's delight?
What brought the kindred spider to that height?
(Make we no thesis of the miller's plight.)　　[miller-moth]
What but design of darkness and of night?
Design, design! Do I use the word aright?*　　　　(1912)

DESIGN

I found a dimpled spider, fat and white,
On a white heal-all, holding up a moth
Like a white piece of rigid satin cloth—
Assorted characters of death and blight
Mixed ready to begin the morning right,
Like the ingredients of a witches' broth—
A snow-drop spider, a flower like a froth,
And dead wings carried like a paper kite.
What had that flower to do with being white,
The wayside blue and innocent heal-all?

*From *The Dimensions of Robert Frost* by Reginald L. Cook. Copyright © 1958 by Reginald L. Cook. Reprinted by permission of Holt, Rinehart and Winston, Publishers.

What brought the kindred spider to that height, *a*
Then steered the white moth thither in the night? *a*
What but design of darkness to appall?— *c*
If design govern in a thing so small.* *c*(1936)

What sonnet-pattern is Frost following? Does he hold to the ten-syllable, five-stress iambic line? What do both poems tell us about the heal-all. Why is this significant to Frost's point? Does Frost change his point? Does he use the word design *aright? Don't miss "white peace" in the first version.*

THE NOVEL AND THE DRAMA

Analyze titles, names, allusions.

A book's title or its characters' names can carry part of the message. Look here for clues to explain to your reader. The "cat's cradle" of Vonnegut's title simultaneously informs us and raises a question. We see in our minds the loops of string interlaced between two hands; we know it is some kind of game, or pastime. In the end, we see it as a symbol of man's aimless and dangerous scientific ingenuity, and its meaningless-ness: "See, no cat, no cradle," as one character says. Browning's "My Last Duchess" tells us, by his title alone, that a duke is speaking, and that he has had several duchesses (a servant could be speaking, of course, but the poem itself soon puts that possibility aside). Look out for these details— and explain them to your reader.

An author may deliberately look for neutral and natural names for his characters, and this in itself tells us that he aims toward realism. If his names seem somehow merely contrived, as in a story that begins "Steph-anie Marsh had spoken to Stephen Blair only once," we suspect the slick and shallow. But an author may also name his characters to tell us what kinds of people they are, or what he wishes them to represent. Fielding's Mr. Allworthy is clearly the ideal worthy man; his Tom Jones, in the very commonness of his name, represents the common human lot. Dickens is a genius at making his names suggestive without labeling his people di-rectly: Podsnap, Gradgrind, Murdstone, Steerforth, Uriah Heep. Introduce your reader to these possibilities. Show how they support your author's meanings.

*From *The Poetry of Robert Frost* edited by Edward Connery Lathem. Copyright 1936 by Robert Frost. Copyright © 1964 by Lesley Frost Ballantine. Copyright © 1969 by Holt, Rinehart and Winston, Publishers. Reprinted by permission of the publisher.

Names may also be allusions. Look up *Uriah* in your dictionary, and
you will discover Uriah the Hittite, an officer in King David's army, whom
David ordered deserted and left to the enemy in the forefront of battle,
so that David could marry Uriah's wife, Bathsheba. A good dictionary will
also tell you that *Uriah* means "Yahweh [God] is my light." Explain
this, and apply it to the story at hand. The creepy Uriah Heep is certainly
the ironic opposite of his namesake: *he* is the treacherous one, as he heaps
up swindles that he hopes will finally include the boss's daughter. Dickens
has alluded, ironically, to one of the Bible's most famous stories. Similarly,
almost any garden may prompt an author to allude to the Garden of Eden,
strengthening his meaning from an even more famous biblical source.
Shakespeare also is a frequent source. When Faulkner names his novel
The Sound and the Fury, he wants us to remember, or discover, Macbeth's
eloquent despair, which ends: "[Life] is a tale/Told by an idiot, full
of sound and fury/Signifying nothing" (V.v.26–28). Faulkner's first section is literally "told by an idiot," the thirty-three-year-old Benjy, whose
impressions and memories flow in sometimes incoherent sounds and
frustrated furies, and the whole novel is a somber comment on life's
fruitless struggles, which seem to signify nothing. Allusions are myriad in
their variety, of course, but keeping alert for them will turn them up, and
will help you explain to your reader what this is all about. Look up every
biblical name—Timothy, Tobias, even Elizabeth—to see if the author may
have had something allusive in mind. Catching an allusion will expand
understanding both for you and your reader.

Look for symbols.

Symbols are a kind of concrete allusion—a physical object that calls
to mind, or acquires, a cluster of meanings—asking you for explanation.
In *The Sound and the Fury,* for instance, clocks and watches recurringly
symbolize the passage and the waste of time, and sometimes the elegance
of good times past as against the tawdry present, sometimes the measure
of time as against the fluid and insubstantial life of memory and thought.
Similarly, a soiled wedding slipper symbolizes spoiled aspirations, empty
institutions, and the failures and hopeless yearnings of love.

Symbols arise naturally from the natural world. Some have become
traditional, accumulating layers of association over the ages—eagles,
doves, snakes, for instance. Others are even more generally and immediately symbolic. A rose, or any flower, immediately symbolizes the
beautiful and transitory. White and black come directly from all our days
and nights. Frost saw a white spider with a dead white moth on an un-

usually white flower, all having come together in black night, as seeming to symbolize some "Design" in the universal way of things.

But unless the author brings his object into sufficient prominence to become a symbol, be cautious: it may be just one more of several objects that together suggest wealth, good taste, bad taste, acquisitiveness, carelessness, or the like. These are not symbols but merely parts of the setting, which you describe as a total impression.

Identify the written voice: point of view.

Every word speaks. In literature, every word is dramatic, since it conveys a human personality, its speaker's, whether that speaker is the author or a character, whether that word speaks from an essay, a poem, a story, or a play. Locate the speaker, assemble in your mind the personality speaking, and then describe it for your reader. The first question any text poses is: "Who is speaking?" The author? A dramatized voice of authority? A character? With Herrick's poem on Julia's clothes, the question of whether the speaker is actually Robert Herrick or some imagined lover is not immediately significant. But in poems or stories where the speaker seems markedly different from the author, the question becomes significant. We know instantly, for example, that Faulkner and Browning are dramatizing an idiot and a duke distinct from themselves. But frequently we must wait some time for certainty as to whose voice utters the enchanting words from the first sentence onward: "She looked around. The world was all white velvet, with nothing beyond. Where were the walls? . . ." The voice may represent one of four speakers:

1. The omniscient narrator
2. A character observing
3. A character participating
4. The protagonist

THE OMNISCIENT NARRATOR. The "all-knowing" narrator speaks in the third person: "she thought; he went; they arrived." The omniscient narrator speaks in a godlike voice, knowing all that has happened, recounting the story, quoting the characters ("she said"), summarizing their thoughts: *Where were the walls?* This third-person narrator—who may be very different from the actual author who is putting him on paper—tells us exactly what he wants us to know, taking us into one character's thoughts, describing another only from the outside, giving us a third only as another character sees him. The voice thus gives us the station—the point—from which we view everything. The narrator seems to locate himself, and us,

just behind the shoulder of one character, or indeed within his consciousness, describing what goes on there, so that our third-person "she" comes
through to us like a first-person protagonist. The narrator may also follow
several persons, like a TV camera that can also transcribe thought. But
the narrator and his omniscient voice can also move off, again like the
camera and its commentator, to survey the large scene or to probe a small
detail somewhere else. His reportage is godlike, and our interpretation
must include both the reportage and the godlike reporter.

FIRST-PERSON OBSERVER. A character observes the action. His first-person
"I" tells us the tale. This "I" is close enough to the principal characters
to know the details, but not so close as to be badly caught in their troubles.
Dramatic irony—in which the speaker does not understand the full implications of what he reports—carries much of the impact. The barber who
tells the story in Ring Lardner's "Haircut" is a classic example. The em-
ployer who tells of Melville's "Bartleby, the Scrivener" is another. You,
as the explicator, explain these implications.

FIRST-PERSON PARTICIPANT. The participating first-person is also observing, of course. The narrating "I" is part of the action, but not the main
character. Conrad's "The Heart of Darkness" is about Mr. Kurtz, but
Marlowe, the first-person narrator, goes through considerable miles of
Congo and throes of activity to get at the enigma of Kurtz. The partici-
pating-observing Nick tells us the story of Fitzgerald's *Great Gatsby*. The
author must weave his participant into the story to get the information we
need, and his skill in making this plausible and evolving his speaker's
personality are what you need to watch and then unfold for your reader.

FIRST-PERSON PROTAGONIST. Defoe's Crusoe tells us all that happened
to him, with some touches of verbal irony at his former mistakes and
limitations. But the first-person protagonist is most effective, again, as
the voice of dramatic irony: he does not understand the full import of what
he does and tells and explains. The speaker, like Browning's duke in "My
Last Duchess," or Henry James's literary thief in *The Aspern Papers*, or
Iris Murdoch's Bradley Pearson in *The Black Prince*, unknowingly reveals
his meanness or other shortcomings in the very act of explaining or ex-
cusing himself. This inadvertent revelation, this dramatic irony, may be
grim, as with Browning, or comic, as with James and Murdoch.

Your analytical question, then, is simply *Who is speaking?* From there
you unfold for your reader what the point of view is—whether
third-person-omniscient or one of the three first-persons—and what that

implies for the reportage. How limited is the view? How reliable the report? How deep the dramatic irony, if any?

Identify the written voice: tone and style.

Tone and style come through together, of course, from the first sentence onward, giving us the author's, or speaker's, tone of voice and the attitude toward his story that this tone conveys. Hemingway's is like a sad bell that strikes a note and floats on in the same mellow resonance from first word to last. Joyce's is immediately ironic, as he looks down on his Leopold Bloom with amused detachment and a touch of scorn. Jane Austen's tone is also that of irony, as she describes her Emma, but warmer and more affectionate. Virginia Woolf's is the yearning inner voice of sensitive perception responding to the wonder and evanescence of life as it passes before us and we pass through it. Their various styles convey these various tones. Look for the typical sentence, the favorite words, and describe them, giving examples, if they are unusual and meaningful enough. You may not need, or want, to describe this for your reader, but you should ask yourself if it is distinctive enough to warrant description.

Determine the setting.

Where are we? As the voice implies its person, it also conjures up a place, even if only some lost mist of nonbeing. Frequently the setting is as dense as a Victorian sitting room, and it conveys the stuffiness of the people who sit in it. Sometimes the setting is so vaguely implied that we must fill it in only with the utmost tentativeness, as with the courtly surroundings that Julia's silks suggest. The setting may signify little or nothing, but you should at least ask yourself *where* and *when* it is, and what, if anything, it does signify—or you may miss a point your reader should know.

Describe the plot.

What happens? Nothing? That, too, is a significant happening. Describe it. Probably the happening is all in the past, put together by re-collections—"flashbacks"—like flashes of lightning vivifying a moment along the trail of the past. Or the story may be highly plotted, one move causing another, invariably different from what the mover intended or we expected, though it may fulfill our general fears or expectations. Describe this too, trying to see how much the author emphasizes chance as against human intention and error. Whether the story is static and open-ended or active and conclusive, something is in conflict. Find out exactly what *is* in conflict. What motives, wishes, beliefs, assumptions collide? Who are the good guys and the bad guys, and what do they represent? Then locate those crucial events, mistakes, moments, that determine the outcome, and ask what the people might have done differently—what and where the crucial mistakes are. These may be the very center of your essay.

In plot, irony of circumstance rides high, since life's contrariness seems to intrigue us. When things go as expected, we hardly notice, and we have little of interest to report. But buy a new car and have it dented, buy a watch for a lifetime and have it stolen the first hour, and you have a tale to tell. Plots are usually a chain of intentions ironically backfiring, or veering off, to the worst, or funniest, consequences. Romeo intends to stop a fight and end a feud, but his intervention kills his friend and seals his own doom. In describing any plot, comic or tragic, or in between, note the force and turn of these circumstantial ironies.

Distinguish plot and plotting.*

An author rations his material. The *plot* is everything that happened—what we would summarize in straight chronological order after we learned the full story—and the storyteller knows its entirety before he begins. The *plotting* is his strategy of letting us discover, eventually, everything that happened, and probably not in the sequence of happening. He must keep us in suspense, in the dark, letting in the light only a bit at a time until the final illumination. What side-trips does he take? How does he delay even as he informs? What red herrings does he drag across the trail to draw us from the scent? Keeping the plot and the plotting distinct will help you to describe the story's effect as it unfolds, and finally achieves its end.

Look especially for those things the author lets us misinterpret. In Austen's *Emma,* Frank Churchill goes all the way to London for a haircut. Everyone, including us, takes this as a sign of his frivolity. He (and Jane Austen) lightheartedly lets everyone cultivate this impression. In the end, we surmise the truth the author never tells us directly: he got his haircut, of course, but he really went to London to buy the slightly mysterious piano everyone has explained in another way. This is plot, after we have assembled all the details. The plotting is in dissociating the two significant details so that we miss their connection, and infer it only after we have learned all the facts of the plot. The author has indulged in, and enjoyed

*This distinction between plot and plotting originated in my "Bridget Allworthy: The Creative Pressures of Fielding's Plot," *Papers of the Michigan Academy of Science, Arts, and Letters,* 52 (1967), 345–356, reprinted in *Tom Jones,* Norton Critical Edition, ed. Sheridan Baker (New York: W. W. Norton & Co., 1973), pp. 906–916.

at our expense, the necessary deception of plotting, allowing room to deepen her characterization of Churchill as well. And we, too, enjoy the deception, as we take in the full light at the end, admiring her deftness and economy, and her accuracy in depicting human personality and human misperceptions. This is the charm of storytelling, the excitement in not knowing, in waiting to learn, in trying to guess and being surprised, until the master storyteller finally lets us fully into the secret. This is the strength of plotting. Your readers will appreciate your pointing it out to them, if it is notably good, as it certainly is in *Emma*.

Characters: individuals or stereotypes?

"Begin with an individual," writes F. Scott Fitzgerald, "and before you know it you find that you have created a type; begin with a type, and you find that you have created—nothing."* The writer has not *created,* in other words; he has merely borrowed a stereotype, a figure so thin and conventional as to be uninteresting or, worse, irritating, because the author thinks he has offered something new when he has given us only the fixed outline of the rich man, the poor man, the merchant, the chief, the Negro, the Jew, the Scotsman, the Irishman—all reflecting the haughty prejudices that produced them. An effective character does seem an individual, a real person, however fanciful the setting, on whatever mission impossible.

But a character must also seem typical of something in the human spectrum, or he will mean nothing. Actually, Fitzgerald is wrong about starting with a type. Probably all good writers often start precisely there— the young lover, the worried parent—and individualize the type as they go, as with Chaucer's marvelous array of types, each vividly individual. The greater the character, the more individualized, the more complex in motives and traits, and yet the more universally typical too, perhaps even *archetypical,* becoming a universal model forevermore, like Don Quixote or Falstaff or Hamlet or Huckleberry Finn.

In analyzing and describing characters, then, look first for their type. Labeling them may help you describe them for your readers—their names may tell something: *Flora* (the goddess of flowers), *Pinchpenny* (the ultimate tightwad). So try to find a label: the budding adolescent, the ineffectual old man, the pushy matron, the wily lawyer. Now you can present them a little more clearly, and show more clearly what energies are conflicting in this fictional drama. Then ask if the author individualizes them or leaves them merely typical. E. M. Forster divided char-

*Opening sentence, "The Rich Boy," first published in two parts, *Redbook Magazine,* January and February, 1926, and now widely anthologized.

acters into "round" and "flat," and the contrast has remained highly useful.* The round character has complexities, contradictions, depths, which make him seem fully rounded into life. The flat character we see only from the outside and from one side, knowing only a few of his typical traits, which remain the same, since his purpose is only to represent something typical. So tell your reader if a character is round or flat, and whether we learn something of his inner life or see him solely in one dimension.

Finally, try to say what individualizes this person, who is, of necessity, also a type. In *Ulysses*, for example, Joyce's Bloom is the typical alienated modern man. He is also Ulysses, tossed on strange shores and seeking home. He is also an Irishman, and also the Wandering Jew. He is a sensualist, who loves scented soap, and eats "with relish the inner organs of beasts and fowls," each sensuality putting a slight but different mark on the negative side of Bloom's ledger. Bloom is also a father seeking the son he has lost, and a jolly good fellow in the pub. In Bloom, we see surprisingly that individuals are bundles of typical traits, the naming of which helps us to define the individual. We apparently individualize the typical by mixing in more typicalities. Any detail of dress, any mannerism that particularizes, any "human touch," as we say, engages our attention because it is typically human. Pinpoint these details for your reader.

Types may also operate powerfully in stylized contexts, as in Japanese No plays, or in those several modern satirical fantasies with characters named Boy, Girl, Stenographer, Machine, and so forth. Describe the odd stamp of these machined abstractions. Conversely, one sign of the great writer is to vitalize some insignificant and momentary character who would usually remain no more than a shadowy type. A highwayman in *Tom Jones* will pay an old woman a saucy compliment as he robs her, and will live forever in her memory, and ours. Shakespeare will let us glimpse an apothecary in Mantua so poor he will sell a deadly poison against his better will, or a soldier in Denmark who knows a piece of farmland when he sees one. These glimpses of vitalized types at the story's edges make the life it portrays broader and more solid. Describe them.

Analyze characterization.

We should therefore explain *how* the author presents his characters. He may tell us about them directly. D. H. Lawrence, for instance, frequently begins with a brilliant, almost breathtaking, summary of his protagonist's situation and personality.

*Aspects of the Novel (New York: Harcourt Brace Jovanovich, Inc., 1927), p. 103.

There was a woman who was beautiful, who started with all the advantages, yet she had no luck. She married for love, and the love turned to dust. She had bonny children, yet she felt they had been thrust upon her, and she could not love them. They looked at her coldly, as if they were finding fault with her. And hurriedly she felt she must cover up some fault in herself. Yet what it was that she must cover up she never knew. Nevertheless, when her children were present, she always felt the centre of her heart go hard. This troubled her, and in her manner she was all the more gentle and anxious for her children, as if she loved them very much. Only she herself knew that at the centre of her heart was a hard little place that could not feel love, no, not for anybody. Everybody else said of her: "She is such a good mother. She adores her children." Only she herself, and her children themselves, knew it was not so. They read it in each other's eyes.*

Lawrence's summarizing characterizations are straight from storyland, with modern psychology added. Most authors shy away from such straight storytelling, describing their characters' appearance—note Lawrence's omission of physical detail—and adding the psychological shading through dialogue and action. But watch out for irony in the author's tone, as when Joyce says "inner organs" instead of liver.

The first question, then, and perhaps the last, is the author's attitude toward his character. Then tell whether he sketches out his portrait gradually, or fills in and colors an initial outline. For your description of an author's method, ask how we come to know his main characters, whether by one or several of the following: (1) how they look, (2) what they do, (3) what they say, (4) what others say of them, or (5) how others react to them. Note especially how your author introduces his characters. Description followed by speech and action? Other characters talking about them first? Dialogue? Inner monologue? These questions will help you explain how your author works, how he puts his portraits together.

Describe the author's blend of narration and scene.

The author tells us what he wants us to know, describes what he wants us to see, and gives us "scenes" of dialogue, in which his story seems much like a play. Each author's proportion of narration to scene,

*"The Rocking-Horse Winner" from *The Complete Short Stories of D. H. Lawrence.* Copyright 1933 by the Estate of D. H. Lawrence, © 1961 by Angelo Ravagli and C. Montague Weekley, Executors of the estate of Freida Lawrence Ravagli. Reprinted by permission of Viking Press, Inc. First published in 1933.

of "telling" to "showing," is different.* Lawrence's tremendously effective "telling," for instance, is much on the side unpopular with modern critics, but his scenes of dialogue are equally compressed and sharp, as in the generalized scene he so swiftly sketches in his opening paragraph: "Everybody else said of her: 'She is such a good mother. She adores her children.' "

So explain how your storyteller handles his scenes. Do they proceed mostly in the author's voice, with astute pinpoints of dialogue? Or are they briefly set, with dialogue carrying almost everything thereafter? In Fielding's *Joseph Andrews*, Lady Booby asks Joseph, her footman, to bring up her teakettle. Notice how Fielding's first sentence moves from description to dialogue with an indirect quotation in italics; his second places it within quotation marks. Then the dialogue becomes direct, with only an occasional descriptive touch, as with Joseph's "Confusion" (Fielding's capitals and italics are typical of the eighteenth century).

> **The Lady being in Bed, called *Joseph* to her, bad him sit down, and having accidently laid her hand on his, she asked him, *if he had never been in Love? Joseph* answered, with some Confusion, 'it was time enough for one so young as himself to think on such things.' 'As young as you are,' reply'd the Lady . . . .†**

Each author moves into his scenes in a slightly different way. So try to describe these transitions especially, and then notice how much, or how little, the author's descriptive comments are present as he sets his dialogue before us.

Consider the structure.

Simply step back from the work for a moment and see how it is built. What follows what? What are the high points, what the transitions? Since all temporal works must begin somewhere, must arch through, or sag through, some middle ground, and then must end somewhere, consider Beginning, Middle, and End. You may find a work neatly proportioned and architectural, constructed in three equal parts, with the center of complexity almost at the exact mathematical center, as in *Tom Jones* or

*This popular and useful distinction originates with Percy Lubbock, *The Craft of Fiction* (London: Jonathan Cape, 1921), p. 62: ". . . the art of fiction does not begin until the novelist thinks of his story as a matter to be *shown*, to be so exhibited that it will tell itself." But Joseph Warren Beach, also writing on Henry James and acknowledging his debt to Lubbock in general, probably popularized the terms: "I like to distinguish between novelists that *tell* and those that *show* ("Introduction: 1954," *The Method of Henry James* [Philadelphia: Albert Saifor, 1954], pp. xxix–xxx).

†Wesleyan ed., I,v.29. First published 1742.

Emma, or in the central scene in the central third act in Shakespeare's five-act plays. Or you may find a work that flows, breaks off, and resumes, to be structured around some physical point, like Virginia Woolf's *To the Lighthouse* or Faulkner's *Light in August.* However it may be, consider the physical construction, and how it contributes to our comprehension of the work. Structure, in itself, may stir you to an essay—it really is, fundamentally, fascinating.

Note the similarities and differences of drama and fiction.

As our terms—plot, character, scene—suggest, fiction and the drama (and film, a vividly pictorial form of drama) share the same stuff of life and its mimesis. The drama tells a story, and the storyteller dramatizes his tale. Our impressions of both, especially if we *read* a play, are so similar that we hardly notice the differences of presentation. But two differences are essential:

1. Drama unfolds in the immediate present; fiction reports something already past.
2. The drama presents directly what fiction can only describe.

Drama is present tense; fiction is past tense. Drama is first person ("I"); fiction is, most frequently, third ("he, she"). The play is before us, minute by minute. The story tells us things that have already happened. Even the narrator's dramatic scenes, which seem to unfold directly before us, as if on a stage, are actually reports from the past (he *said,* she *said*), with the storyteller mimicking the speakers' voices superbly well. But characters in plays (and films) speak *now.* "Now I *am* alone," says Hamlet. "Now he *was* alone," writes the storyteller.

As the narrator's scenes borrow "presentness" from the drama, so the dramatist must fill in some of the narrator's past. How he manages this exposition of past events is an index of his skill. A professional bore called a *nuntius* may come puffing in from Marathon to report triumph or disaster, or Shakespeare's repetitious Nurse may fix Juliet's birthday and age so amusingly in our minds that we do not notice the exposition. Or stark secrets may emerge from the past in intensely dramatic moments, as they do from the lips of Strindberg's Miss Julie, almost at the play's, and her own, tragic end. So look for background from the past (or from across the street a few moments before), and explain how well the playwright disguises its essentially undramatic exposition.

Finally, the drama's "presentness" is physical, it is visual and aural. Music, the dance, gesture, spectacle—royal processions with crowns bestowed or torn asunder—have added meaning to the spoken words ever since the Greeks evolved their drama from pagan ritual. And modern theater, with lighting and sights and sounds at its fingertips, has evoked effects that earlier theaters could approximate only in words, if they could imagine them at all. Your estimate of any play must ponder these wordless effects, or must visualize them from stage directions, estimating what they add to the spoken drama.

EXERCISES

9. *Here is a scene that has proved widely effective on the stage, yet it is almost entirely narrative. It comes from Edward Albee's one-act play* The American Dream, *which he describes as "an examination of the American scene." The curtain rises on Mommy and Daddy sitting on opposite sides of a very dismal living room. From the exposition, as they talk, we gather that, years ago, they bought a child who proved "unsatisfactory" and eventually died. Now they want their money back, and are waiting for satisfaction.*

Write a brief explanation of what Albee is saying about "the American scene" through this stylized "examination" of it. Note especially what he implies by his setting and his brief stage directions. Why "Mommy" and "Daddy" rather than names? How would you have them look and act? What is their relationship like? What is Mommy's relationship with "the chairman of our woman's club"? Why is her husband "adorable"? Why the indistinguishable colors? Why the repeated "lovely"? What is the point about buying and selling? What is the satisfaction Daddy says you can't get today, and what is Mommy's satisfaction? Finally, what does Albee gain or lose by having Mommy narrate the hassle of the hat rather than staging it directly?

From THE AMERICAN DREAM*

MOMMY *(giggles at the thought; then):* All right, now. I went to buy a new hat yesterday and I said, "I'd like a new hat, please." And so, they showed me a few hats, green ones and blue ones, and I didn't like any of them, not one bit. What did I say? What did I just say?

DADDY: You didn't like any of them, not one bit.

MOMMY: That's right; you just keep paying attention. And then they showed me one that I did like. It was a lovely little hat, and I said, "Oh, this is a lovely little hat; I'll take this hat; oh my, it's lovely. What color is it?"

*Copyright © 1960, 1961 by Edward Albee. Reprinted by permission of Coward, McCann & Geoghegan, Inc.

And they said, "Why, this is beige; isn't it a lovely little beige hat?" And I said, "Oh, it's just lovely." And so, I bought it. (*Stops, looks at* DADDY)

DADDY *(to show he is paying attention):* And so you bought it.

MOMMY: And so I bought it, and I walked out of the store with the hat right on my head, and I ran spang into the chairman of our woman's club, and she said, "Oh, my dear, isn't that a lovely little hat? Where did you get that lovely little hat? It's the loveliest little hat; I've always wanted a wheat-colored hat *myself.*" And, I said, "Why, no, my dear; this hat is beige; beige." And she laughed and said, "Why no, my dear, that's a wheat-colored hat . . . wheat. I know beige from wheat." And I said, "Well, my dear, I know beige from wheat, too." What did I say? What did I just say?

DADDY *(tonelessly):* Well, my dear, I know beige from wheat, too.

MOMMY: That's right. And she laughed, and she said, "Well, my dear, they certainly put one over on you. That's wheat if I ever saw wheat. But it's lovely, just the same." And then she walked off. She's a dreadful woman, you don't know her; she has dreadful taste, two dreadful children, a dreadful house, and an absolutely adorable husband who sits in a wheel chair all the time. You don't know him. You don't know anybody, do you? She's just a dreadful woman, but she *is* chairman of our woman's club, so naturally I'm terribly fond of her. So, I went right back into the hat shop, and I said, "Look here; what do you mean selling me a hat that you say is beige, when it's wheat all the time . . . wheat! I can tell beige from wheat any day in the week, but not in this artificial light of yours." They have artificial light, Daddy.

DADDY: Have they!

MOMMY: And I said, "The minute I got outside I could tell that it wasn't a beige hat at all; it was a wheat hat." And they said to me, "How could you tell that when you had the hat on the top of your head?" Well, that made me angry, and so I made a scene right there; I screamed as hard as I could; I took my hat off and I threw it down on the counter, and oh, I made a terrible scene. I said, I made a terrible scene.

DADDY *(snapping to):* Yes . . . yes . . . good for you!

MOMMY: And I made an absolutely terrible scene; and they became frightened, and they said, "Oh, madam; oh, madam." But I kept right on, and finally they admitted that they might have made a mistake; so they took my hat into the back, and then they came out again with a hat that looked exactly like it. I took one look at it, and I said, "This hat is wheat-colored; wheat." Well, of course, they said, "Oh, no, madam, this hat is beige; you go outside and see." So, I went outside, and lo and behold, it *was* beige. So I bought it.

DADDY *(clearing his throat):* I would imagine that it was the same hat they tried
   to sell you before.
MOMMY *(with a little laugh):* Well, of course it was!
DADDY: That's the way things are today; you just can't get satisfaction; you just
   try.
MOMMY: Well, *I* got satisfaction.

EVALUATION

Evaluation sums up the questions we have been asking. Ultimately, all
writing about literature—all criticism, in fact—entails evaluation. Merely
selecting a story or poem to write about is an act of evaluation, since you
are distinguishing it from others of its kind as exceptional, good or bad,
outstanding in some ways, faulty in others. I would not have selected
"Upon Julia's Clothes," for instance, had I not thought it great, and wanted
to find out and explain exactly why. You may wish to explain a novel's
point, making your thesis an assertion of what the novel's implied thesis
is, and this would seem a perfectly neutral kind of exposition. But your
selection has already made the initial evaluation, and your essay will assume that treating this particular novel, whether good or bad, will produce
more illumination than would treating another. Or you may wish explicitly
to take the final step and make your thesis openly evaluative: "This
novel is unusually significant because. . . ."

To discover the thesis of your novel (or poem, play, or film), you
may ask yourself the four essential critical questions:

1. What?
2. How?
3. How well?
4. So what?

These are handy abbreviations for the questions:

1. What is *there?*—describe it.
2. How is it presented?—tell us the author's characteristic ways of
putting his *there* before us. This is the question of technique.
3. How well does the author succeed in hitting his presumed aims
with his technical choices?
4. What does all this effort amount to, really?

The first two questions take you into the area of description, the last two
into evaluation. As you make notes toward answering these questions,

you will develop not only your thesis, but also all the evidence you need to illustrate it. The many ways of addressing the *What?* and *How?* questions, the many elements of a novel, play, or poem to which you direct these questions, we have just surveyed. Now, the most important *what* of all—what does the author imply through these elements? What is his implied thesis, his purpose?

The first of your two evaluative questions—*How well?*—is perhaps a lesser one, of technique and aesthetic effect, of means rather than ends. You may in fact not need to answer it, unless the means—the style, organization, and general management of the book—contribute noticeably to the end, to the book's final power and meaning. Most books are reasonably well written, and you may need little beyond a sentence observing the fact. The *How well?* becomes important only when technique makes an unusual contribution, or when it is noticeably at odds with content, as with a book that is skillfully written but empty, like a clever advertisement. On the other hand, you will occasionally find a book whose lack of art is forgivable because it has something to say. Although Defoe's *Moll Flanders,* for example, is an awkward and cluttered book, its moral vitality has enabled it to endure these two centuries and a half. If you know *Moll Flanders* at all, you understand that by *moral vitality* I do not mean simply "goodness," but any instructive and vital display of the various heavens and hells of existence.

Evaluate firmly—reach a judgment.

The ultimate evaluative question, *So what?*, is one we like to ask but hate to answer. Evaluation is extremely hard, and it is dangerous. When it applies inappropriate standards to something new, it may go badly wrong, as when critics decried Beethoven's dissonance. But warmth of judgment, even though wrong, is better than an eternal freeze of indecision. A mind gathered firmly around a reasoned conviction is better than no mind at all. Try to reach a judgment. Is it a good book (or movie) or a poor one? What does it amount to? What do its particulars tell you about life in general?

Here is a film that takes place in three hours in Hoboken, as two characters search for a lost train and relive their lives, seem to fall in love, but then move off on different tracks, both richer for the experience. It is ably done, perfectly believable, and the characters look and speak like real people. It seems to say that we are all on trains that pass in the night. Well—so what? You know it is good. But to explain to your readers *why* it is good, you must go beyond the movie to what man seems to value in life itself—love over hate, compassion over vindictiveness, sympathy over selfishness, understanding over ignorance—to some perception of the whole agony and wonder of being human.

Here is a book. It has held your attention and moved you, and you feel that it is good. But what has it said, what has it amounted to? What, in short, is its thesis and the worth of its thesis? The story is about a boy in prep school who has run away to the city because everything at school has suddenly turned to ashes in his mouth. Everyone and everything— the whole system—seems false, as if they would turn to dust when touched. He finds the same in the city's more devious ways. But he also comes to see that life, at its center, can sustain its false surfaces if one can give something of himself to others equally lost, if one can find some mutual support in the family. He may not have a stable center himself, but he sees that life does have this center, whereas he formerly saw only a void.

You have been describing, of course, Salinger's amusing and moving *The Catcher in the Rye.* You have summarized *what is there* until you have come to a statement of the novel's thesis. Although working unseen among the details, the thesis also has been *there* for you to find and state, if you are to grasp the novel as anything more than a series of serio-comic episodes. Now you can write your first paragraph:

> **J. D. Salinger's *The Catcher in the Rye* at first seems no more than a humorous, slangy tale about an adolescent boy in a hunting cap, which he wears turned backward for some obscure adolescent reason. We follow Holden Caulfield's escapades in New York City with amusement, and we listen to his wild, earnest slang with delight. How can anyone resist such good entertainment? But as we read on, we discover that the story is not simply funny: it is also pathetic. For all his distraught immaturity, Holden is a very decent person. We soon find ourselves believing he is right and the world is wrong, until finally we discover, with him, that the wrong, empty world can have a center after all, that the center consists in helping the still more helpless, in an act of protective love much like a parent's for a child. In short, at the center of the sham and chaos is a simple affection and understanding that begins at home, in the family.**

In criticism, write in the present tense.

You will notice that that paragraph describes *The Catcher in the Rye* in the present tense. You should continue in the present tense throughout the rest of your paper. The custom and the rule is this: in describing events in plays or novels, or in writing about a poem, *write in the present tense.* Write "Holden *goes* to New York" not "Holden *went* to New York." Likewise you would write "Herrick *repeats* the rhyme" not "Herrick *repeated* the rhyme." The past tense unveils you, as a student and amateur, experiencing the book last night, now in your own past. The present tense testifies to the timeless present in which literature lives, and it also exhibits your own sophistication as critic in recognizing that timeless present. Herrick will still repeat, and Holden will still go, tomorrow and tomorrow and tomorrow (when you and I can no longer do either), and at the same place in the poem or book. And be careful not to drift into the past without noticing, as you recall reading by the midnight lamp, or think of Herrick himself as long since dead. Now, in the present tense, we can continue with Holden.

Describe and explain.

The middle of your "Holden" paper may now well begin by summarizing the *What,* describing the story and the people, in more detail.

> **The story begins at Holden's prep school, on a Saturday night, when ends are especially loose. . . .**

You tell just enough to establish the book for your reader without telling him everything. But do not assume that he has read the book, or you will not explain the action fully and clearly enough.

Next you will probably want to say something about the *How,* since the book's language is not only striking but important. Holden's improper idiom carries us to the truth, which the proper world has apparently lost. Proper speech seems a sham, and the only true language left is Holden's yearning, vivid, improper slang. So you give an example or two of this.

Another important *How* about the book, one that immediately moves into the question of *How well,* arises at the end. There we discover that Holden's entire story has been a monologue addressed to his psychiatrist. His telling of his story has presumably straightened out his perspectives. You would certainly point out this unusual technical feature to your reader, and comment on whether it works. Salinger gives some clues in the first chapter, but are they sufficient to forestall the reader's surprise at the end? Perhaps you think the end a bit too much the gimmick to come off with complete conviction. Nonetheless, you think the book stands up under the sudden strain of its ending. Explaining the strain and the survival will lead you to the heart of the book's value. You will have come from describing contents and technique to answering the question *So what?,* to which your thesis addressed itself, though briefly, at the start.

Here you are, then, at the last section of your middle and just before your conclusion, ready to answer the question that will give your thesis its fullest explanation: how, exactly, does the book assert its thesis that familial affection triumphs over social chaos? Here you explain the title: Holden's hunting cap symbolizes his role. He is hunting for something, and going about it backwards, running away from, rather than pursuing, his problem. More specifically, his cap symbolizes his role as "catcher" in the rye: he wears it backward, like a baseball catcher's cap, though he does not know why he likes it that way. You explain his curious misunderstanding of the song "Coming Through the Rye," his seeing the little boy on a Sunday stroll with his father and mother, happily walking the gutter's edge, his imagining himself waiting in the rye, the savior of little children, ready to catch them just before they fall over cliffs. Then, of course, you describe his little sister, "old Phoebe," and tell how he gives her his hunting cap, and how *she* saves *him.*

Notice that you have not needed to answer directly the devastating final question of value. You have implied its answer. From the very first, everything you have said has implied, "This book is valuable." You have asserted the grounds for its value: its thesis that love, and familial love, can hold the world together. Few would think to dispute that assertion very strenuously. Furthermore, your paper has shown, without directly saying so, that this valid thesis is convincingly acted out, in Salinger's superb mimesis.

Now I have sketched out a number of the various ways you may write about literature, and the questions to ask to get started. Don't feel that you must answer all of them, all at once, for any one paper. I have tried to cover the possibilities, to make them available if, and when, you may need them. Actually, you write in much the same terms whatever you choose to discuss: the importance of a minor character, let us say, or of a particular speech or scene, the prominence of a particular metaphor, the balance and emphasis of form, the force of a style, the difference between two similar stories or poems. You simply assert that something is significant, then explain how this is so, describing what you *see* and quoting for specific illustration. And you shape your essay in the usual way, following the essential psychology of how we take things in, through time: a thesis to guide and organize, a beginning, middle, and end.

EXERCISES

10. *Here is a story by Joyce Cary, conveniently good and short. Enjoy it, with one eye open for significant details to write about. Then check your impressions against my analysis, which follows it.*

EVANGELIST*

John Pratt, fifty-five, on holiday at the sea, gets up one sunny morning, looks from the window, says, "It won't last," and picks from his seven suits the only dark one. He dresses himself with care, and eats for breakfast one piece of dry toast.

"A touch of liver," he says to himself, takes his umbrella and a bowler, and goes for his morning walk along the Parade.

"Why the bowler?" he asks himself. "I'm not going back to town." And suddenly it strikes him that he is bored. "Impossible," he says; "I've only been here a week and my regular time is always a fortnight."

He looks about him to discover some usual source of pleasure in this charming old place; and immediately he is seized, possessed, overwhelmed with boredom, with the most malignant and hopeless of all boredoms, holiday boredom. It rises from his stomach, it falls from the lukewarm air. Everything in sight is instantly perceived as squalid, mercenary, debased by mean use and vulgar motives. The Regency facades whose delicate taste he has so much admired, which bring him year after year to a place neither smart nor quiet, seem to leer at him with the sly, false primness of old kept women on the lookout for some city lecher, willing to set off cracked plaster against lewd dexterity.

He looks at the sea for freshness. But it appears thick, greasy: he murmurs with horror, "The cesspool of the whole earth." He sees the drains discharging from a million towns, the rubbish unbucketed from ten thousand years of ships, wrecks full of corpses; the splash of glitter beyond the pier is like the explosion of some hidden corruption. The ozone comes to his nose like a stench.

He sees from the distance a friend, the Colonel in his light gray suit, stepping briskly. He is whirling his stick—it is plain that he is in his usual high spirits.

Pratt crosses the road to avoid him. A taxi hoots in an angry and distracted manner, but he does not hurry, he would rather be killed than betray the

*"Evangelist" in *Spring Song and Other Stories* (New York: Harper & Row, Publishers). Copyright, 1952 by Arthur Lucius Michael Cary and David Alexander Ogilvie, Executors of the Estate of Joyce Cary. Reprinted by permission of Harper & Row, Publishers, Inc., and Curtis Brown Ltd., on behalf of the Estate of Joyce Cary.

dignity of his despair. The taxi's brakes squawk like Donald Duck—it comes to a stop at his elbow—a furious young man with upstanding black hair and red-rimmed eyes, thrusts out his neck and bawls insults. Bystanders laugh and stare. Pratt does not turn his head or quicken his walk. He accepts these humiliations as appropriate to such a morning in such a world.

The shopping housewives with their predatory eyes and anxious wrinkled foreheads fill him with a lofty and scornful pity, as for insects generated by a conspiracy of gases and instinct to toil in blind necessity for the production of more insects.

Yes, he thinks, humanity is like the maggots on a perishing carcass. Its history is the history of maggots; the fly, the buzz, the coupling of flies, the dropping of their poison on every clean thing, the hunt for some ordure, some corpse, the laying of eggs, and another generation of maggots. Foulness upon foulness. Tides of disgust and scorn rise in his soul; he stalks more grandly; he has become a giant for whom all history is meaner than the dust on his boot soles.

Suddenly he is accosted by a red-faced man, an hotel acquaintance, who starts out of a shop and seizes him by the hand—impossible to avoid this person. The red-faced man is in a fluster. Has Mr. Pratt seen the news? Is there going to be a war, is this it? Should he sell out his investments and pay his debts; should he fetch back his family from abroad?

Pratt draws himself up and out of mere wrath at this intrusion, utters in severe tones such banalities as amaze his own ears. If war comes, he says, it will come, and if not, then not. There are good arguments on both sides of the question. If we believe our freedom is worth defending, then we should be ready to defend it at all costs. For faith is not faith, not what we truly believe, unless we are prepared to die for it. And in a conflict of faith those alone who are prepared to die for what they believe deserve to win. As for bombs, one can die but once. One will die anyhow and possibly much worse than by a bomb.

And all these panic-mongers, are they not more than foolish? Panic is not only useless, it is a treachery—a defeat—an invitation to the enemy within as well as without.

The red-faced man is taken aback by this rigamarole of eloquence. He listens with surprised attention in his green eyes—then with respect. Pratt's unmoved solemnity, his severe tone born of scornful indifference, impress him. He ejaculates murmurs of approval. He says that this is just what he himself has always thought. And this is probably true. He could scarcely have escaped such reflections.

At last he is greatly moved. He turns even redder, his gooseberry eyes shine. He grasps Pratt's hand with fervor and a glance that means, "This is an important, a solemn occasion. You are a bigger man than I took you for. Men of sense and courage, like ourselves, should be better acquainted.'' He departs exalted.

Pratt walks on alone, his step is still majestic but full of spring. He is exhilarated; he looks at the sea and it appears to him noble in its vastness, transcendent in its unconcern, venerable in its intimation of glorious deeds. The houses are like veteran soldiers in line, meeting with stoic pride the injuries of time. The housewives, striving, saving for their families, wear the brows of angels; the battered angels roughly carved on some primitive church. He salutes with heroic elation a world made for heroes. He perceives with joy that it is going to be a fine day, that he is hungry. He whirls his umbrella.

MOOD AND METAPHOR

Opening
Orientation
with Setting

Joyce Cary's brief story, "Evangelist," gives us a picture of a typical English seaside resort, and a typical British personality. We see the unnamed seaside village through the eyes and disposition of middle-aged John Pratt during a short span in one morning of his annual vacation. Cary's story is a gem of playful comic irony. It shows us with unusual wit and clarity how our disposition colors the world and generates our metaphors.

Thesis

Describing
Character-
ization

Cary makes Pratt very amusingly British. Pratt's reference to "town," together with his bowler and umbrella, denote the man from the "City," London's financial district, the heart of London, of England, of former empire. Pratt is a proper bachelor on a proper holiday, scheduled for two weeks annually, at the same time, to the same place. He is affluent and orderly, with seven suits, one for each day of the week, and, one might surmise, worn in proper succession. All are appropriately light in color for the summer holidays, except one, presumably for Sunday. Pratt has awakened to a sunny day but a gloomy mood. He selects his only dark suit to suit his dark spirits.

Summarizing
and
Describing
Events

He breakfasts only on one piece of dry toast. He feels that he has indigestion. He puts on his bowler, inappropriate for a holiday stroll, and takes his umbrella, inappropriate for a sunny day, since he thinks it cannot last. He goes out in the full black formal rigging of the City for his routine morning walk. He feels boredom rising from his stomach. He sees the village, a "charming old place," as the epitome of mercenary corruption and squalor. The calm sea seems the cesspool of the world.

He turns quickly across the street to avoid his friend, the Colonel, whom he sees at a distance stepping along in a light gray suit, swinging his stick in high spirits, the living opposite of Pratt's black gloom. Pratt, disdainful in his mood, almost steps in front of a taxi, "whose brakes squawk ridiculously like Donald Duck," bringing laughter from the bystanders as the uncouth and weary young cab-driver shouts insults. This raises Pratt's contempt for the world, as he stalks grandly on, generating more metaphors of corruption. Life seems nothing but a senseless toil of flies breeding maggots on corpses.

In this mood, Pratt faces a red-faced acquaintance, with opaque green eyes, like gooseberries, evidently not very bright, who is worried about an impending war. From the story's date (1952) and the talk of bombs, we can **Explication** surmise that Cary is placing Pratt's day in the late 1930's, on the verge of World War II. Pratt's contempt for the world, and for his worried acquaintance, now produces a string of platitudes about facing the inevitable. Pratt's platitudes **More** begin to amaze even himself, and indeed they do sound impressive. His friend's **Describing** green eyes shine even more comically in his even redder face as, his worries relieved, he looks on Pratt as a savior.

Pratt is now the comically ironic "evangelist" of Cary's title, the bringer **More** of good news to lift the spirits. "Evangelist" means exactly that, combining **Explication** Greek *eu* ("good") with Latin *angelos* ("messenger") to designate a preacher of the gospel ("good news"), a "Good Angel." Now the evangelist has converted himself. His accidental triumph, which ironically sprang from his sour mood, lifts his picture of himself into heroic majesty, and his metaphors change to match. Now, like the Colonel whose sprightliness grated against Pratt's mood, Pratt has a spring in his step, and he whirls his inappropriately moody umbrella, as the Colonel had whirled his stick. Pratt sees with joy that the day, sunny from the first, will indeed be fine, because now his spirits are fine.

The point of the story is the comically ironic fact that we think we have **Analysis** rational charge of ourselves, and that we think of reality as steadily one thing, out there, at the very time we are demonstrating that accidents of bodily chemistry and chance are controlling us and coloring reality a great deal more than we admit. The actual facades of the buildings along the seafront work **More** nicely in the story to suggest Pratt's, and our, changing façades. They had **Explication** formerly seemed delicate to Pratt. Now, to his gloomy eyes, they seem like lewd old women, an extreme of moral decay. Next, in his heroic mood, they seem like old soldiers, holding their ranks stoically and proudly against the "injuries of time." His metaphorical projection of old women as bad and old soldiers as good, neatly mirrors his conservative bachelorhood. The sea is now vast and transcendent, made for heroes. The housewives have changed from flies to angels "roughly carved on some primitive church." as the new evangelist walks on. His sourness has turned to joy, and we see the cause he does not: he is hungry. His spirits have cleared up his stomach, which they had probably soured to begin with.

Conclusion

Cary's economy makes his story especially attractive. It is barely 1000 words, as against, let us say, 5000 for stories that still seem quite short. He deftly sketches a very amusingly British Britisher, as he also gives us vividly and amusingly the comic fact of how our moods work, in spite of us, and how insignificant and transitory they are. The story's short scope highlights Cary's skill, making its appreciation part of our enjoyment. We see in clear detail his unusually well-educated and pictorial imagination at work on the image-making few achieve so fully. We see clearly his psychological perception and his comic view of the human lot. Pratt—a comic, impudent name—proves to be an evangelist of nothing but the comic human ego.

Restatement of Thesis

Now, with this story and its analysis for suggestion and encouragement, see what you can do to analyze in a brief essay some story you like.

11. *Pick two of Shakespeare's sonnets and demonstrate that one is better than the other.*

12. *Pick two stories from James Joyce's* Dubliners, *from John Cheever's* Stories, *or from any similar collection of stories by another author, and demonstrate that one is better than the other.*

13. *Write an essay on a novel you have read recently, or a movie you have seen, checking your analysis against the four critical questions: What? How? How well? So what?*

14. *Following the same procedure, write an essay on a work of nonfiction— a book of ideas, political, sociological, philosophical, an autobiography, a biography, a history.*

Chapter 10

BEGINNING RESEARCH: USING THE LIBRARY

Now to consolidate and advance. Instead of one thousand words, you will write three thousand. Instead of a self-propelled debate or independent analysis, you will write a scholarly argument. You will also learn to use the library, and to take notes and give footnotes. You will learn the ways of scholarship. You will learn to acknowledge your predecessors as you distinguish yourself, to make not only a bibliography, but a contribution.

The research paper is very likely not what you think it is. *Research* is searching again. You are looking, usually, where others have looked before; but you hope to see something that they have not. Research is not combining a paragraph from *The Encyclopaedia Britannica* and a paragraph from *The Book of Knowledge* with a slick pinch from *Time*. That's robbery. Nor is it research even if you carefully change each phrase and acknowledge the source. That's drudgery. Even in some high circles, I am afraid, such scavenging is called research. It is not. It is simply a cloudier condensation of what you have done in school as a "report"— sanctioned plagiarism to teach something about ants or Ankara, a tedious compiling of what is already known. That such material is new to you is not the issue: it is already in the public stock.

CHOOSING YOUR SUBJECT

Pick something that interests you.

You need not shake the world. Such subjects as "Subsidized College Football," "Small College Versus Big University," or the worth of "A Best-Selling Novel" well suit the research paper—a threefold elaboration of the simple essay involving: (1) the handling of your argument, (2) the citation of others' facts and arguments *as part of your own argument*, and (3) the managing of footnotes and bibliography. Bigger subjects, of course, will try your mettle: subjects like nuclear power, abortion, federal funding, endangered species as against public need. The whole question of governmental versus private endeavors affords many lively issues for research and decision, perhaps in your own locality and your own local newspaper.

You can stir your own interests and turn up a number of good ideas for research by reading the newspapers—*The Christian Science Monitor* is especially fruitful—and by browsing the current magazines such as *Time, Newsweek, Psychology Today, Scientific American, Harpers, Atlantic Monthly, Saturday Review*, and many another. Other good sources are interviews on TV, film documentaries, and even arguments in the coffee shop or bar.

Find a thesis.

Well, then, since you will be dealing mostly with facts in the public stock and with ideas with other people's names on them, what can you do to avoid copycatting? You move from facts and old ideas to new ideas. In other words, you begin by inquiring what is *already* known about a subject, then, as you collect inferences and judgments, you begin to perceive fallacies and to form conclusions of your own. Here the range is infinite. Every old idea needs new assertion. Every new assertion needs judgment. Here you are in the area of values, where everyone is in favor of virtue but in doubt about what is virtuous. Your best area of research is in some controversial issue, where you can add, and document, a new judgment of "right" or "wrong." I have put it bluntly to save you from drowning in slips of paper. Remember that an opinion is not a private fancy; it is an opinion *about* what the right is, what the truth is, what the facts mean. It is a judgment of what *is*—out there somewhere, not merely in somebody's head. An opinion, when careful and informed, is usually as close as you will get to truth: a statement of what the truth of the matter seems to be. Your opinion may be just as accurate as anybody's, and the major task of the research paper is to sift opinions.

Your sifter, as always, is your thesis, right there at the neck of your beginning paragraph. Your thesis, as always, is your essay in miniature. Make your thesis first, *before you begin research.* Call it a hypothesis (a "subthesis") if that will make you comfortable. It does seem unscientific. But it is nearer the scientific method than it looks. The scientist, too, plays his hunches. James Watt saw the steam condenser in the lid of his aunt's teakettle; Donald Glaser saw the tracks of atomic particles in the bubbles of his beer. As with scientific experiment and the simple essay, if the hypothesis proves wrong, the testing will have furnished means to make it more nearly right. With the research paper, if you do not have a thesis to lead you through the twists and turns of print, you will never come out the other end. Unless you have a working hypothesis to keep your purpose alive as you collect, or at least a clear question to be answered, you may collect forever, forever hoping for a purpose, If you have a thesis, you will learn—and then overcome—the temptations of collecting only the supporting evidence and ignoring the obverse facts and whispers of conscience. If further facts and good arguments persuade you to the other side, so much the better. You will be the stronger for it.

Persuade your reader you are right.

You do not search primarily for facts. You do not aim to summarize everything ever said on the subject. You aim to persuade your reader that the thesis you believe in is right. You persuade him by: (1) letting him see that you have been thoroughly around the subject and that you know what is known of it and thought of it, (2) showing him where the wrongs are wrong, and (3) citing the rights as right. *Your* opinion, *your* thesis, is what you are showing; all your quotations from all the authorities in the world are subservient to *your* demonstration. You are the reigning authority. You have, for now, the longest perspective and the last word.

Pick an argument.

The tactics of the research paper, then, are exactly those of any argumentative essay. Any straight exposition can take a helpful argumentative edge: not "House Cats" but "House cats are more intelligent than most people realize." You can find something to prove even in straight description: "See," you say, "this has been overlooked; this has not been appreciated; this has been misunderstood." But you will be stronger yet in dealing with a controversial topic. Therefore: (1) pick a subject in which much is to be said on both sides; (2) take the side where your heart is; (3) write a thesis-sentence with a *because* in it: (4) gather your material around and about the *pro* and the *con;* (5) write an essay with beginning, middle, and end, and with a *pro-and-con* structure like one of those described on pages 32–34.

ORGANIZING YOUR RESOURCES

Now you are ready to dig in. You have decided on your subject and your tentative thesis. Now for the library—which is rationally organized for research and conveniently staffed with experts to help you. You can easily learn the ways of this organization and apply fundamental procedures to virtually any subject you will ever want to investigate. Research in a library is really no more than the logical discovering of information to answer specific questions, a very reasonable lamp with which you play both Aladdin and the genie at the same time. As with all engagements of mind and matter—like the process of writing itself—the process of research permits, and often inspires, creativity. Only when you are confidently in command of the existing knowledge about a topic can you resolve the age-old ambiguities, make the educated guesses, and ask the questions out of which new knowledge and insights are born.

Getting around.*

Take a tour of the building. Your instructor may have arranged one. If not, see what your library does for its public. Some provide self-guided walking tours through brochures or even earphones and recorded voice. Others have videotape programs to explain their facilities, policies, and services. Every library will have some form of handout to help you. In any case, find (1) the circulation desk, (2) the reference room, (3) the card catalog, (4) the course-reserve area, (5) the microform and documents collections, and (6) the current newspapers and periodicals. And get a general idea of where books on various subjects are shelved. Ask someone how to find out if a book is checked out to another person and what to do to have it held for you when returned. Since many campuses have more than one library, pick up a list or map specifying what and where the other collections are. Explore the library in your dormitory. And find out about the local public library: it may be both superb and uncrowded.

Getting equipped.

For efficiency and peace of mind, you need two kinds of equipment for any but the briefest kind of research: (1) a supply of note-cards and

---

*For advice and help in the writing of this section on research, I am heavily indebted to Mary W. George, Reference Librarian, The University of Michigan.

(2) a notebook. The 3″ × 5″ cards used for cataloging are perhaps most handy, but some people like the larger sizes (4″ × 6″ or 5″ × 7″) affording more room for notes and publication data. Cards in several colors can help you segregate information on various sub-topics in your research. On these cards, you record both your bibliography and your notes—summaries in your own words and direct quotations.

The notebook has another purpose altogether: to help you keep track of your progress. For a brief paper researched in a single day, this is no problem. But for any extended investigation, an informal running diary is indispensable. It will prevent you from wasteful repetitions—going through the same periodical index twice, for instance—a common pitfall when several days elapse between trips to the library. A notebook gives you a handy checklist of your steps, from first analyzing your problem to your final double-check of citations. You can cross off the steps completed, rearrange subsequent ones, jot down relevant subject headings, questions arising, new ideas and insights, and generally keep tabs on how your work and thoughts are flowing. Keeping the same notebook for research projects over several terms gives you a kind of homemade research guide of your own. Finally, your research diary is there for that crucial moment when you ask your professor or reference librarian for help, and they say, "What have you done so far?" No one wants to suggest what you have already tried, so you can help them and help yourself by recapitulating your steps. In general, your entries should record the date, what you did, how it worked, and any ideas or leads it gave you.

Start your notebook with a statement of your subject—with your tentative thesis, if you can manage one. Then jot down which disciplines would seem most productive of the answers you seek—psychology, literary history, anthropology, geography, biography. Then go to the library. In the card-catalog room, you will find the two-volume *Library of Congress Subject Headings,* from which you can jot down in your notebook the likely headings to look under in the catalog. Many of the periodical indexes use the same subject-words. By jotting these terms in your notebook, you will save a great deal of trial and error. You may miss whole areas, or think your library has no books on your subject, because you are looking under the wrong headings. A notorious example is the Library of Congress's custom of listing books on World War I under "EUROPEAN WAR, 1914–1917." Suppose you were researching some phase of cybernetics, the study of biological and automated systems of control. Here is the relevant section from the *Library of Congress Subject Headings,* giving you no less than nineteen headings under which you might find what you are looking for:

Subject heading .... Cybernetics
used by Library ⁣ ⁣ sa ⌐Biological control systems
of Congress │Bionics
(note heavy type │Computers
face) │Conscious automata
 │Information theory
"sa" means "see ....⎰Information theory in aesthetics
also": all of these │Information theory in psychology
terms can also be │Perceptrons
looked under for │Self-organizing systems
other aspects of │System analysis
the same idea. ⎩Systems engineering

Ignore terms *x* ⌐Mechanical brains
preceded by "x" *xx*│Automatic control
or "xx" (these are ....⎰Calculating-machines
for use by │Communication
catalogers). │Electronics
 ⎩System theory

These .... ⎰—Juvenile literature
subheadings can ⎱—Research *(Direct)*   *(Q317)*
be added to basic
term.

Analyze the problem.

Your tentative thesis has formulated your problem. But the research-problem needs some analysis into its components to discover what kinds of information it requires and what kinds of places to look for it. Suppose you have decided to research the following thesis:

> **Small colleges provide a better education than large universities because they emphasize excellence in teaching.**

This suggests a number of areas to research. Jot them down in your notebook as you think of them:

1. Statistical evidence: relative enrollment, student-teacher ratios, demographic characteristics, grade point averages. . . .

2. Profiles of typical small colleges and large universities: matched geographically, by public funding, private funding. . . .

3. Comparison of curricula and degrees offered.

4. Placement in jobs, representative careers of graduates.

5. Surveys of opinions of administrators, faculty, students, and parents.

You can probably think of others. Your list, of course, would depend on your emphasis and the length of your paper. The point is not to begin researching haphazardly, without thinking your topic through in some detail, looking for possibilities. You won't use them all, of course. But some of them may provide you solid and unexpected information, and give your paper an air of original and creative thinking. If you have trouble coming up with varying approaches, talk with your teacher, or your librarian, or have a friend brainstorm with you. Discussing your thesis with someone with a different point of view is bound to open new possibilities to explore.

Now jot down in your notebook, for preliminary strategy, the disciplines or fields that seem most likely to yield the information you want. Here "Education" and "Sociology" would seem most central. Then jot down what forms of information you will probably need: books, learned journals, governmental reports, statistics, college catalogues. Now you will have something firm to go on.

Distinguish your sources: primary, secondary, tertiary.

Distinguishing the kinds of sources of information simplifies your researching. A *primary source* most closely and accurately records whatever phenomenon is being studied—a book, a document, an observer's report. A *secondary source* is one step removed, deriving from one or several primary sources. A *tertiary source* describes secondary sources. We might represent them like this:

PHENOMENON	PRIMARY SOURCE
Speed of light	Equation
Depth of the ocean	Measurement
Tribal puberty rites	Data from observation
Speed of human reflexes	Data from experiment
Hamlet	Edition of text
Baseball game	Videotape, newspaper-account, box score

SECONDARY SOURCES

Discussion or commentary on primary source: textbooks, treatises, journal articles, conference papers . . . .

TERTIARY SOURCES
Syntheses and lists of primary and secondary sources:
reference tools, bibliographies, indexes

To get the best coverage, to identify your secondary and primary sources, and to get a synthesis or clarification of the information they contain, you must start with the tertiary sources and move up the chart to the more and more specific. This is exactly the logical procedure you have probably followed many times in the past. Suppose you want to buy an elaborate stereo set, bringing together components of various makes to achieve the ultimate. You begin with catalogues to find out what is available, your tertiary sources. You then read through consumers' guides and the recommendations of experts, your secondary sources. You then draw up a list of the components to investigate further, based on quality, cost, and compatibility. Finally, you go to a stereo store and spend hours listening and asking questions—examining and evaluating your primary sources. When at last you decide on exactly the equipment you want— the primary data of your research, selected and arranged—you go back to the tertiary level again, turning the yellow pages and watching the sales and shopping the stores to get the very best piece of primary data at the most attractive price. Research in the library follows this same everyday procedure, investigating, narrowing, and selecting as the researcher focuses more and more closely on the phenomenon in question.

Get acquainted with the tools.

The tertiary sources are your reference tools. Like a good tourist bureau, they either give you information directly or tell you where to go to get it—they are what the librarians call either fact tools or finding tools. You have certainly already used a number of them:

FINDING TOOLS
Bibliographies
Catalogs
Indexes
Lists of book reviews, paintings, sound recordings . . . .

HYBRIDS
Encyclopedias
Directories
Textbooks
Gazetteers

FACT TOOLS
Dictionaries
Almanacs, yearbooks
Handbooks, companions
Summaries of current events

FACT TOOLS (cont.)   Histories, chronologies
Biographical sketches
Statistical tables
Collections of quotations

Encyclopedias and dictionaries are very handy hybrids because of their dual nature. An article in an encyclopedia will give you not only a vast number of facts and a thorough background, but also citations and a brief bibliography of the most important books and articles, thus serving as a finding tool, too. If someone's initials appear at the end, this is also an important "find." He is an authority. Look him up in the index or contributors' list, which may also cite his important works. You can find more by looking him up in the card catalog. The index also helps you find data scattered through all the volumes. Under "Medicine," for instance, it directs you to such topics as "Academies," "Hypnotism," "Licensing," "Mythology," and so on.

Your desk dictionary is primarily a factual tool, of course, but it also is a handy finder locating people and things in their areas of geography, time, and thought, for further investigation. Along with the usual meanings and derivations of words, your dictionary can give you quickly some needed biographical details, like the birth and death dates of Harriet Beecher Stowe or the real name of Voltaire. The great *Oxford English Dictionary* (twelve volumes and a supplement, abbreviated *OED* in your footnotes) gives the date a word like *highwayman* first appeared in print, and traces changing usages through the years, points both factual and suggestive of other things to investigate.

In a somewhat different sense, a directory—whether a phone book or a list of schools that teach bee-keeping—is also a hybrid since it indicates not only who or what does something but where to find him or it. Textbooks function like encyclopedias; gazetteers (geographical dictionaries), like dictionaries. These are your finders. In general, you will cite your fact tools in footnotes, but not your finding tools, unless, like encyclopedic articles by authorities, they turn out to be sources themselves.

Follow a basic strategy.

In researching, as in buying your stereo, you start with a general analysis and then move in for the particulars. Once you have defined your problem and jotted down its components and possibilities, the intelligent manipulation of factual and finding tools will provide an efficient and creative strategy. You move back and forth, merging the two. You begin with the factual and those seminal hybrids, the encyclopedias. You begin with the factual tools for background. You move to the finding tools for your primary and secondary sources, for your raw data and its interpretation by others. You move back again to the factual tools for support and embellishment. Your procedure might look like this:

(1) NOTEBOOK	(2) FACT TOOLS
The problem analyzed	The possibilities clarified

(3) FINDING	(4) FACT TOOLS
Relevant primary and secondary sources discovered	Your argument embellished

Your topic will require only a few of the many tools available. You have two super-tools. The first is your reference librarian. Come with your problem blocked out in your notebook, and your librarian will probably hand you the tools in fur-lined geniality. The second is the librarian's librarian, Constance M. Winchell's constantly revised *Guide to Reference Books*. You can ask for it at the reference desk, and use it for your preliminary list of sources for your topic. You will probably see your librarian reach for it to suggest tertiary and secondary sources to get you started. The *Guide to Reference Books* follows the logical pattern of research, first sources by discipline, then types of tools in each discipline, finally those beautiful hybrids, encyclopedias and dictionaries.

A STRATEGY OUTLINED

THE ASSIGNMENT: Write an 8–10-page research paper on the major issues surrounding any political conflict of the 1970's, outside the U.S.

TENTATIVE TOPIC: To discuss the background and issues underlying the unrest in Northern Ireland.

TENTATIVE THESIS: Nationalistic forces outweigh the religious in the unrest in Northern Ireland.

YOUR ANALYSIS:

Sub-Problems: History of the unrest in the twentiety-century Catholic, Protestant, and British stands. Close scrutiny of the causes and aftermath of a single incident

Formats: Newspaper reports (primary)
Population and casualty figures (primary)
Speeches and resolutions in Parliament (secondary)
Newspaper editorials (secondary)
Articles and books on the Irish situation (secondary)

Disciplines: Mostly political science, but also history, journalism, law

STEP I: Surveying and clarifying the problem—fact tools and hybrids.

    A. *Encyclopedias,* for both an overview and citations to basic works.

        1. *Encyclopedia Americana*

        2. *Encyclopedia Britannica* (in the "New Britannica" or 15th edition, articles appear in the "Macropae-dia" volumes). Despite its name, this is an American work.

        3. *Chambers's Encyclopaedia* is crucial to this topic because it is British.

    B. *Dictionaries.* Not only would English-language and place-name dictionaries be helpful for this topic, but also specialized ones, for example, Jowitt's *Dictionary of English Law.*

    C. *Handbooks and almanacs.* These are usually one-volume annual compilations of essential facts and figures on such matters as population and governmental organization. Similar compendia for current events are the yearbook supplements to encyclopedias and news summaries such as *Keesing's Contemporary Archives,* a British publication.

    D. *Biographical sketches,* e.g., *Who's Who.*

STEP II: Finding tools, to identify relevant writing by others.

    A. *Card catalog.* Use your library's catalog, thumbing through the appropriate headings as found in *Library of Congress Subject Headings.*

    B. *Bibliographies* on the topic can be found carded under appropriate subject headings, "NORTHERN IRELAND, BIBLIOGRAPHY" in the card catalog or by using *Bibliographic Index* under subject. Bibliographies, once found, will in turn lead to books, articles, and other materials.

    C. Indexes

        1. Newspaper: *Index to the Times* [London] and *New York Times Index.*

2. Periodical: *Reader's Guide to Periodical Literature, British Humanities Index* (like the *Reader's Guide* for Great Britain), *Essay and General Literature Index, Public Affairs Information Service, Social Sciences Index.*

D. *Card catalog again,* this time under names of book authors and journal titles found via bibliographies and indexes, to find call numbers.

E. *Browse* very current issues of relevant newspapers and journals of latest information.

STEP III: Return to factual tools for necessary supporting data.

EXERCISES

1. *To get a sense of how research changes knowledge in quantity and esteem, and of how encyclopedias differ in personality, compare two articles on the same subject in two different encyclopedias. The 1911 edition of the* Britannica *and the most recent one, published and continually updated by the University of Chicago, make interesting contrasts on such subjects as* Egoism, Poetry, Public Health, *or almost anything. Or you may contrast an article in one of the specialized encyclopedias, such as the* Catholic Encyclopedia, *the* Encyclopedia of World Art, *or the* Cyclopedia of American Government, *with an article on the same subject in one of the general encyclopedias like the* Britannica *or* Collier's. *Write an analysis that compares and evaluates the differing treatments.*

2. *Consult the current* World Almanac and Book of Facts, *or some other from the* Guide to Reference Books, *for the date of some memorable event; the sinking of the* Titanic *or the* Lusitania, *Lindbergh's flight over the Atlantic, the United States' entry into war, the founding of the United Nations, the great stock-market crash, or the like. Now go to another collection, such as* Facts on File, *and some of the other almanacs for the year of your event, and write an essay entitled, let us say, "1929"—a synopsis of the monumental and the quaint for that year, as lively and interesting as you can make it.*

3. *Go to the* World Almanac *and see what you can find out about the items listed below. Remember that if you want details about 1979, you must go to the* World Almanac *for 1980. Each succeeding year's* Almanac *will repeat many of the same facts, of course, but it will also drop many, such as last year's postal rates and former presidents of small countries: you must go back to the pertinent year for these.*

1. To whom were the first five Pulitzer Prizes in American Poetry awarded?
2. What was the best selling nonfiction book in 1978?
3. What was the best selling book of fiction in 1978?
4. Who is the head of state, and with what title, of: Afghanistan? Algeria? Canada? Kenya? Mali?
5. Who is the premier or prime minister of: Canada? China? Japan? North Vietnam? Yugoslavia?
6. Find the following facts about Canada: the capital, the population in 1978, the largest group by ethnic origin, the second largest, the smallest.
7. Write a paragraph on the history of Canada, being particularly cautious not to plagiarize (see pp. 268–269).

4. *Look up "Ecology" in the* Reader's Guide, *March 1977–February 1978, and translate the entries into complete statements by writing out the abbreviations. This will help you to use the table of abbreviations in the front of the book, and accustom you to getting the complete information before you go to the card catalog and stacks to find the articles themselves. Then, below each written-out translation, write a full bibliographical entry, as it would appear in your finished bibliography, looking up the article itself to complete the details.*

5. *Choose some subject like "Dog Racing," "Saudi Arabia," "Bowling," "Mushrooms,"—anything that interests you—and write a short statistical report on the listings under this subject in the* Reader's Guide to Periodical Literature *over the past ten years. Does your subject have unusually fat or lean years? What kinds of magazines treat the subject? Can you infer anything from your data about fashions in magazines, or happenings in the world? Go to one article in the most prolific year to discover the reason for your subject's popularity.*

6. *Choose a subject like the origin of man, Watergate (or a similar affair), apartheid—anything that interests you—and compile a bibliographical list of the articles given in the* Reader's Guide, *beginning with the most recent issue and going backward in time until you have eight or ten titles. You may have to look under several headings, such as "archeology," "anthropology," and "evolution," for the origin of man; under "U.S. Government" and others in addition to "Watergate" itself for the Watergate affair; and under "South Africa," "racism," and "apartheid" itself for apartheid. Then look in the* Humanities Index *and the* Social Sciences Index, *and make another bibliographical listing of your subject for the same period. Which articles appear in the* Humanities *or* Social Sciences Index *(or both) only? Which articles appear in the* Reader's Guide *only? Which appear in both the* Indexes *and the* Guide? *Write a brief commentary about the differences in coverage in these two (or three) indexes. What does comparing them tell you about research?* .

7. *Look up some event of the recent past (after 1913) in the* New York Times Index. *Write a paper on how the event is reported in the* Times *and in the other newspapers available in your library.*

8. *Learn to use the valuable* Essay and General Literature Index *by taking the following steps:*

1. What essays on "Skepticism" appeared in books published between 1941 and 1947? Give the author, the essay's title, the book's title, the book's editor if different from the essay's author, and the pages.
2. Now, go to the card catalog and record the call numbers and full bibliographical data on three of these.
3. Look up an essay entitled "Pornography, Art, and Censorship" that appeared in a book of essays published sometime after 1969. Record the entry given in the *Essay and General Literature Index,* then give below it the call number of the book, together with the book's editor, title, place of publication, publisher, and date, all from the card catalog.
4. Find an essay on the moon by Harold Urey, published in a collection sometime after 1968. Again, record the entry in the *Essay and General Literature Index,* and full information from the card catalog.
5. Look up three essays published in anthologies between 1965 and 1969 on Gerard Manley Hopkins, recording each entry in the *Essay and General Literature Index,* and then following it by full data on the book, with call number, from the card catalog.

INSIDE THE SYSTEM

Understand the machinery.

The card catalog contains the library's system. Its 3×5 cards list all the library's holdings—books, journals, newspapers, atlases, microfilms—with approaches by (1) author, (2) title, and (3) subject. The next page illustrates the three kinds of cards (filed alphabetically) on which the catalog lists the same book—by author, by title, and by subject. Some libraries file all cards in one alphabet, so that you will find *Adams, John* and *The Anatomy of Melancholy* and *Atomic Energy* in that order, in the *A* drawers. Other libraries divide their catalog into separate alphabets for authors, titles, and subjects. In any case, drawers will be clearly marked, and cross-references will direct you around.

On the cards in the illustration, notice the call number, the same on all cards for that book, typed by your library according to its system of classification. This number locates the book on the shelves, leads you

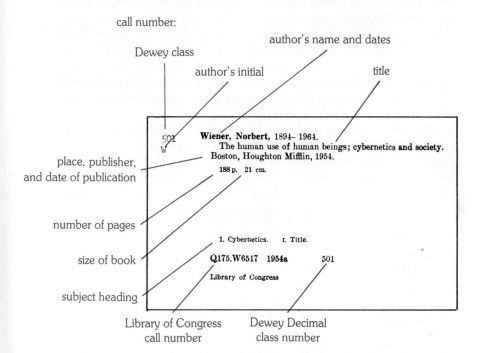

call number:

Dewey class

author's initial

author's name and dates

title

place, publisher,
and date of publication

number of pages

size of book

subject heading

Library of Congress
call number

Dewey Decimal
class number

501
W

Wiener, Norbert, 1894– 1964.
　　The human use of human beings; cybernetics **and** society.
　Boston, Houghton Mifflin, 1954.

　188 p.　21 cm.

　　1. Cybernetics.　ɪ. Title.

　Q175.W6517　1954a　　　501

　Library of Congress

Subject Card

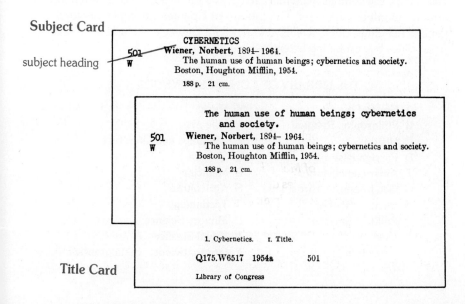

subject heading

501
W

CYBERNETICS
Wiener, Norbert, 1894– 1964.
　　The human use of human beings; cybernetics and society.
　Boston, Houghton Mifflin, 1954.

　188 p.　21 cm.

501
W

The human use of human beings; cybernetics
　　and society.
Wiener, Norbert, 1894– 1964.
　　The human use of human beings; cybernetics and society.
　Boston, Houghton Mifflin, 1954.

　188 p.　21 cm.

　　1. Cybernetics.　ɪ. Title.

　Q175.W6517　1954a　　　501

　Library of Congress

Title Card

to it (in open stacks), and identifies it on your call slip, if you wish to "call" for it. Notice that the subject card is made simply by adding the subject to the top of an extra author card. Title cards are made in the same way. The author card is filed under W (for Wiener), the subject card under C (cybernetics), and the title card under H (Human). You will notice that the bottom of the card shows the Library of Congress's cataloging number (Q175.W6517) and the number from the older Dewey Decimal System (501), devised by Melvil Dewey in 1876, and still broadly in use, as this card shows (501/W).

The following table shows the Dewey system, with its ten divisions of knowledge, easily subdivided by decimals. Bringing order out of confusion, it became virtually standard throughout the United States, and made considerable headway in Great Britain.

THE DEWEY DECIMAL SYSTEM

000 General Works	500 Natural Sciences
100 Philosophy	600 Useful Arts
200 Religion	700 Fine Arts
300 Social Sciences, Govern-	800 Literature
ment, Customs	900 History, Travel, Biography
400 Philology	

But Library of Congress is gaining ground, particularly in the larger collections. Big libraries need more and more subdivisions, to place a book among hundreds of a class. The Library of Congress, using letters for its general headings, offers twenty categories for Dewey's ten, and additional possibilities by combining letters with numbers.

THE LIBRARY OF CONGRESS SYSTEM

A General Works	M Music
B Philosophy, Religion	N Fine Arts
C History	P Language and Literature
D Foreign History	Q Science
E,F American History	R Medicine
G Geography, Anthropology	S Agriculture
H Social Sciences	T Technology
J Political Science	U Military Science
K Law	V Naval Science
L Education	Z Library Science, Bibliography

Letters present some difficulties, of course. *I* and *O* have been skipped to avoid their confusion with numerals, and only three letters stand as initials for their categories. But in the older and the newer systems, you can see some interesting changes in the shape of human knowledge. "Religion" has lost some distinction, now sharing a category with "Philosophy"; "Philology" has became "Language" and has moved in with "Literature"; "History" has proliferated; "Politics" has become a science, with a category of its own. The newer system is far from perfect: "American History" has two letters, for instance, but "Anthropology" shares one with "Geography," which no longer seems its nearest relative. Knowledge, and the categories of knowledge, will change; the stock of books, and microfilms, will fluctuate in proportion; and our librarians will adjust their systems, endlessly and faithfully keeping their cards up to date.

Learn how libraries alphabetize.

If you have ever tried to find your library's file of the *New Yorker*, or the *New York Times*, your heart probably sank before the drawers and drawers in the N-section labeled "New York." The alphabet seems to have collapsed under the dominance of our city of cities. You discover that you need to know a little more than the alphabet to find your way. Here are some finer details of arrangement in the card catalog:

1. Not only men, but organizations and institutions, can be "authors" if they publish books or magazines, as do the following:

Parke, Davis & Company, Detroit
The University of Michigan
U.S. Department of State

2. Initial *A, An, The,* and their foreign equivalents *(Ein, El, Der, Une,* and so forth) are ignored in alphabetizing a title. *A Long Day in a Short Life* is alphabetized under *L.* But French surnames are treated as if they were one word: De la Mare as if *Delamare,* La Rochefoucauld as if *Larochefoucauld.*

3. Cards are usually alphabetized *word by word: Stock Market* comes before *Stockard* and *Stockbroker.* "Short before long" is another way of putting it, meaning that *Stock* and all its combinations with other separate words precede the longer words beginning with *Stock-.* Whether a compound word is one or two makes the apparent disorder. Hyphenations are treated as two words. The sequence would run thus:

Stock
Stock-Exchange Rulings
Stock Market
Stockard

4. Cards on one subject are arranged alphabetically by author. Under *Anatomy,* for instance, you will run from "Abernathy, John" to "Yutzy, Simon Menno," and then suddenly run into a title—*An Anatomy of Conformity*—which happens to be the next large alphabetical item after the subject *Anatomy.*

5. Identical names are arranged in the order (a) person, (b) titles and places, as they fall alphabetically.

Washington, Booker T.
Washington, George
Washington (State)
Washington, University of
Washington, D.C.
Washington Square **[by Henry James]**

"Washington," the state, precedes the other "Washingtons" because "State" (which appears on the card only in parentheses) is not treated as part of its name. The University of Washington precedes "Washington, D.C." because no words or letters actually follow the "Washington" of its title.

6. Since *Mc, M',* and *Mac* are all filed as if they were *Mac,* go by the letter following them: *M'Coy, McDermott, Machinery, MacKenzie.*

7. Other abbreviations are also filed as if spelled out: *Dr. Zhivago* would be filed as if beginning with *Doctor; St. Joan* as if with *Saint; Mrs. Miniver* as if with *Mistress*—except that many libraries now alphabetize *Mr.* and *Mrs.* as spelled, and *Ms.* has found its place in the alphabet.

8. Saints, popes, kings, and people are filed, in that order, by name and not by appellation (do not look under *Saint* for St. Paul, nor under *King* for King Henry VIII). The order would be:

Paul, Saint
Paul VI, Pope
Paul I, Emperor of Russia
Paul, Jean

9. An author's books are filed first by collected works, then by individual titles. Different editions of the same title follow chronologically. Books *about* an author follow the books *by* him.

That is the system. Now you can thumb through the cards filed under your subject—"Cancer," or "television," or "Hawthorne"—to see what books your library has on it, and you can look up any authorities your encyclopedia has mentioned. Two or three of the most recent books will probably give you all you want, because each of these will refer you, by footnote and bibliography, to important previous works.

EXERCISES

9. *Go to the card catalog and pick a card at random. Write down everything you can learn from it about the author and the book. Is it classified according to Dewey Decimal or the Library of Congress? Whichever way, what would its number be in the other system? What general category is it in—Philosophy, Agriculture? What can you surmise from the other numbers and letters of the call number? What other cards have probably been made for it? Record everything you can learn or guess from the single card. Now, find the book itself, and report everything else you learn about it from the title page and the back of the title page.*

10. *Select some well-known literary work:* Walden, David Copperfield, Huckleberry Finn, Alice in Wonderland, The Wind in the Willows, A Farewell to Arms. *Describe how thoroughly it is cataloged by your library. Check cards for author, title, and subject. How many editions does the library have? Is the work contained within any* Works? *How many cards treat it as a subject? Does your library own a first edition? This last may require that you find the date of the first edition by looking up your author in an encyclopedia, checking available books about him, and perhaps checking in the British Museum's* General Catalogue of Printed Books, *or, for a twentieth-century book,* United States Catalog of Printed Books *or* Cumulative Book Index *to discover the earliest cataloging.*

MAKING YOUR CARDS

Your notebook will have formulated your problem, blocked out the likely areas to investigate, and listed some of the tools for the initial dig. It will be a diary of your progress, a log of what you have done on each trip, and the luck you have had. But your actual notes, from which you will write your paper, are much more handy if you put them directly on your bibliographical cards.

Suppose you are assigned a three-thousand-word paper, about twelve pages of double-spaced typescript. Some ten or fifteen sources will probably suffice for ample information and solid coverage, giving your thesis an air of conviction and your reader a sense that you have been thoroughly around the question. As you pick up an author or two, and some titles, start a bibliographical card for each: *one card for each title*. Leave space to the left to put in the call number later, and space at the top for a label of your own, if needed. Put the author (last name first) on one line, and the title of his work on the next, leaving space to fill in the details of publication when you get to the work itself—for books, place of publication, publisher, and date; for magazine articles, volume number, date, and pages. Italicize (that is, underscore) titles of books and magazines; put titles of articles *within* books and magazines in quotation marks. The card catalog will supply the call numbers, and much of the other publishing data you need; but check and complete all your publishing data when you finally get the book or magazine in your hands, putting a light √ in pencil to assure yourself that your card is authoritative, that quotations are word for word and all your publishing data accurate, safe to check your finished paper against. Get the author's and the publisher's names as they appear on the title page, adding details in brackets, if they would be helpful: Smith, D[elmar] P[rince]. Get all the information, to save repeated trips to the library. See the completed cards for a book and an article.

When picking up bibliographical items from encyclopedias and in-

---

828
W60
A43sn
Allen, Gay Wilson

The Solitary Singer :

A Critical Biography of Walt

Whitman (New York: The

Macmillan Co., 1955).

```
AP        Ghodes, Clarence L.
2           "Whitman and Emerson,"
.S52
          Sewanee Review, 37 (1929),

          79-93.
```

dexes, be sure to get all the information they have, translating out fully on your card the abbreviations they are apt to use, and leaving space to fill in full names, publishers, dates, and so forth, when you look at the book or article itself. You will usually find lists of abbreviations inside the front cover or in the first few pages. Here is an entry from the *Reader's Guide to Periodical Literature,* for example:

> **GAMBLING**
> It's bye! bye! blackjack. D. E. Scherman. il Sports Illus 20:18-20 +
> Ja 13 '64

By consulting the list of abbreviations and the accompanying explanatory guide, you learn that the article is illustrated ("il") and in volume 20, which you may need for finding it. You also learn that the article continues on back pages: "18–20 +—which you would complete after you had found the article and read it through, as: "pp. 18–20, 43, 46–47." Your initial translated bibliographical card would come out like this:

> **Scherman, D. E., "It's Bye! Bye! Blackjack,"** *Sports Illus-*
> *trated,* **January 13, 1964, pp. 18–20. . . .**

If you forget to write out as full a translation as you can on your biblio-graphical card, while you have the index in front of you, you may not understand the abbreviations when going to find the magazine or writing your bibliography.

Take brief notes.

Many people dislike putting notes on bibliographical cards. But I find the economy well worth the slight clutter. Limiting yourself to what you can put on the front and back of one bibliographical card will restrain your notes to the sharp and manageable. You can always add another note-card if you must. If you find one source offering a number of irresistible quotations, put each one separately on a 3 × 5 card (with author's name on each), so you can rearrange them later for writing. You can use some obvious abbreviations to save space and time— *&* for "and," for instance—as long as you remember that they are your own, standing for full words in your source.

However you do it, keep your notes brief. Read quickly, with an eye for the general idea and the telling point. Holding a clear thesis in mind will guide and limit your note taking. Some of your sources will need no more than the briefest summary: "Violently opposed, recommends complete abolition." This violent and undistinguished author will appear in your paper only among several others in a single footnote to one of your sentences: "Opposition, of course, has been tenacious and emphatic.²"

Suppose you are writing a paper to show that great books are usually not recognized at first (as the student in our sample paper did, pp. 289–304). You find in Randall Stewart's biography of Hawthorne that *The Scarlet Letter* was very well received. Here is a perfect piece of opposition, a *con,* to set your thesis against, to explain and qualify. But don't copy too much. Summarize the author's point, jot down some facts you might use, and copy down directly, within distinct quotation marks, only the most quotable phrase: "The leading critics were lavish in their praise."

Let us assume, however, that you and your instructor prefer keeping bibliographical cards and note-cards separate. (He may also suggest that you write on the front of each card only, for the easiest arranging for writing.) See at the right three note cards that you have labeled for sorting. Since you have the author's name, the book's title, and all the publishing data in full on your bibliographical card, you identify the author only briefly at the foot of the card.

Take care with page numbers. When your passage runs from one page to the next—from 29 over onto 30, for instance—put "(29–30)" after it, *but also mark the exact point where the page changed.* You might want to use only part of the passage and then be uncertain as to which of the pages contained it. An inverted L-bracket and the number "30" after the last word of page 29, will do nicely: "All had ⌐**30** occurred earlier." Do the same even when the page changes in mid-word with a hyphen: "having con- ⌐**21** vinced no one."

When preparing a research paper on a piece of literature, you would also make a bibliographical card for the edition you are using, and would

Hawthorne – Info

"One day a big man, with a broken beard and shining brown eyes, who bubbled over with enthusiasm and fun, made his appearance and talked voluably about something & went away again, & my father & mother smiled at each other. _The SL_ had been written, & James T. Fields had read it, & declared it the greatest book of the age." ✓

Hawthorne, Julian p. 18 ✓

Hawthorne - Con

E. P. Whipple (_Graham's Mag._) answered objections of gloominess: "The Custom House" showed H's ability to mix tragedy and comedy, like Shakespeare, but hopes "pathos and power" will be "more relieved by touches of that beautiful and peculiar humor, so serene and searching, in which he excells almost all living writers." ✓ – in his next book.

Stewart, p. 97 ✓

Hawthorne - Pro

"A group of hostile critics were violently proclaiming ... the gross immorality of the book." _Brownson's Review_, by Orestes A. Brownson, led the attack: "There is an unsound state of public morals when the novelist is permitted, without a scorching rebuke, to select such crimes, & to invest them with all the fascination of genius, & all the charms of a highly polished style." ✓

Stewart, p. 97 ✓

probably need a number of note-cards for summaries and quotations from the work itself—one card for each item, for convenience in sorting.

Take care against plagiarism.

Plagiarism is presenting someone else's work as your own. Since in research you will be dealing with what others have written, and with a number of ideas already stated and shared, plagiarism, inadvertent or intentional, may seem hard to avoid. But simple honesty will guide you, and care in your note-taking will protect you. Actually, care against plagiarizing will make your research self-evidently more solid and thorough. If you borrow an idea, footnote your source (see pp. 274–279 for footnoting). If you have an idea of your own and then discover that someone has beaten you to it, swallow your disappointment and footnote your predecessor, seeing what more you can add to get back some of your own. Or you can keep even more of your own by saying, in footnote, "I discover that James Smith agrees with me on this point," explaining, if possible, what Smith has overlooked, or his differing emphasis, and again giving a full citation of Smith's article for all future reference.

In taking notes, copy out possible quotations accurately, with full details of source and page, and mark them clearly so that you will know they are quotations later. Quote them directly in your paper, and footnote your source:

```
According to Freud, establishing the ego is

a kind of "reclamation work, like the

draining of the Zuyder Zee."1
```

```
    1New Introductory Lectures on Psycho-
Analysis, trans. W. J. H. Sprott (New York:
W. W. Norton & Co., 1933), p. 112.
```

The author's name does not appear in the footnote because I have already named him in my text, which is the best place. Notice also that I have quoted the shortest possible segment of Freud's sentence to get the sharpest focus, and that I have run it into my own sentence within quotation marks. You would indent and single-space a long quotation, and omit the quotation marks: for further details see, pp. 68–69.

Or you may quote indirectly, rephrasing unmistakably in your own words:

```
Freud likens psychotherapy to reclaiming

territory from the sea.1
```

The danger lies in copying out phrases from your source as you summarize what it says, and then incorporating them in your essay, with or without realizing that those phrases are not yours. The solution is, again, to take down and mark quotations accurately in your notes, or to summarize succinctly in your own words, words as far away from the original as possible, keeping the two as distinct as you can, so that nothing from your source will leak through your notes, unmarked, into your paper, arousing your reader's suspicions. Remember that the word *plagiarism* comes from the Latin word for kidnapping (from *plaga,* "net"), and that it is indeed a crime—one that can bring lawsuits and expulsions from college. Remember, too, that your instructor can almost invariably detect changes in your vocabulary and style that indicate a kidnapping of someone else's brainchild. Be honest, and your papers and prose will reflect that honesty.

EXERCISES

11. *Go to the card catalog and find* PMLA: Publications of the Modern Language Association of America. *(This contains the world's most comprehensive literary bibliography, listing the annual international crop of scholarly articles and books on literary subjects.) Then, from the shelf, pick Vol. 84 (1969), which contains the "1968 MLA International Bibliography." Now, give the full bibliographical form of the first four entries concerning Emily Dickinson. Again, you will have to consult the list of abbreviations at the front of the magazine, completing your entries—and checking them—by consulting the works themselves. Do the same for any British author of your own choosing.*

Chapter 11

WRITING THE RESEARCH PAPER

YOUR FIRST DRAFT

Plot your course.

Formal outlines, especially those made too early in the game, can take more time than they are worth, but a long paper with notes demands some planning. First, draft a beginning paragraph, incorporating your thesis. Then read through your note-cards, arranging them roughly in the order you think you will use them, getting the opposition off the street first. If your thesis is strongly argumentative, you can sort into three piles: *pro's, con's,* and *in-between's* (often simple facts). Now, by way of outline, you can simply make three or four general headings on a sheet of paper, with ample space between, in which you can jot down your sources in the order, *pro* and *con,* that is best for your argument. The very act of ordering your thoughts and notes through such an arrangement will bring your thesis to sharp focus, if its edges have been uncertain before. Our paper on the American classics would block out something like this:

I.   Generally poor reception

PRO	CON
	Hawthorne's instant fame
But gloom, indecency	
	Henry James
Declining sales Uncle Tom Ben Hur	

II. Melville's poor sales
     Hostile English reviews

	London Herald Lewes The first six days in America
But hostility, then silence	

III.

	Praise for Thoreau
But not unanimous (Canby) Poor sales-- Lamplighter Canby--nature reading	
	George Eliot Recognition abroad

IV. Whitman unknown

	Emerson Thoreau Lincoln Notoriety

Outline more fully, if you wish.

   You can easily refine this rough blocking (probably more nearly complete here than yours would actually be) into a full topic outline, one that displays your points logically, not necessarily in the actual sequence of your writing. The principle of outlining is to rank equivalent headings—keeping your headings all as nouns, or noun phrases, to make the ranks apparent (see pp. 40–43, and the full outline on p. 289).

But, *begin to write soon.* You have already begun to write, of course, in getting your thesis down on paper, and then drafting a first paragraph to hold it. Now that you have blocked out your argument, however roughly, plunge into your first draft.

Put in your references as you go.

Your first draft should have all your footnotes, abbreviated, right in the text. Otherwise you will lose your place, and go mad with numbers. Put the notes at the *end* of the last pertinent sentence or word, with as many references as possible grouped in one note. Make your quotations in full, all distinctly set within quotation marks, and include the author's surname and the page number with each citation. You will change these in your final draft, of course, filling in the names or leaving them out of the note altogether if they appear in the text. But it will help you in checking against your cards to have an author's name and a page number for each citation. *Don't number your footnotes yet.* When your draft is finished, add the numbers in pencil, so you can change them; circle them in red pencil, so you can see them. As you type along, mark your notes with triple parentheses: (((. . .)))—the easiest distinction you can make. See page 294 for a sample first-draft page, with its accompanying transformation into smooth and final copy.

YOUR FINAL DRAFT

Reset your long quotations.

Your final draft will change in many ways, as the rewriting polishes up your phrases and turns up new and better ideas. But some changes are merely presentational. The triple parentheses of your first draft will disappear, along with the quotation marks around the *long* quotations, since you will single-space and indent, *without quotation marks,* all quotations of more than fifty words, to simulate the appearance of a printed page. You will do the same with shorter quotations, if you want to give them special emphasis, and also with passages of poetry. Some instructors prefer, and some handbooks recommend, that you double space your long inset quotations, setting them off by triple spacing, above and below, as you would with an essay submitted for publication. Either way, if your quotation begins as a paragraph, indent its first line farther, to reproduce the paragraphing. Again, pp. 294–295 show how a first-draft quotation is transformed in the final draft. Check the rules about quotation marks on pp. 391–393. Use brackets for inserting your own words within a quotation. See pp. 390–391.

Allow space for notes at the foot of the page.

Some instructors like footnotes gathered all together in a section at the end, as they would be in a manuscript prepared for the printer. But many prefer them at the foot, where the reader can see them, as if on a printed page. From your preliminary draft, you can see about how many footnotes will fall on your page, and about how much space to allow at the bottom. Allow plenty. You will begin your notes three spaces below your text (you have been double-spacing your text). Do *not* type a solid line between text and notes: this indicates a footnote continued from the preceding page. Single-space each note, but double-space between notes. Indent as for a paragraph. Type the number, then roll down about half the height of a capital letter, and begin typing your note immediately at the next letter-space:

```
4Stewart, p. 97.
```

After the first line, notes return to the left margin, as in paragraphs.

Footnotes carry only information not mentioned in the text. At first mention in text or note, give your author's full name, in normal order—"Randall Stewart"—and use only his last name thereafter. (Your alphabetized bibliography will give last name first.) If your text names the author, the note carries only the title of his work, the publishing data, and the page number. If your text names the author and his work, the note carries only the publishing data and the page number. Once you have cited a source, you can put the page numbers of further citations directly in your text, within parentheses. Note in the first of the following two examples where the quotation marks go and how the period (like the comma) follows the parenthesis:

```
     Henry James describes how the book "was

 a great success, and [Hawthorne] immediately

 found himself famous" (p. 108).
```

```
Henry James (p. 108) describes the book's

success.
```

At the end of a long indented, single-spaced quotation from a work already cited, the page number in parentheses *follows* the period (see the inset quotations in our sample paper):

```
. . . had a mysterious charm. (p. 108)
```

Make and punctuate your footnotes meticulously.

The three principal kinds of references produce three forms of footnotes:

BOOK

```
¹Watson G. Branch, Melville, The Critical
Heritage (London and Boston: Routledge &
Kegan Paul, 1974), p. 2.
```

QUARTERLY MAGAZINE

```
²Ernest W. Baughman, "Public Confession
and The Scarlet Letter," The New England
Quarterly, 40 (1967), 548–49.
```

When giving the volume number, "40," you omit the "p." or "pp." before page numbers. (If such a periodical numbers its pages by issue rather than volume, give volume *and* issue numbers: "... *Affairs*, 16, No. 3 (1967), 145–52.") With consecutive page numbers, hyphenated, give the full second number up through 99. For larger numbers, use only the last two figures of the second if it is in the same hundred or thousand: 27–29 (not 27–9), 107–08, 695–907, 999–1006, 1006–09, 1503–601.* Convert all Roman volume numbers into Arabic: "XL" becomes "40."

POPULAR MAGAZINE OR NEWSPAPER

Popular Magazine

```
³Norman R. Collins, "More Frenzied
Fiction," News Chronicle, 20 Apr. 1931, p. 4.
```

Ignore volume number, if any. As in this last example, give the full date for a popular magazine, instead of volume number and year, and *use no parentheses*. Newspaper articles sometimes need more detail:

---

*This rule, and these examples of footnoting, reflect the current usage of the Modern Language Association of America. In the text, I have retained full consecutive numbers for slightly more clarity, and less chance for error.

Newspaper
Article

```
    4"The Trouble with Fiction" (editorial),
New York Times, 10 Apr. 1984, Sec. 4, p. 8.
```

Notice the comma here: omitted after "Fiction" and inserted after the parenthesis. Do the same with any parenthetical explanation of a title. With this newspaper, you need to give the section number because each section begins numbering anew.

Here are some further complications:

One Source
Quoting
Another

```
    5Abraham B. Caldwell, "The Case for a
Streaming Consciousness," American Questioner,
20 June 1979, p. 37, quoted in Albert N.
Mendenhall, Modern Commentary (Princeton:
Little House, 1979), p. 308.
```

You have found the quotation in Mendenhall's book.

Quotation
from Article in
Edited
Collection

```
    6D. C. Hill, "Who Is Communicating
What?" in Essays for Study, ed. James L.
McDonald and Leonard P. Doan (New York:
Appleton Hall, 1973), p. 214.  Reprinted from
Era, 12 (1972), 9-10.
```

McDonald and Doan have edited the collection, or casebook. Note that a title ending in a question mark should not take a comma.

Citation from
Volume in
Series of
Bound Books

```
    7David R. Small, "The Telephone and
Urbanization," in Annals of American
Communication, ed. Walter Beinholt (Boston:
Large, Green and Co., 1969), III, 401.
```

The *Annals of American Communication* is a series of bound books, not a magazine: the volume number is in Roman numerals, and it *follows* the parenthesis. Had this been a magazine, the entry would have omitted the "in," the editor, and the place of publication, and would have read ". . . *Annals of American Communication,* 3 (1969), 401."

You indicate books without place or date of publication as follows:

No Place of
Publication

```
    8Annette Segal, The Question of Rights
(n.p.: Bell Press, 1983), p. 16.
```

No Date of
Publication

```
    9Annette Segal, The Question of Wrongs
(San Francisco: Bell Press, n.d.), p. 17.
```

The point is to give the fullest information available, and to indicate what the title page and its back (the copyright page) omit.

Abbreviation
of Familiar
Title

10Arnold Peters, "Medicine," Encyc.
Brit., 11th ed.

Abbreviate familiar titles, so long as they remain clear. You need neither volume nor page numbers in alphabetized encyclopedias; and only the number (*or the year of publication*) of the edition you are citing, without parentheses. Here the article was initialed "A.P.," and you have looked up the author's name in the contributors' list.

11"Prunes," Encyc. Brit., 11th Ed.

Here the article was not initialed.

Quotation in
Title

12George L. Gillies, "Robert Herrick's
'Corinna,'" Speculation, 2 (1881), 490.

This hypothetical example shows where to put the comma when the title of a magazine article ends in a quotation, and you have to use both single and double quotation marks. Gillies's original title would have looked like this: Robert Herrick's "Corinna."

Editions sometimes need more detail if you are citing only a preface, introduction, foreward, or afterword:

Afterword

13Colby Quackenbush, Afterword [no
quotation marks], The Scarlet Letter, by
Nathaniel Hawthorne (New York: Dunne Bros.,
Inc., 1984), p. 481.

Introduction

14John Quirk Haskell, Introd.
[abbreviated], The Dog's Eye, by Sarah Kettle
(Philadelphia: Bleak House, Inc., 1983),
p. xxi.

Your first footnote identifying a quotation from this edition would look like this (if including the chapter is significant to the point you are making):

15Sarah Kettle, The Dog's Eye, introd.
John Quirk Haskell (Philadelphia: Bleak House,
Inc., 1983), Ch. xiii (p. 183).

If you do not need the chapter, that note would end: **. . . Inc., 1983), p. 183.** Here is a more conventional citation:

¹⁶Romeo <u>and</u> <u>Juliet</u> II.iii.94, in <u>An</u>
<u>Essential</u> <u>Shakespeare</u>, ed. Russell Fraser
(New York: Prentice-Hall, 1972).

Play

Note the absence of the comma after the play's title, and the periods and close spacing between Act.scene.line. Subsequent references would go directly in your text within parentheses: (IV.iii.11–12). Or, if you are quoting several of Shakespeare's plays: (*Romeo* IV.iii.11–12). See further instructions below (pp. 282–283).

¹⁷P[aul] F[riedrich] Schwartz, <u>A</u> <u>Quartet</u>
<u>of</u> <u>Thoughts</u> (New York: Appleton Hall, 1943),
p. 7.

Added Details

¹⁸[George H. Lewes], "Percy Bysshe
Shelley," <u>Westminster</u> <u>Review</u>, 35 (April
1841), 303-44.

These two footnotes show how to use brackets to add details not actually appearing in the published work. Of course, famous initials are kept as initials, as with T. S. Eliot, H. G. Wells, or D. H. Lawrence. You also need brackets to replace parentheses when your comments in a footnote require a parenthesis around your entire source:

¹⁹. . . (cited in John E. Basset,
<u>William</u> <u>Faulkner</u>: <u>An</u> <u>Annotated</u> <u>Checklist</u> <u>of</u>
<u>Criticism</u> [New York: David Lewis, 1972],
p. 35).

**Entire Source
in Parentheses**

Pamphlets and other oddities just require common sense:

²⁰"The Reading Problem," mimeographed
pamphlet, Concerned Parents Committee, Center
City, Arkansas, 25 Dec. 1975, p. 8.

Pamphlets

²¹U. S. Congress, House Committee on
Health, Education, and Welfare, <u>Racial</u>
<u>Integration</u>, 101st Cong., 2nd sess., 1969,
H. Rep. 391 to accompany H. R. 6128.

Pamphlets like these you must play by instinct, including all the details, as briefly as possible, that would help someone else hunt them down.

Recordings, films, and tapes also require some ingenuity. Do not cite microfilms and other reproductions of things in print. Simply cite the book, article, or newspaper as if you had it in hand. But other media are forms of publications in themselves, to be cited as clearly as possible if you use them. The American Library Association* recommends the following ways of citation:

MOTION PICTURE
[22]Valley Forge [Motion Picture] (New York: Steve Krantz Productions, Released by Encyclopaedia Britannica Educational Corp., 1972).

DISC
[23]Eugene O'Neill, Long Day's Journey into Night [Sound Recording] (Caedmon, [1972], 3 discs TRS350), Disc 3, Side 2.

FILMSTRIP
[24]Limericks [Filmstrip], Enjoying Poetry (Jamaica, N.Y.: Eye Gate House, 1964), Frame 27.

TAPE
[25]Herbert Frank York, The Missile Race— Destination Unknown [Sound Recording] (Santa Barbara, Calif.: Center for the Study of Democratic Institutions, [1972], Tape No. 576.

[26]Rachael McDuff, "Interpreting the Media" [Sound Recording], Lecture presented at the Department of Journalism, Winston State College, 20 Apr. 1980.

CASSETTE
[27]"Ree-deep, ribbid": Herpetologist Charles Bogard Studies the Frog and Its Call [Sound Recording] (Center for Cassette Studies, 1971), Cassette 010 13460.

---

*Eugene B. Fleischer, *Style Manual for Citing Microform and Nonprint Media* (Chicago: American Library Association, 1978).

These examples, together with the footnotes in our sample research paper (next chapter), should cover most footnoting problems, or suggest how you can meet them.

EXERCISES

1. *Assume that you are quoting the following passage in its entirety, and that you have not mentioned it, or its author, earlier in your paper. Devise a sentence to introduce the passage, quote the passage and give it a footnote-number, then write a footnote covering the necessary bibliographical data. The author is Gilbert K. Chesterton. The book, Heretics, was published in 1905 by John Lane, in London. The passage is on page thirty-eight:*

> When Byron divided humanity into the bores and bored, he omitted to notice that the higher qualities exist entirely in the bores, the lower qualities in the bored, among whom he counted himself. The bore, by his starry enthusiasm, his solemn happiness, may, in some sense, have proved himself poetical. The bored has certainly proved himself prosaic.

2. *Now write a sentence referring to Chesterton's point that a bore may be poetical, quoting directly only the phrase* his starry enthusiasm. *Assume that you have already fully cited Chesterton, and give your reader whatever bibliographical information this new quotation demands.*

3. *Write four footnotes illustrating the four different kinds of sources, described below, for the same hypothetical fact:* 300 dropouts annually.

1. You found this in an article with these characteristics:

   Quarterly magazine entitled: Schools and Scholars
   Volume number: Forty-nine
   Author: Gladys P. Spencer
   Page: One hundred three
   Date: January 1976
   Title: Our Local Schools

2. Write the same footnote as if the magazine were a popular weekly dated January 10, 1976.
3. Write the same footnote to your statistic as if you had found it, together with a full citation of this article in the popular monthly, on page 460 of a book entitled *Education for Educators* by Featherbush Brown published in Philadelphia in 1980 by the P. J. Slacks Company, Incorporated.
4. Write the same footnote assuming that you found Spencer's statistic on page forty-nine in a collection of essays entitled *Readings for Reading*, which Beatrice

Long and Bernard Short edited, and which the Grimm Publishing Company produced in 1980, in New York City.

4. *W. L. Cranberry has written the following two studies, both of which you want to cite:*

Book: The Dying Locomotive

Article: Transportation No Problem

First, write a footnote for the book—Verity and Company published it in Miami in 1981—in which you inform your reader that the author's full name is Walter Lightfoot Cranberry. You have quoted from page one.

Next, assume that you have already given the first full citation for both the book and the article. Now write footnotes 3 and 4, footnote 3 for the book, footnote 4 for the article, making up and providing suitable page numbers.

Abbreviate your references after the first full citation.

Three old favorite abbreviations are now mercifully out of style. Do NOT USE:

ibid.—*ibidem* ("in the same place"), meaning the title cited in the note directly before. Instead, USE THE AUTHOR'S LAST NAME, AND GIVE THE PAGE.

op. cit.—*opere citato* ("in the work cited"), meaning a title referred to again after other notes have intervened. Again, USE THE AUTHOR'S LAST NAME INSTEAD, AND GIVE THE PAGE: "Stewart, p. 97." If you have two Stewarts, simply include their initials. If Stewart has two articles or books on Hawthorne, devise two convenient short titles for subsequent references:

²Stewart, <u>Hawthorne</u>, p. 97.

³Stewart, "Symbols," p. 301.

loc. cit.—*loco citato* ("in the place cited"). Simply repeat the page number: ". . . as Smith says (p. 62). He cites, however, some notable exceptions (p. 62)."

But two old standbys are still used and especially useful (do *not* italicize them):

cf.—*confer* ("bring together," or "compare"); do not use for "see."

et al.—*et alii* ("and others"); does not mean "and all"; use after the first author in multiple authorships: "Ronald Elkins et al."

Two more Latin terms, also not italicized, are equally handy:

passim—Not an abbreviation, but a Latin word meaning "throughout the work; here and there." Use when a writer makes the same point in many places within a single work; use also for statistics you have compiled from observations and tables scattered throughout his work.

sic—a Latin word meaning "so"; "this is so"; always in brackets—[sic]—because used only within quotations following some misspelling or other surprising detail to show that it really was there, was "so" in the original and that the mistake is not yours.

Other useful abbreviations for footnotes are:

c. or **ca.**	*circa,* "about" (c. 1709)
Ch., Chs.	chapter, chapters ("Ch. iii"—lowercase Roman numerals—or Arabic "Ch. 3.")
ed.	edited by, edition, editor
f., ff.	and the following page, pages
l., ll.	line, lines
ms, mss	manuscript, manuscripts (Capitalize MS and use a period when citing a specific manuscript: "Bodleian MS. Cotton 92.")
n.d.	no date given
n.p.	no place of publication given
p., pp.	page, pages
rev.	revised
tr., trans.	translated by
vol., vols.	volume, volumes ("Vol. III of 4 vols.")

A footnote using some of these might go like this (you have already fully cited Weiss and Dillon):

> 16See Donald Allenberg et al., <u>Population in Early New England</u> (Boston: Large, Green and Co., 1974), pp. 308ff.; cf. Weiss, p. 60. Dillon, passim, takes a position even more conservative than Weiss's. See also A. H. Hawkins, ed., <u>Statistical Surveys</u> (Chicago: Nonesuch Press, 1960; rev. 1973), pp. 71–83 and Ch. 10. Records sufficient for broad comparisons begin only ca. 1850.

EXERCISES

5. *Write a summarizing footnote, including the following phrases and abbreviations:* c. cf., ed., see also, Ch., ff., rev., et al., passim, *and dealing with the following supposed items:*

1. An essay entitled Too Many Cars by L. A. Crump, in an anthology called Traffic edited by Arlene Pringle and several others, which the Willing Company published in New York in 1978 and then revised in 1983—you wish to refer your reader to an extended account beginning on page ten.
2. Certain statistics have become available only from about 1920.
3. Wilma May Smithers, whom you have already cited in full, says something on her page four that the reader should compare with Crump; the reader should also look at her sixth chapter.
4. Griffin, another writer you have already cited, takes a generally hostile view of Crump's work.
5. You want the reader to consult also the entry about automobiles in The Encyclopaedia Britannica, volume dated 1987.

Abbreviate books of the Bible, even the first time.

The Bible and its books, though capitalized as ordinary titles, are never italicized. Biblical references go directly into your text, within parentheses—no footnote, no commas, *lowercase* Roman numerals for chapter, Arabic for verse: Mark xvi.6; Jer. vi.24; 1 Sam. xviii.33. No comma—only a space—separates name from numbers; periods separate the numbers, *with no spacing.* The dictionary gives the accepted abbreviations: Gen., Exod., Lev., Deut. Make biblical references like this:

```
There is still nothing new under the sun

(Eccl. i.9); man still does not live by bread

alone (Matt. iv.4).

As Ecclesiastes tells us, "there is no new

thing under the sun" (i.9).
```

Abbreviate plays and long poems after the first time.

Handle plays and long poems like biblical citations, after an initial footnote that identifies the edition (see page 277). Italicize the title (underscore the title with your typewriter): *Merch.* II,iv.72–75 (this is *The*

Merchant of Venice, Act II, Scene iv, lines 72–75); *Caesar* V.iii.6, *Ham.* I.i.23, *Iliad* IX.93, *P.L.* IV.918 (*Paradise Lost,* Book IV, line 918). Use the numbers alone if you have already mentioned the title, or have clearly implied it, as in repeated quotations from the same work.

Match your bibliography to your footnotes.

When your paper is finally typed, arrange the cards of the works cited in your footnotes in alphabetical order (by authors' last names or, with anonymous works, by first words of titles—ignoring initial *The, A,* or *An*). You will not have used all your notes, nor all the articles you have carded. In typing your bibliography, pass over them in decent silence. *Include no work not specifically cited.* Your bibliographical entries will be just like your footnotes except that: (1) you will put the author's last name first; (2) you will give the total span of pages for book or magazine articles—none at all for books as a whole; (3) you will reverse identation so that the author's name will stand out; and (4) you will punctuate differently—putting one period after the alphabetized name or title, and another (no parentheses) after a book's place and date of publication. Here are some special cases:

> Hill, D. C. "Who Is Communicating What?" In <u>Essays</u> <u>for</u> <u>Study</u>. Ed. James L. McDonald and Leonard P. Doan. New York: Appleton Hall, 1973, pp. 211–19. Reprinted from <u>Era</u>, 12 (1972), 9–18.

Article in Edited Collection

When listing other works by the same author, use a solid line (your underscorer) and a period instead of repeating the name:

> Jones, Bingham, and Samuel Baher. <u>The</u> <u>Kinescopic</u> <u>Arts</u> <u>and</u> <u>Sciences</u>. Princeton: Little House, 1970.
>
> _____. "Television and Vision: The Case for Governmental Control." <u>Independent</u> <u>Review</u>, 7 (1969), 18–31.

Two Authors; More Than One Entry for Same Author(s)

Alphabetize by the name of the *author* of an article, not the editor of the collection containing it:

> Small, David R. "The Telephone and Urbanization." In <u>Annals</u> <u>of</u> <u>American</u> <u>Communication</u>. Ed. Walter Beinholt. Boston: Large, Green and Co., 1969. III, 398–407.

Article in Multivolume Set

But alphabetize by the name of the editor, when you have referred to his Introduction and notes:

Editor, When
Quoted

```
Cowley, Malcolm, ed. The Portable Hawthorne,
    with Introduction and Notes. New York:
    Viking Press, 1948.
```

Alphabetize the first significant word in anonymous works ("Trouble" in the first following example):

Anonymous
Works

```
"The Trouble with Puritans." Anon. editorial.
    The New York Times, 10 Apr. 1984, Sec.
    4, p. 8.

Valley Forge [Motion Picture] (New York: Steve
    Krantz Productions.  Released by
    Encyclopaedia Britannica Educational
    Corp., 1972).
```

I have based these instructions on the 1977 edition of *The MLA Handbook for Writers of Research Papers, Theses, and Dissertations* (compiled by the Modern Language Association of America), following the customs for work in literature and the humanities. The social and natural sciences use slightly different conventions. An article would look like this in a botanical bibliography (no quotation marks, no parentheses, fewer capitals):

Entry in
Scientific
Bibliography

```
Mann, K. H. 1973.  Seaweeds: their
    productivity and strategy for growth.
    Science 182:975—981.
```

This article might be referred to in text as (Mann, 1973), or simply as, say, (14), if the bibliographic entries are not alphabetized but numbered (for example, "14. K. H. Mann, *Science.* 182:975–981"—title of article omitted). Footnotes would be reserved for the author's additional comments. For papers in the social and natural sciences, consult your instructor about the correct style, or style manual, to follow.

A good general manual is the current edition of Kate L. Turabian, *A Manual for Writers of Term Papers, Theses, and Dissertations* (Chicago and London: The University of Chicago Press). A larger reference popular with scholars is *A Manual of Style* (the "Chicago Style Manual"), also published by the University of Chicago Press. Both the *MLA Handbook* and the Chicago *Manual* list other manuals for the various disciplines— engineering, geology, linguistics, psychology, and medicine, for example.

EXERCISES

6. *Make a bibliography, listing one entry each from Exercises 1, 3, 4, and 5, adding hypothetical page numbers, if necessary.*

7. *Using* The New York Times Index, *play researching detective on one of the following murder cases or Indian uprisings, tracing your case through the newspapers and subsequent indexings, and any other sources you may discover.* Look under "Murders" and the victim's name both; for Indian uprisings, check "Editorials," "Political," "War," and "Miscellaneous." Write a paper (2,000-3,000 words) presenting and evaluating the case or the affair.*

MURDERS (an asterisk marks unsolved cases)

The Sickles Tragedy (1859)
John Smedick (1868)
C. M. Rogers (1869)
*Benjamin Nathan (1870)
William J. Sharkey (1872)
James Fisk (1872)
*Kelsey Tar and Feather Case (1873)
Coroner Croker (1874)
James Noe (1875)
Judge Chisolm (1877)
Staten Island Mystery (1878)
R. H. Smith (1878)
Judge Elliot (1879)
Capt. A. C. Nutt (1882)
*Rose Clark Ambler (1883)
Benjamin Pitzel (1884)
Mrs. H. H. Bliss (1885)
*Rahway Murder Mystery (1887)
Dr. P. H. Cronin (1889)
Josephine Barnaby (1891)

William Guedensuppe (1897)
Kate Adams (1898)
William Marsh Rice (1900)
Robert Thorpe (1900)
F. J. Young (1904)
Herman Rosenthal (1912)
Barnet Baff (1914)
Mrs. William Bailey (1914)
*Charles Murry (1915)
Charles F. Stielow (1915)
Arthur Warren Waite (1916)
Ruth Cruger (1917)
Virginia Rappe (1921)
Mills Hall (1922)
West End Bank Messenger (1923)
Red Cassidy (1929)
*The 3-X Murders (1930)
E. A. Ridley (1933)
Major Cofran et al (1946)
Willie Earl (1947)

INDIAN UPRISINGS

Sioux Uprising (1862)
Genl. Sully, Indian Fighter (1862)
Black Kettle, Indian Chief (1868)
Spotted Tail, Indian Chief (1869)
Piegans Indians (1870)

Modoc War (1872)
Bannock War (1877)
Nez-Perce War (1877)
Poncas Indians (1879)
Ute Uprising (1879)

*I am indebted to W. Keith Kraus, Shippensburg State College, Pennsylvania, who invented the game and who provides enough cases for every member of the class ("The Research Paper Revisited," *The PCTE Bulletin* [Official Publication of the Pennsylvania Council of Teachers of English], No. 27 [April, 1975], pp. 14–20).

Chapter 12

THE FULL RESEARCH PAPER

Here is a sample, a complete research paper from one of my classes, to show what the final product can look like. I had suggested, among several topics, that the unusual cluster of four of America's greatest books in the 1850's might be worth looking into. A few students took one or another of the books, defined its quality as they and several modern critics saw it, and then checked that against the early reactions. This student took all four books, going first to the *Encyclopaedia Britannica,* then to the leading biographies. I had also suggested that the 1911 *Britannica* was particularly strong on literary topics falling before that date. From a reference to *Uncle Tom's Cabin* in one of the books, without sales figures, the student simply went to the *S* shelf and found in Mrs. Stowe's introduction to a later edition the figures he wanted.

To convey an idea of the whole process, the backs of the first two pages show bibliographical cards with notes—the "combined" cards that save space—corresponding to the first four footnotes, and the back of the third page (opposite p. 3 of the paper) shows a page of the first draft, which matches the final text beginning with the James quotation at the bottom of p. 2.

This research paper, for the most part, follows the conventional format: title page with outline (unnumbered if one page, numbered with small Roman numerals if more than one page); double-spaced text with single-spaced footnotes, each page except the first numbered in Arabic at the top; and the bibliography at the end, on a separate page or pages. Our paper combines title page with outline; perhaps more common is a separate title page. To set up a separate title page, center the title on the width of the page somewhat above the middle and the other elements—name, designation of course, instructor's name, date—below as shown:

America's Classics:

When 1850 Was Today

Vincent Cross

[12 to 15 lines of space]

English 270

Mr. Baker

April 16, 1980

Our bibliography is alphabetized by authors' last names or by titles when the author is unknown or anonymous. Keeping this alphabetization for each group, you can divide a longer bibliography into *primary sources*—works of literature, historical documents, letters, and so on—and *secondary sources,* or works *about* your subject.

Vincent Cross
English 270
Mr. Baker
April 16, 1981

AMERICA'S CLASSICS: WHEN 1850 WAS TODAY

Thesis: Though some readers recognized their greatness, all

four of America's classics of the 1850's went into

a fairly early eclipse.

Topic Outline

I.   Hawthorne's The Scarlet Letter (1850)
    A. Instant fame
       1. Fields's enthusiasm
       2. Early reviews
           a. Favorable
           b. Unfavorable
       3. Henry James's recollection
    B. Low sales as against best sellers

II. Melville's Moby-Dick (1851)
    A. Mixed but balanced reception
       1. England
           a. Favorable
           b. Unfavorable
       2. America's early praise turned sour
    B. The almost total eclipse

III. Thoreau's Walden (1854)
    A. Mixed reception
    B. America's neglect
    C. George Eliot and growing recognition abroad

IV. Whitman's Leaves of Grass (1855)
    A. Total silence
    B. Whitman's gift-copies and self-advertising
    C. Influential readers
       1. Emerson
       2. Thoreau
       3. Lincoln
    D. Notoriety and fame

828   Stewart, Randall
H40   Nathaniel Hawthorne : A
S85   Biography (New Haven : Yale
1961   University Press, 1948)

1st ed., March 16, 1850 - 2,000 copies sold
in 10 days.
2nd ed., 3,000 copies, sales good at first, soon
dropped. 2 yrs. later SL advertised
as in its "sixth thousandth" (96).
"The leading critics were lavish in their
praise." (97)

828   James, Henry
H40   Hawthorne (Ithaca : Cornell Univ.
J27   Press, 1967 -- first printed 1879)
1967

James gts. James T. Fields (H's publisher). F. called
on H. in Salem, found him depressed. H. gives him
unfinished MS. of Scarlet Letter ("thrust
upon him") as he was leaving. H.
depressed because earlier stories not
well nor widely received. F. goes back
to Boston, reads MS. with mounting

excitement. Sends letter saying so and
announcing his return next day to
arrange publication. When he arrived:
    "I went on in such an amazing
state of excitement... that he would
not believe I was really in earnest.
He seemed to think I was beside
myself, & laughed sadly at my
enthusiasm." (107)

290 THE FULL RESEARCH PAPER

AMERICAN CLASSICS: WHEN 1850 WAS TODAY

In the eighteen-fifties, American literature came of
age. Four of America's greatest books appeared in the first
five years of that decade: Nathaniel Hawthorne's The Scarlet Letter (1850), Herman Melville's Moby-Dick (1851), Henry
David Thoreau's Walden (1854), and Walt Whitman's Leaves of
Grass (1855). But was their greatness recognized at the
time? Would we recognize them today? How did these new and
unknown books seem to the reviewers who received them or
the people who bought them? Were they best sellers? Actually, none of them was. Though each of them had readers
who recognized their quality, all of them also received
negative criticism, some very severe, and all went into a
fairly early eclipse.

Hawthorne's The Scarlet Letter (1850) is the nearest
to an exception to this rule. Randall Stewart reports that
the leading critics were lavish in their praise,[1] reflecting
the same enthusiasm that James T. Fields, Hawthorne's publisher, had felt on reading the unfinished manuscript.
Fields tells of calling on Hawthorne in Salem, finding him
depressed, having the unfinished manuscript given him on
leaving, and reading it that night with growing excitement.
He returned to Salem the next day to arrange for publication: "I went on in such an amazing state of excitement

_____

[1]Nathaniel Hawthorne: A Biography (New Haven: Yale
University Press, 1948), p. 97.

Beginning

(Funneling to)

Thesis

Opposition

Footnote:
Author
Named in Text

THE FULL RESEARCH PAPER **291**

ALL ON ONE SIDE

828 Hawthorne, Julian
H40 *Hawthorne and His Circle* (New
H39h York: Harper & Bros., 1903)

"One day a big man, with a broken beard
and shining brown eyes, who bubbled
over with enthusiasm and fun, made his
appearance and talked volubly about something &
went away again, & my father & mother smiled at each
other. *The SL* had been written, and James T. Fields
had read it, & declared it the greatest bk. of the age."(18)

SECOND "STEWART" CARD—FRONT

Stewart— ②
E. P. Whipple (*Graham's Mag.*) answered objections of
gloominess: "The Custom House" showed H's ability
to mix tragedy & comedy, like Shakespeare, but hopes
"pathos and power" will be "more relieved by touches
of that beautiful and peculiar humor, so
serene and searching, in which he excells
almost all living writers." — in next bk. (97)

"A group of hostile critics were
violently proclaiming ... the gross im—

BACK

morality of the book." (97) *Brownson's
Review*, by Orestes A. Brownson, led the attack:

"There is an unsound state of public morals
when the novelist is permitted, w'out a
scorching rebuke, to select such crimes, &
to invest them w. all the fascination of
genius, and all the charms of a highly
polished style." (97)

. . . that [Hawthorne] would not believe I was really in
earnest. He seemed to think I was beside myself, and
laughed at my enthusiasm."[2] Julian Hawthorne, Hawthorne's
son, remembers the occasion:

Ellipsis and
Bracket

> One day a big man, with a broken beard and shin-
> ing brown eyes, who bubbled over with enthusiasm and
> fun, made his appearance and talked volubly about
> something, and went away again, and my father and
> mother smiled at each other. The Scarlet Letter had
> been written, and James T. Fields had read it, and de-
> clared it the greatest book of the age.[3]

Extended
Quotation,
with Footnote

Nevertheless, even the most favorable critics thought
the book was too uninterruptedly gloomy. E. P. Whipple,
who compared Hawthorne to Shakespeare for mixing the comic
tone of "The Custom House" section with the tragic main
story, hoped that in Hawthorne's next book the "pathos and
power" would be "more relieved by touches of that beautiful
and peculiar humor, so serene and searching, in which he
excels almost all living writers."[4] Moreover, as Stewart
notes, hostile critics attacked the book as immoral, especially Orestes A. Brownson in Brownson's Review:

Topic
Sentence

> There is an unsound state of public morals when the
> novelist is permitted, without a scorching rebuke, to
> select such crimes, and to invest them with all the
> fascination of genius, and all the charms of a highly
> polished style. (p. 97)

Extended
Quotation;
Same-Page
Reference to
Stewart

Henry James best describes how the book "was a great

---

[2]Henry James, Hawthorne (Ithaca: Cornell University
Press, 1967, first published 1879), p. 107.

Author Not
Named in Text

[3]Hawthorne and His Circle (New York: Harper & Brothers,
1903), p. 18.

Second
Citation
Abbreviated

[4]Stewart, p. 97.

and to the forefront of it" (p. 109). ~~Henry~~ James ~~reports that:~~ *writes*

> The writer of these lines, who was a child at the time,
> remembers dimly the sensation the book produced, and the
> little shudder with which people alluded to it, as if a
> peculiar horror were mixed with its attractions. He was
> too young to read it himself, but its title, upon which
> he fixed his eyes as the book lay upon the table, had
> a mysterious charm. ✓(p. 108)

Little Henry thought of the "scarlet letter" as a red envelope being sent
~~James wondered why a letter should be crimson,~~ until ~~later~~ his *through the mails*

mother showed him a painting in the National Gallery of Hester

and her scarlet A, with little Pearl touching it, which indicates *teasingly*

the fame the book had ~~achieved.~~ *already*

But the great acclaim died down. Sales soon dropped off.
(March 16, 1850) had
The first edition of 2,000 copies sold out in ten days, but the

second edition of 3,000 began to slow down. Two years later,

the publishers advertised that the book was in its "sixth

thousandth." (((Stewart, p. 96.))) This is almost nothing ⑤

compared to Uncle Tom's Cabin (1852), which sold 10,000 copies

"in a few days" and over 300,000 in the first year, or Ben Hur, *to*

which sold 200,000 copies in 1887. (((Harriet Beecher Stowe, ⑥

"The Author's Introduction," Uncle Tom's Cabin, or, Life Among

the Lowly (Boston and New York: Houghton Mifflin and Co., 1896),

p. lxii; Hugh W. Hetherington, Melville's Reviewers, British and

American, 1846-1891 (Chapel Hill: University of North Carolina

Press, 1961), p. 221.)))

Melville's Moby-Dick sold even more poorly, and soon ~~nobody~~ *was almost*
completely forgotten.
~~was reading it.~~ It was published first in London as The Whale
and additions,
(October 16, 1851), and then, with ~~some~~ revisions, it was published

in America as Moby-Dick (November 14, 1851). Many readers were
in not finding
disappointed ~~to find that it did not have~~ the adventures they

success, and [Hawthorne] immediately found himself famous" (p. 108). There was a general pride "in the idea of America having produced a novel that belonged to literature, and to the forefront of it" (p. 109). James writes:

Supporting View; Further References in Parentheses, Followed by Period

> The writer of these lines, who was a child at the time, remembers dimly the sensation the book produced, and the little shudder with which people alluded to it, as if a peculiar horror were mixed with its attractions. He was too young to read it himself, but its title, upon which he fixed his eyes as the book lay upon the table, had a mysterious charm. (p. 108)

Quotation from Work Already Cited, with Reference in Parentheses at End, Not Followed by Period

Little Henry thought of the "scarlet letter" as a red envelope being sent through the mails, until his mother showed him a painting in the National Gallery of Hester and her scarlet A, with little Pearl touching it teasingly, which indicates the fame the book had already achieved.

But the great acclaim died down. Sales soon dropped off. The first edition of 2,000 copies (March 16, 1850) had sold out in ten days, but the second edition of 3,000 began to slow down. Two years later, the publishers advertised that the book was in its "sixth thousandth."[5] This is almost nothing compared to Uncle Tom's Cabin (1852), which sold 10,000 copies "in a few days" and over 300,000 in the first year, or to Ben Hur, which sold 200,000 copies in 1887.[6]

Date in Parentheses

Publication Date in Parentheses

[5]Stewart, p. 96.

[6]Harriet Beecher Stowe, "The Author's Introduction," Uncle Tom's Cabin, or, Life Among the Lowly (Boston and New York: Houghton Mifflin and Co., 1896), p. lxii; Hugh W. Hetherington, Melville's Reviewers, British and American, 1846-1891 (Chapel Hill: University of North Carolina Press, 1961), p. 221.

Footnote Covering Two Sources

Melville's Moby-Dick sold even more poorly, and soon was almost completely forgotten. It was published first in London as The Whale (October 16, 1851), and then, with revisions and additions, it was published in America as Moby-Dick (November 14, 1851). Many readers were disappointed in not finding the adventures they had expected from Melville's earlier books, and many "decried the mixture of modes and of subjects in what they considered an extravagant though often powerful production."[7] In London, both on the same day (October 25, 1851), The Spectator and The Athenaeum published hostile reviews. The Athenaeum called it "an ill-compounded mixture of romance and matter-of-fact," and The Spectator wrote:

> This sea novel is a singular medley of naval observation, magazine article writing, satiric reflection upon the conventionalisms of civilized life, and rhapsody run mad.[8]

Nevertheless, also on October 25, a review in John Bull praised the book:

[sic]Pointing to Error in Punctuation— Period Instead of Question Mark

> Who would have looked for philosophy in whales, or for poetry in blubber.[sic] Yet few books which professedly deal in metaphysics, or claim the parentage of the muses, contain as much true philosophy and as much genuine poetry as the tale of the Pequod's whaling expedition.[9]

Moreover, London's Morning Herald, five days earlier (October 20, 1851) had already come out with unqualified praise:

---

[7]Watson G. Branch, Melville: The Critical Heritage (London and Boston: Routlege & Kegan Paul, 1947), p. 1.

Two Pages Not Consecutive

[8]Branch, pp. 253, 257.

[9]Branch, p. 255.·

"Melville is on the right track." Melville's new book now shows "a concentration of the whole powers of the man." The reviewer continues:

> Resolutely discarding all that does not bear directly on the matter at hand, he has succeeded in painting such a picture--now lurid, now ablaze with splendour --of sea life, in its most arduous and exciting form, as for vigor, originality, and interest, has never been surpassed.[10]

George Henry Lewes, a leading critic, says that "No European pen still has the power to portray the Unseen so vividly . . . ."[11] In the three months in which the book was reviewed in England, says Hetherington, the reception was "evenly balanced," though the ultimate reception was "completely negative" (p. 201).

Quotation, Elipsis at End

Quotation Sharpened to Key Phrases

In America, when Moby-Dick was published on November 15, 1851, the reception was similar. On that day, The Courier and New York Enquirer, the biggest paper in the city of New York, praised the book's "freshness," "vividness," and "witching interest"; Melville showed "the gusto of true genius."[12] In spite of some protests over "profaneness" and "indecency," all reviewers in the first six days were favorable.

But the tide began to turn. Soon the book was "sad stuff, dull and dreary, or ridiculous" (p. 218). In the first ten days, it had sold 1,835 copies, but by February

[10]Hetherington, p. 191.

[11]Hetherington, p. 196.

[12]Hetherington, p. 204.

7 of the next year (1852), it had sold only 471 more.
Thirty-six years later, through 1887, the year of Ben Hur's
200,000 copies, it had sold only 3,797. Melville's earlier
book, Typee (1846), had sold 6,392 copies in three years
(p. 221). The 1911 Encyclopaedia Britannica gives Melville only a paragraph, mentioning Moby-Dick with Typee,
Omoo, and White Jacket as portraying "seafaring life with
vigour and originality," and ends by saying that Melville
wrote in a period "when fiction written by writers below
Irving, Poe, and Hawthorne was measured by humble artistic
standards." Moby-Dick was far from the classic it is considered today.

The reception of Thoreau's Walden (August 9, 1854)
was similar to that of Moby-Dick, though without the open
hostility on the negative side. "Praise . . . was hearty
but by no means unanimous."[13] On July 29, 1854, Horace
Greeley announced the forthcoming book in the New York
Tribune, a widely read and very influential paper, with a

summary and extracts of about 2,000 words (p. 289), and long
approving reviews appeared in Graham's Magazine and Putnam's
Monthly.[14] But sales were poor. In the same year that Maria
Cummins's sentimental novel The Lamplighter became a tremendous success, Walden's 2,000 copies were more than enough,

---

[13]Henry Seidel Canby, Thoreau (Boston: Houghton Mifflin Co., 1939), p. 289.

[14]Philip Van Doren Stern, The Annotated Walden (New
York: Clarkson and Potter, Inc., 1970), p. 43.

lasting for eight years, when it finally went out of print in 1862.[15]

According to Canby, although America eventually relegated Walden "to the humble position of accessory reading about nature," it "picked up admirers, one by one, all over the world" and eventually "won its place as a world classic of literature" (p. 293). George Eliot's long review, with excerpts from Walden, in the Westminster Review in London in 1856, indicates the beginning of this bit-by-bit European trend. She says that Walden is "quite interesting enough" for her to break the magazine's rule against "retrospective" reviewing. The book shows "a refined as well as a hardy mind" and contains "plenty of sturdy sense":

> . . . we have a bit of pure American life (not the "go ahead" species, but its opposite pole), animated by that energetic, yet calm spirit of innovation, that practical as well as theoretic independence of formulae, which is peculiar to some of the finer American minds.[16]

Recognition was on its way, but in America it was long in coming.

Walt Whitman's Leaves of Grass (1855) has a different history from the other three classics of the 1850's. Although it was received in almost total silence, Leaves of Grass, with a one-by-one gaining of readers, started its very slow uphill climb about two weeks after publication,

---

[15]Stern, p. 41.

[16]"Contemporary Literature," Westminster Review, January 1856, p. 166. This unsigned article is identified as George Eliot's by Stern's reference to it (p. 41).

Margin notes:

Quotation Shifting from Summary to Full Passage, Set Off

Article in Periodical, with Explanation

mostly through Whitman's own efforts in distributing gift-
copies and advertising himself. Hawthorne, Melville, and
Thoreau were already known as authors before their new
"classics" appeared. Whitman, though active as a journalist
and newspaper editor, was totally unknown. Leaves of Grass
was his first book. He financed it himself, but the first
edition of 1,000 (July 6, 1855) was a total failure. Gay
Wilson Allen estimates that it had as few as two or three
dozen readers.[17] According to Allen, Whitman himself said
in old age that not a single copy had sold, contradicting
an early boast that it "sold readily" (p. 150). Certainly, Whitman and his publisher gave most of the 1,000
copies to reviewers, who failed to review, or to influential
people and acquaintances.

One of these was Ralph Waldo Emerson, then America's
leading man of letters. He had never heard of Whitman, but
the letter he wrote thanking Whitman for his gift-copy was
eventually to bring Leaves of Grass to public attention.
Emerson wrote that he felt like coming to Brooklyn immediately to meet "my benefactor," calling the book "the most
extraordinary piece of wit and wisdom that America has yet
contributed."[18] But this was a private letter. Only one
review--in the influential New York Tribune, July 23, 1855--

---

[17]The Solitary Singer: A Critical Biography of Walt
Whitman (New York: The Macmillan Co., 1955), p. 150.

[18]Richard Rupp, Critics on Whitman (Coral Gables, Florida: University of Miami Press, 1972), p. 14; see also Clarence L. Ghodes, "Whitman and Emerson," Sewanee Review, 37
(1929), 79-93.

300 THE FULL RESEARCH PAPER

broke the public silence until Whitman himself, apparently despairing, wrote three anonymous reviews in September. These seem to have stirred Putnam's Magazine to review the book as "a mixture of Yankee transcendentalism and New York rowdyism." Conceding a certain "original perception of nature, a manly brawn, and epic directness," the reviewer nevertheless found Whitman's mixed vocabulary making some passages "downright laughable."[19]

Next year (1856), Whitman financed a second edition, and advertised it in the Tribune by publishing Emerson's letter without his permission, which Emerson thought "a strange rude thing to do."[20] But the reaction, as Allen reports, was now hostile. Whittier is said to have thrown his gift-copy into the fire, perhaps because it contained a clipping of Emerson's letter, which Whitman had pasted into a number of his gifts (p. 174). Boston's Christian Examiner called the book "impious libidinousness"; the Criterion wrote:

> . . . it is impossible to imagine how a man's fancy could conceive such a mass of stupid filth, unless he were possessed of the soul of a sentimental donkey that had died of disappointed love. (p. 174)

Ellipsis at Beginning of Set-Off Quotation

The second edition, like the first, failed to sell, and the third (1860) failed also when the publisher went bankrupt at the outbreak of the Civil War.[21]

Nevertheless, Whitman was gaining readers one by one.

[19]Allen, p. 173.

[20]Allen, p. 174.

[21]Allen, "Walt Whitman," Encyclopaedia Britannica (1967).

Emerson continued to recommend <u>Leaves of Grass</u> to his friends, in spite of Whitman's "strange rude" publishing of his letter. Thoreau, to whom Whitman had sent a gift of the second edition, found it "exhilarating, encouraging," writing a friend that "it has done me more good than any reading for a long time," though he disliked its sensuality.[22] Out in Springfield, Illinois, in the law offices of Lincoln and Herndon, some law students began to discuss the newly-published <u>Leaves of Grass</u>, which William Herndon had put on the office table. One of the students wrote that Lincoln,

Long
Quotation
Summarized

"who during the criticisms had been apparently in the unapproachable depths of one of his glum moods of meditative silence," picked up the book and read it for over an hour, then turned back to the beginning, "and to our general surprise, began to read aloud," revealing "a charm of new life" in Whitman's poem. He praised its "vitality, freshness, unconventional sentiments, and unique form of expression, and claimed that Whitman gave promise of a new school of poetry." Lincoln took the book home that night, but returned it to the office table next day, saying that he had saved it "from being purified by fire by the women, and asked that it be kept there, where he often picked it up and read it aloud."[23]

Whitman kept expanding the poem, bringing out unsuccessful editions, and publicizing both it and himself. By June

Short Title,
When Author
(Allen) Has
Several Works
Cited

[22]Rupp, p. 15.

[23]Allen, <u>Singer</u>, pp. 175-76.

302 THE FULL RESEARCH PAPER

30, 1865, the book had become notorious for being "full of indecent passages," as the Secretary of the Interior, James Harlan, said on firing Whitman, then a government clerk, when he discovered his authorship.[24]   In 1881, the Attorney General of Massachusetts threatened a Boston publisher with prosecution for obscenity unless he withdrew some sections in the seventh edition. Whitman shifted to Philadelphia, and, at last, with the new publicity, Leaves of Grass began to make money and to get the wide attention it holds to this day.[25]

    None of these great classics, then, was a best seller in its day. Though The Scarlet Letter made Hawthorne instantly famous, and though Moby-Dick received favorable reviews at first, both went into early eclipse, with Moby-Dick almost totally forgotten, or misunderstood, until well into the twentieth century. America more or less overlooked Thoreau, and Whitman met almost total silence, broken only by his own efforts to advertise himself. Nevertheless, one thing seems clear: from the first, with each of these American classics, some readers, however few, recognized their greatness. Although The Scarlet Letter and Moby-Dick quietly faded, and Leaves of Grass failed from the beginning, someone, somewhere, read them, remembered them, and recommended them to others, until they became generally recognized as the classics they are.

Thesis Restated

Clincher

[24]Allen, Walt Whitman Handbook (Chicago: Packard and Co., 1946), p. 5.

[25]Allen, Encyc. Brit.

BIBLIOGRAPHY

Article   Allen, Gay Wilson. "Walt Whitman." <u>Encyclopaedia Britannica</u> (1967).

Books by Same Author   _____. <u>Walt Whitman Handbook</u>. Chicago: Packard and Co., 1946.

_____. <u>The Solitary Singer</u>: <u>A Critical Biography of Walt Whitman</u>. New York: The Macmillan Co., 1955.

Two Cities of Publication   Branch, Watson G. <u>Melville</u>: <u>The Critical Heritage</u>. London and Boston: Routlege & Kegan Paul, 1947.

Canby, Henry Seidel. <u>Thoreau</u>. Boston: Houghton Mifflin Co., 1939.

Author Anonymous on Publication   [Eliot, George.] "Contemporary Literature." <u>Westminster Review</u>, January 1856, pp. 124–72.

Ghodes, Clarence L. "Whitman and Emerson." <u>Sewanee Review</u>, 37 (1929), 79-93.

Hawthorne, Julian. <u>Hawthorne and His Circle</u>. New York: Harper & Brothers, 1903.

Hetherington, Hugh W. <u>Melville's Reviewers</u>, <u>British and American</u>, <u>1846-1891</u>. Chapel Hill: University of North Carolina Press, 1961.

James, Henry. <u>Hawthorne</u>. Ithaca: Cornell University Press, 1967.

Further Identification for City of Publication   Rupp, Richard. <u>Critics on Whitman</u>. Coral Gables, Florida: University of Miami Press, 1972.

Stern, Philip Van Doren. <u>The Annotated Walden</u>. New York: Clarkson and Potter, Inc., 1970.

Stewart, Randall. <u>Nathaniel Hawthorne</u>: <u>A Biography</u>. New Haven: Yale University Press, 1948.

Introduction in Book   Stowe, Harriet Beecher. "The Author's Introduction," <u>Uncle Tom's Cabin, or, Life Among the Lowly</u>. Boston and New York: Houghton Mifflin and Co., 1896, pp. liii-xc.

304 THE FULL RESEARCH PAPER

THE
HANDBOOK

Section A

THE ENGLISH LANGUAGE

In your writing course, as in the rest of your life, you deal with and through an extraordinary language. The speech you are born to—or have since acquired—is rich and supple because of the many historic threads that constitute its weave. For a century or so it has been, and for at least the near future it will continue to be, a worldwide language, constantly absorbing greater variety of expression and enlarging its communicative power. This global language of ours began in the distant past among other peoples and other tongues. Fascinating in itself, this story can help you to understand your medium, and to use it more effectively.*

---

*For this survey, I am basically indebted to a splended course in philology with Professor Arthur Brodeur, University of California, 1947–48, and, in addition to Murray, Pyles, and Dillard, as cited, to Albert H. Marckwardt, *American English* (New York: Oxford University Press, 1958), Richard Middlewood Wilson, "English Language," *Encyc. Brit.* (1967), from whom I have selected a number of word-lists, James R. Hulbert, *Bright's Anglo-Saxon Reader,* revised and enlarged (New York: Henry Holt and Co., 1936), and Calvert Watkins, "Indo-European and the Indo-Europeans," *The American Heritage Dictionary* (1969), pp. 1496–1502. I am also grateful to Professor John H. Fisher of the University of Tennessee and Professor William Labov of the University of Pennsylvania for informed and helpful comments.

THE INDO-EUROPEANS

The story of English begins about 5000 B.C. with a late Stone Age people in the Eurasian grasslands of what is now western Russia, where man first domesticated the horse. Words surviving in many of the eight big groups of languages descending from their speech show that they were an inland people, living among rivers and lakes, among waterfowl and grazing animals, knowing wolves, bears, deer, and beavers, in open country with deciduous trees, and snow—all suggesting a Eurasian terrain, perhaps near modern Lithuania, rather than the deserts and jungles of the countries farther east and south where their language also eventually thrived.

They were hunters and herdsmen. They had horses, and were acquiring bronze and gold. They were also warriors, as the dominance and spread of their language suggest, since they had no writing. Their language spread very slowly, over thousands of years and many generations, as one segment or another moved to new grass and hunting grounds, displacing and absorbing other peoples before them, slowly separating into divers races and derivative languages. Their general movement to new territories was probably underway by 3500 B.C., when the Egyptians had already begun to write and to build the world's first great civilization. The modern world has named these people *Aryans*, or, better, *Indo-Europeans*, a name indicating the ultimate span of their language from Europe to India.

Derivatives of Indo-European speech and people eventually covered Europe, and Russia, flowing gradually down the peninsulas and subcontinents of Spain, Italy, Greece, Asia, and India, and northward into Scandinavia, and westward into the British Isles—possibly dry-soled over ridges not yet sunken under the North Sea, or not broken at the Straits of Dover. The English language itself arrived several thousand years later, a very late comer, a division of a small subdivision that had evolved in Germany to become, today, the most widespread of any of the Indo-European languages—virtually an international language. And, oddly, most of the basic Indo-European words modern scholars can reconstruct are still represented in modern English, through inheritance or borrowing from other Indo-European languages—words like *father, mother, east,* for instance, and *name, bear,* and their combination *number.*

Here is a table of the Indo-European languages, to help you visualize this astonishing linguistic dispersal that eventually produced English:

INDO-EUROPEAN LANGUAGES

I. "SATEM" LANGUAGES*

A. Indo-Iranian
1. Indic: Sanskrit, Pakrit, Pali, Hindi, Urdu, Hindustani, Bengali, Gujarati, Marathi, Punjabi, Singhalese, Romany
2. Iranian: Avestan (the oldest of the Indo-Iranian group), Old Persian, Pahlavi (Middle Persian), Sogdian (ancient Central Asia), Scythian (ancient southeastern Europe and Asia), Baluchi (modern Baluchistan, India), Pashtu (Afghanistan), Persian, Kurdish, Ossetic (Russia, between the Black and Caspian seas)
B. Armenian: Classical Armenian, Eastern, and Western Armenian
C. Albanian: Thracian, Illyrian (ancient coastal Yugoslavia), Albanian
D. Balto-Slavic
1. Slavic: Old Bulgarian, Bulgarian, Serbo-Croatian, Slovenian, Czech, Slovak, Polish, Wendish (ancient German area), Great Russian, White Russian, Ukrainian
2. Baltic: Old Prussian, Lithuanian, Latvian

II. "CENTUM" LANGUAGES

A. Hellenic: Mycenean Greek, Attic, Ionic (ancient Greeks of western Asia Minor), Doric (ancient central Greece), Aeolic (ancient eastern Greece), Cyprian, Modern Greek
B. Italic
1. Oscan (ancient southern Italy)
2. Umbrian (ancient central Italy)

*Linguists divide the Indo-European languages into two groups according to whether they have kept the Indo-European *k*-sound or changed it to *s*. Linguists arbitrarily chose the word for "hundred," *statem* in Avestan, *centum* in Latin, to designate the two groups. As you probably know, the Latin *c* is "hard," pronounced as *k*.

Sir William Jones, a learned orientalist and lawyer appointed to the British supreme court in Calcutta, took the first step toward uncovering the Indo-European languages. He put forward, for the first time with sufficient evidence and force (1786), the theory that Sanskrit had derived from the same source as Greek and Latin. Nineteenth-century German scholars—notably Jacob Grimm, who, with brother Wilhelm, wrote the famous fairy tales, and Karl Verner, whose law explains some changes beyond Grimm's law—completed the basic analysis, identifying the related languages and the principles by which they had changed the sounds of the consonants in the parent tongue.

Modern scholars identify two other small groups, separate from the Satems and Centums: (1) ancient Hittite and related Anatolian languages in Turkey about 2000 B.C. (the oldest), and (2) two Tocharian languages in Chinese Turkestan about 1000 B.C.

3. Latin: Faliscan (around prehistoric Rome), Latin, Italian, Provençal, French, Spanish, Catalan, Portuguese, Rumanian
C. Celtic: Gaulish, Welsh, Cornish, Breton, Irish, Manx, Gaelic
D. Germanic
   1. East Germanic (Gothic)
   2. North Germanic
      a. East Norse: Swedish, Danish, Gutnish
      b. West Norse: Norwegian, Faroese, Icelandic
   3. West Germanic
      a. High German: Alemannic, Bavarian, Yiddish
      b. Low Germanic (*Plattdeutsch*)
         i. Franconian: Flemish, Dutch
       ii. Frisian
      iii. English

THE ANGLO-SAXONS (449)

Before "English" came to Britain (named by the Romans for some of its inhabitants, the Brythonic Celts, a western Indo-European branch), the Roman Empire had risen, flourished, and begun to totter. Caesar invaded Britain in 55 B.C., though serious conquest and colonization began almost a century later. Nevertheless, by the time that Angles, Saxons, and Jutes landed in southern England in A.D. 449, bringing the language that was to become "Old English," Romans had lived and died in Britain, representing the dominant culture, for almost five hundred years—a century longer than Europeans have lived in America. Latin (a southern Indo-European branch) was the language of England. "English," under some other name, might well have become another Romance language, like Italian, Spanish, and French.

But the Roman Empire slipped. Alaric the Goth, after sieges in 408 and 409, finally sacked Rome in 410. Other Gothic tribes were raiding into Roman Gaul (modern France). Britain was the empire's farthest outpost. Emperor Honorius wrote the British cities in 409 that they must fend for themselves. The legions withdrew, and many citizens with them. The elegant resort city of Bath, abandoned, sank back into the sulphur marsh, totally lost and forgotten for another two hundred years. Native chieftains began to gather strength, and to squabble. One, Vortigern, invited two "Saxon" lords and their men to help him fend off raiding Picts and Irish. Hengist and Horsa, two brothers (the first means "stallion," the second, "horse's"), of the Jutes, landed at Ebbsfleet, Kent, on the coast south of the Thames, in 449. They continued to dominate Kent; and other Angles and Saxons—all closely related in race and language—landed, first, on the southern coast, and later, on the eastern coast to the north. The invaders' power as well as their language prevailed over the scattered Celtish fragments left behind by the Romans.

ANGLO-SAXON BORROWINGS

The Anglo-Saxons picked up very few Celtic words, and even fewer from British Latin, probably because the Celts had mostly stayed clear of the Romans, and because the new invaders from Europe had the dominant culture. But many place-names in England survived from Roman-Celtic times, notably *ceaster* (from Roman *castrum,* fortified camp), which still remains in names like *Winchester, Westchester,* and *Worcester* (pronounced "Wooster" now, for more than four hundred years). Shakespeare's river Avon is a Celtish name for "river," as are others like Usk, Ouse, Stour, and Wye. London and York are Celtish names (the Romans had called the great city *Londinium,* from the Celtish *Londos,* for "wild"). Of the few other Celtish words the Anglo-Saxons adopted, even fewer remain today, among them *binn,* for "manger," now our flourbins and coalbins, and *cursian,* "to curse."

The Anglo-Saxons had already acquired a stock of Latin words from fighting and trading with the Romans in continental Europe, many of which are still in the language. *Copor,* "copper," from Latin *cuprum/coprum,* comes in very early, before the Latin in Gaul had shifted pronunciation to *covrum.* Similarly, *wīn* ("wine," pronounced "ween") came in when classical Latin *vinum* was still pronounced "weenum." Our word *vine,* which grows the grapes for the wine, comes from the same Latin word, but six or seven centuries later, after the Norman Conquest, as the English borrowed the French word for the *vines* in the *vineyards* of Bordeaux, which were producing their *wines.* From the Romans, the continental Anglo-Saxons, with the other Germanic peoples, had also borrowed *naep,* now "turnip," *peose* "pea," *culter* "colter" (plowblade), *weall* "wall," *cēap* "to bargain" (hence "cheap"), *pund* "pound," and *mynet* "money" (hence "mint"). They also took the *flasce* for the *wīn* they poured in their *cuppe* to put under their *belt,* and they bought from the Romans *cyse* "cheese," *pipor* "pepper," and *butere* for the *cycene* "kitchen." Roman *cealc* "chalk," *pic* "pitch," and *tigele* "tile" went into buildings. The early continental Germans also borrowed "street" from Roman *via strata* and "mile" from *mil*—a thousand paces of the marching Roman legions. *Segl* "sail" from Latin *sagulum* is the same in almost every Germanic language, as the northerners, especially the Vikings, saw how much it improved the Roman galley. A ruler became *cāsere*, after Caesar, which also produced the German *Kaiser* and the Russian *Czar* or *Tsar*. The last day of the week became *Saeternesdaeg*, "Saturn's day"—the only Roman among a week of Germanic sun, moon, and gods. Christianity, in 597, brought a new flood of Latin words into Anglo-Saxon England.

THE OLD ENGLISH PERIOD (450–1100)

The Anglo-Saxons referred to themselves and their language as *Anglisc* or *Englisc,* probably because the Angles in Northumbria, in northern England, developed the first literature, centuries earlier than any literature in any of the other Germanic languages. Their language was nearer modern German than English. It was a "synthetic," or inflected language, signaling its grammar by word-endings, as in German or Latin. Here are the opening lines of the *Beowulf,* the greatest remaining Old English epic (pronounce the *ae* like *hat,* but the other vowels separately, with the qualities of Spanish or Italian; the *y* pronounces like the *u* in French *lune;* þ and ð are "th"):

> Hwaet, wē gār-Dena   in gēardagum,
> þēodcyninga,   þrym gefrūnon,
> **hū ðā aeþ elingas**   ellen fremedon!

Literally:

> **What! we, of spear-Danes',**   **in yore-days,**
> **People-kings',**   **power have heard,**
> **how the noblings**   **valor performed!**

Only the simple words—*what, we, in, how, the*—remain in English today, pretty much as they were. Notice that we still pronounce the beginning of *what* in the Anglo-Saxon way, *hw,* although the Middle-English scribes changed it to *wh,* for some obscure reason. Here the Anglo-Saxon harper uses it as a call for the audience's attention: it is usually translated "Lo" or "Behold." The blocky half-lines, incidentally, pausing in the middle and alliterated across the gap, probably coordinated with the harper-reciter's sweeps across the strings, one sweep for each half-line. We can also recognize the outlines of modern *Dane, yore, day,* and *king,* but all the rest are entirely foreign to us, lost from the language along with the seemingly backward word-order, and the inflectional grammatical endings that support it. In its fifteen hundred years of history, English has changed from a "synthetic," inflected language to an "analytic," almost uninflected one, where position in the sentence (subject-verb-object), together with such indicators as *with, in, to, by,* expresses meaning, the former function of the vanished word-endings. And it has traded off a major portion of its old vocabulary for new.

THE NORSEMEN (789)

Because the Germanic languages characteristically accent the beginnings of words, Anglo-Saxon had already begun to slur and to lose older and more complicated inflectional endings before the Norsemen came. But invading Norsemen, in two waves three hundred years apart, accelerated the change from synthetic to analytic. The Norsemen, or Vikings, began their raids on England in 789, when, as *The Anglo-Saxon Chronicle* tells us, three ships, "the first ships of Danish men," raided a seaport on the southern coast. Raids continued on eastern and northern coasts, Scotland, and Ireland, until the Danes had settled the whole of central England as their territory, known as the "Danelaw." Alfred, the West Saxon king, who had held the Danes out of southern England and had established the last great period of Anglo-Saxon literature and culture, signed the Peace of Wedmore with them in 878. Since the Old Norse of the Danes and the Old English of the Anglo-Saxons were similar Germanic languages but with differing word-endings, people went for the word and forgot the endings, smoothing out the grammar. Nevertheless, only about forty Norse words appear in the written language, still classically Anglo-Saxon under Alfred—notably *lagu* "law," *hūsbonda* "householder," and *ræl* "thrall" (slave, now in *enthrall*)—until after the next and very different Norse invasion, that of the Norman French.

THE NORMAN CONQUEST (1066)

The raids and settlement of Norsemen southward—the Age of the Vikings—lasted from the first appearance of Danish ships off southern

England (789) until the treaty of St. Clair-sur-Epte (912), which established the Norsemen in Normandy, France. Some social upheaval, perhaps over-population, had turned the Nordic custom of sea-raiding ("Viking" means "sea-raider") into conquest. By land, the Norsemen pushed into western Russia, and southward into the Burgundy of modern France, which bears the tribal name of its Norse invaders and settlers. By sea, they raided the coasts of France and Spain, and pushed into the Mediterranean to settle in Sicily (where, at Monreale, near Palermo, you can still see a magnificent Norman cathedral built by their Christianized descendants).

But the most significant of the Norse settlements was in Normandy, which, like Burgundy, bears the invaders' name. While Alfred was fighting the Vikings in England, other Norsemen sailed up the Seine to Rouen, devastating the countryside and eventually repopulating it with a Nordic-Gallic admixture. But France (or French women) prevailed after all, for the conquerors lost their language, ultimately adopting both Christianity and French. When the Norman William, the Conqueror, landed at Hastings, in England, in 1066, about the only Norse remaining was his battle cry, *Tur ai!*, "Thor, aid!" The rest of the swearing was in French.

MIDDLE ENGLISH (1100–1500)

The language of English upper-class culture was now Norman French. Anglo-Saxon went underground, the speech of peasants. All the riches of Anglo-Saxon poetry, like *hron-rād*, "whale-road," for "sea," and *eard-stapa*, "earth-stepper," for a wandering outcast, never found in common prose, disappeared from the language. But all the Old Norse words acquired in common parlance in Anglo-Saxon days now begin to appear in writing, many of them eventually replacing their Old English synonyms with such central words as *sky, die, take, fellow, leg, low, egg, awe.* Some Old English words acquired an Old Norse synonym of slightly differing mean-ing: *rear/raise, from/fro, craft/skill, hide/skin, to/til, sick/ill,* and *shirt/skirt,* which became the female version of the belted Anglo-Saxon smock, or "shirt," worn by both sexes. Any *sk* word in modern English is very likely from Old Norse. Old Norse also endowed us with the pronoun *she,* a clearer distinction than the Old English *hēo,* and with the other pronouns *they, their, them,* for the same reason. Other important Old Norse words still with us, surfacing after the Norman Conquest, are *though, aloft, ath-wart,* and *seemly.*

But the Noresman's most significant imprint on English was not of Norse but of his more recent Norman French, which cut Anglo-Saxon off from writing and accelerated its incipient change from synthetic to analytic grammar, offering as reinforcement a language already analytic in structure. Many new words came in directly from Latin, still the language of learning and science, and many more French words derived directly from their ancestral Latin. English and French words, surviving side by side, give us some interesting opportunities for one-upmanship: *hearty/cordial, ask/demand, answer/reply, house/mansion, ghost/spirit, room/chamber, shun/avoid, seethe/boil, yearly/annual.* In most of these pairs, the French half, the second one, still carries an air of social superiority—*house/mansion,* for instance. While the Anglo-Saxon peasantry herded, in their own language, the *calves, steers, swine,* and *sheep,* and refrained from killing the *deer,* the French lords and ladies ate in French: *veal, beef, pork, mutton, venison.* Since Anglo-Saxon *lamb* is our word for both the animal and the meat, we may assume that the French lords liked their *mutton* mature, and that roast leg of lamb came into favor only after the lordly descendants of the Normans had shifted to English. Synonyms also borrowed later from both Norman and Parisian French give us some other interesting pairs: *catch/chase, canal/channel, real/royal, wage/gage, warden/guardian, warrant/guarantee.*

But although the Norman Conquest deposed and then largely rebuilt much of our vocabulary, English, as evolving from Anglo-Saxon, continued to work itself upward. By the reign of Edward III (1327–1377), the nobility were speaking English. About 1350, "John Cornwal, a maystere of gramere," changed the language of teaching in grammar school from "Freynsch into Englysch."* A statute of Edward's in 1362-1363 made English the language for pleadings in the lawcourts. And Chaucer's great works, beginning in 1359 and culminating in the *Canterbury Tales* (1387), though heavily influenced by French, are, of course, in Middle English. French is again a foreign language.

The opening lines of Chaucer's *Canterbury Tales* well show what has happened to the Old English inflectional endings, which had signaled subjects, objects, indirect objects, and so forth: they have all rounded down to a meaningless final *e,* pronounced "uh," or not pronounced at all when the meter (or the rush of conversation) crowds it against the vowel of a word following. *Aprille* is pronounced "Ah-PRÍLL-uh," and

---

*John de Trevisa, translation of Ranulf Higden's *Polychronicon,* 1387, quoted in Sir James A. H. Murray, "English Language," *Encyc. Brit.,* 11th ed. (1910), p. 594.

shoures soote is pronounced "SHOOR-uhs SOHT-uh''; but *veyne* is pronounced exactly like modern *vein* because the *i* of the following *in* absorbs the final *e*, or at least most of it. *Drought* sounded about like modern "looked" with a guttural *gh* for the *k*, like a clearing of the throat. I have scanned the lines into their iambic pentameter (which allows for an extra light syllable at the end of its usual ten-syllable line), so you can see how the word-endings work, and how Middle English sounded at its very best. Pronounce the *a's* as in *ah*, long *e's* as in "SWAYT-uh brayth," long *i* like the double *ee* in "peer," and long *u* and *o* as in "SHOOR-uhs SOHT-uh.''

∪ — |∪ —|∪ —|∪   —|∪ —|∪
Whan that Aprille with his shoures soote

∪   —| ∪ — | ∪ —|∪ —|∪ —|∪
The drought of March hath perced to the roote,

∪ —|∪ —|∪ — |∪ — |∪ —|
And bathed every veyne in swich licour

∪   —| ∪ —| ∪ —|∪ —|∪   —|
Of which vertu engendred is the flour;

∪ —|∪ —| ∪   —| ∪ — |∪ —|
Whan Zephirus eek with his sweete breeth

∪ — |∪ —| ∪ —|∪ —|∪   —|
Inspired hath in every holt and heeth

∪   — |∪ — |∪
The tendre croppes. . . .

(When April, with his sweet showers, has pierced the drought of March to the root, and bathed every vein in such liquor of whose strength the flower is engendered, when Zephyr, moreover, with his sweet breath has inspired the tender crops in every field and heath. . . .)

This opening sentence of Chaucer's runs on for another four and a half lines before reaching its main clause (*Thanne longen folk to goon on pilgrimages,* "Then folk long to go on pilgrimages"), and for another six lines beyond that before the period. His sentence is 128 words long. English has loosened, and flexed, and sophisticated considerably since the hardy, blocky phrases of the *Beowulf*.

To illustrate further the change from Old English to Middle English to Modern English, here are three translations of the same passage from the Latin Bible—New Testament, St. Mark iv. 2–9:

OLD ENGLISH
WEST-SAXON GOSPELS (c. 1000)

(2) And hē hi fela on bigspellum lǣrde, and him tō cwæ ð on his lāre, (3) Gehȳraþ: Ūt ēode sē sǣdere his sǣd tō sāwenne. (4) And þā hē sēow, sum fēoll wið þone weg, and fugelas cōmon and hit frǣton. (5) Sum fēoll ofer stānscyligean, þār hit næfde mycele eorðan, and sōna ūp ēode; and for þām hit næfde eorðan þiccnesse, (6) þā hit ūp ēode, sēo sunne hit forswǣlde, and hit forscranc, for þām hit wyrtruman næfde. (7) And sum fēoll on þornas; þā stigon ðā þornas and forðrysmodon þæt, and hit wæstm ne bær. (8) And sum fēoll on gōd land, and hit sealde ūppstīgendne and wexendne wæstm; and an brōhte þrītigfealdne, sum syxtifealdne, sum hundfealdne. (9) And hē cwæð, Gehȳre, sē ð e ēaran hæbbe tō gehȳranne.

MIDDLE ENGLISH
JOHN WYCLIFF'S BIBLE (1382)

(ʒ = The Old English gutteral *gh*-sound; v = u, and
u sometimes = v, as in *heuene, vp,* and ʒ *aue)*

And he tauʒte hem in parablis many thingis. And he seide to hem in his techynge. Heere ʒee. Loo! a man sowynge goth out for to sowe. And the while he sowith, an other seed felde aboute the wey, and briddis of heuene, or of the eire, camen, and eeten it. Forsothe an other felde doun on stony placis, wher it had nat myche erthe; and anoon it sprong vp, for it hadde nat depnesse of erthe. And whenne the sunne rose vp, it welwide for heete, and it dried vp, for it hadde not roote. And an other felde doun into thornes, and thornes stieden vp, and strangliden it, and it. ʒaue not fruyt. And an other felde doun in to good lond, and ʒaue fruyt, styinge vp, and wexinge; and oon brouʒte thritty fold, and oon sixtyfold, and oon an hundridfold. And he seide, He that hath eris of heeryng, heere.

MODERN ENGLISH
KING JAMES VERSION (1611)

(2) And he taught them many things by parables, and he said unto them in his doctrine, (3) Hearken; Behold, there went out a sower to sow: (4) and it came to pass, as he sowed, some fell by the wayside,

and the fowls of the air came and devoured it up. (5) And some fell on stony ground, where it had not much earth; and immediately it sprang up, because it had no depth of earth: (6) but when the sun was up, it was scorched; and because it had no root, it withered away. (7) And some fell among thorns, and the thorns grew up, and choked it, and it yielded no fruit. (8) And other fell on good ground, and did yield fruit that sprang up and increased, and brought forth, some thirty, some sixty, and some a hundred. (9) And he said unto them, He that hath ears to hear, let him hear.

After English had firmly reestablished itself by the middle 1300's, a new tide of Latin borrowings came in, alongside the French words, which also derived from Latin. From the days of the Roman Empire onward, steadily through the Dark Ages, the Middle Ages, the Renaissance, and well into modern times, the international language of learning and science was Latin. All discourse at the universities was in Latin. Today, ceremonial lectures at Oxford and Cambridge continue to be delivered in Latin. The new tide of Latin brought into Middle English such familiar words as *client, psalm, equivalent, allegory, formal, library, dissolve, ascension, impediment, alienate,* and *dissent.* But it reached its height in the fifteenth century with a number of self-conscious poetic inventions, like *dispone,* and *equipolent,* known as "aureate [that is, gilded] diction." Most of these faded away, but some became permanent, like *laureate, mediation, oriental,* and *prolixity.* From the early 1500's, as the Modern period opened, and up through the days of Queen Elizabeth and Shakespeare, similar immense borrowings from Latin came into English, many literary and self-conscious, which were soon called, in reaction, "inkhorn terms." But most came in naturally as the Renaissance moved into England, as interest in the Greek and Roman classics revived under the stimulus of humanists like John Colet, William Lyly, and Erasmus, and as scientists and voyagers expanded their discoveries.

MODERN ENGLISH (1500 onward)

The Modern period of the English language really begins when William Caxton brought the printing press to England, and London, in 1476. On the continent, where he learned the craft he had already issued, probably in 1474 and 1475, the first two books printed in English: his translation of a French romance concerning the Trojan War, *Recuyell of the Historyes* *of Troye,* and *The Game and Playe of Chesse,* also translated from the French. Setting up at Westminster, he issued almost eighty books, many his own translations, in his remaining fourteen years of life. His books confirmed the English of London as the national standard, though great variety in dialect and usage persisted as perfectly acceptable well into the seventeenth century. Throughout the sixteenth century, the language "seems to be in a plastic, unformed state, and its writers, as it were, experiment with it, bending it to constructions which now seem indefensible," writes Sir James A. H. Murray.* Nevertheless, Caxton did a great deal toward stabilizing a language even more fluid and diversified, worrying about what words to use so the largest number could understand him, whether to write *eggs* as *egges* (from Old Norse), which a country woman could not understand, or as *eyren* (from Old English), which presumably would puzzle others.†

By Shakespeare's day, English had somewhat settled down, but was still exploring its riches, with a sense of freedom. The civil war that tore England apart in the middle 1600's also shook the language into further transition, but with the Restoration of 1660 and the general reaching out for postwar stability, the language settled into a recognizably modern form, with the Bloodless Revolution of 1688 usually taken as the final watershed into modernity, as the language attained a new smoothness and fluency under the pen of John Dryden.

Samuel Johnson's *Dictionary* of 1755 helped to stabilize English spelling, and Bishop Robert Lowth's *A Short Introduction to English Grammar* (1762) did much the same for grammar, setting the pattern for school texts almost down to our own time. Johnson and Lowth shared the age's wish for stability, definition, and clarity. Both looked at the classical languages, particularly Latin, as fountainheads, at which modern languages ought again to refresh themselves. Their works, and others following, answered the urge of a new mercantile society moving upward to affluence and literacy, and wanting to know what was deemed correct in cultivated circles. Nineteenth-century America, sprawling rapidly to new and newer frontiers, pursued correctness in pronunciation and usage even more persistently than England, toward which America continued to feel secretly and chronically inferior.

The influence of Latin on English has been, from the first, considerable. Some sixty percent of our modern vocabulary comes, one way or another, from Latin, and many influential writers from the sixteenth

Encyc. Brit., 11th ed. (1910), p. 601.
†In his Preface to his translation of Virgil's *Aeneid* (1490); see below, pp. 327–328.

through the nineteenth centuries have had Latin in their heads as they wrote their English. Schooling of *every* boy in England from Shakespeare through Fielding and on to about 1866, consisted basically of studying the classics and memorizing Lyly's *Latin Grammar* (c. 1513), used in all schools in England, and later in America, with almost no change for three and a half centuries. This classical cast of mind helped frame the Declaration of Independence and the U.S. Constitution—note the "Senate" straight from ancient Rome—and shaped the linguistic habits of those who wrote and spoke English well into the twentieth century. A certain learned eloquence persisted in correspondence and conversation, as men and women read George Eliot and Dickens aloud, quoted poetry to each other, and attended to the ornate oratory of the pulpit and the popular lecture platform. Before World War I, most American universities still required a proficiency in Latin for admission.

AMERICAN ENGLISH

The language the people of Jamestown and Plymouth first brought to America was not only ample in heritage and potential, but was in the especially fluid and fluent state of the late Renaissance. The most significant shift in pronunciation since 449, though almost completed, was still in progress. The English long vowels—*ah, ay, ee, oh, oo*—shifted from the "continental" quality they shared with their sister languages to the diphthongs of modern English, the double vowels all of us say, though we hear them as single letters: we think *a,* but pronounce it to rhyme with something like "May-ee." Beginning in the fifteenth century, *a* shifted from *ah* to the "May-ee" of *make*. Long *e*, which had sounded like modern *make,* shifted to *ee; i* became *ai; o* became *oh-oo; u* changed from *oo* to the *au* in *ouch*. In Virginia to this day, people retain something of the older *u*, because their ancestors came over before the *u* had fully shifted, calling a *house* a "huh-oos" and a *mouse* a "muh-oos," after the Old English *hūs* ("hoos") and *mūs* ("moos"). English-speaking Canadians, whose ancestors came largely from Scotland two centuries later, say these words very much like Virginians, because in Scotland the Old English *u* never fully shifted to *au*.

British and American pronunciations now differ considerably, with New England and the South being somewhat nearer to British in their dropping of the final *r*, but differing from educated British and from each other in many other ways. These areas were settled mostly by people from the old East-Anglian region—southeastern England, including London. The middle area—New Jersey, Delaware, Maryland, Pennsylvania, which now stretches to the west coast and northwest—came mostly from more northern English regions where the r remained hard, or even trilled. Consequently, most Americans say *water* not *watah.*

Aside from "New England" and "Southern," the vast majority of Americans can hardly detect regional differences among themselves, though these exist both in qualities of pronunciation and in vocabulary. Radio, TV, and the movies have evened out American pronunciation considerably. Although levels of education and affluence still produce marked differences, as do the many minority dialects, particularly Black English, the lines between regional and social groups in America are not so explicitly drawn in pronunciation and vocabulary as they are between upper class and working class in England, or among the numerous regional and rural dialects of Britain, which retain many differing traces from old Anglo-Saxon-Nordic times—dialects that many Americans and some Britishers have great difficulty in understanding.

These Old English traces remain in American regional usages also. America keeps the Anglo-Saxon *dune,* but limits it to a sandhill; England uses the later vowel-shifted version, *down,* for its hills (which mixes Americans up). American English frequently retains these older forms that British has long since lost: *gotten,* for instance, as against British (and American) *got.* The British say "his attitude *to* sports"; Americans, "his attitude *toward* sports," keeping the more elaborate and less frequent of the two Anglo-Saxon alternatives. The Old Germanic habit of accenting beginnings and swallowing endings is stronger in England, producing what Americans call the "clipped" British way of speaking, with "Thank you" sounding like "kyup!" and *extraordinary* like *strórdnr,* and even *got* and *that* now swallowed back in the throat, in common parlance, to the briefest *ga'* and *tha',* so that the modern Londoner sounds like the traditional Scot with his "Will y' na' come back again." Americans have followed the printed word more closely than have the British, tending to pronounce syllables and letters slurred over by Britishers—evidently, as we have seen, from the early feeling of cultural inferiority and the drive to be educated. Nevertheless, in rural American speech, some words the city-dweller thinks mere country ignorance actually reflect the oldest forms, as they do also in rural England: *lookee,* for instance, from the archaic *look ye* that goes straight back to Anglo-Saxon, and *ax,* for "ask," which still seems to reflect the dominant Anglo-Saxon verb, *ācsian* or *āxian,* of which *āscian* was then only a minor variant.

Many such differences in American speechways reflect the region of England (and sometimes the historical period) from which a particular group of settlers came. But since most groups included people widely assorted from different old Anglo-Saxon dialectical areas, the reasons for one American region's saying, for instance, *pail* and another's saying *bucket* are obscure. *Pail* goes back to Anglo-Saxon; *bucket,* to the Normans. But why one should prevail in Maine and the other in Pennsylvania eludes certainty. The different choices in America simply demonstrate how language will develop independently in any region not consistently communicating with another. So an American's car has a *hood;* a Britisher's, a *bonnet.* One buys *gas;* the other, *petrol. Two-lane traffic* is a *dual carriageway;* an *overpass,* a *flyover;* a *drugstore,* a *chemist's shop. Corn,* in England, is wheat, or any grain; in America it's on the cob, or in something generally rural or *corny.* And an American's *crotch* is a Britisher's *crutch.*

American English has always been inventive, and highly absorptive, and many Americanisms have gone back to England and around the world. *O.K.* may be the world's most universal word.* Our Thomas Jefferson invented the ever-popular *belittle. Cocktail, jackpot, know-how, fizzle, bingo, honk* are all American innovations as are most of our terms of racial contempt, like *honky,* first applied (in the form *Bohunk,* "Bohemian-Hungarian") to Hungarian immigrants of the steel mills and coal mines by established whites, now applied to all whites by blacks. *Honky-tonk,* which seems to have come from a tinking-tonking piano, and *jazz,* which arose, with the music, from the Black culture of New Orleans, both with an African origin (Pyles, p. 47), have become international English words. Another is *Yankee,* perhaps from *Janke,* the diminutive of *Jan* (Dutch for "John"), as a nickname for New York's early Dutch settlers.

---

*Allen Walker Read traces it to the O.K. Club, supporting Martin Van Buren against William Henry Harrison in the presidential campaign of 1840. "O.K." stood for "Old Kinderhook," Van Buren's nickname, from his birthplace, Kinderhook, New York. "The O.K. Club" first appeared in print on March 23, 1840. But the opposition decided to smudge the Democrats by an article "explaining" O.K. as an illiterate abbreviation of "All Correct" by the incumbent President, Andrew Jackson, Van Buren's sponsor ("The Evidence on O.K." *The Saturday Review of Literature,* July 19, 1941, summarized and discussed by Thomas Pyles, *Words and Ways of American English* [New York: Random House, Inc., 1952], pp. 158–165). O.K. had indeed originated as an abbreviation for humorously misspelt "oll korrect" in a spate of abbreviations in the Boston newspapers in the 1830's, along with *N.G.* ("no go"), *R.T.B.S.* ("remains to be seen"), and *S.P.* ("small potatoes"), according to Merriam-Webster researchers (*Christian Science Monitor,* December 2, 1977). The O.K. Club was apparently exploiting a coincidence with popular slang. A later theory, that *O.K.* derived from Choctaw *hoke* ("it is so"), a theory much liked by President Woodrow Wilson, who wrote it *okeh,* gave the term a certain respectable boost.

But the most curious thing about American English is the great difference in pronunciation between New England and the South—areas both settled mostly from southeast England in the same span of history. New Englanders apparently tended to nasalize, especially the Puritans, whom an Englishman in 1770 reported as having a "whining cadence" in their speech (Pyles, p. 241). On the other hand, Southern speech seems to have mellowed.

However one may attempt to explain this distinction—the languid climate and slower pace in life, for instance—the greatest single distinction between North and South was, almost from the first, a considerable population of African slaves. Black slaves, often deliberately assorted from different tribes to minimize revolts on shipboard and ashore, had no common language.* The slave's greatest need was to talk with his fellow captives. The white master had little to say to him. A *git,* a *wuk,* a *come,* a *go,* and a whip, would probably suffice. For communication among themselves, slaves used whatever lingua franca they could acquire from their captors and each other. In the fourteenth century, Sabir, the French-Italian-Spanish pidgin of the Arab slavers, the oldest in the business, was current. When the Portuguese began to dominate world trade in the fifteenth and sixteenth centuries, the West African slaving areas began to acquire Pidgin Portuguese. *Pickaninny, savvy,* and *Negro* (reinforcing the earlier Sabir-Spanish) testify to their Portuguese origin. The simplified grammar of Pidgin Portuguese probably copied that of Sabir, and the simplified grammar of Pidgin English probably followed that of both.†

But African intonations and words were shaping whatever pidgin or creole a slave community acquired. In Louisiana, a French pidgin evolved into an indigenous French Creole. Slaves who escaped to islands offshore of South Carolina, Georgia, and Florida evolved from the pidgins of Portuguese and English, and their native African, an independent creole language known as Gullah, a language which in turn put many Africanisms first into Black English, then into general American usage: *jazz,* most notably, and *tote, gumbo, buckaroo, banjo, okra, juke, bozo, voodoo,* and probably other special usages like *hip, hep,* and *cat* (Dillard, pp. 118–119). *Mon,* or "man," almost universal for address and exclamation in black dialects around the Caribbean, has now become almost equally universal in young American speech.

*For this point and a number of others following, I am indebted to J. L. Dillard, *Black English* (New York: Random House, Inc., 1972), pp. 73 ff.

†Keith Whinnon, "The Origin of the European-based Creoles and Pidgins," *Orbis* (1968), pp. 509–526, cited Dillard, p. 21.

Thus, even as blacks were acquiring English, something of their intonations and idioms was tempering the English of their white masters. The white pidgin-speaker, when giving orders, would naturally imitate the black to make himself understood, and some of that imitation would eventually remain. Even more significant was the black mammy, and her children, with whom the white child spent much of his time from infancy onward. William Faulkner's short story "That Evening Sun" illustrates the process still at work in relatively modern times. Conversely, Southern vowels were changing in ways wholly unrelated to West African, Caribbean, or Gullah,* and blacks were acquiring them as they learned the white community's speech. From the first, the early pidgins and Plantation Creole moved steadily over toward the evolving Standard English,† and moved outward to virtually every state in the nation. The dual process continues from coast to coast, as whites acquire black idioms and intonations, and blacks acquire the shared standard usages.

Writing makes the ultimate selection, and is perhaps the ultimate educator. Like Caxton in 1490, the modern writer ponders which words will reach the widest audience, which will connect him with the largest sharing of culture, which will persuade, which may lose him the credit he needs to be convincing. His choices, and their social nuances, are richly varied, since English has gathered and kept synonyms not only from its Germanic-Latin-Norse-French mainstream but from most of the other languages one can name. English probably has the largest living vocabulary in the world, because its literature—the written language—keeps alive, in great works, those words that speech alone would have long since lost.

Literature continually breathes new life into the inevitable decay of daily usage as metaphors and precisions fade into gobbledegook, and prominent people can utter with satisfaction such densities as *fuel economy program success.* A word like *sanction,* for instance, which means "a blessing," comes in official jargon to mean also its opposite, a "penalty," its precision impaired, until some poet comes along to remind us again of what it means, at the root, in the holy sanctions of the heart. The spoken word dies on our breath. The written word endures—*litera scripta manet*—because the writer makes words mean what they say, and renews their durable life. As Auden reminds us, Time, who is

---

*William Labov, commenting on my earlier draft of this section.

†Dillard notes that runaway slaves—people of nerve and ability—"were likely to be just those slaves who did attain a relative mastery of Standard English" (p. 86): a runaway would need to communicate with a wide diversity of people who would not understand Plantation Creole, and reading and writing Standard English was greatly to his advantage.

. . . indifferent in a week
To a beautiful physique,

Worships language and forgives
Everyone by whom it lives.*

To join that timeless crowd by whom language lives is the writer's secret obsession, as he searches the clutter of everyday usage for the real riches of the world's most extended language.

The process of writing, then, brings these riches into our personal usage, and our speech acquires the breadth and span of the written language, moving into the mainstream from whatever regional or dialectical point we may have started. This mainstream, this Standard English, is constantly gathering new vitalities from its edges and dropping others no longer of use. To use it well is to share a living entity, perhaps with some wonder at the strange energy in Indo-European that slowly flowed outward over Europe and Asia, and then, in a much changed and minor dialect, reached southern England in 449 to carry itself on around the world.

EXERCISES

1. *Pick five common words now in slang or dialectical usage*—joint, *or* roach, *or* grass, *for a marijuana cigarette, for instance. Write a clear definition of each in Standard English anyone could understand, then look up the word's origin in the dictionary. Put this origin, together with a brief speculation on how the slang term may have derived, in parentheses after your definition.*

EXAMPLE *joint:* a cigarette made from dried flower clusters and leaves of the hemp plant, *cannabis sativa,* usually rolled loosely in paper by the user. (Middle English, from Old French, from the past participle of *joindre,* "to join," possibly because the user "joins" the materials.)

If your term is not in the dictionary, try another that is. If you can see no connection between its origin and its slang usage, say "slang origin obscure."

2. *Translate the following passage of standard prose into your own local or regional dialect of English, or into contemporary college slang. You will need to*

*W. H. Auden, from "In Memory of W. B. Yeats," in *Collected Shorter Poems 1927–1957* (New York: Random House, 1966). Copyright 1940, renewed 1968 by W. H. Auden. Reprinted by permission of Random House, Inc.

keep some of the author's words and phrases, of course, but make the transformation as thorough as possible. Would Schlesinger's article be more effective or less, if it moved some of the way toward your version? All the way? Does your translation change the meaning?

What more astonishing adventure could there have been than that of the settlement of America? Anonymous men and women, renouncing a familiar and traditional existence, abandoning places where their families had lived for centuries, embarked on frail ships, crossed perilous seas and put down roots in an unknown and alien continent. It requires a violent thrust of the contemporary imagination to comprehend the courage—the courage and the despair and the hope—that lay behind countless individual decisions in quiet European villages. And so they came, laid their lives on the line, endured hardship and vicissitude. Many gave up or starved or were killed by disease or Indians. The survivors gradually came to terms with the new land.

Roanoke Island, 1585: the lost colony, the settlers mysteriously vanished, only the word CROATOAN carved on a post to mark the fact that Englishmen had tried to live there, the enigma of their disappearance unsolved to this day. Jamestown, 1607: two-thirds of the first settlers dying from famine and sickness. "There were never Englishmen left in a forreigne Country in such miseries as we," wrote one of them. "So lamentable was our scarcity," wrote another, "that we were constrained to eat dogs, cats, rats, snakes, toadstools, horsehides and what not; one man out of the misery that he endured, killing his wife, powdered her up to eat her, for which he was burned." Plymouth, 1620: half the colonists dying in the first year.

But the survivors hung on. "It is not with us as with other men," the Pilgrims said, "whom small things can discourage, or small discontentments cause to wish themselves at home again." They built their dwellings, organized their governments, enacted their laws, cleared their forests, discovered new crops and new ways to farm, heard the call of the dark and silent wilderness beyond. Nor was the invasion of America an English monopoly. The Dutch settled on Manhattan Island, Swedes along the Delaware, Scotch-Irish and Germans in Pennsylvania, French and Spanish in Florida. Whether sustained by relish of adventure or by the search for gold or by the desire to worship God as they saw fit, they were men and women beyond the reach of small discontentments.*

---

*From Arthur Schlesinger, Jr., "The Birth of a Nation—A Journey into America's Past," *Travel & Leisure* (American Express Publishing Corp.), July 1974. Copyright © 1974 by Arthur Schlesinger, Jr.

3. *Translate into clear contemporary English the following famous passage from William Caxton's Prologue to his translation (from the French) of Virgil's Aeneid, which he spelled* Eneydos *(1490). Remember that printed* u *frequently stood for* v, *as in* ouer, *and that printed* v *frequently stood for* u, *as in* vnderstande. *In his* yᵗ, *he is using* y *for the Old English thorn,* þ, *the th-sound, which, combined with the little superscript* t *was an abbreviation for* that. *(The* ye *of Middle English and the sixteenth century, incidentally, similarly stood for the sound* the *when used as an article, as in* ye booke, *not* ye, *as we now read it; but* ye, *meaning "you" was pronounced "yee.") Caxton's* tamyse *is the river Thames;* zelande *is Zeeland (southern Holland);* forlond *is Foreland, the farthest tip of land on the southern shore of the Thames estuary, just north of where the Jutes landed in 449.*

. . . I delybered and concluded to translate it in-to englysshe, And forthwyth toke a penne & ynke, and wrote a leef or tweyne whyche I ouersawe agayn to corecte it. And whan I sawe the fayr & straunge termes therin I doubted that it sholde not please some gentylmen whiche late blamed me, sayeng, yᵗ in my translacyons I had ouer curyous termes whiche coude not be vnderstande of comyn peple and desired me to vse olde and homely termes in my tran-slacyons. and fayn wolde I satysfye euery man and so to doo, toke an olde boke and redde therin and certaynly the englysshe was so rude and brood that I coude not wele vnderstande it. And also my lorde abbot of westmynster ded do shewe to me late, certayn euydences wryton in olde englysshe, for to reduce it in-to our englysshe now vsid. And certaynly it was wreton in suche wyse that it was more lyke to dutche than englysshe; I coude not reduce ne brynge it to be vnderstonden. And certaynly our langage now vsed varyeth ferre from that whiche was vsed and spoken whan I was borne. For we englysshe men ben borne vnder the domynacyon of the mone, whiche is neuer stedfaste but euer wauerynge, wexynge one season and waneth & dyscreaseth another season. And that comyn englysshe that is spoken in one shyre varyeth from a nother. In so moche that in my dayes happened that certayn marchauntes were in a shippe in tamyse, for to haue sayled ouer the see into zelande and for lacke of wynde, thei taryed atte forlond, and wente to lande for to refreshe them; And one of theym named sheffelde, a mercer, cam in-to an hows and axed for mete; and specyally he axyd after eggys; And the goode wyf answerde, that she coude speke no frenshe. And the marchaunt was angry, for he also coude speke no frenshe, but wolde haue hadde egges and she vnderstode hym not. And thenne at laste a nother sayd that he wolde haue eyren. then the good wyf sayd that she vnderstod hym wel. Loo, what

sholde a man in thyse dayes now wryte, egges or eyren. certaynly it is harde
to playse euery man by cause of dyuersite & chaunge of langage. For in these
dayes euery man that is in ony reputacyon in his countre, wyll vtter his com-
mynycacyon and maters in suche maners & termes that fewe men shall vnderstonde theym. And som honest and grete clerkes haue ben wyth me, and
desired me to wryte the moste curyous termes that I coude fynde. And thus
bytwene playn rude & curyous, I stande abasshed. but in my Iudgemente the
comyn termes that be dayli vsed, ben lyghter to be vnderstonde than the olde
and auncyent englysshe

4. *Translate into clear contemporary English the following passage from
Herman Melville's* Typee *(1846, Chapter 17). Melville (1819–1891) was a young
New Yorker, who, after trying schoolteaching, shipped out as a sailor before the
mast at nineteen. With a companion, he jumped ship at Nuku Hiva, Marquesas
Islands, in 1842. They crossed the mountainous island, and dropped into the
steeply enclosed valley, opening seaward, that was the territory of the Typees, a
tribe of cannibals. The chiefs and warrier-élite ate enemies slain in battle, at rit-
ualized feasts from which all commoners were excluded, but Melville had no way
of knowing how far their dietary habits might extend. His friend escaped in two
weeks, and he, eventually, in four. He had caught a fever, accompanied by a
painfully swollen leg, in crossing the mountains. Kory-Kory was the man assigned
to serve and guard him. The "Happy Valley" is the blissfully utopian mountain-valley
in Samuel Johnson's* Rasselas *(1759), from which no one who enters can escape.*

*After you have made your translation, list ten of Melville's words (or short
phrases) that sound odd in modern English, and for which you found modern
synonyms. Look up their derivations in your dictionary, and record them in parentheses. Then put down your words and derivations beneath each of Melville's.
What can you say about the differences in vocabulary between Melville's American
English of the 1840's and yours of the 1980's? What other differences can you
see between his passage and yours? What things have remained fairly stable?*

Day after day wore on, and still there was no perceptible change in the
conduct of the islanders towards me. Gradually I lost all knowledge of the
regular occurrence of the days of the week, and sunk insensibly into that kind
of apathy which ensues after some violent outbreak of despair. My limb suddenly healed, the swelling went down, the pain subsided, and I had every
reason to suppose I should soon completely recover from the affliction that
had so long tormented me.

As soon as I was enabled to ramble about the valley in company with
the natives, troops of whom followed me whenever I sallied out of the house,
I began to experience an elasticity of mind which placed me beyond the reach

of those dismal forebodings to which I had so lately been a prey. Received wherever I went with the most deferential kindness; regaled perpetually with the most delightful fruits; ministered to by dark-eyed nymphs; and enjoying besides all the services of the devoted Kory-Kory, I thought that for a sojourn among cannibals, no man could have well made a more agreeable one.

To be sure there were limits set to my wanderings. Toward the sea my progress was barred by an express prohibition of the savages; and after having made two or three ineffectual attempts to reach it, as much to gratify my curiosity as anything else, I gave up the idea. It was in vain to think of reaching it by stealth, since the natives escorted me in numbers wherever I went, and not for one single moment that I can recall to mind was I ever permitted to be alone.

The green and precipitous elevations that stood ranged around the head of the vale where Marheyo's habitation was situated effectually precluded all hope of escape in that quarter, even if I could have stolen away from the thousand eyes of the savages.

But these reflections now seldom obtruded upon me; I gave myself up to the passing hour, and if ever disagreeable thoughts arose in my mind, I drove them away. When I looked around the verdant recess in which I was buried, and gazed up to the summits of the lofty eminence that hemmed me in, I was well disposed to think that I was in the "Happy Valley," and that beyond those heights there was nought but a world of care and anxiety.

As I extended my wanderings in the valley and grew more familiar with the habits of its inmates, I was fain to confess that, despite the disadvantages of his condition, the Polynesian savage, surrounded by all the luxurious provisions of nature, enjoyed an infinitely happier, though certainly a less intellectual existence, than the self-complacent European.

A WRITER'S GRAMMAR

GRAMMAR AS THERAPY

You have already seen, in THE RHETORIC, many of the ills of writing—the ailing thesis that weakens the whole system, the *of*-and-*which* disease, the recurring rashes of wordiness. But many a sentence suffers from ailments more deeply genetic. You can probably tell when a sentence feels bad, especially after your instructor has marked it up. You can, in other words, detect the symptoms, but to work an efficient cure you need also to find the causes and to treat them directly. You need some skill in the old household remedies of grammar.

Indeed, grammatical ignorance—even in everyday conversation—is not exactly bliss. When you put it in writing, it is worse. You try to impress or persuade, and you fall on your face. And since the telltale slips are so easily corrected, letting them go is a shame. They can only distract your reader from what you are saying, and start him thinking, probably unflatteringly, about you. Keep your mind and your language alert, and you will retain his attention and respect. Keep the parts of your sentence well fitted, your prose active and spare, your meanings clearly working together. Keep trimly to the essential structure of the active sentence. Rid yourself of all inconsistencies in tense, voice, and mood. Above all, make your thoughts complete, with every noun and pronoun and verb in proper form, with nothing dangling, and with your meaning unmistakable. Good grammatical prose takes exercise, but it will increase your confidence and your effectiveness wherever you go.

GRAMMAR AS MEANING

Grammar, simply, fits a sentence together most meaningfully. On paper, you can see where the meanings slide. Here are fifteen sliding sentences, each with slippage noted, each slippage discussed on the text pages given at the right.

They *study hard, but* you *do not have to work all the time.* [You *does not agree with* They]   339

Holden goes *to New York and* learned *about life.* [Learned *does not agree in tense with* goes]   339

A citizen *should support the government, but* they *should also be free to criticize it.* [They *does not agree with* citizen.]   339

The professor, *as well as the students,* were *glad the course was over.* [Were *does not agree with* professor]   341

As *he looked up,* a *light could be seen* in the window. [*The subject has shifted awkwardly from* he *to* light, *and the verbal construction from active to passive.*]   338; 345

Now we knew: it was him. [Him *does not agree in case with the subject,* it.]   352

Let's keep this between you and I. [I *cannot be the object of* between]   353

Can you and Shirley play doubles next Sunday with Bob and I? [I *cannot be the object of with—with* I?]   353

They accuse William Singleton Stone and I *of mismanaging their accounts.* [I *cannot be the object of a verb—*accuse I?]   353

The students always elect whomever *is popular.* [Whomever *cannot be the subject of the verb* is.]   354

She hated me leaving so early. [*She hated not* me *but the* leaving.]   355

Bill told *Fred* that he failed the exam. [*He can mean either* Bill *or* Fred.]   356

Each of the laborers performed their *task.* [*Each and* their *disagree in number.*]   358

Father felt *badly.* [*Badly* describes Father's *competence, not his condition.*]   359

They walked leisurely. [*The verb requires an adverb, like* slowly.]   359

She said on Tuesday *she* would call. [*The position of* on Tuesday *confuses the times of* saying *and* calling.]   361

Walking to class, her book *slipped from her grasp.* [*Walking* refers illogically to *book.*]   363

While playing *the piano, the* dog *sat by me and* howled. [*Dogs don't play pianos.*]   363, 364

With each of these, you sense that something is wrong. With a little thought you can usually find the trouble. But what to do may not be so readily apparent. We first need to understand something of the basic structure of grammar.

Know the basic parts of speech.

The parts of speech are the elements of the sentence. A grasp of the basic eight—nouns, pronouns, verbs, adjectives, adverbs, prepositions, conjunctions, and interjections—will give you a sense of the whole.

NOUNS. Nouns name something. A *proper noun* names a particular person, place, or thing. A *common noun* names a general class of things; a common noun naming a group as a single unit is a *collective noun*. A phrase or clause functioning as a noun is a *noun phrase* or a *noun clause*. Here are some examples:

COMMON: **stone, tree, house, girl, artist, nation, democracy**
PROPER: George, Cincinnati, Texas, Europe, Declaration of Independence
COLLECTIVE: **committee, family, quartet, herd, navy, clergy, kind**
NOUN PHRASE: *Riding the surf* takes stamina.
NOUN CLAUSE: *What you say* may depend on *how you say it.*

PRONOUNS. As their name indicates, pronouns stand "for nouns." The noun a pronoun represents is called its *antecedent*. Pronouns may be classified as follows:

> PERSONAL *(standing for persons):* I, you, he, she, we, they; me, him, her, us, them; my, his, our, and so on
> REFLEXIVE *(turning the action back on the doer):* I hurt *myself.* They enjoy *themselves.*
> INTENSIVE *(emphasizing the doer):* He *himself* said so.
> RELATIVE *(linking subordinate clauses):* who, which, that, whose, whomever, whichever, and so on
> INTERROGATIVE *(beginning a question):* who, which, what
> DEMONSTRATIVE *(pointing to things):* this, that, these, those, such
> INDEFINITE *(standing for indefinite numbers of persons or things):* any, each, few, some, anyone, no one, everyone, somebody, and so on
> RECIPROCAL *(plural reflexives):* each other, one another

VERBS. Verbs express actions or states of being. A verb may be *transitive,* requiring an object to complete the thought, or *intransitive,* requiring no object for completeness. Some verbs can function either transitively or intransitively. *Linking verbs* link the subject to a state of being.

> TRANSITIVE: He *put* his feet on the chair. She *hit* the ceiling. They *sang* a sad old song.
> INTRANSITIVE: He *smiled.* She *cried.* They *sang* like birds. They *are coming.*
> LINKING: He *is* happy. She *feels* angry. This *looks* bad. It *is* she.

ADJECTIVES. Adjectives describe nouns or pronouns. An *adjectival phrase* or *adjectival clause* functions in a sentence as a single adjective would.

> ADJECTIVES: The *red* house faces west. He was a *handsome* devil. The *old haunted* house was *empty. These* books belong to *that* student. [In the last example, demonstrative pronouns serve as adjectives.]
> ADJECTIVAL PHRASE: He had reached the end *of the book.*
> ADJECTIVAL CLAUSE: Here is the key *that unlocks the barn.*

ADVERBS. Adverbs describe verbs, adjectives, or other adverbs, completing the ideas of *how, how much, when,* and *where.* An *adverbial phrase* or *adverbial clause* functions as a single adverb would.

> ADVERBS: Though *slightly* fat, he runs *quickly* and plays *extremely well.*

ADVERBIAL PHRASE: **He left** *after the others.*

ADVERBIAL CLAUSE: **She lost the gloves** *after she left the store.*

PREPOSITIONS. A preposition links a noun or pronoun to another word in the sentence. A preposition and its object form a *prepositional phrase,* which acts as an adjective or adverb:

> BY *late afternoon,* **Williams was exhausted.** [as adverb, modifying *was*]
>
> He walked TO *his car* and drove FROM *the field.* [as adverbs, modifying *walked* and *drove*]
>
> The repairman opened the base OF *the telephone.* [as adjective modifying *base*]

Certain forms of verbs, alone or in phrases, serve as nouns, adjectives, and adverbs. *Participles* act as adjectives. *Present participles* are verbs plus *-ing,* and *past participles* are regular verbs plus *-ed* (see pp. 348–349 for *Irregular verbs*). *Gerunds,* like present participles, are verbs plus *-ing* but work as nouns; past participles occasionally function as nouns, also. *Infinitives*—*to* plus a verb—serve as nouns, adjectives, or adverbs. Unlike participles and gerunds, infinitives can have subjects, which are always in the objective case.

> PRESENT PARTICIPLES: *Feeling* **miserable and** *running* **a fever, she took to her bed.** [adjectives]
>
> PAST PARTICIPLES: **The nurses treated the** *wounded* **soldier.** [adjective]
> **The nurses treated the** *wounded.* [noun]
>
> GERUND PHRASE: *His going* **ended the friendship.** [noun, subject of sentence]
>
> INFINITIVES: *To err* **is human;** *to forgive,* **divine.** [nouns, subjects of sentence]
>
> **I saw** *him* [*to*] *go.* [phrase serving as noun, object of *saw; him* subject of *to go*]
>
> **Ford is the man** *to watch.* [adjective]
>
> **Coiled, the snake waited** *to strike.* [adverb]

CONJUNCTIONS. Conjunctions join words, phrases, and clauses. *Coordinating* conjunctions—*and, but, or, yet*—join equals:

> **Mary** *and* **I won easily.**
> **Near the shore** *but* **far from home, the bottle floated.**
> **He was talented,** *yet* **he failed.**

Subordinating conjunctions attach clauses to the basic subject-and-verb:

> *Since* it was late, they left.
> He worked hard *because* he needed an A.
> They stopped *after* they reached the spring.

INTERJECTIONS. Interjections interrupt the usual flow of the sentence to emphasize feelings:

> But, *oh,* the difference to me.
> Mr. Dowd, *alas,* has ignored the evidence.
> The consumer will suddenly discover that, *ouch,* his dollar is cut in half.

SENTENCES

Learn to identify the simple subject and its verb.

Grammar conveniently classifies the words in your sentences into parts of speech. With the natural and logical joining of parts, thought begins. And the very beginning is the subject and its verb. A noun expresses a meaning, which, when expressed, gathers other meanings to it. The mere idea of *tree* moves on to include some idea of a verb: *tree is.* And other subject-verb thoughts are probably not far behind: *tree sways; it drops its leaves.* With *The poplar tree sways in the wind, dropping yellow leaves on the lawn,* you have a full-grown sentence. At its heart are *tree*— the simple subject (the subject shorn of all modifiers)—and *sways,* the verb. All the rest is filling out, or explaining, of the simple subject and its verb. You should accustom yourself to locating these two parts in an ailing sentence. They will help you see how its other parts are behaving— or ought to behave. First, find the verb, since that names the action: *sways.* Then ask *who* or *what.* The answer gives you your subject, *tree,* which, with modifiers cut away, is the simple subject. Having found the heart—*simple subject* plus *verb*—you are well on the way to understanding the rest of your sentence's anatomy.

Know the structure—and modifications—of the simple sentence.

The simple English sentence can take one of three essential forms:

I. Subject-Verb

II. Subject-Verb-Object
III. Subject-Is-Something

These three incorporate the three major kinds of verbs (indicated in brackets):

I. Subject-Verb [*intransitive*]

She *smiles.*
He *laughs* like a perfect idiot.
The tree *sways* in the wind.

II. Subject-Verb [*transitive*]-Object

Boy *meets* girl.
He *liked* her minibus.
They *cashed* the check.

III. Subject-Is [*linking*]-Something

The temperature *is* up.
They *are* here.
This *tastes* salty.
The pie *smells* good.

Is is the most common linking verb; but, as you see, a number of other verbs may serve: *taste, smell, feel, look, seem, appear, act, get, grow, turn, become.*

Simple Sentence   Although the structure is simple, the simple sentence may exhibit considerable variation. It may contain compounds in subject or predicate:

The *boy* and the *girl,* the *aunt, and* the whole hypocritical *family* smile. [compound subject]
He *hit* the right note with her *and struck* a full sympathetic chord with her parents. [compound predicate]
The *president* of the company *and* the *chairman* of the board *stormed and raged.* [compounds in subject and predicate]

Or it may attach modifiers to subject and verb:

Beautiful beyond imagination, glowing with health, *she* won the contest. [*She* is the subject]
He *swam,* unaware of sharks, indifferent to snipers' bullets, as if he were merely racing again in the varsity pool. [*Swam* is the verb.]

Or put the verb before the subject:

> **Near the window** *stood* **a folding** *screen.*
> **Behind it** *was* **the** *murderer.*
> **There** *is* **a problem.** [The expletive *there* can never be a subject.]
> **It** *was* **too bad** *that he quit.* [*That he quit,* a noun clause, is the
> subject. Like *There, It* is an expletive introducing the sentence.
> You will write more concisely if you avoid these expletives
> altogether: *Unfortunately, he quit. We have a problem.*]

Or use a verbal form for subject:

> *To see* **it will be enough.**
> *Seeing* **it will convince you.**

Or omit the subject (*you* implied) in a command or request—an *imperative*
sentence:

> **Get smart.**
> **If it is not too much trouble, please punctuate accurately.**
> **Take, oh take, those lips away.**

Two or more simple sentences can combine into a *compound* sentence: **Compound
Sentence**

> **He drove the car, and she did the talking.**
> **He liked the scenery, she liked the maps, and they both enjoyed the
> motels.**
> **The food was good; the prices were reasonable.**
> **Either the plan was bad, or the instructions failed.**

A simple sentence with one or more subordinate clauses added becomes **Complex
Sentence**
a *complex* sentence:

> **When the weather cleared, they started their vacation.**
> **Although the weather was fine, although the timing was perfect,
> although expenses were no problem, their vacation was miserable.**
> **They returned home as soon as they could.**

Two or more simple sentences combined with one or more subordinate **Compound-
Complex
Sentence**
clauses become a *compound-complex* sentence:

> **When the weather cleared, they started their vacation, but they
> returned home as soon as they could.**

EXERCISES

1. *Treat these ailing sentences. In your cured versions, underline the simple subject of each clause once, and the subject's verb twice. Underline any other changes, and put brackets around subordinate clauses where you find them.*

SIMPLE SENTENCES

1. The old and the young, the feeble and the sprightly, joins the dance.
2. John Stevenson liked everything about the old town, her relatives, and she most of all.
3. There is one or two things left to do.
4. Solving several specific problems are good exercise.
5. Ann, as well as her mother, like to sew.

COMPOUND SENTENCES

6. He drives the car, and she, a friendly girl, do the talking.
7. Jim drove the car, and her friends think him crazy.
8. They liked the dinner, but they forgot to thank Gertrude and I.
9. Either the bed was too hard, or it is too expensive for one night.

COMPLEX SENTENCES

10. While leaving the stadium, the game was over.
11. Whenever he comes, a party could be expected to begin.
12. Them who gets there first gets the best seats.
13. After all these years, they still envied him succeeding in everything he tried.
14. Winding the grandfather clocks that stand in several rooms are easy, since they just pull the chains that lifts the weights.
15. All the people, whoever happened to be in the village, was welcome.

SUBJECTS

Avoid awkward changes of subject in midsentence.

Unnecessary shifts in structure can confuse a sentence's vision and its sense of direction. A needless change in subject may make a sentence appear unsure whether it is coming or going.

> FAULTY: **As *I* entered the room, *voices* could be heard.**
> REVISED: **As *I* entered the room, *I* could hear voices.**

> FAULTY: **The *audience* was pleased by his performance, and *he* earned a standing ovation.**

REVISED: His performance pleased the audience and earned him a standing ovation.

FAULTY: The first *problem* is political, but there are *questions* of economics that are almost entirely involved in the second problem.
REVISED: The first *problem* is political; the second, principally economic.

FAULTY: *Jim* rolled up his sleeves, the *axe* was raised, and the *sapling* came down with four powerful strokes.
REVISED: *Jim* rolled up his sleeves, raised the axe, and cut the sapling down with four powerful strokes.

Avoid illogical shifts in person and number.

Person refers to the form a pronoun and verb take to indicate who is speaking, who is being spoken to, and who is being spoken about:

I am—first person   Person
You are—second person
He is, they are—third person

Numbers refers to the form a noun or pronoun and verb take to indicate one *(singular)* or more than one *(plural)*. A sentence that shifts illogically in person or number is almost completely unhinged: it cannot distinguish between persons, or it has forgotten how to count.

FAULTY: *They* have reached an age when *you* should know better.   Number
REVISED: *They* have reached an age when *they* should know better.

FAULTY: *The reader has* difficulty in following the argument. *You get* lost in qualifications.
REVISED: *The reader has* difficulty in following the argument. *He gets* lost in qualifications.

FAULTY: If *someone asks* her a question, *they get* a straight answer.
REVISED: If *someone asks* her a question, *he gets* a straight answer.

FAULTY: A motion *picture can improve* upon a book, but *they* usually *do* not.
REVISED: A motion *picture can improve* upon a book, but *it* usually *does* not.

EXERCISE

2. *Revise the following sentences, correcting the awkward shifts of subject, person, and number.*

1. A stitch was dropped, and Barbara sighed.
2. Whenever a stitch was dropped, Barbara would sigh.
3. First he investigated the practical implications, and then the moral implications that were involved were examined.
4. Sam sat down at the counter, catsup was poured on the hamburger, and there was hunger in his face as he ate it.
5. These statistics are impressive, but error is evident in them.
6. The United Nations is not so firmly established that they can enforce international law.
7. One should never assume that they have no faults.
8. A person is overwhelmed by the gardens. Everywhere you look is beauty.
9. The buffalo is far from extinct. Their numbers are actually increasing.
10. People distrust his glibness. One feels they are being taken in by him.

VERBS

Keep your verb and its subject in agreement.

Match singulars with singulars, plurals with plurals. You will have little trouble except when subject and verb are far apart, or when the number of the subject itself is doubtful. (Is *family* singular or plural? What about *none?*—about *neither he nor she?*)

Sidestep the plural constructions that fall between your singular subject and its verb:

FAULTY: **The *attention* of the students *wander* out the window.**
REVISED: **The *attention* of the students *wanders* out the window.**

FAULTY: ***Revision* of their views about markets and averages *are* mandatory.**
REVISED: ***Revision* of their views about markets and averages *is* mandatory.**

FAULTY: **The *plaster,* as well as the floors, *need* repair.**
REVISED: **The *plaster,* as well as the floors, *needs* repair.**

Collective nouns (*committee, jury, herd, group, family, kind, quartet*) are single units; give them singular verbs, or plural members:

FAULTY: Her *family were* ready.
REVISED: Her *family was* ready.

FAULTY: The *jury have disagreed* among themselves.
REVISED: The *members* of the jury *have disagreed* among themselves.

FAULTY: *These kind* of muffins *are* delicious.
REVISED: *This kind* of muffin *is* delicious.

Remember that in clauses introduced by expletive *there* (which can never be a subject though it may look like one), the subject follows the verb and governs its number:

> There *is* only one good *choice*.
> There *are* several good *choices*.

"There"

But expletive *it* always takes a singular verb:

> It *is* [*was*] the *child*.
> It *is* [*was*] the *children*.

"It"

Watch out for the indefinite pronouns *each, either, neither, anyone, everyone, no one, none, everybody, nobody*. Each of these is (not *are*) singular in idea, yet each flirts with the crowd from which it singles out its idea: each of *these*, either of *them*, none of *them*. They all take singular verbs. *None of them are*, of course, is very common. From Shakespeare's time to ours, it has persisted alongside the more precise *none of them is*, which seems to have the edge in careful prose.

Indefinite Pronouns

FAULTY: *None* of these men *are* failures.
REVISED: *None* of these men *is* a failure.

FAULTY: *None* of the class, even those best prepared, *want* the test.
REVISED: *None* of the class, even those best prepared, *wants* the test.

FAULTY: *Everybody* on the committee *are* present.
REVISED: *Everybody* on the committee *is* present.

FAULTY: *Neither* the right nor the left *support* the issue.
REVISED: *Neither* the right nor the left *supports* the issue.

When one side, or both, of the *either-or* contrast is plural, the verb conventionally matches the closer side:

> Either the players or the coach *is* bad.
> Neither the rights of man nor the needs of the commonwealth *are* relevant to the question.

In the first example, though, *players is* disturbs some feelings for plurality. The best solution is probably to switch your nouns:

> **Either the coach or the players *are* bad.**

Relative Pronouns
When a relative pronoun *(who, which, that)* is the subject of a clause, it takes a singular verb if its antecedent is singular, a plural verb if its antecedent is plural:

> **The *person* who *tries* cannot fail.**
> **The *people* who *try* cannot fail.**

FAULTY: **Phil is one of the best *swimmers* who *has* ever been on the team.**

REVISED: **Phil is one of the best *swimmers* who *have* ever been on the team.**

FAULTY: **Phil is the only *one* of our swimmers who *have* won three gold medals.**

REVISED: **Phil is the only *one* of our swimmers who *has* won three gold medals.**

Don't let a plural noun in the predicate lure you into a plural verb:

FAULTY: **His most faithful rooting *section are* his girl and his family.**
REVISED: **His most faithful rooting *section is* his girl and his family.**

Use the tense that best expresses your idea.

Tense means time (from Latin *tempus*). Using verbs of the right tense means placing the action in the right period of time. Usually, you have no trouble choosing the forms to express simple past, present, and future; but you may have trouble expressing "perfected" forms of past, present, and future—especially when they must appear in the same sentence or paragraph with the simpler forms.

Here, with active and passive examples, are the six principal tenses found in English:

TENSE	ACTIVE VOICE	PASSIVE VOICE
Present	He asks	He is asked
Past	He asked	He was asked
Future	He will ask	He will be asked
Present Perfect	He has asked	He has been asked
Past Perfect	He had asked	He had been asked
Future Perfect	He will have asked	He will have been asked

Each tense has its own virtues for expressing what you want your sentences to say.

Use the *present tense* to express present action:

> Now she *knows.* She *is leaving.*

Use the present also for habitual action:

> He *sees* her every day.

Or for future action:

> Classes *begin* next Monday.

Or for describing literary events:

> Hamlet *finds* the king praying, but he *is* unable to act; he *lets* the opportunity slip.

Or for expressing timeless facts:

> The Greeks knew the world *is* round.

Or for the "historical present":

> King Alfred *watches* as the spider *mends* her web. He *determines* to rebuild his kingdom.

But reserve the historical present for such deliberate literary effect. In ordinary narration or exposition, *avoid* this kind of thing:

> One day I *am watching* television when the phone *rings;* it *is* the police.

Use the *past tense* for all action before the present:

> He just *left.*
> One day I *was watching* television when the phone *rang;* it *was* the police.

Use the *future tense* for action expected after the present:

> He *will finish* it next year.
> When he *finishes* next year, ... [the present functioning as future]
> He *is going to finish* it next year. [The "present progressive" *is going* plus an infinitive, like *to finish,* commonly expresses the future.]

Use the *present perfect tense* for action completed ("perfected") but relevant to the present moment:

I *have gone* there before.
He *has sung* forty concerts.
She *has driven* there every day.

Past Perfect
Tense

Use the *past perfect tense* to express "the past of the past":

When we *arrived* [past], they *had finished* [past perfect].

Notice that the present perfect (*have* plus past participle) becomes the past perfect (*had* plus past participle) when you step from present to past. Everything moves back one step:

The flare *signals* that he *has started*.
The flare *signaled* that he *had started*.

Future Perfect
Tense

Use the *future perfect tense (or the present perfect tense* if appropriate) to express "the past of the future":

When we *arrive* [future], they *will have finished* [future perfect].
You *will have worked* thirty hours by Christmas [future perfect].
The flare *will signal* [future] that he *has started* [present perfect].

Avoid unnecessary shifts in tense, voice, and mood.

Inconsistencies in verbal forms will bother your reader, and usually muddle your ideas as well. Choose your tense and stay with it, stepping away only when the thought demands some other tense to make a distinction of time.

Agreement of
Tenses

FAULTY: Then Antony *looked up* from the body and *begins* to speak.

REVISED: Then Antony *looks up* from the body and *begins* to speak.

FAULTY: King Alfred *thanks* the peasant, and *went* his way. He *gathered* his men. They *are* overjoyed.

REVISED: King Alfred *thanks* the peasant, and *goes* his way. He *gathers* his men. They *are* overjoyed.

FAULTY: While the executives *stayed* in the plant, the strikers *picket* outside.

REVISED: While the executives *stayed* in the plant, the strikers *picketed* outside.

FAULTY: Although the government *has stated* its policy [present perfect], the people *have* still *been* confused [present perfect].

REVISED: **Although the government** *has stated* **its policy [present perfect], the people** *are* **still confused [present].**

AWKWARD: **We** *will have left* **[future perfect] by the time they** *will have arrived* **[future perfect].**

REVISED: **We** *will have left* **[future perfect] by the time they** *arrive* **[present functioning to express future action].**

English has only two "voices"—the active (I *see*) and the passive (I *am seen*)—of which, as we have seen, the active is by far the more efficient. But whether using active or passive, avoid awkward shifts, especially if they also bring awkward shifts of subject.

FAULTY: **This plan** *reduces* **taxes and** *has been proved* **workable in three other cities.**

REVISED: **This plan** *reduces* **taxes and** *has proved* **workable in three other cities.**

Active and Passive

FAULTY: **He** *had paid* **for the new tires and the new upholstery; and now even the car** *was paid for.*

REVISED: **He** *had paid* **for the new tires and new upholstery; and now he** *had* **even** *paid* **for the car.**

FAULTY: **After they** *laid out* **the pattern, electrical shears** *were used* **to cut around it.**

REVISED: **After they** *laid out* **the pattern, they** *cut* **around it with electrical shears.**

Mood (also called *mode:* "manner") is the attitude of the speaker toward the action his verb names. English has three moods. The *indicative mood* declares a fact or asks a question:

Indicative Mood

This pie *is* **good. Susan** *baked* **it.**
Susan *baked* **it?** *Is* **there any left?**

The *imperative mood* expresses a command or request:

Imperative Mood

Get **out. Please** *be* **careful.** *Take* **two aspirin.**

The *subjunctive mood* expresses an action or condition not asserted as actual fact. Such conditional, provisional, wishful, suppositional ideas are usually subjoined (*subjunctus,* "yoked under") in subordinate clauses. The form of the verb is often plural, and often in a past-tense form, even though the subject is singular, and the condition is present or future.

<table>
<tr><td>Subjunctive
Mood</td><td>He looked as if he *were* confident.
If I *were* you, Miles, I would ask her myself.
If this *be* error, and upon me [*be*] proved. . . .
Had he *been* sure, he would have said so.
I demand that he *make* restitution.
I move that the nominations *be closed,* and that the secretary *cast* a unanimous ballot.</td></tr>
</table>

Avoid awkward or faulty shifts of mood:

<table>
<tr><td>Change in
Mood</td><td>FAULTY: **If I *was* you, John, I would speak for myself.**
REVISED: **If I *were* you, John, I would speak for myself.**</td></tr>
<tr><td></td><td>FAULTY: **If he *would have known,* he never would have said that.**
REVISED: **If he *had known,* he never would have said that.**
REVISED: ***Had* he *known,* he never would have said that.**</td></tr>
</table>

Be careful not to write *would of* or *should of* for *would have* (*would've*) or *should have* (*should've*).

FAULTY: **He moved that the club buy the picture, and that the secretary *shall bill* the members.**

REVISED: **He moved that the club buy the picture, and that the secretary *bill* the members.**

FAULTY: **You *should read* carefully and *don't miss* his irony.**

REVISED: **You *should read* carefully *to avoid missing* his irony.**

REVISED: ***Read* carefully, and *don't miss* his irony.**

Master the tenses of the troublesome verbs.

Six short verbs are among the most troublesome in English: *lie, lay; sit, set; rise, raise.* These are six separate verbs, with six separate meanings. Master their meanings and their "principal parts" (present tense, past tense, and past participle—the form used with *has* or *had* in compound verbs). Indeed, three of the six suggest the convalescing patient: *lie, sit, rise.* These three are intransitive: they never take an object. The other three function more aggressively, always transitively, always taking an object: *lay, set, raise.* Now for the meanings, principal parts, and uses of them all.

First, the intransitive verbs, *lie, sit, rise.*

Lie, lay, lain (present, past, past participle) means to recline, or to be at rest.

> PRESENT: **The patient *lies* quietly asleep.**
> **The patient *is lying* quietly asleep.**
> PAST: **After the visitors left, the patient *lay* quietly asleep.**
> **The purse *lay* unnoticed on the chair.**
> PAST PARTICIPLE: **He has *lain*, quiet and asleep, all afternoon.**

Since this one gives the most trouble, memorize this simple set:

> **I *lie* down.**
> **I *lay* down yesterday.**
> **I have *lain* down often.**

When someone says incorrectly "He is *laying* down," ask yourself the impudent questions "Who is Down?" or "Is he laying feathers?"—and you might remember to say, and write: "He is *lying* down."

Sit, sat, sat means to assume, or remain in, a sitting position.

> PRESENT: **I *sit* by the bed.**
> **A clock *sits* on the table near the bed.**
> PAST: **The patient *sat* in the sun today.**
> PAST PARTICIPLE: **He had *sat* by the window yesterday.**

Rise, rose, risen means to stand up, or to move upward.

> PRESENT: **When supply is short, prices *rise*.**
> PAST: **To my surprise, he *rose* to greet me.**
> PAST PARTICIPLE: **To my surprise, he had *risen* to greet me.**

Here are the transitive verbs, *lay, set, raise.*

Lay, laid, laid means to place or put something.

> PRESENT: **He *lays* the suitcase on the bed.**
> **He *is* already *laying* plans for a new life.**
> PAST: **Yesterday he *laid* new tile in the playroom.**
> PAST PARTICIPLE: **By now he has *laid* the cornerstone of the new city hall.**

Set, set, set means to place something in position.

> PRESENT: **I *set* the chair near the window.**

He *sets* the checkerboard on the table.

PAST: He *set* the chair near the window.

PAST PARTICIPLE: He has *set* the checkerboard on the table.

Don't confuse it with *sit* or *sit down:*

FAULTY: He *sat* the chair near the window.

REVISED: He *set* the chair near the window.

FAULTY: He *set* himself *down* by the entrance.

REVISED: He *sat* himself *down* by the entrance

Finally, *raise, raised, raised* usually means to make something move up or grow.

PRESENT: When supply is short, businessmen *raise* prices.

PAST: He *raised* his hand in greeting.

PAST PARTICIPLE: She has *raised* three beautiful children.

Part of the difficulty is that the first five of these six troublemakers are *irregular verbs*—verbs not forming the past and the past participle by adding the usual *-ed*, as in **worked, graduated, danced.** Here are some more to watch; learn to control their past and past-participial forms. Alternate forms are in parentheses, in italics.

arise, arose, arisen
awake, awoke, awaked [but *was awakened*]
bear, bore, borne [but: "She was *born* in 1960."]
beat, beat, beaten
begin, began, begun
bid ("order"), *bade* [pronounced "bad"], *bidden*
bid ("offer"), *bid, bid*
burst, burst, burst
drag, dragged, dragged [not *drag, drug, drug*]
draw, drew, drawn
drink, drank, drunk
fit, fitted [or *fit,* especially intransitively], *fitted*
fling, flung, flung
get, got, got (gotten)
hang ("suspend"), *hung, hung* [but: *hang* ("execute"), *hanged,*
   hanged]
lead, led, led [Don't let the *lead* in *lead pencil* trick your spelling.]
lend, lent, lent
light, lit (lighted), lit (lighted)

prove, proved, proved (proven)
ride, rode, ridden
ring, rang, rung
sew, sewed, sewn (sewed)
shine ("glow"), *shone, shone* [distinct from "polish"—*shine, shined, shined*]
show, showed, shown (showed)
shrink, shrank (shrunk), shrunk (shrunken)
sing, sang, sung
sink, sank, sunk
sow, sowed, sown (sowed)
slink, slunk, slunk
spring, sprang, sprung
swim, swam, swum
swing, swung [not *swang*], *swung*
wake, woke (waked), waked

EXERCISES

3. *Treat these troubles, mostly verbal:*

1. Conservatism, as well as liberalism, are summonses for change in American life as we now know it.
2. These kind of questions are sheer absurdities.
3. The lion shall lay down with the lamb, and the hen will have lain the golden egg.
4. The committee were miles apart.
5. None of these proposals are unworkable.
6. Neither the tweed of his jacket nor the silk of his tie impress us.
7. The house set on a low hill. A brick patio had been lain in back.
8. Neither the question nor the answers seems pertinent to the issue.
9. None of us are perfect.
10. He swang out of the upper bunk, before he had really woke up.
11. John was the second one of the fifty boys who has volunteered.
12. Each who have come this far have shown real determination.
13. His idea of fine foods are hamburgers and French fries.
14. Toys were laying all over the floor, and the babysitter had laid down and fallen asleep.
15. Doug is the only one of the tall boys who always stand straight.
16. Last year we are warned of higher taxes and getting lower taxes. This year

we are promised lower taxes and getting higher taxes. What next year is holding, we can only guess. But sooner or later we are being promised and taxed into disbelief.

17. He looked like something the cat had drug in when he flang open the door.
18. They laid on the beach all afternoon, talking and just laying around, until after the sun had sank in the ocean. A few may have swam a little.
19. He had rang the bell and lead the posse that hung him.
20. If our defense would of been tighter, we would of won.

4. *Clinch your mastery of lie, lay, sit, set, rise, and raise by writing three active sentences for each, the first using the present tense, the second using the past tense, the third using the past participle.*

5. *Straighten out the inconsistencies of tense, voice, and mood in this passage:*

A third principle that industry should recognize was the need for constant appraisal by management of an employee's progress. Management would determine what a person, when he or she would of been hired, were expected by it to achieve; and it then judges whether it now had had that person poorly assigned. They probably know their own limitations, and jobs beyond their capacity are poorly handled by them. But it is not enough that a manager sit down periodically with employees and reviews their performance. The important thing is that the manager understands a person well enough and be articulate enough to make sure the person has become conscious of needs for further development. If the manager will have been sufficiently observant, he might have helped his employees to an accurate evaluation of their own potential.

PRONOUNS AS SUBJECTS AND OBJECTS

Match a pronoun's form to its function.

Unlike nouns, pronouns change form when they change from subject to object. *John* remains *John*, whether on the giving or receiving end of the verb: *John* hits Joe; Joe hits *John*. But the pronoun changes from subjective to objective form: *He* hits Joe; Joe hits *him*. We all know the difference between *who* (subject) and *whom* (object), if only because we are so often uncertain about them. We tend to say, "*Who* did you see," because *who*, though really the object of the verb *see*, comes first—in the slot usually reserved for subjects. "*Whom* did you see" is historically correct. Though *who*, as object, is displacing *whom* in some uses, knowing the distinction will help your writing in tricky constructions. We are also sometimes skittish about "between you and me," which is solidly correct, *me* being the object of the preposition *between*. Pronouns can cause considerable uncertainty—but they need not if you merely remember which forms are subjective and which objective. Here are the pronouns that give trouble:

SUBJECTIVE	OBJECTIVE
I	me
he	him
she	her
we	us
they	them
who	whom
whoever	whomever

Use subjective pronouns for subjective functions.

Compound subjects, like "Bill and I," are a common source of trouble. For an easy way to check whether *I* or *me* (*he* or *him*) is right, drop the "Bill" and see how well the pronoun alone stands as subject of the verb. You would not, for instance, say "Me reported the accident."

FAULTY: *Me* and Bill reported the accident.
REVISED: Bill and *I* reported the accident.

Compound
Subject

FAULTY: Sally and *her* rode up front.
REVISED: Sally and *she* rode up front.

FAULTY: *Us* and *them* should have cooperated on this.
REVISED: *We* and *they* should have cooperated on this.

FAULTY: Pierce, Finch, and *myself* have resigned.
REVISED: Pierce, Finch, and *I* have resigned. [Keep *myself* where it belongs, as an intensive (I *myself*) or reflexive (I hurt *myself*), and be unashamed of *me* where it properly fits.]

A *complement* is a word that "complements" or completes the meaning of a verb. *Subjective complements* are words that complete the meaning of a linking verb, like *is*, while referring back to the subject ("Tom is *chairman*"). Pronouns serving as subjective complements must, of course, be subjective in form:

Subjective
Complement

FAULTY: **This is *him*.**
REVISED: **This is *he*.**

FAULTY: **He discovered that it was *me*.**
REVISED: **He discovered that it was *I*.**

FAULTY: **It was *them* who signed the treaty.**
REVISED: **It was *they* who signed the treaty.**

A pronoun *in apposition* with the subject (that is, positioned near, and meaning the same thing as, the subject), or in apposition with a subjective complement, must also take the subjective form:

Apposition
with Subject

FAULTY: ***Us* students would rather talk than sleep.**
REVISED: ***We* students would rather talk than sleep.**

FAULTY: **Both of us—Mike and *me*—should have gotten the credit.**
REVISED: **Both of us—Mike and *I*—should have gotten the credit.**
   [*Mike and I* are in apposition with the subject, *Both*, not with the object of the preposition, *us*]

FAULTY: **They were both to blame—Lord Hervey and *him*.**
REVISED: **They were both to blame—Lord Hervey and *he*.**

When a pronoun follows *than* or *as*, it must be subjective if it is the subject of an implied verb:

Implied Verb

FAULTY: **She is taller than *me* [am].**
REVISED: **She is taller than *I* [am].**

FAULTY: **You are as bright as *him* [is].**
REVISED: **You are as bright as *he* [is].**

FAULTY: **She loves you as much as *me* [love you].**
REVISED: **She loves you as much as *I* [love you].**

FAULTY: **She loves you better than [she loves] *he*.**
REVISED: **She loves you better than [she loves] *him*. [Here the pronoun is objective, since it is the object of the implied verb.]**

Use objective pronouns for objective functions.

A pronoun functioning as a *direct object*, an *indirect object*, or an *object of a preposition* must be objective in form. Compound objects give most of the trouble. Again, *see if the pronoun would stand by itself.*

FAULTY: The credit goes to *he* who tries.
REVISED: The credit goes to *him* who tries.

FAULTY: Can you have lunch with Mary and *I?*
REVISED: Can you have lunch with Mary and *me?*

FAULTY: She typed the letter for Stuart and *he.*
REVISED: She typed the letter for Stuart and *him.*

FAULTY: Between her and *I,* an understanding grew.
REVISED: Between her and *me,* an understanding grew.

FAULTY: Everyone but Mildred and *she* contributed.
REVISED: Everyone but Mildred and *her* contributed. [*But* is used here
as a preposition with the meaning "except."]

FAULTY: The petition was drafted by Nielsen, Wright, and *myself.*
REVISED: The petition was drafted by Nielsen, Wright, and *me.*

FAULTY: The mayor complimented Bill and *I.*
REVISED: The mayor complimented Bill and *me.*

FAULTY: The clerk sold John and *I* the case.
REVISED: The clerk sold John and *me* the case. [*Case* is the direct
object of *sold.*]

Pronouns in apposition with objects must themselves be objective:

FAULTY: The mayor complimented us both—Bill and *I.*
REVISED: The mayor complimented us both—Bill and *me.*

FAULTY: She gave the advice specifically to us—Helen and *I.*
REVISED: She gave the advice specifically to us—Helen and *me.*

FAULTY: Between us—Elaine and *I*—an understanding grew.
REVISED: Between us—Elaine and *me*—an understanding grew.

FAULTY: He would not think of letting *we* girls help him.
REVISED: He would not think of letting *us* girls help him.

Notice this one:

FAULTY: Will you please help Leonard and *I* find the manager?
REVISED: Will you please help Leonard and *me* find the manager?

Leonard and me are objective both as objects of the verb *help* and as
subjects of the shortened infinitive *to find.* Subjects of infinitives are
always in the objective case, as in "She saw *him* go"; "She helped *him*
find his keys."

Use a subjective pronoun for the subject of a noun clause.

This is one of the trickiest of pronominal problems. When a pronoun is the subject of a noun clause, it will often follow a verb or preposition, and therefore look like an object. But it is the subject, after all, and it must take a subjective form:

After Verb
FAULTY: The sergeant asked *whomever* did it to step forward.
REVISED: The sergeant asked *whoever* did it to step forward. [*Whoever did it* is a noun clause functioning as direct object of the verb *asked*. But *whoever* is the subject of the clause.]

After Preposition
FAULTY: They promised the medal to *whomever* would go.
REVISED: They promised the medal to *whoever* would go. [*Whoever would go* is a noun clause functioning as object of the preposition *to*. But *whoever* is the subject of the clause.]

Similarly, parenthetical remarks like *I think, he says,* and *we believe* often make pronouns seem objects when they are actually subjects:

Parenthetical Remark
FAULTY: Ellen is the girl *whom* I think will succeed.
REVISED: Ellen is the girl *who* I think will succeed.

FAULTY: Jim will vote for *whomever* they say is a winner.
REVISED: Jim will vote for *whoever* they say is a winner.

The *who* pronouns also match form to function in relative adjectival clauses:

In Relative Clause
FAULTY: The man *whom* had lied to her came in.
REVISED: The man *who* had lied to her came in. [*Who* is the subject of the clause *who had lied to her.*]

FAULTY: The man *who* she hated came in.
REVISED: The man *whom* she hated came in. [*Whom* is the direct object of the verb in the clause *whom she hated.*]
BETTER: The man she hated came in.

But the *subject of an infinitive—and its complements—*is objective in form:

With Infinitive
FAULTY: They guessed the author to be *I.*
REVISED: They guessed the author to be *me.*

FAULTY: They will pay *whoever* they find the artist to be.
REVISED: They will pay *whomever* they find the artist to be.

Use the possessive pronoun before a gerund.

Gerunds are verbal forms used as nouns *(hunting, skating, reading, sleeping). Participles* look exactly the same, but serve as adjectives.

> GERUND: *Hunting* **is good exercise.**
> PARTICIPLE: *Hunting* **the southern hills, he came upon an old cabin.**

A gerund accompanied by a pronoun often runs into trouble:

> FAULTY: **She disliked** *him* **hunting.**
> REVISED: **She disliked** *his* **hunting.**

The object of her dislike is not *him* but *hunting;* hence the possessive pronoun merely modifies the true object, the gerund. Sometimes, however, the choice is not so clear:

> **They caught** *him* **cheating on the first exam.**
> **They caught** *his* **cheating on the first exam.**

Here the difference is not one of correctness, since both examples are correct, but of meaning as expressed through grammatical structure. In the first sentence, the object of *caught* is *him,* which is modified by the participle *cheating.* In the second sentence, the object is the gerund *cheating,* which is modified by *his.* In the first sentence, he is caught in the act; in the second, they detect his cheating as they read the completed exam.

> FAULTY: **Her father disapproved of** *me* **dating her.**
> REVISED: **Her father disapproved of** *my* **dating her.**

> FAULTY: **I am bothered by** *him* **not asking me out.**
> REVISED: **I am bothered by** *his* **not asking me out.**

> FAULTY: **He consented to** *them* **making the trip.**
> REVISED: **He consented to** *their* **making the trip.**

EXERCISES

6. *Correct the pronouns:*

1. It was him all right.
2. She disliked him whistling the same old tune.
3. They cheered both of us—Andy and I.

4. I admit it was me to whom they first confided.
5. We all three like it—Helen, Ann, and myself.
6. Us sophomores should all sign the petition. Me and Pete will circulate it.
7. Both her and me were elected.
8. He blamed Winston Atterbury and I for his missing the plane.
9. They always elect whomever is popular.
10. They choose whoever they like.
11. My mother insists on me buying my own clothes.
12. Everybody thinks us girls should go.
13. Little love is lost between him and I.
14. In the end, it was them who succeeded.
15. The child who he adored finally broke his heart.
16. Gladys takes more responsibility than her, and everyone knows it but him.
17. Christmas Greetings from we Bradshanks—Marge, Dave, Pat, and Binkie. Everyone will add their own tale to this, our fifth annual newsletter.
18. Everything comes to he who waits, but not to you and I.
19. No one likes their friends talking behind their back.
20. The child who she had saved was reading a comic book, as calm as you or I.

PRONOUNS AND THEIR ANTECEDENTS

Keep your antecedents specific, unambiguous, and close at hand.

An antecedent states your pronoun's meaning. If an antecedent is missing, ambiguous, vague, or too far away, the pronoun will suffer from "faulty reference" and throw your sentence into disarray. Here are some of the problems:

Missing

FAULTY: **In Texas *they* produce a lot of oil.**
REVISED: ***Texas* produces a lot of oil.**

FAULTY: **My father is a doctor, and *this* is the work I want to do too.**
REVISED: **My father is a doctor, and *medicine* is the profession I want to follow too.**

Ambiguous

FAULTY: **Peter told Sam that *he* had played terribly. [Is *he* Pete or Sam?]**
REVISED: **Pete said that *Sam* had played terribly.**
REVISED: **To Sam, Pete admitted having played terribly.**

FAULTY: Adams told Andrews that he could send *him* to London.
REVISED: Adams threatened Andrews with being sent to London.

FAULTY: Paul smashed into a girl's car *who* was visiting his sister.
REVISED: Paul smashed into the car of a *girl* visiting his sister.

FAULTY: He aimed at the tiger's eye, but *it* ran away.
REVISED: He aimed at the eye, but *the tiger* ran away.

FAULTY: He is an excellent guitarist. *This* is because he began studying *it* as a child.

Vague

REVISED: He is an excellent guitarist because he began taking lessons when a child.

FAULTY: Because Ann had never spoken before an audience, she was afraid of *it*.
REVISED: Because Ann had never spoken before an audience, she was afraid.

FAULTY: He shouted outside the window and pounded on the frame, *which* finally broke the glass.
REVISED: He shouted outside the window and pounded on the frame till he finally broke the glass.

FAULTY: The mayor's committee reported on the remaining problems of polluted air, poor traffic control, inadequate schools, and rat-infested slums. The mayor was proud of *it*.

Remote

REVISED: The mayor's committee reported on the remaining problems of polluted air, congested traffic, inadequate schools, and rat-infested slums. The mayor was proud of *the committee*.

FAULTY: The castle was built in 1337. The rooms and furnishings are carefully kept up for the eyes of tourists, and at the entrance stands a coin-fed turnstile. *It* still belongs to the Earl.
REVISED: The castle, which still belongs to the Earl, was built in 1337. The rooms and furnishings are carefully kept up for the eyes of tourists, and at the entrance stands a coin-fed turnstile.

With an indefinite antecedent, use a singular pronoun.

Prominent among the indefinite antecedents are *anybody, anyone, each, either (neither), everybody, everyone, no one, nobody.* Also included are generic nouns like *kind, sort, man, woman,* and *person,* and the collective nouns like *family, jury,* and *clergy.* All of these, collecting plural items under one head, retain a certain misleading plural feeling, which may wrongly tempt you to plural pronouns of reference.

FAULTY: **Modern woman is frequently unable to pursue *their* true goals.**

REVISED: **Modern woman is frequently unable to pursue *her* true goal.**

FAULTY: ***Everybody* paid for *their* ice cream.**

REVISED: ***Everybody* paid for *his* ice cream.**

FAULTY: ***Each* of the students hoped to follow *their* teacher's footsteps.**

REVISED: **Each of the students hoped to follow *the* teacher's footsteps.**

FAULTY: **After *everybody* in the crowd had contributed, Stan thanked *him.* [The grammar is correct, but the meaning is wrong.]**

REVISED: **After *all* the crowd had contributed, Stan thanked *them.***

FAULTY: **If the *clergy* dares to face the new philosophy, *it* should declare *themselves.***

CLEARER: **If the *clergy* dares to face the new philosophy, *it* should declare *itself.***

REVISED: **If the *clergy* dares to face the new philosophy, the *clergy* should declare *itself.***

EXERCISE

7. *Strengthen the faulty references:*

1. He sent him his high-school pictures.
2. He kicked the child's toy by accident who was visiting.
3. Everyone knows their own best interest.
4. He missed several classes, which in the end defeated him.
5. When industries fail to make plans far enough into the future decades, they often underestimate them.
6. She ended her performance, but it was too late.
7. He opened the bird's cage, and it flew away.
8. My family is always throwing their weight around.
9. Shakespeare has Edgar portray his essential position.
10. These sort of snakes are very deceptive in their coloring.

11. The roofers finished early, after last touches to the trim and shingles, and they had really made it sparkle.
12. She loves swimming especially in the surf, thinking it the best exercise in the world.
13. His article was accepted by *Sport* magazine, for which he acknowledged his gratitude.
14. People should insure themselves against death and accident. These provide for the welfare of their loved ones.
15. There is a sandwich shop by the police station, and we phone them when we get hungry.
16. Coaches sometimes ignore the best interests of their players for the sake of winning games, and they are angry if they lose them because of bad grades, after working them too hard.
17. When he had his last heart attack, it almost stopped beating.
18. A governor should know a little about law and a lot about people, and apply them diplomatically.

MODIFIERS MISUSED AND MISPLACED

Learn the difference between adjectives and adverbs.

Adjectives describe nouns; adverbs describe verbs, adjectives, or other adverbs. ("He *very shrewdly* played a *really* conservative game.") But the adjective sometimes wrongly crowds out the adverb ("He played *real well*"). And the adverb sometimes steals the adjective's place, especially when the linking verb looks transitive but isn't *(feels, looks, tastes, smells)*, making the sense wrong. "He feels *badly*" means incompetence, not misery. "It tastes *wonderfully*" means skill in *it*—some kind of tasting machine. And certain adjectives ending in *-ly (lonely, lovely, leisurely)* tend to masquerade as adverbs:

> WRONG: **She swam lovely.**
> DOUBTFUL: **They walked leisurely.**
> WRONG: **He brooded lonely.**

But notice how quickly you can restore the adjective if you press your words for their meanings:

> **She swam, lovely as a swan.**
> **They walked, leisurely and thoughtful.**
> **I wandered lonely as a cloud.**

Or you can simply assert the adverbial:

> **She swam beautifully.**
> **They strolled slowly.**
> **He brooded solitarily.**

Some words serve both as adjectives and adverbs: *early, late, near, far, only, little, right, wrong, straight, well, better, best, fast,* for example.

> **He waited *late* for the *late* train.**
> **Think *little* of *little* things.**
> **Go *straight* up the *straight* and narrow path.**

Near is both an adverb of place (*near to it, near the barn*) and an adjective (*the near hill, the near future*); and *near,* the adverb of place, is often confused with *nearly,* the adverb of degree, which means "almost."

> RIGHT: **It was *near* Toledo.** [adverb of place]
> RIGHT: **It was *nearly* perfect.** [adverb of degree]

To avoid confusing the two, substitute *almost* or *nearly* for the *near* of degree that tends to slip wrongly into everyone's prose, or convert it into a proper *near* of place, actual or figurative:

> FAULTY: **He was near exhausted.**
> REVISED: **He was nearly exhausted.**
> REVISED: **He was near exhaustion.**

> FAULTY: **It was a near treasonous statement.**
> REVISED: **It was a nearly treasonous statement.**
> REVISED: **The statement was almost treasonous.**

> FAULTY: **We are nowhere near knowledgeable enough.**
> REVISED: **We are not nearly knowledgeable enough.**

> FAULTY: **With Dodge, he has a tie of near-filial rapport.**
> REVISED: **With Dodge, he has a nearly filial rapport.**
> REVISED: **With Dodge, he has an almost filial rapport.**

Slow has a long history as an adverb, encouraged by its crisp antithesis to *fast* (and its convenience for street-signs), but *slowly* keeps the upper hand in print. Notice that adverbs usually go after and adjectives before:

> **The *slow* freight went *slowly*.**

Put your modifiers where their meaning is clear.

Some modifiers seem to look in two directions at once—the so-called "squinting" modifiers. Put them in their proper places. Make clear which way you want them to face.

AMBIGUOUS: **She said on Friday to phone him.**
REVISED: **On Friday, she said to phone him.**
REVISED: **She said to phone him on Friday.**

AMBIGUOUS: **They agreed when both sides ceased fire to open negotiations.**
REVISED: **They agreed to open negotiations when both sides ceased fire.**
REVISED: **When both sides ceased fire, they agreed to open negotiations.**

AMBIGUOUS: **Several delegations we know have failed.**
REVISED: **We know that several delegations have failed.**

AMBIGUOUS: **They hoped to try thoroughly to understand.**
REVISED: **They hoped to try to understand thoroughly.**

AMBIGUOUS: **He resolved to dependably develop plans.**
REVISED: **He resolved to develop dependable plans. [See "Split infinitives," in "A Glossary of Usage."]**

AMBIGUOUS: **Prices moved upward sufficiently to virtually wipe out the loss.**
REVISED: **Prices rose almost enough to wipe out the loss completely. [And you can take out *completely* to save a word.]**

Make your comparisons complete.

Both adjectives and adverbs have "comparative" and "superlative" forms:

ADJECTIVE: **green, green*er*, green*est***
easy, eas*ier*, eas*iest*
ADVERB: **smoothly, *more* smoothly, *most* smoothly**
easily, *more* easily, *most* easily

All comparatives demand some completion of thought, some answer to the question *than what?*—"Greener than what?"; "More smoothly than what?"

FAULTY: **The western plains are flatter.**
REVISED: **The western plains are flatter than those east of the Mississippi.**

FAULTY: **He plays more skillfully.**
REVISED: **He plays more skillfully than most boys his age.**

FAULTY: **He was as tall if not taller than his sister.**
REVISED: **He was as tall as his sister, if not taller.**

The adjectives ending in *y* that have an adverbial companion—*easy, easily, handy, handily*—most frequently stray into the wrong comparative slot.

WRONG: **so she can get around *easier*.**
RIGHT: **so she can get around *more easily*.**

FAULTY: **Jane told her more than Ellen.**
REVISED: **Jane told her more than she told Ellen.**

FAULTY: **His income is lower than a busboy.**
REVISED: **His income is lower than a busboy's.**

FAULTY: **The pack of a paratrooper is lighter than a soldier.**
REVISED: **A paratrooper's pack is lighter than a soldier's.**

Superlatives also sometimes need completion if the context is unclear:

UNCLEAR: **This is the best painting.**
REVISED: **This is the best painting in this exhibit.**

UNCLEAR: **Here was the prettiest if not the fastest car.**
REVISED: **Here was the prettiest car in the show, if not the fastest.**

EXERCISES

8. *Cure the faulty modifiers:*

1. They asked after ten days to be notified.
2. We wanted to win enough to cry.
3. Everyone feels badly about it.
4. She sang melancholy.
5. The bidding began quietly and leisurely.

6. The work of a student is more intense than his parents.
7. It was a near perfect shot.
8. Some girls have expectations beyond a husband.
9. The party planned to completely attempt reform.
10. Industry is as strong if not stronger than before the depression.
11. We were dancing slow when the alarm sounded louder, and we were asked to leave peaceful and quiet but as quick as possible.
12. A number of women she knew had driven trucks, so she could refute his argument easier in the recent negotiations.
13. It was a near perfect pass, but he was near exhausted and too tightly covered to really get it.
14. They agreed to pay last year on January 1, 1985, to fully complete the contract.
15. Eliot respected him more than Pound.

DANGLING VERBAL CONSTRUCTIONS

Connect a modifier clearly to what it modifies.

Verbals are those *-ing* words, the gerunds (verbal nouns) and participles (verbal adjectives): *laughing, cooking, concentrating.* The phrases and clauses growing out of these words have a tendency to slip loose from the main sentence and dangle. "Going home, the walk was slippery" indicates that the *walk* was going home. The writer has actually compressed two sentences:

I was going home.
The walk was slippery.

But the compression has accidentally omitted the true subject of *going,* which we can put back, to keep that *Going* from dangling:

When I was going home, the walk was slippery.

Or we can give the main clause its true subject:

Going home, *I found* the walk slippery.

Make sure your modifying verbal connects with its true subject:

FAULTY: **When getting out of bed, his toe hit the dresser.**
REVISED: **When getting out of bed, he hit his toe on the dresser.**

Infinitive phrases also can dangle badly:

FAULTY: **To work well, keep your bike oiled.**
REVISED: **To work well, your bike needs frequent oiling.**

FAULTY: **To think clearly, some logic is important.**
REVISED: **To think clearly, you should learn some logic.**

Any clause or phrase may dangle:

FAULTY: **When only a freshman, Jim's history teacher inspired him.**
REVISED: **When Jim was only a freshman, his history teacher inspired him.**

FAULTY: **After he had lectured thirty years, the average student still seemed average.**
REVISED: **After he had lectured thirty years, he found the average student still average.**

For more on dangling participles, see page 148.

EXERCISES

9. *Mend these dangling constructions:*

1, What we need is a file of engineers broken down by their specialities.
2. Following the games on television, the batting average of every player was at his fingertips.
3. When entering the door, the lamp fell over.
4. To study well, a quiet room helps.
5. After he arrived at the dorm, the dean phoned.

10. *Straighten these sentences:*

1. The only light coming from machine-gun fire and explosions, it is hard for the audience to see whom is hit.
2. The audience, as well as the cast, were glad when they were finished.
3. In 1965, blacks numbered only 14 out of 863 students at the Bronx High School of Science, 23 out of 629 students at Stuyvesant High School, 45 in 368 at the High School of Music and Art, and out of 907 at Brooklyn Technical School you could only find 22.
4. If the Republicans would have checked into the activities that were being done by the Democrats in an honest manner, they would have avoided the mess of Watergate.

5. Either the report is incomplete or deliberately lying to both the public and he personally.
6. Not only did he delight in youth, but he had an almost pathological fear that it was already too late to enjoy it.
7. They study hard here, but you do not have to work all the time.
8. The contest between Louise and I was decided by only the absentee ballots, and they totaled them inaccurately.
9. Walking to the game, it was decided to give the team their due, whether or not it was going to bring us the championship.
10. Speaking before the committee, everything he said damaged his case.
11. Every member of the committee had tried to keep their minds open.
12. He sat his briefcase carefully on the desk, hoping it would not be too late to use the evidence in it, and left it laying there when he answered the phone.
13. She was awakened by a loud knocking, which turned out to be across the hall where they were installing a new floor.
14. Bordered on each side by steep white cliffs, they entered the valley where Dieppe lays.
15. Norsemen may have lain out the first settlement here, finding it's *diep,* or inlet, right for their ships.
16. Disturbing the peace, the judge decided to leniently sentence them to consecutively work out their penalty on week ends.
17. I would wish that he would have resigned more graceful.
18. Give the award to he who earns it, whether or not someone else may have swam a better race than him.
19. The police drug the river but could of conducted a more thorougher investigation.
20. Everyone and their brother was there, but they always take forever to really start the fireworks.

PUNCTUATING THE SENTENCE

Punctuation gives the silent page some of the breath of life. It marks the pauses and emphases with which a speaker points his meaning and controls his sentences. Loose punctuators forget what every good writer knows: that even silent reading produces an articulate murmur in our heads, that language springs from the breathing human voice, that the beauty and meaning of language depend on what the written word makes us *hear*, on the sentence's tuning of emphasis and pause. Commas, semicolons, colons, periods, and other punctuation transcribe our meaningful pauses to the printed page, and make our sentences fully meaningful.

THE COMMA

The comma is the key to meaningful punctuation. Here are the four basic commas:

I. THE INTRODUCER—after introductory phrases and clauses.
II. THE COORDINATOR—between "sentences" joined by *and, but, or, nor, yet, so, for.*

III. THE INSERTER—a PAIR around any inserted word or phrase.
IV. THE LINKER—when adding other words or phrases.

I. THE INTRODUCER. A comma after every introductory word or phrase makes your writing clearer, more alive with the breath and pause of meaning:

> Indeed, the idea failed.
> After the first letter, she wrote again.
> In the autumn of the same year, he went to Paris.

Without the introductory comma, your reader frequently expects something else:

> After the first letter she wrote, she . . .
> In the autumn of the same year he went to Paris, he . . .

Notice how the introducer changes the meaning of *However* in these two sentences:

> However she goes, she goes in style.
> However, she goes when she feels like it.

You can usually avoid the danger of forgetting the comma and spoiling the sense by substituting *but* for your introductory *however's:* "But she goes . . ." Put your *however's* within the sentence between commas:

> She goes, however, when she feels like it.

But beware! What looks like an introductory phrase or clause may actually be the subject of the sentence *and should take no comma.* A comma can break up a good marriage of subject and verb. The comma in each of these is an interloper, and should be removed:

> That handsome man in the ascot tie, is the groom.
> The idea that you should report every observation, is wrong.
> The realization that we must be slightly dishonest to be truly kind,
>   comes to all of us sooner or later.

If your phrase or clause as subject is unusually long, or confusing, you may relieve the pressure by inserting some qualifying remark after it, between two commas:

> The idea that you should report every observation, *however insig-nificant,* is wrong.

> **The realization that we must be slightly dishonest to be truly kind,**
> *obviously the higher motive,* **comes to all of us sooner or later.**

Commas mark your meaning. A man inquires about bidding on a carload of coal. How does he read the telegram in reply?

No price too high.
No, price too high.

A comma would make a difference in the commissar's telegram:

Pardon impossible, to be sent to Siberia.
Pardon, impossible to be sent to Siberia.

EXERCISES

1. *Master* however *by writing two groups of three sentences on the following pattern:*

However she tried, she could not do it.
She tried, however, a very long time.
She tried; however, she could not do it.

2. *Write three sentences with a long clause or phrase as subject, avoiding the temptation of putting a comma after the subject. Then repeat each of these sentences, but after each clause-or-phrase as subject insert a qualifying remark, between commas, thus setting the subject apart from its verb for clearer distinction.*

II. THE COORDINATOR—between "sentences" joined by coordinate conjunctions. You will often see the comma omitted when your two clauses are short: "He hunted and she fished." But nothing is wrong with "He hunted, and she fished." The comma, in fact, shows the slight pause you make when you say it.

Think of the "comma-and" **(, and)** as a unit equivalent to the period. The period, the semicolon, and the "comma-and" **(, and)** all designate independent clauses—independent "sentences"—but give different emphases:

   .   **He was tired. He went home.**
   ;   **He was tired; he went home.**
  , and **He was tired, and he went home.**

A comma tells your reader that another subject and predicate are coming:

He hunted the hills and dales.
He hunted the hills, and she fished in the streams.
She was naughty but nice.
She was naughty, but that is not our business.
Wear your jacket or coat.
Wear your jacket, or you will catch cold.
It was strong yet sweet.
It was strong, yet it was not unpleasant.

Of course, you may use a comma in *all* the examples above if your sense demands it. The contrasts set by *but, or,* and *yet* often urge a comma, and the even stronger contrasts with *not* and *either-or* demand a comma, whether or not full predication follows:

It was strong, yet sweet.
It was a battle, not a game.
. . . a bird in the hand, or two in the bush.

Commas signal where you would pause in speaking.
The meaningful pause also urges an occasional comma in compound predicates, usually not separated by commas:

He granted the usual permission and walked away.
He granted the usual permission, and walked away.

Both are correct. In the first sentence, however, the granting and walking are perfectly routine, and the temper unruffled. In the second, some kind of emotion has forced a pause, and a comma, after *permission.* Similarly, meaning itself may demand a comma between the two verbs:

He turned and dropped the vase.
He turned, and dropped the vase.

In the first sentence, he turned the vase; in the second, himself. Your **, and** in compound predicates suggests some touch of drama, some meaningful distinction, or afterthought.

You need a comma before *for* and *still* even more urgently. Without the comma, their conjunctive meaning changes; they assume their ordinary roles, *for* as a preposition, *still* as an adjective or adverb:

She liked him still . . . [That is, either *yet* or *quiet!*]
She liked him, still she could not marry him.
She liked him for his money.
She liked him, for a good man is hard to find.

An observation: *for* is the weakest of all the coordinators. Almost a subordinator, it is perilously close to *because. For* can seem moronic if cause and effect are fairly obvious: "She liked him, for he was kind." Either make a point of the cause by full subordination—"She liked him *because* he was kind"—or flatter the reader with a semicolon: "She liked him; he was kind." *For* is effective only when the cause is somewhat hard to find: "Blessed are the meek, for they shall inherit the earth."

To summarize the basic point about the comma as coordinator: put a comma before the coordinator (*and, but, or, nor, yet, so, still, for,*) when joining independent clauses, and add others necessary for emphasis or clarity.

EXERCISES

3. *Write six pairs of sentences, using the six conjunctions* and, but, for, or, yet, still, *on the pattern:*

He hunted the hills and . . .
He hunted the hills, and . . .

4. *Write three pairs of sentences with compound predicates showing how a comma changes verbal meaning, briefly explaining the difference in meaning after each:*

He turned and dropped the vase.
He turned, and dropped the vase.

III. THE INSERTER. Put a PAIR of commas around every inserted word, phrase, or clause—those expressions that seem parenthetical and are called "nonrestrictive." When you cut a sentence in two to insert something necessary, you need to tie off *both* ends, or your sentence will die on the table:

When he packs his bag, however he goes. [, however,]
The car, an ancient Packard is still running. [, an ancient Packard,]
April 10, 1980 is agreeable as a date for final payment. [, 1980,]
John Jones, Jr. is wrong. [, Jr.,]
I wish, Sandra you would do it. [, Sandra,]

You do not mean that 1980 is agreeable, nor are you telling John Jones that Junior is wrong. Such parenthetical insertions need a PAIR of commas:

The case, *nevertheless,* was closed.
She will see, *if she has any sense at all,* that he is right.
Sam, *on the other hand,* may be wrong.
Note, *for example,* the excellent brushwork.
Tom Flint, *M.D.,* and Bill Stone, *Ph.D.,* doctored the punch to
perfection.
He stopped at Kansas City, *Missouri,* for two hours.

The same rule applies to all *nonrestrictive* remarks, phrases, and clauses—all elements simply additive, explanatory, and hence parenthetical:

John, *my friend,* will do what he can.
Andy, *his project sunk, his hopes shattered,* was speechless.
The taxes, *which are reasonable,* will be paid.
That man, *who knows,* is not talking.

Think of *nonrestrictive* as "nonessential" to your meaning, hence set off by commas. Think of *restrictive* as essential and "restricting" your meaning, hence not set off at all (use *which* for nonrestrictives, *that* for restrictives; see pp. 170–171.

RESTRICTIVES:
The taxes that are reasonable will be paid.
Southpaws who are superstitious will not pitch on Friday nights.
The man who knows is not talking.

NONRESTRICTIVES:
The taxes, which are reasonable, will be paid.
Southpaws, who are superstitious, will not pitch on Friday nights.
The man, who knows, is not talking.

The difference between restrictives and nonrestrictives is one of meaning, and the comma-pair signals that meaning. Our first "Southpaw" sentence says that only the superstitious ones lie low on Fridays: our second one, that *all* of them do. Now, how many grandmothers do I have in the first sentence below (restrictive)? How many in the second (nonrestrictive)?

My grandmother who smokes pot is ninety.
My grandmother, who smokes pot, is ninety.

In the first sentence, I still have two grandmothers, since I am distinguishing one from the other by my restrictive phrase (no commas) as the one with the unconventional habit. In the second sentence, I have but one grandmother, about whom I am adding an interesting though nonessential, nonrestrictive detail within a pair of commas. Read the two aloud, and you will hear the difference in meaning, and how the pauses at the commas signal that difference. Commas are often optional, of course. The difference between a restrictive and a nonrestrictive meaning may sometimes be very slight. For example, you may take our recent bridegroom either way (but not halfway):

> **That handsome man, in the ascot tie, is the groom. [nonrestrictive]**
> **That handsome man in the ascot tie is the groom. [restrictive]**

Your meaning will dictate your choice. But use **PAIRS** of commas or none at all. Never separate subject and verb, or verb and object, with just one comma.

Some finer points. One comma of a pair enclosing an inserted remark may coincide with, and, in a sense, overlay, a comma "already there":

> **In each box, a bottle was broken.**
> **In each box, however, a bottle was broken.**

> **The team lost, and the school was sick.**
> **The team lost, in spite of all, and the school was sick.**

> **The program will work, but the cost is high.**
> **The program will work, of course, but the cost is high.**

Between the coordinate clauses, however, a semicolon might have been clearer:

> **The team lost, in spite of all; and the school was sick.**
> **The program will work, of course; but the cost is high.**

Beware: *however,* between commas, cannot substitute for *but,* as in the perfectly good sentence: "He wore a hat, *but* it looked terrible." You would be using a comma where a full stop (period or semicolon) should be:

> WRONG:
> **He wore a hat, however, it looked terrible.**

> RIGHT (*notice the two meanings*):
> **He wore a hat; however, it looked terrible.**
> **He wore a hat, however; it looked terrible.**

But a simple **(, but)** avoids both the ambiguity of the floating *however* and the ponderosity of anchoring it with a semicolon, fore or aft: "He wore a hat, but it looked terrible."

Another point. *But* may absorb the first comma of a pair enclosing an introductory remark (although it need not do so):

> **At any rate, he went.**
> **But, at any rate, he went.**
> **But at any rate, he went.**
> **But [,] if we want another party, we had better clean up.**
> **The party was a success, but [,] if we want another one, we had better clean up.**

But avoid a comma *after* "but" in sentences like this:

> **I understand your argument, but [,] I feel your opponent has a stronger case.**

Treat the "he said" and "she said" of dialogue as a regular parenthetical insertion, within commas, and without capitalizing, unless a new sentence begins:

> **"I'm going," he said, "whenever I get up enough nerve."**
> **"I'm going," he said. "Whenever I get up enough nerve, I'm really going."**

And American usage puts the comma *inside* **ALL** quotation marks:

> **"He is a nut," she said.**
> **She called him a "nut," and walked away.**

Finally, the comma goes after a parenthesis, never before.

> **On the day of her graduation (June 4, 1980), the weather turned boiling hot.**

EXERCISE

5. *Write five pairs of sentences showing the difference between nonrestrictive and restrictive clauses on this pattern:*

The taxes, which are reasonable, will be paid.
The taxes that are reasonable will be paid.

IV. THE LINKER. This is the usual one, linking on additional phrases and afterthoughts:

Additional
Phrases;
Afterthoughts

They went home, having overstayed their welcome.
The book is too long, overloaded with examples.

It also links items in series. Again, the meaningful pause demands a comma:

Items
in
Series

words, phrases, or clauses in a series
to hunt, to fish, and to hike
He went home, he went upstairs, and he could remember nothing.
He liked oysters, soup, roast beef, and song.

Put a linker before the concluding *and* in any series. We pause there in our speech, saying "Hawthorne, Dickens, and Thackeray" and keeping "Dickens and Thackeray" (no comma) from sounding like a comedy team. Again, commas signal those pauses by which the English language distinguishes meanings.

By carefully separating all elements in a series, you keep alive a final distinction long ago lost in the daily press, the distinction Virginia Woolf makes (see p. 161): "urbane, polished, brilliant, imploring and commanding him . . ." *Imploring and commanding* is syntactically equal to each one of the other modifiers in the series. If Woolf customarily omitted the last comma, as she does not, she could not have reached for that double apposition. The muscle would have been dead. These other examples of double apposition will give you an idea of its effectiveness:

Double
Appositions

They cut out his idea, root and branch.
He lost all his holdings, houses and lands.
He loved to tramp the woods, to fish and hunt.

A comma makes a great deal of difference, of sense and distinction.

But adjectives in series, as distinct from nouns in series, change the game a bit. Notice the difference between the following two strings of adjectives:

Strings of
Adjectives

a good, unexpected, natural rhyme
a good old battered hat

With adjectives in series, only your sense can guide you. If each seems to modify the noun directly, as in the first example above, use commas. If each seems to modify the total accumulation of adjectives and noun, as with *good* and *old* in the second phrase, do not use commas. Say your phrases aloud, and put your commas in the pauses that distinguish your meaning.

Finally, a special case. Dramatic intensity sometimes allows you to join clauses with commas instead of conjunctions:

> **She sighed, she cried, she almost died.**
> **I couldn't do it, I tried, I let them all get away.**
> **It passed, it triumphed, it was a good bill.**
> **I came, I saw, I conquered.**

Clauses
Joined with
Commas

The rhetorical intensity of this construction—the Greeks called it *asyndeton*—is obvious. The language is breathless, or grandly emphatic. As Aristotle once said, it is a person trying to say many things at once. The subjects repeat themselves, the verbs overlap, the idea accumulates a climax. By some psychological magic, the clauses of this construction usually come in three's. The comma is its sign. But unless you have a stylistic reason for such a flurry of clauses, go back to the normal comma and conjunction, the semicolon, or the period.

EXERCISE

6. *Write five sentences with concluding double appositives that might look like parts of a simple series but which are not: "They cut out his idea, root and branch."*

FRAGMENTS, COMMA SPLICES, AND RUN-ONS

These are the most persistent problems in using the comma—either missing it or misusing it. We have already looked at the fragment (p. 160), but one more look will consolidate your control. The rhetorical fragment may have great force: "So what." But the grammatical one needs repairing with a comma:

> FAULTY: **She dropped the cup. Which had cost twenty dollars.**
> REVISED: **She dropped the cup, which had cost twenty dollars.**

> FAULTY: **He does not spell everything out. But rather hints that
> something is wrong, and leaves the rest up to the reader.**
> REVISED: **He does not spell everything out, but rather hints . . ., and
> leaves . . ..**

FAULTY: Yet here is her husband treating their son to all that she considers evil. Plus the fact that the boy is offered beer.

REVISED: Yet here is her husband treating their son to all that she considers evil, especially beer.

FAULTY: He points out that one never knows what the future will bring. Because it is actually a matter of luck.

REVISED: He points out that one never knows what the future will bring, because it is actually a matter of luck.

FAULTY: They are off. Not out of their minds exactly but driven, obsessed. (*Time*, August 21, 1978, p. 30)

REVISED: They are off, not out of their minds exactly, but driven, obsessed.

Beware the comma splice, and the run-on.

The comma splice is the beginner's most common error, the exact opposite of the fragment—putting a comma where we need a period, splicing two sentences together with a comma:

Comma
Splice

The comma splice is a common error, it is the exact opposite of a fragment.

The run-on sentence (fortunately less common) omits even the splicing comma, running one sentence right on to another without noticing:

Run-On

The comma splice is a common error it is the exact opposite of a fragment.

Here the writer is in deeper trouble, having somehow never gotten the feel of a sentence as based on subject and verb, and thus needing special help. But most of us can see both the comma splice and run-on as really being two sentences, to be restored as such:

The comma splice is a common error. It is the exact opposite of a fragment.

Or to be coordinated by adding a conjunction after the comma:

The comma splice is a common error, and it is. . . .

Or to be subordinated by making the second sentence a phrase:

The comma splice is a common error, the exact opposite. . . .

Here are some typical comma splices:

> She cut class, it was boring.
> The class was not merely dull, it was useless.
> He was more than satisfied, he was delighted.

Each of these pulls together a pair of closely sequential sentences. But a comma without its *and* or *but* will not hold the coordination. Either make them the sentences they are:

> She cut class. It was boring.

Or coordinate them with a colon or dash (with a semicolon *only* if they contrast sharply):

> The class was not merely dull: it was useless.
> He was more than satisfied—he was delighted.

Or subordinate in some way:

> She cut class because it was boring.
> The class was not merely dull but useless.
> More than satisfied, he was delighted.

Here are some more typical splices, all from one set of papers in advanced freshman composition dealing with Shakespeare's *The Tempest*. I have circled the comma where the period should be:

> She knows nothing of the evil man is capable of, to her every man
>   is beautiful.
> The question of his sensibility hovers, we wonder if he is just.
> Without a doubt, men discourage oppression, they strive to be free.
> Ariel is civilized society, besides being articulate, he has direction
>   and order.
> Stephano and Trinculo are the comics of the play, never presented
>   as complete characters, they are not taken seriously.

You will accidentally splice with a comma most frequently when adding a thought (a complete short sentence) to a longer sentence:

> The book describes human evolution in wholly believable terms,
> comparing the social habits of gorillas and chimpanzees to human
> behavior, it is very convincing.

But your reader will be confused by your drift. Which way is that *comparing* phrase supposed to go? You must help him by repairing your splice with a period, either like this:

> **The book describes human evolution in wholly believable terms, comparing the social habits of gorillas and chimpanzees to human behavior. It is very convincing.**

Or like this:

> **The book describes human evolution in wholly believable terms. Comparing the social habits of gorillas and chimpanzees to human behavior, it is very convincing.**

In short, be sure to attach all accidental fragments—that *comparing* phrase, by itself, would be a fragment—to your main sentence. But be sure each complete sentence—*It is very convincing*—stands clear and alone with its own capital and period.

Conjunctive adverbs *(however, therefore, nevertheless, moreover, furthermore,* and others) may cause comma splices and trouble:

> **She continued teaching, however her heart was not in it.**

Here are three mendings:

> **She continued teaching, but her heart was not in it.**
> **She continued teaching; however, her heart was not in it.**
> **She continued teaching; her heart, however, was not in it.**

Similarly, transitional phrases *(in fact, that is, for example)* may splice your sentences together:

> **He disliked discipline, that is, he really was lazy.**

You can strengthen the weak joints like this:

> **He disliked discipline; that is, he really was lazy.**
> **He disliked discipline, that is, anything demanding.**

Meet the press.

Now, let's face the music of everyday print. A corporation recently told its stockholders "Abilene, Kansas looks promising," as if the chairman were telling his wife that things looked good in Kansas. Much advertising copy is virtually all fragments, and commas in the popular press fall out at random. The following paragraph, from *Time* magazine, is representative:

The *Aquatic,* a noisy, diesel-driven 40-ft. private sub tender chugs out of Warwick Cove into a gray Rhode Island day. Past rows of boats with names like *Many-Ha-Ha's, Daddy's Girl, Lucy M* and *Gyp Sea.* Past a dock where burlap sacks of clams are bought and sold—the seller getting 55¢ per lb. for littlenecks, as high as 80¢ for big quahogs. Past a sandbar where a tourist drowned yesterday clamming in 3 ft. of water. Past the big shingled mansions that trim the shoreline at fashionable Warwick Neck. And so into Narragansett Bay, a body of water variously ravished by long-handled rakes, progress and history.*

Commas and a dash will turn this choppy passage into a smooth sentence that sweeps the panorama into cohesive view from capital to period:

The *Aquatic,* a noisy, diesel-driven 40-ft. private sub tender◌	Inserter
Linker chugs out of Warwick Cove into a gray Rhode Island day◌past rows	
of boats with names like *Many-Ha-Ha's, Daddy's Girl, Lucy M*◌and	Linker,
Gyp Sea◌past a dock where burlap sacks of clams are bought and	Linker
sold — the seller getting 55¢ per pound for littlenecks, as high as	Dash as
80¢ for big quahogs — past a sandbar where a tourist drowned	Paired Inserter
Linker yesterday clamming in 3 ft. of water◌past the big shingled mansions	
that trim the shoreline at fashionable Warwick Neck◌and so into	Linker
Narragansett Bay, a body of water variously ravished by long-handled	
rakes, progress◌and history.	Linker

Commas keep your sentences coherent, meaningful, and attractive; they give your prose some of the breath, and breadth, of life.

EXERCISES

7. *Find a fragmented passage similar to the preceding and see what you can do to repair it, indicating in the margin which commas you are using.*

8. *Correct the following sentences, inserting commas where needed, removing them where not (and, in a few cases, inserting periods). Some of the sentences are correct as they stand.*

1. This report will discuss the equipment to be used, the procedure to be followed the data to be obtained and the format for presenting the results.

*Reprinted by permission from TIME, The Weekly Newsmagazine; Copyright Time Inc. 1978.

2. We find however, that the greatest expense in renovation will be for labor, not for materials.
3. This book, even after seventy-five years is still one of the finest examples of sociological scholarship available and it ought to be required reading in any elementary sociology course.
4. The French Revolution of 1789 sparked a similar revolution led by Toussaint L'Ouverture, in Haiti in 1791 and shortly thereafter, the French recognized the freedom of the slaves.
5. Remote sensing devices exploit parts of the electromagnetic spectrum invisible to the eye.
6. Will Sexton a long-time member of the department will become sales manager on July 1, 1982 but until that time he will remain on convalescent leave.
7. Tight money and a scarcity of jobs have given a boost to graduate school applications.
8. He depended for his quotations upon the Bible Shakespeare and Emerson.
9. A faithful sincere friend he remained loyal to his roommate even after the unexpected turn of events.
10. We were delayed by the heavy snow, and therefore did not arrive in time for the lecture.
11. Although few readers of *The Adventures of Huckleberry Finn* recognize it at first the book is really a somber story of treachery murder and brutality.
12. Robert E. Lee was born at Stratford Virginia on January 19 1807.
13. In America said the Chinese lecturer people sing "Home Sweet Home." In China they stay there.
14. Should the estimate be too high I will seek other bids.
15. Printed in London bound in New York and first released in Chicago, the book cost so much its sales were very limited.
16. The jobs of these machine operators largely assembly-line workers have become as simple repetitive and mechanical as the functions of the machines themselves.
17. Readers of Joseph Heller's book *Catch-22* a comic novel about World War II seem to react in one of two ways. Either they love the book or they can't stand it, in either case the book seems to arouse their passions.
18. Depressed refusing to face the reality of his situation he killed himself it was as simple as that.
19. Writing in a popular magazine the critic said that Rex Harrison as Henry Higgins and Wilfrid Hyde-White as Colonel Pickering stole the show.
20. Jill Crabtree, in her article, "Foreign Relations at Home" says that American students are not interested in the foreign students on this campus despite the campaign by the International Center to promote their interest.

21. I guess I could drive the truck myself, still I really don't want to.
22. Person-to-person calls collect calls credit-card calls and calls to be billed to another number must be placed through the operator.
23. With the advent of refrigeration both in the home and in conveyances, the housewife could feed her family fresh foods in any season, before that she had fresh foods available only in season, and her winter menus were nutritionally weak.
24. In "Indian Camp" Hemingway's short story the reader's attention is on Nick Adams an eight- or ten-year-old observer of the jackknife Caesarean that his father performs on the Indian woman. We watch the watcher so to speak.
25. Although there are areas of overlap this report is divided into five parts: General Activities Criteria The Committee's Influence Upon Classified Research Communications and Future Considerations.

THE SEMICOLON

Use the semicolon only where you could also use a period, unless desperate.

The dogmatic formula that heads this section, which I shall loosen up in a moment, has saved many a punctuator from both despair and a reckless fling of semicolons. Confusion comes from the belief that the semicolon is either a weak colon or a strong comma. It is most effective as neither. It is best, as we have seen (p. 139), in pulling together and contrasting two independent clauses that could stand alone as sentences:

> **The dress accents the feminine. The pants suit speaks for freedom.**
> **The dress accents the feminine; the pants suit speaks for freedom.**

This compression and contrast by semicolon can go even farther, allowing us to drop a repeated verb in the second element (note also how here a comma marks the omission):

> **Golf demands the best of time and space; tennis demands the best**
> **of personal energy.**
> **Golf demands the best of time and space; tennis, the best of personal**
> **energy.**

Used sparingly, the semicolon emphasizes your crucial contrasts; used recklessly, it merely clutters your page. *Never* use it as a colon: its effect is exactly opposite. A colon, as in the preceding sentence, signals the meaning to go ahead; a semicolon, as in this sentence, stops it. The colon is a green light; the semicolon is a stop sign.

Consequently, a wrong semicolon frequently makes a fragment. *Use a semicolon only where you could also use a period*—forget the exceptions—or you will make semicolon-fragments like the underscored phrases following the erroneous semicolons circled below:

> The play opens on a dark street in New York City; one streetlight giving the only illumination.
> The geese begin their migration in late August or early September; several families having started, in small stages, a week or so earlier.

Each of those semicolons should have been a comma.

Of course, you may occasionally need to unscramble a long line of phrases and clauses, especially those in series and containing internal commas:

> You should see that the thought is full, the words well cleaned, the points adjusted; and then your sentence will be ready to go. [*Note that the period rule would still guide you here:* ". . . adjusted. And then. . . ."]
> Composition is hard because we often must discover our ideas by writing them out, clarifying them on paper; because we must also find a clear and reasonable order for ideas the mind presents simultaneously; and because we must find, by trial and error, exactly the right words to convey our ideas and our feelings about them.

But the semicolon is better when it pulls related sentences together, replacing the period (or the comma-plus-conjunction) for some unusual emphasis:

> They worked hard; they never thought of failure; they were wholly self-sufficient.

And better still when it pivots a contrast:

> Work when you work; play when you play.
> The semicolon is a stop sign; the colon, a green light.

Notice that the semicolon (like the colon) goes *outside* quotation marks:

> This was no "stitch in time"; it was complete reconstruction.

EXERCISES

9. *Write five compound sentences, using a semicolon between two contrasting independent clauses.*

EXAMPLES: Compound sentences are strings of thoughts; complex sentences envelop them.

The semicolon is a stop sign; the colon, a green light.

10. *The following selections include examples of both correct and incorrect semicolons. Insert them where needed; remove them where not. Adjust commas and periods as necessary.*

1. The book deals with the folly of war, its stupidity, its cruelty, however, in doing this, the author brings in too many characters, repeats episodes over and over again, and spoils his comedy by pressing too hard.
2. Despite these shortcomings; however the book has remained popular because it is fresh and wacky in its approach.
3. Most men smoked either cigars or pipes, for a long time cigarettes were regarded as unmanly.
4. Most men smokers used either cigars or pipes; most women smokers used cigarettes.
5. Steinbeck's fictional strike in *In Dubious Battle* is not unique, in the 1930's, such strikes were very real indeed.
6. The endowment provides stipends for periods of from six months to a year. The scope of support includes; language, both modern and classical, literature, jurisprudence, philosophy, ancient, historical, and modern, archaeology, history (of Western Europe only) and sociology.
7. Your comments should be specific, pointed, and candid, you should not hold back anything.
8. We need to create a new kind of academic community, one with a spirit of openness, the student must be able to find meaning, coherence, and significance behind the jumble of experiences he gets.
9. Many graduating students are scared to death. The job market hasn't been so tight since the 1930's.
10. The law library will be open from 8 A.M. to 1 A.M. now through December 21; from 8 A.M. to 6 P.M. from December 24 to January 4, and closed Christmas Day and New Year's Day.
11. To let him go unpunished was unthinkable, to punish him, unbearable.
12. In McKay's novel, *Home to Harlem,* Jake's character remains rather constant, however, his friend Ray undergoes a fairly substantial change.

13. Although the story was written in 1933; it shows few of the characteristic marks of the period's popular literature.
14. On the one hand, it is obvious that Mr. Bisko disagrees with the company policy, on the other hand, if he wants to keep his job, he has to put up with it.
15. Probably only 5 percent of the potential jobs for naval architects and marine engineers are actually held by people who are trained for them, in fact, probably 50 percent of these jobs are held by people who aren't college-educated or technically trained at all.

THE COLON

Use a colon as a green light, or arrow.

The semicolon, as we have seen, makes a full stop; the colon waves the traffic on through the intersection: "Go right ahead," it says, "and you will find what you are looking for." The colon is like one of those huge arrows that say HERE IT IS after you have been following the signs for half a continent. It emphatically and precisely introduces the clarifying detail, the illustrative example, the itemized series, the formal quotation:

> Pierpont lived for only one thing: money.
> In the end, it was useless: Adams really was too green.
> Now he speaks in the romantic mode: "Hasten, O damsel" (I.ii.24).
> The Lord helps those who help themselves: Jasper helped himself.
> Several things were missing: the silver service, his gold watch, Beth's pearls, and the moonstone.
> The committee considered three things: (1) how to reduce expend- itures, (2) how to raise more money, and (3) how to handle Smith's unfortunate laxity.
> The point is precisely this: no one can win.
> He thought not only of home: he thought of grandmother's oatmeal cookies.

Use the colon to introduce quotations.

You naturally introduce long quotations with a colon, indenting them and setting them apart from your own words. Do the same with short quotations within your running text, when they need your sentence but are not part of its grammar:

> We remember Sherman's words: "War is hell."

primarily for listing [handwritten annotation]

You may use a comma informally:

> **We remember Sherman's words, "War is hell."**

When a quotation is an integral part of your sentence, punctuate as necessary, but do not use a colon:

> **As Sherman implied, "war is hell" for all concerned.**
> **We remember, as Sherman said, that "war is hell."**

Notice that here you do not capitalize "war," although you would capitalize in the most careful scholarly writing, to preserve exactly all the details of your quotation.

Do not use a colon immediately after a verb, a preposition, or the conjunction *that*, where it would break up grammatical connections:

> WRONG:
> **The trouble was: he never listened.**
> **The trouble was that: he never listened.**
> **She liked the simple things, like: swimming pools, diamonds, and unadorned mink.**
> **She was fond of: swimming pools, diamonds, and unadorned mink.**

Do not capitalize after a colon, unless what follows is normally capitalized, as with a proper name, a quotation beginning with a capital, a title of a work, or, occasionally, a sequence of several sentences.

> RIGHT:
> **All effort is painful: pleasure comes with achievement.**
> **Again we may say with Churchill: "Never have so many owed so much to so few."**
> **But several major considerations remain: Unending leisure is no blessing for the ordinary mortal. We must be occupied, and yet we cannot forever occupy ourselves. Furthermore, . . .**

I still prefer a period after *remain*, since the colon tends to tie the first two sentences too closely.

EXERCISES

11. *Write five sentences using the colon to introduce a complete clarifying "sentence"—that is, write your sentence so that the colon is clearly more meaningful than a period and new capitalization would have been:*

In the end, it was useless: he really was too green.
The point is precisely this: no one can win.

12. *In the following selections, some colons are right, some wrong, some missing: correct all errors, including misused periods, commas, and semicolons.*

1. The music is generally excellent; the tunes are quite good and the singing clear and bright.
2. Ralph Ellison, describing in *Shadow and Act* how he switched his interest from music to literature says; "Writing provided me a growing satisfaction and required, unlike music, no formal study. . . ."
3. There's only one thing we need right now—more time.
4. Remote sensing devices exploit the following parts of the electromagnetic spectrum; infrared radiation, ultraviolet radiation, gamma rays, and microwaves.
5. We're out here for one reason only, to work with Dr. Ravelli.
6. The semicolon, as we have seen, makes a full stop; the colon waves the traffic on through the intersection, "Go right ahead," it says, "and you will find what you are looking for."
7. For assistance call any of the following staff members, Mr. Beatty, 714-1425; Mr. Greenway, 714-2829; Mr. Brooks, 714-4432.
8. A project may be given a national security classification to provide researchers access to classified information, to facilitate visiting classified activities, counseling, and participating in advisory functions; or to allow freer exchange of ideas.
9. There's one thing you can say: the plot is timely.
10. This attitude is caused by two things; first, students in a large university tend to think of themselves as being lost in the crowd: and, second, students tend to view administrators—as administrators sometimes view themselves—as substitute parents.

THE PERIOD

The period affirms your sentence, and should not break it into fragments. It ends a declaration and makes it independent. It concludes each thought you complete with subject, verb, and other attachments, even when you only imply both subject and verb, as in the fragmentary sentence *Of course.* Notice that you may change your declarations to questions and exclamations merely by switching from the declarative period to a question mark or exclamation point: *Of course? Of course!*

Use a period after an indirect question.

The following are not really questions, but declarations of what the question was; hence the period.

> She asked me when I was going to finish college.
> I wonder if you could come tomorrow.
> He wanted to know how I found it and why I hadn't told him.

Use a period after a polite command or request; use exclamations sparingly.

The exclamation point shouts a little, and the question mark can grow a little shrill. My page would startle you had I written: "Use a period after a polite command or request!" Similarly, the question mark may seem too insistent: "Will you kindly remit?"

> But be careful.
> Come when you can.
> Will you kindly give this matter your earliest attention.
> May the council please have your comments at your convenience.

For periods in abbreviations, see pp. 414–416.

EXERCISES

13. *Write five sentences containing indirect questions, ending them properly with periods.*

14. *Some of the following sentences have correct periods; some run together without punctuation; some fumble the period in various ways. Insert the proper punctuation in the faulty sentences.*

1. I have only a faint recollection of the place of my childhood at times, I can close my eyes and call up vague images, but most of the time I just can't remember.
2. Sitting down in front of the TV set, I kicked off my shoes and loosened my belt, still, I felt very nervous and tense.
3. Two of these packages are headed for Washington, D.C., the third is going to Baltimore.
4. Please climb down you'll hurt yourself.
5. The International Brigades, which were formed by Comintern to fight in Spain, were a combination of displaced and dissatisfied people from all over

the world, many of the first to join were people forced by Fascist governments to leave Germany and Italy.

6. During the Depression, Wright held a number of jobs he was a hospital orderly, a counselor in a boys club, a newspaper correspondent.

7. In studying the similarities in the courtroom strategies of Boris Max and Clarence Darrow, one can also find parallels between the characters themselves, their lives, their attitudes.

8. Thank you for your answers to my questionnaire I will be able to use much of your response in my report.

9. The law school has reached an all-time high in applications. With 13 applicants for each of its 370 openings.

10. About 1,000 scientists from 25 foreign countries are expected to attend the workshop. Where 180 papers will be presented.

11. In order to gain a full understanding of any book. One ought to know something of the life and intellectual background of its author.

12. People seldom form their own judgment about politics they let others form it for them.

13. Although the lawyer knew that his client was guilty. He defended him vigorously so that he could gain a reputation for victory, if not for justice.

14. I awoke at midnight, my bones were aching and my back felt as if it were being pricked with electric needles.

15. Like space, time is a natural organizer. Ancient. And simple.

PARENTHESIS AND DASH

The dash says aloud what the parenthesis whispers. Both enclose interruptions too extravagant for a pair of commas to hold. The dash is the more useful—since whispering tends to annoy—and will remain useful only if not overused. It can serve as a conversational colon. It can set off a concluding phrase—for emphasis. It can bring long introductory matters to focus, as in Freud's sentence on page 156. It can insert a full sentence— a clause is really an incorporated sentence—directly next to a key word. The dash allows you to insert—with a kind of shout!—an occasional exclamation. You may even insert—and who would blame you?—an occasional question. The dash affords a structural complexity with all the tone and alacrity of talk.

With care, you can get much the same power from a parenthesis:

Phrase **Many philosophers have despaired (somewhat unphilosophically) of discovering any certainties whatsoever.**

Thus did Innocent III (we shall return to him shortly) inaugurate an age of horrors. [Note no period after *shortly,* and no capital for *we.*]

Sentence in Sentence

General Douglas MacArthur ("We shall return") accomplished his prediction in October, 1944, when American forces invaded the Japanese-held Philippines. [An exception to the previous rule—with quotation marks, a capital, but no period.]

Quoted Sentence in Sentence

Thus did Innocent III inaugurate an age of horrors. (We shall return to him shortly.) [A full sentence in parenthesis positioned thus for more emphasis takes a period, and a capital for the first word.]

Parenthetical Comment After a Sentence

Cross-Reference But in such circumstances (see page 34), be cautious.

Cross-Reference

Delay had doubled the costs (a stitch in time!), so the plans were shelved.

Interjection

But dashes seem more generally useful, and here are some special points. When one of a pair of dashes falls where a comma would be, it absorbs the comma:

If one wanted to go, he certainly could.
If one wanted to go—whether invited or not—he certainly could.

Dashes

Not so with the semicolon:

He wanted to go—whether he was invited or not; she had more sense.

To indicate the dash, type two hyphens (--) flush against the words they separate—not one hyphen between two spaces, nor a hyphen spaced to look exactly like a hyphen.

Put commas and periods *outside* a parenthetical group of words (like this one). (But if you make an entire sentence parenthetical, put the period *inside.*)

Full Sentence

Change has had its way with the parenthesis around numbers. Formal print and most guides to writing, including this one, still hold to the full parenthesis:

The sentence really has only two general varieties: (1) the "loose," or strung-along, in Aristotle's phrase, and (2) the periodic.
For a number of reasons, he decided (1) that he did not like it, (2) that she would not like it, and (3) that they would be better off without it.

Numbered Items

Popular print and secretarial fashion now omit the first half of the parenthesis:

> . . . decided 1) that he did not like it, 2) that she . . . .

But for your papers—keep the full parenthesis.

EXERCISE

15. *Write four sentences, two containing a phrase or clause within dashes, two containing a phrase or clause within parentheses. Try to make your sentences more elaborate than the following simple models—as different from them as possible, and more interesting.*

> He wrote a sentence containing a phrase—he could have used a clause—inserted between dashes.
> He wrote hastily (he pretended to concentrate) as the boss looked over his shoulder.

BRACKETS

Brackets indicate your own words inserted or substituted within a quotation from someone else: "Byron had already suggested that [they] had killed John Keats." You have substituted "they" for "the gentlemen of the *Quarterly Review*" to suit your own context. You do the same when you interpolate a word of explanation: "Byron had already suggested that the gentlemen of the *Quarterly Review* [especially Croker] had killed John Keats." *Do not use parentheses:* they mark the enclosed words—that is, the parenthesis itself—as part of the original quotation. Don't claim innocence because your typewriter lacks brackets. Just leave spaces and draw them in later, or type slant lines and tip them with pencil or with the underscore key:

In the example below, you are pointing out with a *sic* (Latin for "so" or "thus"), which you should not italicize, that you are reproducing an error exactly as it appears in the text you are quoting:

> "On no occassion [sic] could we trust them."

Similarly, you may give a correction after reproducing the error:

> "On the twenty-fourth [twenty-third], we broke camp."
> "In not one instance [actually, Baldwin reports several instances] did our men run under fire."

Use brackets when you need a parenthesis within a parenthesis:

> **(see Donald Allenberg, *The Future of Television* [New York, 1973],**
> **pp. 15–16)**

Your instructor will probably put brackets around the wordy parts of your sentences, indicating what you should cut:

> **In fact, [the reason] he liked it [was] because it was different.**

EXERCISE

16. *Straighten out errors in parentheses, dashes, and brackets in the following sentences.*

1. Many skiers, (hardly the best) have given up Big Bear run.
2. Several members of the expedition (We name no names.) refused to go on.
3. The paper reported (the *Pinkley Currier,* sic) that Ottis had had twenty-one [21] drinks before leaving.
4. When the alarm rang,—it had been tested only once—it sounded like a distant teapot.
5. "The night before the duel, (Hamilton) wrote his wife that he did not intend to kill Burr."
6. "Our tuition is the lowest (*College Index* lists three institutions lower) in the state."
7. (See Alexis Winsome, *All That Matters* (New Haven: Escapist Press, 1981), p. 32).
8. "Many young couples find a condominia (sic) convenient."
9. Quirk ran the option—he got out of the pocket and still had time to throw, and Coffin was wide open, but he at least picked up four yards.
10. Although some researchers have proved marijuana relatively harmless, others (even admitting its medicinal value for some patients) are pointing to the carcinogenic effects of inhalation.

QUOTATION MARKS AND ITALICS

Put quotation marks around quotations that "run directly into your own sentence" (like this), but *not* around quotations set off from your text and indented. You normally inset poetry as it stands, centering it on your page, without quotation marks:

> An aged man is but a paltry thing,
> A tattered coat upon a stick, unless
> Soul clap its hands and sing . . . .

But if you run it into your text, use quotation marks, with *virgules* (slants) showing the line-ends: "An aged man is but a paltry thing,/ A tattered coat . . . ." (See "Mechanics," pp. 68–69). Put periods and commas *inside* quotation marks; put semicolons and colons *outside:*

Quotation
Marks
with Other
Punctuation

Now we understand the full meaning of "Give me liberty, or give me death."

"This strange disease of modern life," in Arnold's words, remains uncured.

In Greece, it was "know thyself"; in America, it is "know thy neighbor."

He left after "Hail to the Chief": he could do nothing more.

Although logic often seems to demand the period or comma outside the quotation marks, convention has put them inside for the sake of appearance, even when the sentence ends in a single quoted word or letter:

Clara Bow was said to have "It."
Mark it with "T."

If you have seen the periods and commas outside, you were reading a British book or a freshman's paper (or some of America's little magazines).

If you are quoting a phrase that already contains quotation marks, reduce the original double marks (") to single ones ('):

Single
Quotation
Marks

ORIGINAL	YOUR QUOTATION
Hamlet's "are you honest?" is easily explained.	He writes that "Hamlet's 'are you honest?' is easily explained."

Notice what happens when the quotation within your quotation falls at the end:

A majority of the informants thought *infer* meant "imply."	Kirk reports that "a majority of the informants thought *infer* meant 'imply.'"

And notice that a question mark or exclamation point falls between the single and the double quotation marks at the end of a quotation containing a quotation:

"Why do they call it 'the Hippocratic oath'?" she asked.
"Everything can't be 'cool'!" he said.

But heed the following exception:

"I heard someone say, 'Is anyone home?' " she declared.

Do not use *single* quotation marks for your own stylistic flourishes; use *double* quotation marks or, preferably, none:

It was indeed an "affair," but the passion was hardly "grand."
It was indeed an affair, but the passion was hardly grand.
Some "cool" pianists use the twelve-tone scale.

Once you have thus established this slang meaning of *cool,* you may repeat the word without quotation marks. In general, of course, you should favor that slang your style can absorb without quotation marks.

Do not use quotation marks for calling attention to words as words. Use italics (an underscore when typing) for the words, quotation marks for their meanings.

This is taking *tergiversation* too literally.   Italics
The word *struthious* means "like an ostrich."

Similarly, use italics for numbers as numbers and letters as letters:

He writes a *5* like an *s.*

Use quotation marks for titles *within* books and magazines: titles of chapters, articles, short stories, songs, and poems, and for unpublished works, lectures, courses, TV episodes within a series. But use italics for titles or names of books, newspapers, magazines, plays, films, long poems, sculptures, paintings, ships, trains, and airplanes.

Poe's description of how he wrote "The Raven" was attacked in the   Titles and
  Atlantic Monthly [or: the *Atlantic*].   Names
We saw Michelangelo's *Pietà,* a remarkable statue in white marble.
We took the Santa Fe *Chief* from Chicago to Los Angeles.
He read all of Frazer's *The Golden Bough.*
His great-grandfather went down with the *Titanic.*
She read it in the *New York Times.*

Handle titles within titles as follows:

"The Prelude" and Nature in Wordsworth [book]
" 'The Prelude' and Natural Imagery" [article]

"The Art of *Tom Jones*" [article]
The Art of Tom Jones [book]

In the last example, notice that what is ordinarily italicized, like the "book" part (Tom Jones) of a larger book title here, is set in roman when the larger setting is in italics.

Italicize foreign words and phrases, unless they have been assimilated into English through usage (your dictionary should have a method for noting the distinction; if not, consult one that has):

> **The statement contained two clichés and one *non sequitur*.**
> **The author of this naïve exposé suffers from an *idée fixe*.**

Foreign Words

Other foreign expressions *not* italicized are: etc., e.g., et al., genre, hubris, laissez faire, leitmotif, mimesis, roman à clef, raison d'être, tête-à-tête.

Sacred Books

Use neither quotation marks nor italics for the Bible, for its books or parts (Genesis, Old Testament), for other sacred books (Koran, Talmud,

Documents

Upanishad), nor for famous documents like the Magna Carta, the Declaration of Independence, the Communist Manifesto, and the Gettysburg Address, nor for instrumental music known by its form, number, and key:

> **Beethoven's C-minor Quartet**
> **Brahms's Symphony No. 4, Opus 98**

When a reference in parentheses falls at the end of a quotation, the quotation marks *precede* the first parenthesis:

> **As Ecclesiastes tells us, "there is no new thing under the sun" (i.9).**

ELLIPSIS

1. Use three spaced periods . . . (the ellipsis mark) when you omit something from a quotation. Do *not* use them in your own text in place of a dash, or in mere insouciance.

2. If you omit the end of a sentence, put in a period (no space) and add the three spaced dots. . . .

3. If your omission falls after a completed sentence, just add the three spaced dots to the period already there. . . . The spacing is the same as for case 2.

Here is an uncut passage, followed by a shortened version illustrating the three kinds of ellipsis (the numbers refer to the foregoing rules):

> **To learn a language, learn as thoroughly as possible a few everyday sentences. This will educate your ear for all future pronunciations. It will give you a fundamental grasp of structure. And start soon.**

> **(1)**
> **To learn a language, learn . . . a few everyday sentences. This**

> **(2)**
> **will educate your ear. . . . It will give you a fundamental grasp**

> **(3)**
> **of structure. . . .**

The three spaced dots of the ellipsis may fall on either side of other punctuation, to indicate exactly where you have omitted something from the text you are quoting:

> **In many instances . . . , our careful words are superfluous.**
> **In many instances of human crisis, . . . words are superfluous.**
> **We have the bombs . . . ; it looks as if they have the troops.**
> **Eighteenth-century prisons were vicious: . . . the people no less than the rats and the fevers.**
> **Alas, poor Yorick! . . . a fellow of infinite jest.**
> **In this sonnet, Shakespeare is well aware of the foolishness of self-pity: "And trouble deaf heaven with my bootless cries,/ . . . and curse my fate. . . ."**

With Other
Punctuation

If you have no compelling reason to show the other punctuation, then you may drop it, retaining the ellipsis only: "We have the bombs . . . it looks as if they have the troops."

If you omit a line or more of poetry, or a paragraph or more of prose, and *if the omission is significant,* use a whole line of elliptical dots:

In Poetry

> **When in disgrace with Fortune and men's eyes,**
> **I all alone beweep my outcast state,**
> **And trouble deaf heaven with my bootless cries,**
> **. . . . .**
> **Yet in these thoughts myself almost despising,**
> **Haply I think on thee. . . .**

If the omission had not been significant, the ellipsis would have followed *cries:*

And trouble deaf heaven with my bootless cries. . . .
Yet in these thoughts. . . .

Be sure that your omissions do not distort your author's meaning. And remember this: *the shorter your quotation, the better.* A short quotation puts your purpose into sharpest focus for your reader's attention. A long quotation may require you to requote or paraphrase to make your point.

If you begin to quote in the middle of a sentence, place three elliptical dots before the first quoted word:

Mid-Sentence
. . . learn as thoroughly as possible a few everyday sentences. This will educate your ear for all future pronunciations. It will give you a fundamental grasp of structure. . . .

But if you quote a full sentence that falls in the middle of a paragraph, omit the initial elliptical dots:

Mid-Paragraph
We have come to dedicate a portion of that field as a final resting place for those who here gave their lives that that nation might live. It is altogether fitting and proper that we should do this.
But, in a larger sense. . . .

When you use a short partial quotation within a sentence, you can omit the beginning and ending ellipses:

Lincoln was determined that the "brave men . . . who struggled here" should be redeemed by a strengthened nation.

In Quotations
Only
Use the ellipsis in quoted material only. If you use it in your own text, you will seem to drift, which is precisely what it means in a novel: the passage of time, or the drifting of thought. Only most rarely can you work it into expository prose. It is dramatic, and risky. You risk seeming affected. I have used it only once in this entire book (p. 7), and I do not recall ever having used it before. You can leave a space after your last word to stress the drift:

Even the dog-lovers will be uninterested, convinced they know better than you. But the cat . . . .

As I threw the cat in after the dogs to emphasize a point already made, the ellipsis seemed right. But the exception does not overturn the rule: use ellipsis marks in quoted material only.

EXERCISE

17. *Repair the following sentences with the necessary quotation marks, italics (underlining to indicate italics), and ellipses.*

1. Like the farmer in Frost's Mending Wall, some people believe that Good fences make good neighbors.
2. Germaine Greer's The Female Eunuch is a book to be remembered, especially in phrases like I'm sick of peering at the world through false eyelashes and I'm a woman, not a castrate.
3. "The swimming pool . . . . desperately needs draining and resurfacing . . ."
4. Some groovy singers seem stuck in one groove.
5. Cleopatra's Husband, I come! seems out of character.
6. Butterfield finds that Cleopatra's Husband, I come! seems out of character.
7. The committee of twelve . . . was a total failure.
8. The San Francisco Chronicle called it a goof.
9. For him, the most important letter is I.
10. . . . In the evening, in the morning, at noon . . . and at 4 P.M. . . . they check the valves.
11. Their favorite books were Huckleberry Finn, the Bible, especially Ecclesiastes, and Henry David Thoreau's Walden.
12. Why does the raven keep crying Nevermore! he asked.
13. She hated what she called excess baggage; she loved the world from A to Z.
14. . . . yet the mains keep bursting, because they are half a century old . . . .
15. Here see means understand.

Section D

SPELLING, WORD-PUNCTUATION, CAPITALIZATION

Now for the needlepoint. Letter by letter, we stitch out words, and most of us have trouble with the lettering, and with questions of punctuating those words with apostrophes, hyphens, capital letters, and other small but meaningful pointings. As always, the details count, either impressing your reader with your mastery, or putting a beginner's sampler on exhibit. So get the stitches down, and don't let them get you down.

SPELLING IT OUT

You can conquer your troubles with spelling more easily than you think—once you put your mind to it. The dictionary is your best friend as you face the inevitable anxieties of spelling, but three underlying principles and some tricks of the trade can help immeasurably:

PRINCIPLE I. Letters represent sounds: proNUNciation can help you spell. No one proNOUNcing his words correctly would make the familiar errors of "similar" and "enviorment." You can even improve your social standing by learning to say *envIRONment* and *goverNment* and *FebRUary* and *intRAmural*. Simply sound out the letters. Of course, you will need to be wary of some words *not* pronounced as spelled: *Wednesday,* pronounced "Wensday," for instance. But sounding the letters can help your spellings. You can even say "convertible" and "indelible" and "plausible" without sounding like a fool, and you can silently stress the *able* in words like "prob*able*" and "immov*able*" to remember the difficult distinction between words ending in *-ible,* and *-able.*

Consonants reliably represent their sounds. Remember that *c* and *g* go soft before *i* and *e.* Consequently you must add a *k* when extending words like *picnic* and *mimic*—*picnicKing, mimicKing*—to keep them from rhyming with *slicing* or *dicing.* Conversely, you just keep the *e* (where you would normally drop it) when making *peace* into *peacEable* and *change* into *changEable,* to keep the *c* and *g* soft—otherwise they would sound like *peekable* and *hangable.*

Consonants

Single *s* is pronounced *zh* in words like *vision, occasion, pleasure.* Knowing that *ss* hushes ("sh-h-h") will keep you from errors like *occassion,* which would sound like *passion.*

Vowels sound short and light before single consonants: *hat, pet, kit, hop, cup.* When you add any vowel (including *y*) the first vowel will say its name: *hate, Pete, kite, hoping, cupid.* Notice how the *a* in *-able* keeps the main vowel saying its name in words like *unmistakable, likable,* and *notable.* Therefore, to keep a vowel short, protect it with a double consonant: *petting, hopping.* This explains the troublesome *rr* in *occuRRence:* a single *r* would make it say *cure* in the middle. *Putting* a golf ball and *putting* something on paper must both use *tt* to keep from being pronounced *pewting.* Compare *stony* with *sonny* and *bony* with *bonny.* The *y* is replacing the *e* in *stone* and *bone,* and the rule is working perfectly. It works in any syllable that is accented: compare *forgeTTable* as against *markeTable, begiNNing* as against *buttoNing,* and *compeLLing* as against *traveLing.*

Vowels

Likewise, when *full* combines and loses its stress, it also loses an *l.* Note the single and double *l* in *fulFILLment.* Similarly, *SOULful, GRATEful, AWful*—even *SPOONful.*

PRINCIPLE II. This is the old rule of *i* before *e,* and its famous exceptions:

I before *e*
Except after *c,*
Or when sounded like *a*
As in *neighbor* **and** *weigh.*

Memorize it, and use it to check your uncertainties. It works like a charm (*achieve, believe, receive, conceive*). Note that *c* needs an *e* to make it sound like *s*. Remember also that *leisure* was once pronounced "lay-sure," and *foreign*, "forayn." Memorize these exceptions: *protein, seize, weird, either, sheik, forfeit, counterfeit.* Note that all are pronounced "ee" (with a little crowding) and that the *e* comes first. Then note that another small group goes the opposite way, having a long *i* sound as in German "Heil": *height, sleight, seismograph, kaleidoscope. Financier,* another exception, follows its French origin with a hint of its original sound.

Derivations PRINCIPLE III. Most big words, following the Latin or French from which they came, spell their sounds letter for letter. Look up the derivations of the words you misspell (note that double *s*, and explain it). You will never again have trouble with *desperate* and *separate* once you discover that the first comes from *de-spero*, "without hope," and that sePARate divides equals, the PAR values in stocks or golf. Nor with *definite* or *definitive*, once you see the kinship of both with *finite* and *finish*. Derivations can also help you a little with the devilment of *-able* and *-ible,* since, except for a few ringers, the *i* remains from Latin, and the *-ables* are either French *(ami-able)* or Anglo-Saxon copies *(workable).* Knowing origins can help at crucial points: *resemblAnce* comes from Latin *simulAre*, "to copy"; *existEnce* comes from Latin *existEre*, "to stand forth."

The biggest help comes from learning the common Latin prefixes, which, by a process of assimilation (*ad-similis*, "like to like"), account for the double consonants at the first syLLabic joint of so many of our words:

AD- (toward, to): *abbreviate* (shorten down), *accept* (grasp to).
CON- (with): *collapse* (fall with), *commit* (send with).
DIS- (apart): *dissect* (cut apart), *dissolve* (loosen apart).
IN- (into): *illuminate* (shine into), *illusion* (playing into).
IN- (not): *illegal* (not lawful), *immature* (not ripe).
INTER- (between): *interrupt* (break between), *interrogate* (ask between).
OB- (toward, to): *occupy* (take in), *oppose* (put to), *offer* (carry to).
SUB- (under): *suffer* (bear under), *suppose* (put down).
SYN- ("together"—this one is Greek): *symmetry* (measuring together), *syllogism* (logic together).

Spelling takes a will, an eye, and an ear. And a dictionary. Keep a list of your favorite enemies. Memorize one or two a day. Write them in the air in longhand. Visualize them. Imagine a blinking neon sign, with the wicked letters red and tall—d e f i n   t e—d e f i n   t e. Then print them once, write them twice, and blink them a few times more as you go to sleep. But best of all, make up whatever devices you can—the crazier the better—to remember the tricky parts:

DANCE **attenDANCE.**

EXISTENCE **is** TENSE.

There's IRON **in this**
envIRONment.

The resISTANCE **took its**
STANCE.

There's an ANT **on the**
defendANT.

LOOSE **as a goose.**

LOSE **loses an** O.

ALLOT **isn't** A LOT.

ALready **isn't** ALL RIGHT.

I **for** gaIety.

The LL **in paraLLel gives me**
el.

PURr **in** PURsuit.

When an unaccented syllable leads to misspelling, you can also get some help by trying to remember a version of the word that accents the troublesome syllable:

academy—acaDEMic

affirmative—affirMAtion

angel—anGELic

apology—apoLOgia

comparable—comPARE

competition—comPETE

definitely—defiNItion

degradation—deGRADE

democracy—demoCRAT

despair—DESperate

dormitory—dorMIR

extravagant—extravaGANza

fantasy—fanTAStic

fertile—ferTILity

hypocrisy—hypoCRItical

imaginative—imagiNAtion

irritable—irriTATE

laboratory—laBORious

liberal—libeRATE

magnet—magNETic

medicine—meDICinal

melody—meLOdious

personal—persoNALity

preparation—prePARE

prevalent—preVAIL

repetition—rePEAT

reservoir—reSERVE

residence—resiDENtial

restoration—reSTORE

ridicule—riDICulous

Sabbath—sabBATical

vigilance—vigiLANtes

Here are most of the perpetual headaches:*

● **accept, except**—you *accept* criticism, *except* from busybodies.
accommodate—frequently misspelled *accomodate.*
acknowledgment, judgment—don't add an extra *e.*

---

*The entries marked by ● indicate confusion in meaning as well as spelling, and are treated more fully in the Glossary of Usage and Common Errors, pp. 424–480.

- **adverse, averse**—you are *averse* to *adversity*.
- **advice, advise**—you give *advice* when you *advise*.
  adviser, advisor—used interchangeably, with *adviser* preferred.
- **affect, effect**—you *affect* a British accent, and the *effect* is ridiculous.
- **allusion, illusion, disillusion, delusion**—an *allusion* refers to something; an *illusion* is unreal; *delusion* is a deception. *Disallusion* is the usual error.
  analysis, analyzing, annual—watch the *n*'s and that *z*.
  apologize—frequently misspelled *apollogize, appologize*.
  argument—frequently misspelled *arguement*.
  athlete, athletics—often misspelled *athelete, atheletics*. Athletics is singular.

  balance—frequently misspelled ballance: think of that *l* balancing an *a* on each side.
  balloon—frequently misspelled *baloon:* it's like a *ball*.
  beginning—frequently misspelled *begining*, which would rhyme with *shining*.
- **beside, besides**—"by the side of" often confused with "in addition to."
  businessman, businesswoman—frequently misspelled *businesman, busines-woman*.

- **capital, capitol**—every *capital is -al*, except in Washington, D.C.
  careful—frequently misspelled *carefull*, and even *carfull*.
  challenge—frequently misspelled *challange*. Remember *revenge*.
- **cite, site, sight**—you *cite* an authority and build a house on a *site*.
  committee—frequently misspelled *commitee* or *comittee*. Think of double *m*'s and *t*'s. Perhaps thinking *double m-t empty* will help.
- **complement, compliment**—*complement* completes; *compliment* flatters.
- **council, counsel, consul**—a *council* governs as a group; a *counsel* advises as a person, as a *counselor*; a *consul* is a foreign diplimat.
- **credible, creditable, credulous**—*credible* is believable; *creditable*, deserving esteem; *credulous*, believing too easily.
  curriculum, career—watch the *r*'s.

  dealt—often misspelled as it sounds: *delt*. Remember *deal*.
  decide, divide, devices—watch the *i*'s and *e*'s.
  defendant—frequently misspelled *defendent*. A person is usually an *ant*.
  defies, deifies—*defies* stands up against; *deifies* turns something into a god.
  definite—frequently misspelled *definate*. Remember *finIte, finIsh, infinIty*.
- **desert, dessert**—the first is sand; the second ice cream.
  despair—often misspelled *dispair*, or *despare*.
  desperate, separate—one of the most common tangles in spelling. Remember what *desperate* means at the root: *de* (without)-*sperare* (hope). For *separate*,

usually misspelled *seperate* on the pattern of *desperate*, remember the *par*, or equal, in golf. You se**PAR**ate equals.

detrimental—frequently misspelled *detramental*.

- **dilemma, condemn**—*dilemma* frequently, and wrongly, takes on the ending of *condemn: dilemna*. A *lemma* is a proposition; a *dilemma*, a double one.

disastrous—frequently misspelled *disasterous*, after *disaster*.

discrete, discreet—*discrete* is separate; *discreet*, diplomatic.

disillusion—not *disallusion*. See *allusion*.

dissatisfied—frequently misspelled *disatisfied*. Think of *satisfied* and *dis-satisfied*.

dissolve—not *disolve*, but *dis-solve*, "to loosen apart."

divide—not *devide*. Remember the Latin *dis*, and *di*, for "apart."

embarrassment—commonly misspelled by forgetting one of the *r*'s or *s*'s. Spelling it *embarassment* is an *embarrassment*.

- **eminent, imminent, immanent**—*eminent* is prominent; *imminent* is soon forthcoming; *immanent* is indwelling.

environment—remember the *iron*; forget the *vior*.

exaggerate—frequently misspelled *exagerate*.

- **exalt, exult**—*exalt* is to raise; *exult* is to rejoice or gloat.

existence—often misspelled *existance* or *existense*.

explanation—*explain* often induces the misspelling *explaination*.

- **faze, phase**—watch the *s* and the *z*. His adolescent *phase* didn't *faze* him.
- **forward, foreword**—*forward* is a direction; *foreword* is a "word before," a preface.

fulfill, fulfillment—often misspelled *fullfil*, *fullfilment*, or with double *ll*'s all around.

genius, ingenious—*genius* is supreme talent; *ingenious* is inventive.

harassment—often misspelled *harrasment*.

height—frequently misspelled *heighth*. Think of *eight*.

hypocrisy—frequently misspelled *hypocracy*, like *democracy*. Remember *hypocrIte*, *hypocrItical*.

- **indite, indict**—to *indite* is to write; to *indict* is to charge with a crime.
- **inequity, iniquity**—an *inequity* is an unfairness; an *iniquity* is a sin.

irritable—not *iritable*, nor *irritible*. Remember *irritATE*.

lead, led—*led* is often misspelled *lead*, after the *lead* in pencils and pipes.

libel, liable—*libel* defames character; *liable* means likely, or obligated.

lonely, loneliness—often misspelled *lonly*, *lonliness*, which would sound like a *lawn*. Remember *alone* and *loner*.

- **loose, lose**—with a *loose* grip, you *lose* the ball.

- **mislead**—mistaking the *lead* in *lead pencil*, you probably mean *misled:* led astray.
  misspell—frequently misspelled *mispell*. Think of the meaning: *misspell*.

  Negroes, heroes, tomatoes—remember the *e*.

  obstacle—frequently misspelled *obsticle*.
  occurred, occurring—frequently misspelled by omitting the second *r*, which you need to keep the *u*-syllable from sounding like *cure*, or *your*.
  operate (opus, opera)—frequently misspelled *opperate*. Think of *opera*.

  possession—frequently misspelled *posession* or *possesion*.
- **predominate, predominant**—to *predominate* is to dominate outstandingly; *predominant* is an adjective: "His *predominant* feature was his nose."
- **prejudiced**—not *prejudice*, as in "He was *prejudice*": you want the past participle, *prejudiced*.
  primitive—often misspelled *primative*. That a primate is either an ape or a bishop confuses the issue a bit, since both *primitive* and *primate* derive from Latin *primus*, "first."
- **principal, principle**—the first heads a school; the second is a natural or moral law. Think of *pal* for the person.
- **proceed, precede, procedure**—the *e*'s are tricky.
  pronunciation—frequently misspelled *proNOUNciation*, after *pronounce*. Remember *eNUNciation*, how one speaks his words.
  pursue—frequently misspelled *persue*, aided by the idea of "through" in *per*.

  questionnaire—misspelled *questionaire*. Its French form, complete with two *nn*'s and an *e*, shows that it is a recent borrowing.

  renown—frequently misspelled *reknown* or *renoun*. Remind yourself that you do not mean "to be *known again*" nor "to replace *nouns*."
  resistance—frequently misspelled *resistence*, on the pattern of *existence*. Remember, take a STANCE for resiSTANCE.

  separate—frequently misspelled *seperate*. Remember PAR, and the idea of sePARating equals. See *desperate*.
  similar—frequently misspelled *similiar*, on the pattern of *familiar*. Avoid the LIAR.
  successful—frequently misspelled *sucessful*.
  suppressed—often misspelled *supressed*.

there's, theirs—the contraction of *there is* is very often misused for the possessive pronoun, *theirs*, which never takes an apostrophe (see p. 406).
till, until—watch the *l*'s. Both words are acceptable but avoid *'til*.
truly—frequently misspelled *truely*.

unnoticed—frequently misspelled *unoticed*. Remember *un-noticed*.

EXERCISE

1. *To help you identify your likely errors, here are some sentences with a number of commonly misspelled words. Correct each misspelling you find. Then list the five words that give you the most trouble.*

1. Marrage seems to be loosing some of it's traditional signifigance as the devorce rate continues to climb and common-law relationships multiply.
2. Writting is neccessary in almost any proffession.
3. Many women feel there achievements go unrecognized.
4. Offering an explaination is uneccessary unless the personal director asks for one.
5. Certainly one of the most contraversial issues to come along in years, abortion reform has sparked heated arguements in most churches.
6. The proffessor said he would reccomend at least three possable sources.
7. I value your opinion, but your mistaken in principal.
8. He had a good sence of rythm but a terrible ear for pitch.
9. The preformance last night was embarassing, a suprise considerring the ammount of rehersal time the actors had.
10. Environmental deterioration is probobly the single most disasterous consequence of overcrowding.
11. The wittness was able to supply a good discription.
12. Ammong the words on this page, your likely to find at least a few you commonly mispell.
13. There is really no point in studing the definations of words unless at the same time you make an effort to incorperate them into your speech.
14. Students who have transfered from other schools will recieve credit only for those courses in which their grades were above C.
15. The audiance wasn't conscience that anything unusual had occured, but during the third act the leading man broke his collarbone when he was topled back over the couch in the fight scene.
16. The principle reason for the written examinition is that it allows us to spot canidates who's work isn't likely to meet company standards.

17. The city counsel studied each of the items on the agenda seperately and in it's proper sequence.
18. George gets embarrassed whenever anyone pays him a complement.
19. The committee voted to except the treasurer's annual report, but decided to delay any final judgement on the new buget till after all the members had time to anilize the implications of the previous year's figures.
20. The sucessful businessman usually combines aggressiveness with caution; he is willing to take risks but carefull to minimize those risks as much as possible.
21. There's no point in exagerating the significants of Saturday's loss.
22. Heros are often apologetic about their accomplishments.
23. The curriculum has changed remarkably during the passed twenty years.
24. He may be ingenius, but he's certainly no genius.
25. To divide is to separate.
26. One of the curious side-affects of long contact with DDT seems to be an increased resistance to cancer.
27. Primative versions of the television receiver had tiny screens, barely four inches accross.
28. Children often become irratable in the late afternoon.
29. The acknoledgements and the forward precede the table of contents.
30. The Secretery sited the current drop in interest rates as an encouraging sign.

APOSTROPHE

It's may be overwhelmingly our most frequent misspelling as in "The dog scratched *it's* ear." No, no! *It's* means *it is. Who's* means *who is.* NO pronoun spells *its* possessive with an apostrophe: *hers, its, ours, theirs, yours, whose, oneself* (but *one's self,* if you are emphasizing the self).

For all other words, however, we do add aspostrophe-*s* to spell the singular possessive:

dog's life	man's world
hour's work	day's end
horse's mouth	Marx's ideas

Even to words already ending in *s:*

Yeats's poems	Charles's crown
Leavis's error	Moses's law
Pericles's Athens	Vassilikos's work

The same is preferred for French names ending in silent *s*-sounds:

Camus's works	**Marivaux's plays**
Delacroix's friends	**Berlioz's Requiem**

A few plurals also form the possessive by adding *'s:*

children's hour	**people's attitudes**
women's rights	**mice's feet**
sheep's bellwether	**fish's habits**

But most plurals take the apostrophe after the *s* (or *s*-sound) already there:

witches' sabbath	**ten cents' worth**
citizens' rights	**the Joneses' possessions**
The Beaux' Stratagem	**doctors' fees**

I repeat, the best rule for making singulars possessive is to add *'s,* regardless of length and previous ending, though many people and some authorities merely add the apostrophe to names of several syllables already ending in *s (Dickens' novels, Adams' horse).* And certainly there is colloquial and auditory cause for so handling the longest names, as with *Themistocles' death* and *Aristophanes' wit.*

But *Sis' plans* and *the boss' daughter* are not what we say. We say *Sissuz* and *bossuz* and *Keatsuz,* and should say the same in our writing: *sis's, boss's, Keats's.* Even with long words, I find the added *s* an improvement in euphony as well as in sense: *ThemIStoCLESes DEATH, ArisTOPHanESes WIT. The same is true for Horace's satires, Catullus's villa, Cummings's style, Dickens's Pip.* The extra *s* makes no mistake, and you may prefer to distinguish Dickens from Dicken and Adams from Adam. If your page grows too thick with doube *s's,* substitute a few pronouns for the proper names, or rephrase: *the death of Themistocles, the Dickens character, Pip.* **Singular Ending in *s***

The apostrophe can help to clarify clusters of nouns, which are actually misspellings that have followed casual pronunciation. These I have actually seen: *Alistair Jones Renown Combo, the church barbecue chicken sale, the uniform policeman training program, the members charter plane.* and of course, *teachers meeting and veterans insurance* are spellings so common as to seem almost normal. But an apostrophe chips one more noun out of the block. It makes your meaning one word clearer, marking *teachers'* as a modifier, and distinguishing *teacher* from *teachers.* Inflections are helpful, and the written word needs all the help it can get: *Jones's* **String of Nouns**

Renowned, church's barbecued, uniformed policeman's, members' chartered. Distinguish your modifiers, and keep your possessions.

Don't forget the *'s* in the possessive before a gerund:

She objected to Bill's smoking. [not *Bill smoking*]
The teacher's leaving upset our plans. [not *teacher leaving*]
He didn't like anyone's working overtime. [not *anyone working*]

Your *'s* makes clear that she is not objecting to Bill and that ''He'' is not disliking anyone: the smoking and the working are being disliked.

Compounds   Compound words take the *'s* on the last word only: *mother-in-law's hat, the brothers-in-law's attitude* (all the brothers-in-law have the same attitude), *somebody else's problem, Governor Cass of Michigan's proposal.* Joint ownerships may similarly take the *'s* only on the last word (*Bill and Mary's house*), but *Bill's and Mary's* house is more precise and preferable.

Double Possessive   The double possessive uses both an *of* and an *'s*: *a friend of my mother's, a book of the teacher's, a son of the Joneses', an old hat of Mary's.* Note that the double possessive indicates one possession among several of the same kind: mother has several friends; the teacher, several books. Note, further in the *Joneses'* example, that the apostrophe falls *before* the comma, instead of after as a single or double quotation mark would.

Omissions   Use the apostrophe to indicate omissions: *the Spirit of '76, the Class of '02, can't, won't, don't.* Finally, use the apostrophe when adding a grammatical ending to a number, letter, sign, or abbreviation: *1920's;* his *3's* look like *8's; p's* and *q's;* he got four *A's;* too many *of's* and *and's;* she *X'd* each box; *K.O.'d* in the first round.

EXERCISES

2. *Think up, or collect from observation, five strings of nouns an apostrophe-s (and perhaps an -ed) would help clarify; then clarify each string:*

the church barbecue chicken sale
the church's barbecued chicken sale
[They were not cooking the church.]

the sophomore cheesecake rally
the sophomores' cheesecake rally
[The cheesecake was no sophomore.]

3. *To strengthen your perception of the possessive before a gerund, write five pairs of sentences on the following pattern, explaining after each pair the difference in meaning:*

> He didn't like anyone working overtime.
> He didn't like anyone's working overtime.

EXERCISE

4. *Handle the question of apostrophes and possessives in the following sentences.*

1. He is indignant about his students asking her advice.
2. She went to the governors convention. Its the place where state government gets it's chance to be heard.
3. Aiken objected to them leaving early, no matter who's work was finished.
4. They wont support Converse bid for nomination, even if she keeps running until 88.
5. The teachers lounge is a slum, with everything at 6s and 7s.
6. They Xd him from the list at Lois and Matthews apartment.
7. A friend of her brothers cant keep from prying into everybody else problems.
8. The President of the United States proposal carries some weight with Lewis supporters and Malraux enemies.
9. They stayed at Bates' house and met his boss' wife.
10. Some sponsor of their's complained of him appearing on the program, since it's purpose is educational.

HYPHEN

"*Time* abhors the hyphen," someone once said, and, ever since James Joyce's *hoofirons* and *steelyringing,* modern print has tended to compound the work of time, and *Time,* by squeezing the hyphens out of compounds. But the unfamiliar compound is hard on the eye, and the hyphens come back in—until another burst of editorial housekeeping.

The oldest and most useful compounds have coalesced from their original two words, first through hyphenation, then into one solid compound. *Housekeeping,* with the *housekeeper,* has scrubbed out the hyphen entirely. But many very common compounds live happily separated:

horse racing, Adam's apple, all right, blood pressure, stock market, girl friend. And many very common compounds go steadily hyphenated, and go no farther: *blue-pencil* (verb), *clear-cut, deep-freeze, good-bye, mother-in-law.* Check your dictionary.

But one rule remains solid: hyphenate two or more words serving together as an adjective. Unhyphenated words acquire hyphens when moved to an adjectival position:

Compound
Adjectives

She teaches in high school.
She is a high-school teacher.

He was sick of olive drab.
He was sick of his olive-drab uniform.

He was well known.
He was a well-known drifter.

His serve is red hot.
He has a red-hot serve.

It was never to be forgotten.
It was a never-to-be-forgotten gesture.

Some attitudes from the eighteenth century puzzle us.
Some eighteenth-century attitudes puzzle us.

Southern crocus blooms early, cheering us at winter's close.
Early-blooming southern crocus cheers us at winter's close.

You will have to check the hyphenation of prefixes and suffixes in your dictionary, but you can be sure of hyphenating prefixes to proper names:

Prefixes to
Proper Names

anti-Semitism   trans-Russian
post-Crimean War   un-American

Similarly, hyphenate suffixes to single capital initials:

Suffixes
to Capitals

F-sharp   U-turn
I-beam   V-neck
T-shirt   X-ray

Hyphenate *ex-*, meaning former, and *self-* (except *selfhood, selfish, self-less,* and *selfsame* where *self* is the root):

Self-

ex-champion   self-reliance
ex-president   self-respect

Hyphenate to distinguish meanings:

co-op from coop	**re-collect from recollect**	For
re-cover from recover	**re-creation from recreation**	Meaning

Hyphenate to avoid doubling *i*'s and tripling consonants:

anti-intellectual	**bell-like**	Double *i*;
semi-invalid	**wall-less**	Triple Consonants

Hyphenate compound words expressing numbers:

twenty-one	**three-fourths**	
ninety-nine	**one ten-thousandth**	Numbers
three hundred twenty-four	**twenty-one forty-fourths**	

Use the "suspensive," or hanging, hyphen for hyphenated words in series:

We have ten-, twenty-five-, and fifty-pound sizes.	In
He still prefers the six- to the eight-cylinder job.	Series

Or, with only two items, you can avoid the truncated look by using a few more words:

He still prefers the six-cylinder job to the eight-cylinder one.

When you must break a word at the end of a line, put your hyphen where your dictionary marks the syllables with a dot: *syl·lables, syl-lables.* If you must break a hyphenated word, break it after the hyphen: *self-/ sufficient.* Don't hyphenate an already hyphenated word: *self-suf-/ficient.* It's hard on the eyes and the printer. When you write for print, underline those line-end hyphens you mean to keep as hyphens, making a little equals sign: self = /sufficient.

Hyphenate those slants that are popping up all over: not "psychic/ social complex" but "psychic-social complex." See "Virgule" (next page).

EXERCISE

5. *Write five pairs of sentences to show your control of the hyphen:*

She teaches in high school.
She is a high-school teacher.

It was never to be forgotten.
It was a never-to-be-forgotten gesture.

VIRGULE

Don't use the virgule, or slant-mark, for a hyphen: not "male/female conflict" but "male-female conflict." Spare this "little rod" (/), and don't spoil your work with the legalistic *and/or*. Don't write "bacon and/or eggs"; write "bacon or eggs, or both." Use the virgule when quoting poetry in your running text: "That time of year thou mayst in me behold/ When yellow leaves. . . ."

DIACRITICAL MARKS

Many foreign words, though very common in English, retain their native markings, as in *naïveté*. Diacritical marks occasionally appear in spelling native words, as when a writer wishes to distinguish the *learnèd man* from what he has learned. (For italicizing foreign words, see page 394.) Here are some specifics:

DIERESIS *(coöperation, coördinate, naïve, Chloë, Danaë).* Let your dictionary be your guide. Newspapers tend to omit the dieresis, and some very common doubles go unmarked in the most meticulous print, as with *coordination* in this book, and with *cooperation* and *zoology*. But ö; ü *coördination, coöperation,* and *zoölogy* are perfectly acceptable. You also use the dieresis to indicate the umlaut in German words: *über, Fräulein, Götterdämmerung.*

ACUTE ACCENT. For spelling certain words borrowed from French. The *é* sounds like the *a* in *hay:*

é

attaché	fiancé, fiancée
blasé	habitué
café	naïveté
cliché	outré
communiqué	passé
décor	précis
décolleté	protégé, protégée
éclat	résumé
exposé	séance

GRAVE ACCENT. For words from French. The *à* sounds like *a* in *ah;* the *è* like the *e* in *bet.*

à la carte   mise en scène   à; è
à la mode   Molière
crème de la crème   pièce de résistance

CIRCUMFLEX ACCENT. Also for words from French. The *â* sounds like *ah;* the *ê* like the *e* in *bet;* the *ô,* like the *o* in *holes:*

bête noire   raison d'être   ê; ô
coup de grâce   table d'hôte
papier-mâché   tête-á-tête

CEDILLA. For words from French, the *ç* being pronounced *s:*

aperçu   garçon   ç
façade   Provençal
français   soupçon

TILDE. For Spanish words pronouncing *n* like the *ny* in *canyon: doña,* ñ
mañana, señor, vicuña.

Spelling foreign names requires their native diacritical markings: *Müller, Gödel, Göttingen, Poincaré, Brontë, García Lorca, Havlíček.* As always, your dictionary is your best guide, as it is, indeed, to all words transliterated to English from different alphabets and systems of writing (Russian, Arabic, Chinese, Japanese, and so on).

NUMBERS

In general, spell out numbers that take no more than two words: *two,* Spelling
twelve, thirty-one dollars, one hundred, five hundred percent, forty thou-sand, six billion—forty-foot sub tender, three feet of water. You also spell out numbers with fractions: *sixty-three and two-thirds.* Use numerals for the rest: *101; 1976; 200,000.* When a two-word number, like *five hundred,* for example, contrasts with a numeral, make them both numerals: *Even with a short assignment of 500 words, you still have 490 to go.*

Similarly, use numerals and signs in any statistical comparison: *14 as* Comparisons
against 19; only 2 in 96; 30% as compared to 28.5% (otherwise, spell out "percent").

Also use numerals in dates, times, measurements, money, and per- More Uses
centages requiring more than two words, and for streets: *April 1, 1984;* of
6:30 a.m.(but *half-past six*), *3 x 5 cards; 240 by 100 feet; 6'3"* (but *six* Numerals
feet tall); *$4.99* (but *two dollars a ticket; 69 cents a bunch*); *8½ percent*

(but *forty-two percent*); *42nd Street, 5th Avenue* (but *Fifth Avenue* is equally frequent), *1st Street, 3rd Avenue.*

Dates   Dates come with commas around the year: *April 1, 1884, was grim.* Or you may follow the European style without commas—*1 April 1884*—as long as you are consistent throughout. You may write either *February 1918* (no commas) or *February, 1918,* but not both in the same paper. Centuries come uncapitalized: the *twentieth century* (hyphenated when an adjective: *twentieth-century viewpoint*). Put A.D. before the year, and B.C. after: *A.D. 1066; 750 B.C.* Times are in small letters: *2:10 a.m.; 3 p.m.*

Commas with Numbers   As a rule, a comma goes with numbers of four or more digits: *1,986; $6,145; 11,669* (but the sciences usually omit the comma in four-digit numbers: *4589 kilometers* [*km*]). Further exceptions are addresses—*5112 Broadway*; page numbers—*page 1334*; and years—*2985 B.C.* (but *32,000 B.C.*).

Page Numbers   When connecting page numbers, give all numbers in full up through ninety-nine: *pp. 88–99.* For the hundreds and thousands, use only the last two digits of the second figure: *204–06, 1071–85* (but *296–304, 1098–1103*).* (For Roman numerals, see p. 467.)

Numbered Points in Text   Put full parentheses around numbered points in your text:

We will discuss (1) wages and hours, (2) fringe benefits, and (3) sick leave and vacation.

ABBREVIATIONS

Use only those conventional abbreviations your reader can easily recognize: *Dr., Mr., Mrs., Ms., Messrs.* (for two or more men, pronounced "messers," as in *Messrs. Adams, Pruitt, and Williams), Jr., St., Esq.* (Esquire, following a British gentleman's name, between commas and with *Mr.* omitted), *S.J.* (Society of Jesus, also following a name). All take periods. College degrees are equally recognizable: *A.B., M.A., Ph.D., D. Litt., M.D., LL.D.* Similarly, dates and times. *B.C., A.D., a.m., p.m.,* Though B.C. and A.D. are conventionally printed as small capitals, regular capitals in your classroom papers are perfectly acceptable. Write them without commas: *2000 B.C. was Smith's estimate; A.D.* precedes the year, and B.C. follows: *from 2000 B.C. until A.D. 2000.* A number of familiar abbreviations go without periods: *TV, FBI, USSR, USA, YMCA,* though

---

*Largely for less chance of error in reading or writing, some writers prefer full numbers for such connections; see footnote on p. 274. Whichever way you go, follow it consistently.

periods are perfectly OK or O.K. Acronyms ("tip-names" made from the initials or "tips" of longer titles, as in NOW, or UNESCO) usually go without periods, as do radio and television stations (WQXR-FM, NBC-TV) and tuberculosis (TB). *U.N.* and *U.S. delegation* are customary. Note that *U.S.* serves only as an adjective; write out *the United States*, serving as a noun. Certain scientific phrases also go without periods, especially when combined with figures: *55 mph, 300 rpm, 4000 kwh.*

Abbreviations conventional in running prose, unitalicized, are **e.g.** (*exempli gratia*, "for example"), **i.e.** (*id est*, "that is"), **etc.** (*et cetera*, better written out "and so forth") and **viz.** (*videlicet*, pronounced "vi-DEL-uh-sit," meaning "that is," "namely"). These are followed by either commas or colons after the period: Conventional Abbreviations in Prose

> **The commission discovered three frequent errors in management, i.e., failure to take appropriate inventories, erroneous accounting, and inattention to costs.**
> **The semester included some outstanding extracurricular programs, e.g.: a series of lectures on civil rights, three concerts, and a superb performance of *Oedipus Rex.***

The abbreviation *vs.*, usually italicized, is best spelled out, unitalicized, in your text: "The antagonism of Capulet versus Montague runs throughout the play." The abbreviation *c.* or *ca.*, standing for *circa* ("around") and used with approximate dates in parentheses, is italicized: "Higden wrote *Polychronicon* (*c.* 1350)."

For further abbreviations in footnoting, see pp. 280–283.

Avoid making abbreviations of your own. In your running text, spell out names of persons, places, months, and such words as *Street, Road,* and *Boulevard;* for example, *Oxford Street,* not *Oxford St.* (Obvious exceptions are St., Mr., Ms., initials in names, and so on.) Corporate names should follow the firms' preferences. When in doubt, spell *Company* and *Incorporated* in full. Spelling in Full

Here are some special problems:

1. An abbreviation at the end of a declarative sentence. End the sentence with the final abbreviating period.

> **He asked her to mail it C.O.D. [not C.O.D..]**

2. An abbreviation at the end of a question or exclamation. Add the question mark or exclamation point after the abbreviating period.

> **C.O.D.? Yes—but not to Washington, D.C.!**

3. An abbreviation inside a sentence. Let the abbreviating period stand as it comes, and add other punctuation as necessary.

All prices are F.O.B. at our nearest warehouse.
The joy of his life, i.e., his mother-in-law, arrived.

Note that common abbreviations like *i.e., etc., viz.,* and the like, are enclosed in commas, since they are parenthetical remarks. But, except for heavy irony, as with the *i.e.* before *mother-in-law,* your phrase will be smoother if you omit these abbreviations completely, or use *that is, and so on,* and *namely.*

4. Abbreviations like *Mr., Mrs., Ms., Mlle., Mme., Dr., St.* (Saint), *Co.,* and *Ltd.* occur without the period in some British papers and books. Follow U.S. usage, which requires the period.

EXERCISES

6. *Amend the errors in hyphenation, virgules, diacritical marks, numbers, and abbreviations in the following sentences.*

1. At about 10000 BC, man made settlements appear, but probably 80 % of subsistence still came from hunting and gathering.
2. At three P.M., the crowd dwindled, having lost its raison detre—tete a tete with the brass.
3. A twenty ft. gap in the hedge marked the path of 10 tanks and 1222 soldiers, after the attache, protege of the chancellor, misinterpreted a comminique while thinking of his fiancee over a soupcon of vichyssoise at the table d hote.
4. Here came the once in a life time piece de resistance, a 500 pound side of ox, roasted slowly by Godel for 24 hours over an open pit fire.
5. Each guest exhibited his/her naivete, as a learned observer observed, by squealing in delight at the never to be forgotten spectacle at two thirty one third ave.
6. He noticed among the crowd, three fourths of whom were strangers, a matron who taught in the local high-school, a noted antiintellectual, a semiinvalid selfreliant sculptress in a T shirt, and an ex president of the pta.
7. This house, the largest on Rivington Rd., has a living and/or dining area, ten or twelve foot ceilings, a three and a half acre lot, a three car garage, and 4500 square feet of flooring.
8. This is 1980 AD, almost 6000 years since writing was invented in Sumeria at some dim point beyond 3,500 B.C.
9. He had a PHD in herpetology and joined Messrs Wallach, Stein, and Crouch

as their chief consultant with the UN and the US; eg, he solved the problem of frogs in fish weir cultures.

10. Polyphemous Goode, born April 1, 1789 accomplished 40 manuscript pages a day well into his 80s, VIZ almost one hundred and twenty pages/month, or about one hundred and eighty thousand scientific/philosophic pages in his last 30 yrs.

PROBLEMS IN CAPITALIZATION

You know about sentences and most names, certainly; but the following points are troublesome. Capitalize:

1. Names of races, languages, and religions—Negro, Caucasian, Mongolian, Protestant, Jewish, Christian, Roman Catholic, Indian, French, English, Black (as in Black English). But "blacks and whites in this neighborhood," "black entrepreneurs," "white storekeepers"—especially in phrases that contrast blacks and whites, since *white* is never capitalized.

2. Adjectives formed from names—the Shakespearean sonnet, a Joycean sentence, the Renaissance outlook, the American way. But when such adjectives become common allusions, they drop their capital: *jeremiad, draconian measures, platonic love, herculean effort.*

3. Titles of officers, *but not of offices:* "Dean Metzlar is the first dean to subscribe"; "District Attorney Whelan is everyone's district attorney." The President of the United States is generally capitalized: *He was our best President, from his Presidential address throughout his Presidency.*

4. The *complete* names of churches, rivers, hotels, and the like—the First Baptist Church, the Mark Hopkins Hotel, the Suwannee River (*not* First Baptist church, Mark Hopkins hotel, Suwannee river).

5. Nouns and pronouns of diety—God, our Father, Messiah, Son, Savior, He, His, Him, Allah, Krishna, Siva. Pronouns referring to godheads outside the Judeo-Christian tradition are usually not capitalized.

6. North, south, east, and west *only when they are regions*—the mysterious East, the new Southwest (but southwestern flora, midwestern farmland)—or parts of proper nouns: the West Side, East Lansing.

7. All words in titles, except prepositions, articles, and conjunctions. But capitalize even these if they come first or last, or if they are longer

than five letters—"I'm Through with Love," *Gone with the Wind,* "I'll Stand By," *In Darkest Africa.* Capitalize all members in hyphenated compounds—*The Eighteenth-Century Background, The Anti-Idealist* (but *The Antislavery Movement), Pre-Engineered Parts for Heavy-Duty Make-Up.* But the names of numbered streets and the written-out numbers on your checks are *not* capitalized after the hyphen: *Forty-second Street. Fifty-four . . . Dollars.* When referring to magazines, newspapers, and reference works, you may drop *The* as part of the title—the *Saturday Evening Post,* the *Kansas City Star,* the *Encyclopaedia Britannica.*

8. References to a section of work—the Index, his Preface, Introduction, Afterword, Chapter 1, Volume IV, Act II. But "scene iii" is usually not capitalized because its numerals are also in lower case. Smaller numbered items within a work are less certain: Table— and Figure— are customary, but Section [section], Problem [problem], and Exercise [exercise] often go either way. In such instances, capitalize (be sure to do so consistently) when in doubt.

9. Abstract nouns, when you want emphasis, serious or humorous— ". . . the truths contradict, so what is Truth?"; Very Important Person; the Ideal.

10. The first word of a quoted phrase, if originally capitalized, falling within a sentence:

> Horace Greeley advised, "Go west, young man," and stayed home to make a fortune.

But do not capitalize, except for proper nouns, indirect quotations:

> Horace Greeley advised young men to go west, and stayed home to make a fortune.

For sentences in parentheses, see p. 389.

11. *Do not* capitalize the seasons—spring, winter, midsummer.

12. *Do not* capitalize after a colon, unless what follows is normally capitalized (see p. 385):

> Again we may say with Churchill: "Never have so many owed so much to so few."
> *Culture, People, Nature: An Introduction to General Anthropology* [title of book]

Many lost everything in the earthquake: their homes had vanished
along with their supplies, their crops, their livestock.

13. *Do not* capitalize proper nouns serving as common nouns: *china,
cognac, napoleon* (a pastry), *chauvinist, watt* (electricity). (Usage divides
on some proper adjectives: *French* [*french*] *pastry, Cheddar*
[*cheddar*] *cheese, German* [*german*] *measles, Venetian* [*venetian*] *blinds.* Breeds of animals, as in *Welsh terrier,* and products of a
definite origin, as in *Scotch whiskey,* are less uncertain.) When in doubt,
your best guide, as in spelling, is your dictionary.

14. As a rule, articles and prepositions not capitalized in full names
become capitalized when used without forename or title: *De la Mare's
poems* [Walter de la Mare]; *Von Neumann's computers* [John
von Neumann]; *De Gaulle's policies* [Charles de Gaulle, *or* General
de Gaulle]. An excellent help with names is *Webster's Biographical
Dictionary.*

EXERCISES

7. *Capitalize the following, where necessary:*

go west, young man.
the south left the union.
the east side of town
the introduction to
   re-establishing toryism
east side, west side
the tall black spoke french.
she loved the spring.
health within seconds [book]
clear through life in time
   [book]
a doberman pinscher
the methodist episcopal church

the missouri river
my christian name begins
   with *c*
the new york public library
the neo-positivistic approach
   [book]
the st. louis post-dispatch [add
   italics]
twenty-five dollars [on a check]
33 thirty-third street
the tundra occupies a large
   portion of northern canada.
Bohr's and de Broglie's theories

8. *Review the ways to italicize (pp. 393–394) and see if you can restore the
original capitals and italics in the following paragraphs.*

1. the oldest independent black people in the western hemisphere are the bush-
men of surinam on the north coast of south america, the descendants of negro
slaves who escaped from their dutch masters early in the 1600's, according

to the greenhill star-advertiser. They set up strategically scattered villages, raided plantations for black women and supplies, and successfully fought all campaigns against them, even those conducted by experienced european commanders. aphra behn, in her novel oroonoko, or the royal slave (1688), especially in her preface, praises the handsomeness, intelligence, and bravery of the surinam negro. thomas southerne repeats the impression in oroonoko a tragedy (1695), a play based on mrs. behn's book, especially in act i, scene iii. two u.s. blacks from harvard, s. allen counter, jr., a neurobiologist, and david l. evans, admissions officer, have studied the bush people for five years and have produced a documentary film entitled the bush afro-americans of surinam and french guiana: the connecting link. "these people," says counter, "represent to american blacks a mirror of the best example of what we would have been like had we chosen not to live in slavery and had removed ourselves to another place."

2. religious wars are the worst, as we can see in both the near east and the british isles, specifically in lebanon and northern ireland. the german motto gott mit uns ("god is with us") of world war i becomes an attitude excluding the other side from all justification and humanity. it generates fanatical dedication and hatred, as a recent article in the new republic suggests. when moslem fights christian, and catholic fights protestant, each sees his side as right with a religious fervor, as unlike his enemy's as day and night, yet all are identical in their fanaticism unto death, like the ancient zealots, in their unquenchable dedication to revenge and ultimate victory for the cause even in the distant future. dr. roger shinn, reinhold niebuhr professor of social ethics at union theological seminary, new york city, points out that war and religion both ask dedication beyond self. when the two combine, the dedication doubles, and all compromise seems evil, a betrayal of truth, and faith, and the right way.

Section E

USAGE

Speech keeps a daily pressure on writing, and writing returns the compliment, exacting sense from new twists in the spoken language and keeping old senses straight. Usage, generally, is "the way they say it." Usage is the current in the living stream of language; it keeps us afloat, it keeps us fresh—as it sweeps us along. But to distinguish yourself as a writer, you must always swim upstream. You may say, *hooja-eatwith?;* but you will write: *With whom did they compare themselves? With the best, with whoever seemed admirable.* Usage is, primarily, talk; and talk year by year gives words differing social approval, and differing meanings. Words move from the gutter to the penthouse, and back down the elevator shaft. *Bull,* a four-letter Anglo-Saxon word, was unmentionable in Victorian circles. One had to use *he-cow,* if at all. Phrases and syntactical patterns also have their fashions, mostly bad. *Like unto me* changes to *like me* to *like I do; this type of thing* becomes *this type thing; -wise,* after centuries of dormancy in only a few words (*likewise, clockwise, otherwise*), suddenly sprouts out the end of everything: *budgetwise, personalitywise, beautywise, prestigewise. Persuade them to vote* becomes *convince them to vote.* Suddenly, everyone is saying *hopefully.* As usual, the marketplace changes more than your money.

But the written language has always refined the language of the marketplace. The Attic Greek of Plato and Aristotle (as Aristotle's remarks about local usages show) was distilled from commercial exchange. Cicero and Catullus and Horace polished their currency against the archaic and the Greek. Mallarmé claimed that Poe had given *un sens plus pur aux mots de la tribu*—which Eliot rephrases for himself: "to purify the dialect of the tribe." It is the very nature of writing so to do; it is the writer's illusion that he has done so:

> **I have laboured to refine our language to grammatical purity, and to clear it from colloquial barbarisms, licentious idioms, and irregular combinations. Something, perhaps, I have added to the elegance of its construction, and something to the harmony of its cadence.**

—wrote Samuel Johnson in 1752 as he closed his *Rambler* papers. And he had almost done what he hoped. He was to shape English writing and speech for the next hundred and fifty years, until it was ready for another dip in the stream and another purification. His work, moreover, lasts. We would not imitate it now; but we can read it with pleasure, and imitate its enduring drive for excellence.

Johnson goes on to say that he has "rarely admitted any word not authorized by former writers." Writers provide the second level of usage, the paper money. But even this usage requires principle. If we accept "what the best writers use," we still cannot tell whether it is valid: we may be aping their bad habits. Usage is only a court of first appeal, where we can say little more than "He said it." Beyond that helpless litigation, we can test our writing by asking what the words mean, and by simple principles: clarity is good, economy is good, ease is good, gracefulness is good, fullness is good, forcefulness is good. As with all predicaments on earth, we judge by appeal to meanings and principles, and we often find both in conflict. Do *near* and *nearly* mean the same thing? Do *convince* and *persuade? Lie* and *lay?* Is our writing economical but unclear? Is it full by cumbersome? Is it clear but too colloquial for grace? Careful judgment will give the ruling.

Which is right, "I feel *bad*" or "I feel *badly*"? "The dress looks *good* on her" or "The dress looks *well* on her"? The man on the street would say, "I feel *bad*" and "The dress looks *good*," and he would be right: because *badly* would indicate shaky fingers and *well* a dress with good eyes. "Tie it tight" means "Tie it so that it is tight." Unfortunately, people trying to be proper follow the pattern of "He writes badly" and fall into the errors of "I feel badly" and "Tie it tightly." But *writes badly* is a verb with an adverb telling how the action is done, and *feel bad* is a verb with a predicate adjective modifying the subject and telling how the subject *is*. The predicate adjective describes existences, as in *ring true* and *come thick:* "they ring, and they are true"; "they come, and they are thick." So it is with other verbs pointing to states of being—*seem, appear, become, grow, sound, smell, taste*—on which "good usage" might rule the wrong way. English simply has an unresolved problem between usage and logic: *he doesn't feel well* says that his feelers are faulty but means that his health is hurting him. Just remember that you don't say "I feel goodly," and let reason be your guide.

Likewise with *the reason . . . is because.* You can find this colloquial redundancy on many a distinguished page. But everything a good writer writes is not necessarily good. The phrase is a collision between two choices, as the mind rushes after its meaning: between (1) *the reason is that . . .* and (2) *it is . . . because.* Delete *the reason . . . is,* the colloquial pump primer, and you save three words, sometimes four (the following eminent sentence, in which I have bracketed the surplus words, also suffers some redundancy of the *be's*):

> **In general it may be said that [the reason why] scholasticism was held to be an obstacle to truth [was] because it seemed to discourage further inquiry along experimental lines.**

And so, usage is perhaps where we begin; but if we end there, we may end in wordiness and mediocrity. Remember that usage sanctions all those horrors of dense nouns like *personnel application clearance center manager* and *teacher credentialization,* and all those nouns turned overnight into verbs: *to host, to parent, to finalize.* Clarity and economy are better guides than mere usage. Make your words mean what they say.

The following prescriptions are just about what the doctor ordered to keep you ticking, and in good company. They summarize the practices of the most careful writers—those who constantly attend to what words mean. They provide tips on avoiding wordiness, and avoiding those slips in diction that sometimes turn your reception a little chilly. I have also included comments on common problems with meanings, contradictions, and tautologies, and on other informational things like "Irony" and "Letter Writing," to supplement the discussions in the text.

A GLOSSARY OF USAGE AND COMMON ERRORS

A, an. Use *a* before *h* sounded in a first syllable: *a hospital, a hamburger.* Use *an* before a silent *h*: *an honor, an heir, an hour.* An *hypothesis*, accented on the second syllable, presents a problem, since the *h* is also sounded: *a hypothesis* is fully acceptable. For the distinction between *a (an)* and *the, see The.*

Abbreviations. See pp. 280–283, 414–416.

Above. For naturalness and effectiveness, avoid such references as "The above statistics are . . .," and "The above speaks for itself." Simply use "These" or "This."

Abrogated, arrogated. To *abrogate* is to abolish authority; to *arrogate* is to claim haughtily.

Accept, except. Frequently mistaken for each other in writing. *Accept* is to receive willingly; to *except* is to exclude, to make an *exception.* As a preposition, except means "other than," "but."

Adapt, adopt. To *adapt* is to modify something to fit a new purpose. To *adopt* is to take it over as it is.

Adverse, averse. Both turn away. But *adverse* means bad luck, and *averse* means opposed.

Advice, advise. Frequently confused. *Advice* is what you get when advisers *advise* you.

Aesthetic. An adjective: *an aesthetic judgment, his aesthetic viewpoint. Aesthetics* is singular for the science of beauty: "Santayana's *aesthetics* agrees with his metaphysics."

Affect, effect. *Affect* means "to produce an *effect*." Avoid *affect* as a noun; just say *feeling* or *emotion. Affective* is a technical term for *emotional* or *emotive*, which are clearer.

Aggravate. Means to add gravity to something already bad enough. Avoid using it to mean "irritate."

WRONG	RIGHT
He aggravated his mother	He *irritated* his mother.
	The rum *aggravated* his mother's fever.

Agreement. A pronoun should agree with its antecedent; a verb, with its noun; a demonstrative adjective, with its noun. Faulty agreement is usually between singulars and plurals. Also *see* text, pp. 340–342; 356–358.

FAULTY	REVISED
Everyone should roll *their* own.	*Everyone* should roll *his* own.
It was *her.* [Disagreement in case]	*It* was *she.* [Both *It* and *she* are subjective case]
A politician should be fair, but *they* usually are not.	*Politicians* should be fair, but they usually are not.
Those kind of sausages *are* bad.	*That kind* of sausage *is* bad.
Revision of their views about markets and averages *are* mandatory.	*Revision* of their views about markets and averages *is* mandatory.

All, all of. Use *all* without the *of* wherever you can to economize: *all this, all that, all those, all the people, all her lunch.* But some constructions need *of: all of them, all of Faulkner* (but *all Faulkner's novels*).

All ready, already. Two different meanings. *All ready* means that everything is ready; *already* means "by this time."

All right, alright. *Alright* is not *all right;* you are confusing it with the spelling of *already.*

Alliteration. See "Versification," p. 215.

Allusion, illusion, disillusion. The first two are frequently confused, and *disillusion* is frequently misspelled *disallusion.* An *allusion* is a reference to something; an *illusion* is a mistaken conception. You disillusion someone by bringing him back to hard reality from his illusions.

Alot. Wrong. You mean *a lot,* a whole *lot* of things, not *allot.*

Also. Do not use for *and,* especially to start a sentence; not "*Also,* it failed," but simply "And it failed."

Ambiguous. If your instructor marks *Amb* in the margin, he means "this has two meanings," one of which you probably have not noticed. Have you said, "Socrates admitted he was wrong"? This could mean that Socrates admitted that he, Socrates, was wrong, or it could mean that Socrates admitted that Crito was wrong. Check your statements to see that they cannot mean something else to the innocent reader.

Among. See *Between*.

Amount of, number of. Use *amount* with general heaps of things; use *number* with amounts that might be counted: *a small amount of interest, a large number of votes.*

And/or. An ungainly hairsplitter and thought stopper. You never *say* it. Don't write "for stage and/or screen"; write "for stage or screen, or both." Or just write "for stage and screen," and skip the finer possibilities.

Ante-, anti-. *Ante-* means "before": *an antebellum house* (a house built before the [Civil] War); *antedate* (to date before). *Anti-* means "against": *antifeminine, antiseptic.* Hyphenate before capitals, and before *i* and other vowels that confuse the reading: *anti-American, anti-intellectual,* anti-acid, anti-ego.

Anxious. Use to indicate *Angst*, agony, and anxiety. Does not mean cheerful expectation: "He was *anxious* to get started." Use *eager* instead.

Any. Do not overuse as a modifier:

POOR	GOOD
She was the best of *any* senior in the class.	She was the best senior in the class.
If *any* people know the answer, they aren't talking.	If *anyone* knows the answer, he's not talking.

Add *other* when comparing likes: "She was better than *any other* senior in the class." But "This junior was better than any senior."

Anybody. Don't write it as two words—*any body*—unless you mean "any corpse," or other inanimate object (stellar body, body of water).

Any more. Written as two words, except when an adverb in negatives and questions:

She never wins *anymore.*
Does she play *anymore?*

Anyone. Don't write it as two words—*any one*—unless you mean "any one thing."

Anyplace, someplace. Use *anywhere* and *somewhere* (adverbs), unless you mean "any *place*" and "some *place*."

Appear. Badly overworked for *seem.*

Appearing. Don't write "an expensive-appearing house." "An expensive-looking house" is not much better. Write "an expensive house," or "the house looked expensive."

Apostrophe-*s*. It signals possession. Use it as pronounced: *boss's daughter, Kraus's great idea.* Use it to distinguish the possessor's name: *Adams's, Dickens's, Jones's.* Use it to indicate the plurals of letters, dates, and words: *four a's, the 1960's, too many which's.* See also pp. 406–408.

Appreciate. Means "recognize the worth of." Do not use to mean simply "understand."

LOOSE	CAREFUL
I *appreciate* your position.	I *understand* your position.
I *appreciate* that your position is grotesque.	I *realize* that your position is grotesque.

Apt to, likely to, liable to. *Apt* is the more colloquial and dubious choice, but acceptable for known physical tendencies: *He is apt to overshoot his volleys. Likely to* is for general probabilities: *It is likely to rain; She is likely to succeed. Liable to* implies vulnerability: *He is liable to lose on powder snow; Over-confidence is liable to end in disappointment.* Don't use *liable* or *apt* for mere probability: *She is liable [apt] to come tomorrow* for *She may come tomorrow.*

Area. Drop it. *In the area of finance* means *in finance.* Be specific.

POOR	GOOD
This chart is conclusive in all *areas.*	This chart is conclusive.
	This chart thoroughly displays all departments.

Around. Do not use for *about:* it will seem to mean "surrounding."

POOR	GOOD
Around thirty people came.	*About* thirty people came.
He sang at *around* ten o'clock.	He sang at *about* ten o'clock.

As. This is the right one, where many have *like:*

FAULTY	REVISED
Nobody loves you *like* I do	Nobody loves you *as* I do.

Use where the cigarette people have *like:* "It tastes good, *as* a goody should." (*See also Like.*)

Do not use for *such as:* "Many things, *as* nails, hats, toothpicks. . . ." Write "Many things, *such as* nails . . . ."

Do not use *as* for *because* or *since;* it is ambiguous:

AMBIGUOUS	PRECISE
As I was walking, I had time to think.	*Since* I was walking, I had time to think. *Because* I was . . . . [even clearer]

Do not use *as* to mean "that" or "whether" (as in "I don't know *as* he would like her").

As . . . as. Use positively, not forgetting the second *as:*

WRONG	RIGHT
as long if not longer than the other.	*as* long *as* the other, if not longer.

Negatively, use *not so . . . as,* it is clearer (but more formal) than *as . . . as:*

It is *not so* long *as* the other.
His argument is *not so* clear *as* it ought to be.
His argument is *neither so* clear *nor so* thorough *as* it ought to be.

As far as. A wordy windup.

WORDY	IMPROVED
As far as winter wraps are concerned, she is well supplied.	She has a good supply of winter wraps.

As if. Takes the subjunctive:

as if he *were* cold

As of, as of now. Avoid, except for humor. Use *at,* or *now,* or delete entirely.

POOR	IMPROVED
He left *as of* ten o'clock.	He left at ten o'clock.
As of now, I've sworn off.	I've just sworn off.

As to. Use only at the beginning of a sentence: "As to his first allegation, I can only say. . . ." Change it to *about,* or omit it, within a sentence: "He knows nothing *about* the details"; "He is not sure [as to] [whether] they are right."

As well as. You may mean only *and.* Check it out. Avoid such ambiguities as *The Commons voted as well as the Lords.*

Aspect. Overused. See *Jargon.*

Assignment, assignation. An *assignment* is a job to be done; an *assignation* is a rendezvous.

At. Do not use after *where.* "Where is it at?" means "Where is it?"

Awake, awakes. See *Wake.*

Awhile, a while. You usually want the adverb: *linger awhile, the custom endured awhile longer.* If you want the noun, emphasizing a period of time, make it clear: *the custom lasted for a while.*

Bad, badly. Remember that *bad* is an adjective: *a bad trip, a bad book.* And that *badly* is an adverb: *he traveled badly, he wrote badly.* Confusion arises with the linking verbs. *He is bad* is clear enough. But the logic extends to *he looks bad, he smells bad, he acts bad, the dress looks bad, the air seems bad, I feel bad.* These are right! Don't be tricked into using *badly.*

Back of, in back of. *Behind* says it more smoothly.

Balance, bulk. Make them mean business, as in "He deposited the balance of his allowance" and "The bulk of the crop was ruined." Do not use them for people.

POOR	IMPROVED
The *balance* of the class went home.	The *rest* of the class went home.

The *bulk* of the crowd was indifferent.	*Most* of the crowd was indifferent.

Basis. Drop it: *on a daily basis* means *daily*.

Be sure and. Write *be sure to.* See *Try and.*

Because of, due to. See *Due to.*

Behalf—in your behalf, on your behalf. A nice distinction. "He did it *in your behalf"* means he did it in your interest. "He did it *on your behalf"* means he was representing you, speaking for you.

Beside, besides. *Beside* means "by the side of." *Besides* means "in addition to," not "other than."

POOR	IMPROVED
Something *besides* smog was the cause [unless smog was also a cause].	Something *other than* smog was the cause.

Better than. Unless you really mean *better than,* use *more than.*

POOR	IMPROVED
The lake was *better than* two miles across.	The lake was *more than* two miles across.

Between, among. *Between* ("by twain") has *two* in mind; *among* has several. *Between,* a preposition, takes an object; *between us, between you and me.* ("Between you and I" is sheer embarrassment; see *Me,* p. 456.) But words sometimes fail us. "Between you and me and the gatepost" cannot conform to the rule and become "among you and me and the gatepost." *Between* connotes an intimate sharing *among* all concerned, each to each. *Between* also indicates geographical placing: "It is midway between Chicago, Detroit, and Toledo." "The grenade fell between Jones and me and the gatepost"; but "The grenade fell among the fruit stands." Keep *between* for two and *among* for three or more—unless sense forces a compromise. "Between every building was a plot of petunias" conveys the idea, however nonsensical "between a building" is. "Between all the buildings were plots of petunias" would be better, though still a compromise.

Bimonthly, biweekly. Careless usage has damaged these almost beyond recognition, confusing them with *semimonthly* and *semiweekly.* For clarity, better say "every two months" and "every two weeks."

But, cannot but. "He can but fail" is old but usable. After a negative, however, the natural turn in *but* causes confusion:

POOR	IMPROVED
He cannot *but* fail.	He can only fail.
He *could not* doubt *but* that it	He could not doubt that it . . . .
He *could not* help *but* take . . .	He could not help taking. . . .

Similarly, *but*'s too close or frequent keep your reader spinning:

POOR	IMPROVED
The campaign was successful *but* costly. *But* the victory was sweet.	The campaign was costly, but victory was sweet.

When *but* means "except," it is a preposition.

WRONG	RIGHT
Everybody laughed *but* I.	Everybody laughed *but* me.

But rather. Acceptable, though sometimes redundant and open to ambiguity: *She was aloof, but rather nice.* It can be effective following negatives: *The course offers no amusement, but rather information and insight.*

But that, but what. Colloquial redundancies.

POOR	IMPROVED
There is no doubt *but that* John's is the best steer.	There is no doubt *that* John's is the best steer.
	John's is clearly the best steer.
There is no one *but what* would enjoy it.	Anyone would enjoy it.

c., ca. Indicates an approximate date, used only in a parenthesis with numerals, always italicized: "(*c.* 1496)." It stands for *circa*, "around."

Can, may (could, might). *Can* means ability; *may* asks permission, and expresses possibility. *Can I go?* means, strictly, "Have I the physical capability to go?" In speech, *can* usually serves for both ability and permission, though the salesgirl will probably say, properly, "May I help you?" In assertions, the distinction is clear: "He can do it." "He may do it." "If he can, he may." Keep these distinctions clear in your writing.

Could and *might* are the past tenses, but when used in the present time they are subjunctive, with shades of possibility, and hence politeness: "*Could* you come next Tuesday?" "*Might* I inquire about your plans?" *Could* may mean ability almost as strongly as *can*: "I'm sure he could do it." But *could* and *might* are usually subjunctives, expressing doubt:

Perhaps he *could* make it, if he tries.
I *might* be able to go, but I doubt it.

Cannot, can not. Use either, depending on the rhythm and emphasis you want. *Can not* emphasizes the *not* slightly.

Can't hardly, couldn't hardly. Use *can hardly, could hardly,* since *hardly* carries the negative sense.

Can't help but. A marginal mixture in speech of two clearer and more formal ideas *I can but regret* and *I can't help regretting.* Avoid it in writing.

Capability. Often "scientific" jargon. Say *it does* or *can do,* not *it has a capability for.*

Capital, capitol. Frequently confused. You mean *capital,* the head thing (from Latin *capitalis,* "of the head"), whether writing of the head city of a state or national government, the head letter of a sentence, or the top (the "head") of a Greek column, the money that heads your investment, or the offense that once would have gotten your head chopped off—capital punishment. *Capitol,* always capitalized, is the special name of the Temple of Jupiter on the Capitoline Hill in Rome, and also of the Capitol building where Congress sits in Washington, D.C., or the Capitol Hill in Washington on which the Capitol stands (the American founders named their new headquarters, and the hill they stood on, after the Roman ones). Confusion comes especially when you think of Washington:

WRONG	RIGHT
Washington, D.C., is the *capitol* **of the United States.**	**Washington, D.C., is the** *capital* **of the United States.**

Capitalization. Capitalize the first letters of sentences, the names of people, places, books, magazines, organizations, races, nationalities, religions, languages, a Supreme Diety and pronouns referring to Him, the first-person pronoun *I.* For further details, see Section D, "Capitalization" (pp. 417–419).

Case. Chop out this deadwood:

POOR	IMPROVED
In many cases, ants survive.	Ants *often* . . . .
In such a case, surgery is recommended.	*Then* surgery is recommended.
In case he goes	*If* he goes . . . .
Everyone enjoyed himself, *except in a few scattered cases.*	*Almost* everyone enjoyed himself.

Cause, result. Since *all* events are both causes and results, suspect yourself of wordiness if you write either word.

WORDY	ECONOMICAL
The invasions *caused* depopulation of the country.	The invasion depopulated the country.
He lost *as a result* of poor campaigning.	He lost *because* his campaign was poor.

Cause-and-effect relationship. Verbal adhesive tape. Recast the sentence, with some verb other than the wordy *cause:*

POOR	IMPROVED
Othello's jealousy rises in a *cause-and-effect* relationship when he sees the handkerchief.	Seeing the handkerchief *arouses* Othello's jealousy.

Censor, censure. Frequently confused. A *censor* cuts out objectionable passages. *To censor* is to cut out or prohibit. *To censure* is to condemn: "The *censor censored* some parts of the play, and *censured* the author as an irresponsible drunkard."

Center around. A physical impossibility. Make it *centers on,* or *revolves around,* or *concerns,* or *is about.*

Character development. A common cliché, literary jargon. Avoid it. It is ambiguous and cumbersome (noun-on-noun). You mean either *char-*

acterization, the way an author fills out his portraiture, or something like *maturity, evolution, growth in perception or integrity*—the way a literary personality develops. Make clear to your reader which you mean, and avoid the term altogether. See *Jargon.*

Circumstances. *In these circumstances* makes more sense than *under these circumstances,* since the stances are standing around (*circum*), not standing under. Often jargon: *The economy is in trouble* (not *in difficult circumstances*).

Cite. See *Site, sight, cite.*

Clichés. Don't use unwittingly. But they can be effective. There are two kinds: (1) the rhetorical—*tried and true, the not too distant future, sadder but wiser, in the style to which she had become accustomed;* (2) the proverbial—*apple of his eye, skin of your teeth, sharp as a tack, quick as a flash, twinkling of an eye.* The rhetorical ones are clinched by sound alone; the proverbial are metaphors caught in the popular fancy. Proverbial clichés can lighten a dull passage. You may even revitalize them, since they are frequently dead metaphors (see page 194). Avoid the rhetorical clichés unless you turn them to your advantage: *tried and untrue, gladder and wiser, a future not too distant.*

Colloquial, colloquialism. A characteristic of speech, frequently too personal, informal, or unclear for writing.

Come and, try and, go and, be sure and. All colloquial ways of saying *come to, try to, go to, be sure to. Come and see us* means "Come to see us," and so forth.

Comma splice, comma fault. The most common mistake in writing: putting a comma where you need a period, or, occasionally, a colon, dash, or semicolon. See *Run-on sentence,* and Section C, "Punctuating the Sentence" (pp. 375–379).

COMMA SPLICE	REPAIRED
The car, already ten years old, and looking twenty, collapsed in a heap of oily steam, it had run its last mile.	The car, already ten years old, and looking twenty, collapsed in a heap of oily steam. It had run its last mile.
	. . . oily steam, having run its last mile.

Compare to, compare with. To compare *to* is to show similarities (and differences) between different kinds; to compare *with* is to show differences (and similarities) between like kinds.

> **Composition has been compared *to* architecture.**
> **He compares favorably *with* Mickey Spillane.**
> **Compare Shakespeare *with* Ben Jonson.**

Comparisons. Make them complete; add a *than:*

> **It is more like a jigsaw puzzle *than a rational plan.***
> **They are more thoughtful *than the others.***
> **The first is better *than the second.* (Or "The first is *the* better.")**

Complected. A dialectical variant of *complexioned.* Better avoid the problem altogether by phrasing another way: *Her coloring was light; his complexion was dark.*

Complement, compliment. Frequently confused. *Complement* is a completion; *compliment* is a flattery: "When the regiment reached its full *complement* of recruits, the general gave it a flowery *compliment.*"

Comprise, compose, is comprised of. A frequent confusion. Say "The federal government *comprises* [not *is comprised of*] the legislative, judicial, and executive branches." Here, *compose* is correct: "The legislative, judicial, and executive branches *compose* the federal government." Or, as a slightly more wordy passive, "The federal government *is composed of* the legislative, judicial, and executive branches." *Comprise,* because it denotes only the whole containing the parts, lacks a passive voice, that is, is intransitive.

Concept. Often jargonish and wordy.

POOR	IMPROVED
The *concept* of multiprogramming allows	Multiprogramming allows . . . .

Connected with, in connection with. Always wordy. Say *about, with,* or *in.*

POOR	IMPROVED
They discussed several things *connected with* history.	They discussed several historical questions.

They liked everything *in connection with* the university.	They liked everything *about* the university.
He is *connected with* the Smith Corporation.	He is *with* the Smith Corporation.

Connotation. *See Denotation.*

Consensus. A *consensus of opinion* has seemed redundant to many stylists, since consensus means "feeling together," or "an agreed opinion." But you can write "they reached a consensus" and "they reached a consensus of opinion" with equal confidence that your words are saying what they mean. *They agreed* or *Their opinions coincided* would be original and economical, however.

Consider, consider as. The first means "believe to be"; the second, "think about" or "speak about": "I consider him excellent." "I consider him first as a student, then as a man."

Contact. Don't *contact* anyone: get in touch with him, call him, write him, find him, tell him. Don't make a good *contact*, make a helpful friend.

Contemptible, contemptuous. *Contemptible* is deserving contempt; *contemptuous* is giving it.

Continual, continuous. You can improve your writing by *continual* practice, but the effort cannot be *continuous*. The first means "frequently repeated"; the second, "without interruption."

It requires continual practice.
There was a continuous line of clouds.

Contractions. We use them constantly in conversation: *don't, won't, can't, shouldn't, isn't.* Avoid them in writing, or your prose will seem too chummy. But use one now and then when you want some colloquial emphasis: *You can't go home again.*

Contrast. *See Compare to.*

Convince, persuade. *Convince* THAT and *persuade* TO are the standard idioms: *I am convinced that he is right.* Resist the frequent *convince . . . to:*

POOR	IMPROVED
He *convinced* him *to* run.	He *persuaded* him *to* run.
	He *convinced* him *that* he should run.

Could, might. See *Can, may.*

Could care less. You mean *couldn't care less.* Speech has worn off the *n't,* making the words say the opposite of what you mean. A person who cares a great deal could care a great deal less; one who does not care "*couldn't* care less."

Could of, would of. Phonetic misspellings of *could've* ("could have"), and *would've* ("would have"). In writing, spell them all the way out: *could have* and *would have.*

Couldn't hardly. Use *could hardly..*

Council, counsel, consul. *Council* is probably the noun you mean: a group of deliberators. *Counsel* is usually the verb "to advise." But *counsel* is also a noun: an adviser, an attorney, and their advice. Check your dictionary to see that you are writing what you mean. A *counselor* gives you his *counsel* about your courses, which may be submitted to an academic *council.* A *consul* is an official representing your government in a foreign country.

Couple. Use *two, a few,* or *several.* In some breezy moments, you can lighten your prose with *a couple of.*

Credible, creditable. Sometimes confused. *Credible* means "believable." *Creditable* means "worthy of praise"—putting something down to your credit: "His catching the pass at third hand was *credible,* but not really *creditable,* since after Jones's fumble he hardly knew he had the ball."

Curriculum. The plural is *curricula,* though *curriculums* will get by. The adjective is *curricular.*

> **The school offers three separate curricula.**
> **Extracurricular activities also count.**
> **The dean has asked for curricular innovations.**

Dangling modifier. An introductory phrase dangles, with nothing to relate to: "Bowing to the crowd, the bull caught him unawares"; "Driving across country, the prices get higher and higher." You have left out the real subject your modifier modifies: "Bowing to the crowd, the toreador . . .", "Driving across country, we . . ." Other mismatches are frequent: "Having broken the dam, the sandbags could not hold the water" ("The water, having broken the dam, rushed through the sand bags"); "Born in Hungary, his knowledge of American folklore was minimal" ("Born in Hungary, he knew little about American folklore"). For further details *see* pp. 147–148; 363–364.

Data. A plural, like *curricula, strata, phenomena:*

The data are inconclusive.

Definitely. A high-school favorite, badly overused. Avoid "I definitely want to go"; "I want to go" is strong enough.

Defies, deifies. Frequently misspelt. *Defies* resists; *deifies* turns into a god.

Denotation, Connotation. Words denote things, acts, moods, whatever: *tree, house, running, anger.* They usually also *connote* an attitude towards these things. *Tree* is purely neutral denotation, but *oak* connotes sturdiness and *willow* sadness in addition to denoting different trees. *A House Is Not a Home* wrote a certain lady, playing on connotations and a specific denotation: a house of prostitution. *Woman* and *lady* both denote the human female, but carry connotations awakened in differing contexts:

> **A *woman* usually outlives a man. (Denotation)**
> **She is a very able *woman*. (Connotation positive)**
> **She is his *woman*. (Connotation negative)**
> **She acts more like a *lady* than a *lady* of pleasure.**
> **(Connotations plus and minus)**

Usage changes denotations: *a gay party* changes from a festive to a homosexual gathering. Usage also changes connotations: *chairman*, once a neutral denoter, now has acquired enough negative connotations to change a number of letterheads and signatures.

Beware of unwanted, or exaggerated, or offensive connotations: your reader may find you prejudiced.

Depreciate, deprecate. *Depreciate* is to talk something down; *deprecate* is to "pray away," to wish the removal of. You usually mean *depreciate* ("reduce the price of").

Desert, dessert. Frequently confused. You usually mean *desert*, either the sandy place, running away, or getting what you deserve, your "just deserts." *Dessert* comes after dinner. Remember one *s* for sand, two *ss*'s for the sweet stuff.

Different from, different than. Avoid *different than*, which confuses the idea of differing. Things differ *from* each other. Only in comparing several differences does *than* make clear sense: "All three of his copies differ from the original, but his last one is *more* different *than* the others." But here *than* is controlled by *more*, not by *different*.

WRONG	RIGHT
It is different *than* I expected.	It is different *from* what I expected.
	It is not what I expected.
This is different *than* all the others.	This is different *from* all the others.

Dilemma. Frequently misspelled *dilemna*, or *dillema*. A *lemma* is a proposition in logic, an argument; a *di-lemma* is a two-pronged proposition of equal choices that leave one puzzled.

Discreet, discrete. Frequently confused. *Discreet* means someone careful and judicious; *discrete* means something separate and distinct: "He was discreet in examining each discrete part of the evidence."

Disinterested. Does not mean "uninterested" nor "indifferent." *Disinterested* means impartial, without private interests in the issue.

WRONG	RIGHT
You seem *disinterested* in the case.	You seem *uninterested* in the case.
	The judge was *disinterested* and perfectly fair.
He was *disinterested* in it.	He was *indifferent* to it.

Disprove, disapprove. "To prove wrong" as against "to dislike."

Dissemble, disassemble. "To pretend" as against "to take apart."

Double negative. A negation that cancels another negation, making it accidentally positive: "He couldn't hardly" indicates that "He could easily," the opposite of its intended meaning. "They can't win nothing" really says that they *must* win something.

The double negative was standard in Middle English, patterned as it was on French, notably the French *ne . . . pas* ("no . . . not") that frames the verb. Chaucer's Absolon, the young priest in "The Miller's Tale," for instance, liked the women so well *That of no wyf ne took he noon offrynge* ("that of no wife no took he none offering"). We still double our negatives to intensify: "No, no, not so." And the habit most languages share of putting affirmative questions in the negative—"Isn't that so?" when we mean it *is so (N'est-ce pas? Nicht wahr?)*—makes some other double negatives also emphatic: "Don't think he couldn't care" means something like "He cares a great deal, but you *seem* to think he doesn't." A doubled negation carries the same kind of indirect emphasis—a mild irony, really—in such tentative assertions as "One cannot be certain that she will not prove to be the century's greatest poet," or "a not unattractive offer." But make sure your negatives don't cancel each other out, as in *couldn't hardly,* or land you in some mind-boggling absurdity like *No Trespassing Without Permission.*

Due to. Never begin a sentence with "*Due* to circumstances beyond his control, he . . . ." *Due* is an adjective and must always relate to a noun or pronoun: "The catastrophe *due to* [modifies *catastrophe*] circumstances beyond his control was unavoidable," or "The catastrophe was *due* to circumstances beyond his control" (predicate adjective). But you are still better off with *because of, through, by* or *owing to. Due to* is usually a symptom of wordiness, especially when it leads to *due to the fact that.*

WRONG	RIGHT
He resigned *due to* sickness.	He resigned *because of* sickness.
He succeeded *due to* hard work.	He succeeded *through* hard work.
He lost his shirt *due to* leaving it in the locker room.	He lost his shirt *by* leaving it in the locker room.
The Far East will continue to worry the West, *due to* a general social upheaval.	The Far East will continue to worry the West, *owing to* a general social upheaval.

Due to the fact that. A venerable piece of plumbing meaning *because.*

JARGON	IMPROVED
The program failed *due to the fact that* a recession had set in.	The program failed *because* a recession had set in.

Economic, economical. *Economic* deals with the economy, with business:

an economic disaster; economical saves money: *an economical purchase.*

Effect. As a noun, it means "result"; as a verb, "to bring about" (not to be confused with *to affect,* meaning "to concern, impress, touch, move"—or "to pretend." See *Affect.*

What was the *effect*?
He *effected* a thorough change.
How did it *affect* you?

But note that "He effected a change" is wordy for "He changed."

E.g. "For example" (*exempli gratia*). Not in italics. Preceded by a comma, followed by comma or colon. "They lost through errors, e.g., Wilson's fumble, Mitchell's miscall." See "Abbreviations," p. 415.

Either, neither. One of two, taking a singular verb: *Either is a good candidate, but neither speaks well. Either . . . or (neither . . . nor)* are paralleling conjunctions (see p. 155).

Eminent, imminent, immanent. Often confused. *Eminent* is something that stands out; *imminent* is something about to happen. *Immanent,* much less common, is a philosophical term for something spiritual "remaining within, indwelling." You usually mean *eminent.*

Enormity. Means "atrociousness"; does not mean "enormousness."

the *enormity* of the crime
the *enormousness* of the mountain

Enthuse. Don't use it; it coos and gushes:

WRONG	RIGHT
She *enthused* over her new dress.	She gushed on and on about her new dress.
He was *enthused.*	He was enthusiastic.

Environment. Frequently misspelled *enviorment* or *envirnment.* It is business jargon, unless you mean the world around us.

WORDY	IMPROVED
in an MVT *environment*	in MVT; with MVT; under MVT
He works in the *environment* of cost analysis	He analyzes costs.

We need to improve the landscaping in the *environment* of the offices.	We must improve the landscaping around the offices

Equally as good. A redundant mixture of two choices, *as good as* and *equally good.* Use only one of these at a time.

Erring, errant. *Erring* makes mistakes; *errant* wanders.

Eruption, irruption. An *eruption* is a bursting out, as with lava from a volcano, or a tooth through a gum; a *irruption* is a breaking up of things, like a bull in a china shop.

Etc. Substitute something specific for it, or drop it, or use something like "and so forth." See "Abbreviations," p. 415.

POOR	IMPROVED
She served fruit, cheese, candies, *etc.*	She served fruit, cheese, candies, and little sweet pickles. She served fruit, cheese, candies, *and the like.*

Ethic. A mannered rendition of *ethics,* the singular and plural noun meaning a system or science of moral principles. Even poorer as an adjective for *ethical.*

POOR	IMPROVED
The Muslim ethic forbids interest on loans.	Muslim ethics forbids interest on loans.

Everyday, every day. You wear your *everyday* clothes *every day.*

Everyone, everybody. Avoid the common mismatching *their:*

"Everyone does *his* [or *her* but not *their*] own thing."

Evoke, invoke. To *evoke* is to call for the emotions; to *invoke* is to call upon gods for assistance.

Exalt, exult. To *exalt* is to raise on high; to *exult* is to rejoice, or gloat.

Except. See *Accept, except.*

Exclamation. *Exclaim* often induces the misspelling *exclaimation.* Avoid overusing exclamation marks !!!!

Exists. Another symptom of wordiness.

POOR	IMPROVED
a system like that *which exists* at the university	a system like that at the university

Facet. This means "little face," as on a diamond. Use metaphorically or not at all.

POOR	IMPROVED
This problem has several *facets.*	This problem has five *parts.*
	Each *facet* of the problem *sparkles* with implications.

The fact that. Deadly with *due to,* and usually wordy by itself.

POOR	IMPROVED
The fact that Rome fell due to moral decay is clear.	*That* Rome fell through moral decay is clear.
This disparity is in part a result *of the fact that* some of the best indicators make their best showings in an expanding market.	This disparity arises in part *because* some of the best indicators look best in an expanding market.
In view of the fact that more core is installed	*Because* it has more core . . . .

Factor. Avoid it. We've used it to death. Try *element* when you mean "element." Look for an accurate verb when you mean "cause."

POOR	IMPROVED
The increase in female employment *is a factor in* juvenile delinquency.	The increase in female employment *has contributed to* juvenile delinquency.
Puritan self-sufficiency *was an important factor in* the rise of capitalism.	Puritan self-sufficiency *favored* the rise of capitalism.

Farther, further. The first means more distance; the second means more in time or degree. You look *farther* and consider *further,* before you go further into debt.

Faze, phase. See *Phase.*

Feasible. See *Viable.*

Fewer, less. See *Less, few.*

The field of. Try to omit it—you usually can. It is trite and wordy.

POOR	IMPROVED
He is studying in *the field of* geology.	He is studying geology.
He changed from *the field of* science to fine arts.	He moved from science to the fine arts.

Firstly. Archaic. Trim all such terms to *first, second, third,* and so on.

Fix. The word means "to establish in place"; it means "to repair" in speech and colloquial writing, where it can occasionally help fix a ponderous passage.

Flaunt, flout. *Flaunt* means to parade, to wave impudently; *flout* means to scoff at. The first is metaphorical; the second, not: "She *flaunted* her wickedness and *flouted* the police."

Folks. Use *parents, mother and father,* or *family* instead.

For. Be sure to distinguish the conjunction with a comma, or it will look like a preposition.

MISLEADING	ACCURATE
He went *for* the time was ripe.	He went, *for* the time was ripe.

Former, latter. Passable, but they often make the reader look back. Repeating the antecedents is clearer.

POOR	IMPROVED
The Athenians and Spartans were always in conflict. *The former* had a better civilization; *the latter* had a better army.	The Athenians and Spartans were always in conflict. Athens had the better culture; Sparta, the better army.

Forward, foreword. The first is direction; the second, an introduction to a book, a "fore" word or two.

Fragment. An incomplete sentence. A piece of a sentence. Both those statements are, grammatically, fragments, since they contain no verb. Complete your sentences by giving each subject its existence, or its action: its verb. But you can use a *rhetorical* fragment, one that your reader will not mistake as a mistake, most effectively, especially at the beginning of a paragraph: *Not so. Overwhelmed completely. Of course.* These are forceful trimmings from a complete sentence, the rest of which is left understood. See pp. 159–161; 375–376; 382.

Fun. *Fun thing, fun time, fun party*—all popular jargon. Keep *fun* as a noun: "It was fun." Or try something more vivid and original: "The party was hilarious from start to finish."

Funny. Avoid it, especially when you must explain "not funny 'ha-ha,' but funny queer."

Further. See *Farther.*

Gerund. The verb-form ending in -*ing* when it acts as a noun: "*Swimming* is healthful." Also see *Participle for gerund,* and discussion, pp. 334, 355, 408.

Go and see, come and see, be sure and see, try and see. All conversational versions of *go to, come to,* and so forth.

Good, well. *Good* is the adjective: *good time. Well* is the adverb: *well done.* In verbs of feeling, we are caught in the ambiguities of health. *I feel good* is more accurate than *I feel well,* because *well* may mean that your feelers are in good order. But *I feel well* is also an honest statement: "I feel that I am well." Ask yourself what your readers might misunderstand from your statements, and you will use these ambiguous terms clearly.

Got, gotten. Both acceptable and equivalent. Your rhythm and emphasis will decide. America prefers the older *gotten* in many phrases; Britain goes exclusively for *got.*

Gray. America prefers *gray;* England, *grey*—matching each country's initials.

Hand, on [the] one. See *On [the] one hand.*

Hanged, hung. *Hanged* is the past of *hang* only for the death penalty.

> They hung the rope and hanged the man.

Hardly. Watch the negative here. "I can't *hardly*" means "I *can* easily." Write: "One can hardly conceive the vastness."

Healthy, healthful. Swimming is *healthful;* swimmers are *healthy.*

Height. Not *heighth.*

His/her, his (her). Shift to the neutral plural, or otherwise rephrase to avoid this awkwardness. *His* stands for both sexes, if you can stand it.

Historically. A favorite windy throat clearer. Badly overused.

Historic, historical. *Historic* means momentous, but avoid it. *Historical* means recorded, or like history—*an historical novel.*

History. The *narrative,* written or oral, of events, not the events themselves. Therefore, avoid the redundancy "*recorded* history," likewise "*annals* of history," "*chronicles* of history." *History* alone can suffice, or even itself disappear:

PASSABLE	BETTER
Archeologists have uncovered evidence of events previously unknown to history.	Archeologists have uncovered evidence of events previously unknown.
World War II was the most devastating conflict in history.	World War II was the most devastating conflict the world had known.

Homogenous, homogeneous. You probably mean *homogeneous,* "of the same kind, uniform throughout." To *homogenize* is to "make homogeneous." Homogenous, on the other hand, is a biological term meaning "of common origin."

Honorable. See *Reverend.*

Hopefully. An inaccurate dangler, a cliché. "Hopefully, they are at work" does not mean that they are working hopefully. Simply use "I hope": not "They are a symbol of idealism, and, hopefully, are representative," but "They are a symbol of idealism and are, I hope, representative."

Host. A jargonish verb. Try *entertain, has invited, will hold, will preside.*

However. Bury it between commas, or replace it with *but* or *nevertheless.*

POOR	IMPROVED
However, the day had not been entirely lost.	*But* the day had not been entirely lost.
However, the script that Alcuin used became the forerunner of modern handwriting.	The script that Alcuin used, *however,* became the forerunner of modern handwriting.

Initial *however* should be an adverb:

However long it takes, it will be done.
However she did it, she did it well.

Humanism (mistaken for "Human nature" or "humanitarianism"). The intellectual awakening in the late Renaissance when men like Erasmus (1466–1536) rediscovered the culture and literature of ancient Greece and Rome, and began to shift attention from God and eternity to man and his capacities. Since the term has this specific historical meaning, find something else when you want to express, more generally, some focus on human nature.

MISLEADING	CLEARER
This study will be based on *humanism.*	This study will focus on *human nature.*
They pardoned him for *humanistic* reasons.	They pardoned him for *humanitarian* reasons.

Hung. See *Hanged.*

Hyphenation. See pp. 409–411.

I (we, you, one). See discussion, pp. 18–20. Also see "Pronouns as Subjects and Objects," pp. 350–355, and *Me,* p. 456.

The idea that. Like *the fact that*—and the cure is the same.

POOR	IMPROVED
He liked the idea that she was going.	He was pleased she was going.
The idea that space is infinite is difficult to grasp.	That space is infinite is difficult to grasp.

Identify. Give it an object:

He *identified the wallet.*

He *identified himself* with the hero. ("He identified with the hero"
is acceptable but not preferred.)

I.e. *Id est,* "that is." See "Abbreviations," p. 415.

If, whether. *If* is for uncertainties; *whether,* for alternatives. Usually the
distinction is unimportant: *I don't know if it will rain; I don't know
whether it will rain [or not].* To be absolutely clear, use *if* unless
you express an *or.*

Image. Resist its popularity, make it mean what it says, and never make
it a verb. Do NOT say, "The university should *image* the handsome
intellectual."

Imminent, Immanent. *See Eminent.*

Imply, infer. The author *implies;* you *infer* ("carry in") what you think he
means.

He *implied* that all women were hypocrites.
From the ending, we *infer* that tragedy ennobles as it kills.

Importantly. Often an inaccurate (and popular) adverb, like *hopefully.*

INACCURATE	IMPROVED
More *importantly,* he walked home.	More *important,* he walked home.

He did not walk home importantly, nor more importantly.

In back of. Use *behind.*

Includes. Jargonish, as a general verb for specific actions.

POOR	IMPROVED
The report includes rural and urban marketing.	The report analyzes rural and urban marketing.

Indite, indict. *Indite,* meaning "to write," is a common misspelling for
indict (pronounced "indite") meaning "to charge with a crime."

Individual. Write *person* unless you really mean someone separate and
unique.

Inequity, iniquity. "Injustice" as against "sin."

Infer. See *Imply, infer.*

Infinitive. The form of the verb with *to*—*to be, to know, to swim*. It functions as a noun: *To run is fun*. But, being a verb, it also may have an object and take a qualifying adverb: *To run a shop is fun; To run fast is fun*. Often *to* is understood: *We can make the car [to] run fast*. See *Split infinitives*.

Ingenious, ingenuous. Sometimes confused. *Ingenious* means clever; *ingenuous*, naïve.

Inside of, outside of. "They painted the *outside of* the house" is sound usage; but these expressions can be redundant and inaccurate.

POOR	IMPROVED
inside of half an hour	*within* half an hour
He had nothing for dinner *outside of* a few potato chips.	He had nothing for dinner *but* a few potato chips.

Instances. Redundant. *In many instances* means *often, frequently*.

Interesting. Make what you say interesting, but never tell the reader *it is interesting:* he may not believe you. *It is interesting* is merely a lazy preamble.

POOR	IMPROVED
It is interesting to note that nicotine is named for Jean Nicot, who introduced tobacco into France in 1560.	Nicotine is named for Jean Nicot, who introduced tobacco into France in 1560.

Intransitive. A verb not taking an object: "She *weeps*."

Irony. Not the same as *sarcasm* (which see). A clash between appearance and reality. Irony may be either comic or tragic, depending on your view. But, comic or tragic, irony is of three essential kinds:

VERBAL IRONY. You say the opposite of what you mean: "It's a *great* day," appearing to mean "great" but really meaning "terrible."

DRAMATIC IRONY. Someone unwittingly states, or acts upon a contrariety to the truth. A character in a play, for example, might say "This is my great day," and dance a jig, when the audience has just seen his daughter abducted and the mortgage foreclosed.

IRONY OF CIRCUMSTANCE. The opposite of what ought to happen happens (it rains on the day of the Weather Bureau's picnic; the best man of all is killed); and we are sharply aware of the contrast.

Irregardless. A faulty word. The *ir-* (meaning *not*) is doing what the *-less* already does. You are thinking of *irrespective,* and trying to say *regardless.*

Irregular verbs. See pp. 348–349.

Is when, is where. Avoid these loose attempts.

LOOSE	SPECIFIC
Combustion *is when* oxidation bursts into flame.	Combustion *is* oxidation bursting into flame.
"Trivia" *is where* three roads meet.	"Trivia" *is* the place three roads meet.

It. Give it a specific reference, as a pronoun. Avoid the expletive, non-referential *it:* it is wordy and often ambiguous (see also *There is*):

FAULTY	IMPROVED
She quit smoking. *It* is said that it is harmful.	She quit smoking. Doctors say it is harmful.

It's, its. *It's* means "it is": *It's a nice day.* When you write *the book and* IT'S *message,* you are saying "the book and it is message." But *it's* for *its* may be our most popular error. Try to remember that NO pronoun takes an apostrophe in the possessive: *yours, hers, ours, theirs, whose, its.* Write *the book and* ITS *message.*

Italics. See pp. 393–394.

-ize. A handy way to make verbs from nouns and adjectives *(patron-ize, civil-ize).* But handle with care. Manufacture new *-izes* only with a sense of humor and daring ("they Harvardized the party"). Business overdoes the trick: *finalize,* a relative newcomer, has provoked strong disapproval from writers who are not commercially familiarized.

Jargon. A technical, wordy phraseology that becomes characteristic of any particular trade, or branch of learning, frequently with nouns modifying nouns, and in the passive voice. Break out of it by making words mean what they say:

JARGON	CLEAR MEANING
The *plot structure* of the play provides no *objective correlative.*	The play fails to act out and exhibit the hero's inner conflicts. The plot is incoherent. The structure is lopsided.
The *character development* of the heroine is excellent.	The author sketches and deepens the heroine's personality skillfully. The heroine matures convincingly.
Three *motivation profile studies* were developed *in the area of production management.*	The company studied its production managers, and discovered three patterns of motivation.

Jingles. Avoid jingling your sounds together inadvertently.

> Use ample *illumination* for every *examination.*
> A *visionary revision* of the *decision.*
> A *beautiful* example of *dutiful* bureaucrats.

Judgment, judgement. Americans have made *judgment* standard; the British prefer *judgement,* along with *labour, colour,* and so forth.

Kind of, sort of. Colloquialisms for *somewhat, rather, something,* and the like. "It is *kind of* odd" will not get by. But "It is a *kind of* academic hippopotamus" will get by nicely, because *a kind of* means *a species of.* Change "a kind of a poor sport" to "a kind of poor sport," and you will seem as knowledgeable as a scientist.

Lay. Don't use *lay* to mean *lie. Lay* means "to put" and needs an object; *lie* means "to recline." Memorize both their present and past tenses, which are frequently confused:

> I *lie* down when I can; I *lay* down yesterday; I have *lain* down often [Intransitive—no object.]
> The hen *lays* an egg; she *laid* one yesterday; she has *laid* four this week. [Transitive—hen *lays* an object.]

Now I *lay* the book on the table; I *laid* it there yesterday; I have *laid* it there many times.

Lend, loan. Don't use *loan* for *lend*. *Lend* is the verb; *loan,* the noun: "Please *lend* me a five; I need a *loan* badly." Remember the line from the song: "I'll *send* you to a *friend* who'll be willing to *lend*."

Less, few. Do not use one for the other. *Less* answers "How much?" *Few* answers "How many?"

WRONG	RIGHT
We had *less* people than last time.	We had *fewer* people this time than last.

Letter-writing. Except for private correspondence, type your letters, with date, names and titles, addresses, and salutations in full, keeping a copy for reference. Though official correspondence frequently aligns everything flush with the left margin, including signature, such styling may seem pretentious from a private person. The following form and spacing are usual:

```
                              12345 Elmwood Drive
                              Tracy, Illinois 50123

                              July 1, 1976


    Professor Alan P. Kurtz, Chairman
    Department of English
    University of Michigan
    Ann Arbor, Michigan 48109

    Dear Professor Kurtz:

        You may remember me from your class in freshman
    composition, English 123, last spring. I do not
    recall the section number. But perhaps you will
    remember that I did not appear for the final
    examination. My name in class was Kathy Miller.

        I have recently received my grades, indicating
    a C in English.  Since my average had been at least
    a strong B, or even B+, as I remember, I thought
    this was a little severe.
```

I am writing to ask if I might make up the final, and receive some adjustment in my grade. I would be happy to come to Ann Arbor, at your convenience, or to arrange some time early in the fall term. Please let me know what the regulations are, and if I can hope for a second chance. I had some extreme problems right at the end of the semester. I really enjoyed the course.

Sincerely yours,

Kathy Miller Albright

(Mrs.) Kathy Miller Albright

Space long names of institutions equally in two (or more) lines in your salutation:

Dr. Robert A. Nordham, President
Society for Developing
Countries in Asia and
the Western Hemisphere
9876 Central Street
Clintdale, West Virginia 11213

Use "Dear Sir:" or "Dear Sirs:" for salutation to organizations when you do not know a person to address. To women's organizations "Dear Madam:" is customary. "Sincerely" or "Sincerely yours" will meet most situations.

Level. Usually redundant jargon. *High level officials* are *high officials* and *college level courses* are *college courses*. What is a *level official*, or a *level course* anyway?

POOR	IMPROVED
This high school offers a college level course in the senior year.	This high school offers a college course in the senior year.

Lie, lay. See *Lay*.

Lighted, lit. Equally good past tenses for *light* (both "to ignite" and "to descend upon"), with *lit* perhaps more frequent. Rhythm usually determines the choice. *Lighted* seems preferred for adverbs and combinations: *a clean well-lighted place; it could have been lighted better.*

Like, as, as if. Usage blurs them, but the writer should distinguish them before he decides to go colloquial. Otherwise, he may throw his readers off.

> He looks *like* me.
> He dresses *as* I do.
> He acts *as if* he were high.

Note that *like* takes the objective case, and that *as*, being a conjunction, is followed by the nominative:

> She looks like *her.*
> He is as tall as *I* [am].
> He is tall, like *me.*

The pattern of the prepositional phrase *(like me, like a house, like a river)* has caused *like* to replace *as* where no verb follows in phrases other than comparisons *(as . . . as):*

> It works *like* a charm. (. . . *as* a charm *works.*)
> It went over *like* a lead balloon. (. . . *as* a lead baloon *does.*)
> They worked *like* beavers. (. . . *as* beavers *do.*)

Notice that *as* would give these three statements a meaning of substitution or disguise: "It works as a charm" (but it really isn't a charm); "It went over as a lead balloon" (disguised as a lead balloon).

Literally. Often misused, and overused, as a general emphasizer: "We *literally* wiped them off the field." Since the word means "by the letter," a *literal* meaning is distinct from a *figurative* meaning. *His heart was stone* means, literally, that his blood pump was, somehow, made of stone; it means, figuratively, "He was cruel." Avoid *literally* unless you mean to show exactly what a word, or a statement, means: *To decapitate means literally to take the head off.*

Loan. See *Lend.*

Loath, loathe. You probably mean *loathe*, "to hate": *loath* is a slightly archaic word meaning "reluctant."

Loose, lose. You will *lose* the game if your defense is *loose.*

Lots, lots of, a lot of. Conversational for *many, much, great, considerable.* Try something else. *See Alot.*

CASUAL	IMPROVED
Henry VIII had *lots of* problems.	Henry VIII had *many* problems.
Latimer showed *lots of* courage.	Latimer showed *considerable* courage.
Their diet included *a lot of* pepper.	Their diet included *much* pepper.

Majority. More than half the votes, sometimes loosely used for a plurality, the highest number of votes but less than half, when more than two are running. Erroneously applied to quantities rather than numbers.

ERRONEOUS	ACCURATE
He ate *the majority* of the watermelon.	He ate *most* of the watermelon.
The majority of the play is comic.	*Most* of the play is comic.

Often wordy, even when applied to numbers:

WORDY	IMPROVED
The majority of the students take composition.	*Most* students take composition.

Manner. Drop this from your working vocabulary. *In a . . . manner* is a favorite redundancy. Replace it with an adverb: *in a clever manner* means "cleverly"; *in an awkward manner* means "awkwardly." *Manner* usually reveals your amateur standing, unless you really mean a mannerism in gesture or speech, or social manners, good and bad. Use *way,* or something else.

AMATEURISH	IMPROVED
In this *manner,* we learn . . .	In this *way,* we learn . . .
The play proceeds in this *manner* for three more acts.	The play goes on *like this* for three more acts.

Martial, marital. *Martial,* meaning "military," is a frequent misspelling for those *marital* troubles that lead to divorce, embattled though they may be.

Maximum (minimum) amount. Drop *amount*. The minimum and the maximum *are* amounts. Don't write *a minimum of* and *as a minimum:* write *at least*.

May. See *Can, may*.

Maybe. Conversational for *perhaps*. Sometimes misused for *may be*. Unless you want an unmistakable colloquial touch, avoid it altogether.

FAULTY	IMPROVED
The book *maybe* popular, but *maybe* it will endure.	The book *may be* popular, but perhaps it will endure.
It has sold *maybe* a million copies.	It has sold *perhaps* a million copies.

Me. Use *me* boldly. It is the proper object of verbs and prepositions. Nothing is sadder than faulty propriety: "between you and *I*," or "They gave it to John and *I*," or "They invited my wife and *I*. Test yourself by dropping the first member: "between *I*" *(no)*, "gave it to *I*" *(no)*, "invited *I*" *(no)*. And do NOT substitute *myself*. See "Pronouns as Subjects and Objects," pp. 351–353.

Medium, media. The singular and the plural. Avoid *medias*, and you will distinguish yourself from the masses.

Might. See *Can, may*.

Mislead, misled. Frequently confused in spelling. To *mislead* is to *lead* astray. To be *misled* is to have been *led* astray.

Misplaced modifier. A word or phrase misplaced so that it confuses. Frequently marked "DM," or "Dangling Modifier" for convenience. "She said *on Friday* to phone him" could mean "On Friday, she said . . ." or "to phone him on Friday." See pp. 361–364.

MISPLACED	CLARIFIED
She *only* loved her mother.	She loved *only* her mother.
They decided *when the teams tied* to end the game.	*When the teams tied*, they decided to end the game.
	They decided to end the game *when the teams tied*.
He liked people *in his way*.	*In his way*, he liked people.

Most. Does not mean *almost*.

WRONG	RIGHT
Most everyone knows.	*Almost* everyone knows.

Must, a must. *A must* is popular jargon. Try something else.

JARGON	IMPROVED
Beatup is really a *must* for every viewer.	Everyone interested in film should see *Beatup*.
This is a *must* course.	Everyone should take this course.

Myself. Use it only reflexively ("I hurt *myself*"), or intensively ("I *myself* often have trouble"). Fear of *me* leads to the incorrect "They gave it to John and *myself*." Do not use *myself, himself, herself, themselves* for *me, him, her, them.*

Nature. Avoid this padding. Do not write *moderate in nature, moderate by nature, of a moderate nature;* simply write *moderate.*

Near. Avoid using it for degree:

POOR	IMPROVED
a *near* perfect orbit	a *nearly* perfect orbit
	an *almost* perfect orbit
We are *nowhere near* knowledgeable enough.	We are *not nearly* knowledgeable enough.
This tribe is *nowhere near* self-sufficient.	This tribe is *far from* self-sufficiency.
It was a *near* disaster.	It was *nearly* a disaster [*or: nearly* disastrous].

No one. Two words in America, not *noone*, nor *no-one* (which the British prefer).

None. This pronoun means "no one" and takes a singular verb, as do *each, every, everyone, nobody,* and other distributives. *None are* has been common and admissible for centuries, but *none is* holds its own, with a certain prestige, even in the daily newspaper. Another pronoun referring back to any of these must also be singular:

POOR	IMPROVED
None of them *are* perfect.	None of them *is* perfect.
Every one of the men *eat* a big breakfast.	Every one of the men *eats* a big breakfast.
None of the discoveries *appear* significant.	None of the discoveries *appears* significant.
Everybody thinks *they have* the worst of it.	Everybody thinks *he has* the worst of it.

Nonrestrictive. See *Restrictive, nonrestrictive.*

Not . . . as, not . . . so. See *As . . . as.*

Not un-. *A not unwelcome interruption.* Some good writers—most notably George Orwell—find this construction redundant for *a welcome interruption.* It is nevertheless an example of *litotes,* a form of irony that has endured in our thinking for centuries—underlining an affirmative by a roundabout double negative: *not bad, no small achievement, not unusual mistake.* Use it for irony, where it works.

Noun habit, noun-on-noun. Modifying nouns with nouns. Characteristic of wordy writing and jargon. If you find yourself writing *plot structure* or *character trait* or *production management* or *student survey,* suspect yourself of both. See *Jargon,* and the discussion on pp. 173–176.

NOUN-ON-NOUN	REPAIRED
A lower volume of *product sales*	A lower volume of *sales* . . . .
His *character involvement* is	He *involves* his *characters.* . . .
At the root of *health care inflation* is the doctor.	At the root of the *inflating costs of illness* is the doctor.
. . . slashing *health care costs.*	. . . slashing the *costs* of *illness.*

Nowhere, noplace. Use *nowhere* (not *nowheres*), and reserve *no place* (not *noplace*) only for literal meanings: "He could find no place that would hold it."

Nowhere near. Use *not nearly,* or *far from,* unless you really mean *near:* "He was nowhere near the end." See *Near.*

AWKWARD	IMPROVED
It was *nowhere near* long enough.	It was *not nearly* long enough.
They had *nowhere near* enough food.	They had *far from* enough food.

Numbers. See pp. 413–414, and *Roman numerals,* p. 467.

Number of. Usually correct. See *Amount of.*

Off of. Write *from:* "He jumped *from* his horse."

On behalf, in behalf. See *Behalf.*

On [the] one hand. For one side of an issue, to be followed by *on the other hand* or *on the other,* to guide the reader. *On one hand* (*the* omitted) is more economical and preferable, as is *on the other,* if it follows closely and without confusion.

> *On one hand,* logging can leave land eroded and destitute of wildlife. *On the other,* trees prosper in forests thinned of competing and dying timber.

Be careful to place *on one hand* to avoid an unwanted hand:

> On one hand, she wore a hat.

What did she wear on the other?

On the part of. Wordy.

POOR	IMPROVED
There was a great deal of discontent *on the part of* those students who could not enroll.	The students who could not enroll were very discontented.

One. Avoid this common redundancy.

POOR	IMPROVED
One of the most effective ways of writing is rewriting.	The *best* way to write is to rewrite.

> The Ambassadors is one of the most interesting of James's books.
>
> The meeting was obviously a poor one.

> The Ambassadors is James at his best.
>
> The meeting was obviously poor.

In constructions such as "one of the best that . . ." and "one of the worst who . . .," the relative pronouns often are mistakenly considered singular. The plural noun of the prepositional phrase (the best, worst), not the one, is the antecedent, and the verb must be plural too:

WRONG

one of the best players who has ever swung a bat

RIGHT

one of the best players who have ever swung a bat

One (I, we, you). See discussion pp. 18–20.

Only. Don't put it in too soon; you will say what you do not mean.

WRONG

He only liked mystery stories.

RIGHT

He liked only mystery stories.

Outside of. See Inside of.

Overall. Jargonish. Use general, or rephrase.

DULL

The overall quality was good.

IMPROVED

The lectures were generally good.

Parallelism. Putting similar ideas into the same grammatical construction, for emphasis and clarity, usually in the same sentence. See discussion, pp. 152–157.

Parent. One of those nouns aping a verb: to rear, to bring up, to supervise, to raise, to love, to be concerned.

Participle. A form of the verb that functions as an adjective: a going concern, a gone goose; Liking candy, he bought two pounds; He is well liked. Going and liking are present participles; gone and liked, past particles. See pp. 147–148; 363–364.

Participle for gerund. Avoid this frequent confusion of the *-ing's*. The participle works as an adjective; the gerund, as a noun. You want gerunds in the following constructions, and you can get them by changing the misleading noun or pronoun to the possessive case:

WRONG	RIGHT
Washington commended *him passing* through the British lines.	Washington commended *his passing* through the British lines.
Do you mind *me staying* late?	Do you mind *my staying* late?
She disliked *Bill smoking*.	She disliked *Bill's smoking*.
We all enjoyed *them singing* songs and *having* a good time.	We all enjoyed *their singing* songs and *having* a good time.

You can catch these errors by asking yourself if you mean that "You mind *me*," or that "She disliked *Bill*" (which you do not).

Per. Use *a:* "He worked ten hours *a* day." *Per* is jargonish, except in conventional Latin phrases: *per diem, per capita* (not italicized in your running prose).

POOR	IMPROVED
This will cost us a manhour *per* machine *per* month a year from now.	A year from now, this will cost us a manhour a machine a month.
As *per* your instructions	According to your instructions

Per cent, percent, percentage. *Percent* (one word) seems preferred though *percentage*, without numbers, still carries polish: "A large *percentage* of non-voters attended"; "a significant *percentage* of the students." Use both the % sign and numerals only when comparing percentages as in technical reports; elsewhere, use numerals with *percent* when your figures cannot be spelled out in one or two words (2½ percent, 150 percent, 48.5 percent). Otherwise, spell out the numbers as well: *twenty-three percent, ten percent, a hundred percent*. See "Numbers," pp. 413–414.

Perfect. Not "more perfect," but "more nearly perfect."

Personal. Change "personal friend" to "good friend," and protect him from seeming too personal.

Personally. Always superfluous.

POOR	IMPROVED
I want to welcome them *personally.*	I want to welcome them [myself].
Personally, I like it.	I like it.

Phase. *Phase* is not *faze* ("daunt"), nor does it mean *aspect* or *part;* it is a stage in a familiar cycle, like that of the moon or the caterpillar. Unless you can carry the specific metaphor, avoid it, along with *facet.*

Phenomena. Frequently misused for the singular *phenomenon:* "This is a striking *phenomenon*" (not *phenomena*).

Phenomenal. Misused for a general intensive: "His popularity was *phenomenal.*" A phenomenon is a fact of nature, in the ordinary nature of things. Find another word for the extraordinary: "His success was *extraordinary*" (*unusual, astounding, stupendous*).

Picket. A pointed fence post, or a person so staked. *To picket* is to deploy people as pickets, or to join with others as a protesting fence against wrongs.

POOR	IMPROVED
They began *a picket* of	They began *to picket* . . . .
They began *their picket*	They began *picketing* . . . .
Until they withdraw their pickets	Until they withdraw their pickets . . . .

Plan on. Use *plan to.*

WRONG	RIGHT
He *planned on* going.	He *planned to* go.

Plot structure. Jargon. See *Noun habit,* and *Jargon.*

Possessives. See "Apostrophe," pp. 406–408.

Power vacuum. A physical contradiction, since a vacuum is the absence of power. Delete *power,* or put it where it belongs, and your phrase will be accurate. See *Noun habit.*

INACCURATE	IMPROVED
The junta rushed into the *power vacuum* created when the big three withdraw their support.	The junta rushed into the *vacuum* left as the three big *powers* withdrew.

Predominate, predominant. A frequent confusion. To *predominate* means to dominate everything. *Predominant* is the adjective you probably mean—The *predominant* opinion, the *prevailing* opinion, the *major* opinion.

Prejudice. When you write "He was *prejudice*," your readers may be *puzzle*. Give it a *d*—"He was *prejudiced*," —so they won't be *puzzled*.

Presently. Drop it. Or use *now*. Many readers will take it to mean *soon*: "He will go *presently*." It is characteristic of official jargon.

POOR	IMPROVED
The committee is meeting *presently*.	The committee is meeting.
	The committee is meeting *soon*.
He is *presently* studying Greek.	He is studying Greek.

Principle, principal. Often confused. *Principle* is a noun only, meaning an essential truth, or rule: "It works on the *principle* that hot air rises." The *pal* is the adjective: remember the *a*'s, and the *pal* in the princi*pal* person at our schools. The high-school *principal* acts as a noun because usage has dropped the *person* the adjective once modified. Likewise *principal* is the principal amount of your money, which draws interest.

Our *principal* is a woman of *principle*.
If you withdraw your *principal* from the bank, you will lose some interest.
His *principal* motive was greed.
The committee formulated two basic *principles*.

Proceed, precede, procedure. Continually mixed up in spelling. *Proceed* is to go ahead; *precede* is to go before. *Procedure* is a way of doing. The only solution here is memorizing, after you get the three meanings clearly in mind.

Process. Often verbal fat. For example, the following can reduce more often than not: *production process*, to *production; legislative* (or *leg-*

islation) process, to *legislation; educational* (or *education) process,* to *education; societal process* to *social forces.*

Proof, evidence. *Proof* results from enough *evidence* to establish a point beyond doubt. Be modest about claiming proof:

POOR	IMPROVED
This *proves* that Fielding was in Bath at the time.	Evidently, Fielding was in Bath at the time.

Proved, proven. *Proved* is the preferred past participle, which may serve as an adjective meaning "successfully tested or demonstrated"; *proven* is best kept an adjective meaning "tested by time," immediately before a noun:

INACCURATE	IMPROVED
It has proven true. [past part.]	It has proved true.
The theory was proven. [same]	The theory was proved.
a proved remedy [pure adj.]	a proven remedy

Provide. If you *absolutely cannot* use the meaningful verb directly, you may say *provide,* provided you absolutely cannot *give, furnish, allow, supply, enable, authorize, permit, facilitate, force, do, make, effect, help, be, direct, cause, encourage* . . . .

Providing that. Use *provided,* and drop the *that. Providing,* with or without *that,* tends to make a misleading modification. See *Dangling modifier.*

POOR	IMPROVED
I will drop, *providing that* I get an incomplete.	I will drop, *provided* I get an incomplete.

In "I will drop, *providing* I get an incomplete," *you* seem to be providing, contrary to what you mean.

Put across. Try something else: *convinced, persuaded, explained, made clear. Put across* is badly overused.

Quality. Keep it as a noun. Too many *professional quality writers* are already producing *poor quality* prose, and *poor in quality* means *poor.* See *Noun habit* and *Jargon.*

Quite. An acceptable but overused emphatic: *quite good, quite expressive, quite a while, quite a person.* Try rephrasing it now and then: *good, very good, for some time, an able person.*

Quote, quotation. Quote your quotations, and put them in quotation marks. Distinguish the verb from the noun. The best solution is to use *quote* only as a verb and to find synonyms for the noun: *passage, remark, assertion.* See "Punctuating the Sentence," pp. 391–394, for further details.

WRONG	RIGHT
As the following *quote* from Milton shows:	As the following *passage* from Milton shows: . . . .

Rarely ever. Drop the *ever:* "Shakespeare *rarely* misses a chance for comedy."

Real. Do not use for *very. Real* is an adjective meaning "actual":

WRONG	RIGHT
It was *real* good.	It was *very* good.
	It was *really* good.

Reason . . . is because. Knock out *the reason . . . is,* and *the reason why . . . is,* and you will have a good sentence.

[The reason] they have difficulty with languages [is] because they have no interest in them.

Regarding, in regard to. Redundant or inaccurate.

POOR	IMPROVED
Regarding the banknote, Jones was perplexed. [Was he *looking* at it?]	Jones was perplexed by the banknote.
He knew nothing *regarding* money.	He knew nothing *about* money.
She was careful *in regard to* the facts.	She respected the facts.

Regardless. This is correct. See *Irregardless* for the confusion.

Repetition. Avoid saying again what you have already said sufficiently. Avoid also inadvertent repetitions:

Of *course,* the *course* itself was boring.
By this time, people could *buy* some things *by* means of money.
The banking *interests* were *interested* in peace.

But you may repeat words and phrases for effective emphasis. See "Parallel Construction," pp. 152–157, and "Reiteration," p. 215. Repeating a necessary word is far better than trying for synonyms that may mislead your reader by making nonexistent distinctions.

POOR	IMPROVED
In London, most *shops* were small. The owner frequently lived above *the establishment.* Some *stores* were large.	In London, most *shops* were small, though some were large. The owner frequently lived above his *shop.*

Reputed, reputable. *Reputed* means "has the false reputation," or "rumored reputation." *Reputable* means respected. When you write "This is a *reputed* restaurant," you say that it is called a restaurant but really isn't one.

Respective, respectively. Redundant.

POOR	IMPROVED
The armies retreated to their *respective* trenches.	The armies retreated to their trenches.
Smith and Jones won the first and second prize *respectively.*	Smith won the first prize; Jones, the second.

Restrictive, nonrestrictive. A restrictive clause limits and designates what it modifies, *without surrounding commas:* "The book *that was open* was new" (that is, among several other books); "The girl *who sang* was Mildred." Nonrestrictive clauses merely add detail, with *which* and commas: "The book, *which was open,* cost twenty dollars." See pp. 170–171; 370–372.

Reverend, Honorable. Titles of clergymen and congressmen. Use both with first names or initials: "Reverend Smith" and "Honorable Jones" should be *Mr. Smith* and *Mr. Jones,* omitting the title altogether. The fully proper forms, as in the heading of a letter (*the* would not be capitalized in your running prose), are:

The Reverend Mr. Claude C. Smith
The Honorable Adam A. Jones [omit *Mr.*]

In running prose, *the Reverend Mr. Smith* is most proper; *Rev. Claude Smith* and *Hon. Adam Jones* will get by, but the best procedure is to give the title and name its full form for first mention, then to continue with *Mr. Smith* and *Mr. Jones.*

Rise, raise. Frequently confused. *Rise, rose, risen* means to get up. *Raise, raised, raised* means to lift up. "He *rose* early and *raised* a commotion."

Roman numerals. The following table includes most of the Roman numerals you will need:

ROMAN NUMERALS
(Subtract a smaller number preceding a larger: IV = 4, XL = 40)

1	I	14	XIV	30	XXX	110	CX
2	II	15	XV	40	XL	199	CIC
3	III	16	XVI	41	XLI	200	CC
4	IV	17	XVII	49	XLIX	400	CD
5	V	18	XVIII	50	L	500	D
6	VI	19	XIX	60	LX	900	CM
7	VII	20	XX	70	LXX	1000	M
8	VIII	21	XXI	90	XC	1500	MD
9	IX	22	XXII	91	XCI	1600	MDC
10	X	23	XXIII	98	XCVIII	1700	MDCC
11	XI	24	XXIV	99	IC	1865	MDCCCLXV
12	XII	25	XXV	100	C	1492	MCDXCII
13	XIII	29	XXIX	101	CI	1980	MCMLXXX

Use Roman numerals together with Arabic to designate act, scene, and line in plays, and book, chapter, and page in the novels that use them:

Romeo lies on the floor and cries like a child (III.iii.69–90).
When Tom Jones finds the banknote (XII.iv.483), ...

You would have already identified, in a footnote, the edition you are using. For further details see pp. 274–275; 277; 281–283.

Round. British for *around.*

Run-on sentence. Two or more sentences run together as one, with no punctuation where a period or semicolon should go. See *Comma splice* and pp. 376–378.

RUN-ON	REPAIRED
The hero can no longer think he nearly goes insane.	The hero can no longer think. He nearly goes insane.
The book is well written it is full of fascinating information.	The book is well written. It is full of fascinating information.
The novel fails to make Gatsby convincing the movie brings him to life.	The novel fails to make Gatsby convincing; the movie brings him to life.

Sanction. Beatifically ambiguous, now meaning both "to approve" and "to penalize." But why contribute to confusion? Stick to the root; use it only "to bless," "to sanctify," "to approve," "to permit." Use *penalize* or *prohibit* when you mean just that.

POOR	IMPROVED
They exacted *sanctions.*	They exacted *penalities.*

Sarcasm. The student's word for irony. Sarcasm intends personal hurt. It may also be ironic, but need not be. "Well, little man, what now?" is pure sarcasm when a dwarf interrupts the class; it is ironic sarcasm when a seven-footer bursts in. See *Irony.*

Seldom ever. Redundant. Cut the *ever.*

Set, sit. Frequently confused. You *set* something down; you yourself *sit* down. Confine sitting mostly to people *(sit, sat, sat),* and keep it intransitive, taking no object. *Set* is the same in all tenses *(set, set, set).*

CONFUSED	CLARIFIED
The house *sets* too near the street.	The house *stands* [*sits*] too near the street.
The package *sat* where he left it.	The package *lay* [*set*] where he left it.
He *has set* there all day.	He *has sat* there all day.

Shall, will; should, would. The older distinctions—*shall* and *should* reserved for *I* and *we*—have faded; *will* and *would* are usual: "I will go"; "I would if I could"; "he will try"; "they all would." *Shall* in the third person expresses determination: "They shall not pass." *Should,* in formal usage, is actually ambiguous: *We should be happy to comply,* intended to mean "would be happy," seems to say "ought to be happy."

Should of. See *Could of, would of.*

[sic]. Latin for "so," put in brackets within a quotation, unitalicized, after some error or detail that might puzzle the reader. See "Brackets," pp. 390–391.

Similar to. Use *like:*

POOR	IMPROVED
This is *similar to* that.	This is *like* that.

Sit. See *Set, sit.*

Site, sight, cite. Often confused. *Site* is a piece of land to put a building on, or holding a building. You do not see the *sites;* you see the *sights.* To *cite* is to quote or mention an authority, or other evidence.

Situate. Usually wordy and inaccurate. Avoid it unless you mean, literally or figuratively, the act of determining a site, or placing a building.

FAULTY	IMPROVED
Ann Arbor is a town *situated* on the Huron River.	Ann Arbor is a town on the Huron River.
The building is *situated* in the slums.	The building is in the slums.
The control panel is *situated* on the right.	The control panel is on the right.
He is well *situated.*	He is rich.
The company is well *situated* to meet the competition.	The company is well *prepared* to meet the competition.

Situation. Usually jargon. Avoid it. Say what you mean: *state, market, mess, quandary, conflict, predicament . . .*

Size. Often redundant. *A small-sized country is a small country. Large in size is large.*

Slash, slant-line (/). See *Virgule,* and p. 412.

Slow. GO SLOW is what the street signs and the men on the street all say, but write "Go slowly."

So. Should be followed by *that* in describing extent: "It was *so* foggy *that* traffic almost stopped." Avoid its incomplete form, the gushy intensive—*so nice, so wonderful, so pretty*—though occasionally this is effective.

So . . . as. See *As . . . as.*

Someplace, somewhere. See *Anyplace.*

Sort of. See *Kind of, sort of.*

Split infinitives. Improve them. They are cliché traps: *to really know, to really try, to better understand.* They are misleaders: *to better . . . , to further . . . , to well . . . , to even . . . ,* all look and sound like complete infinitives: *to further investigate* starts out like *to further our investigation,* throwing the reader momentarily off the track. *To better know* is to make *know* better, *to even like* is to make *like* even, all of which is nonsense. Indeed, in perverse moments *to eventually go* seems to say that *go* is being "eventualied." They are one of the signs of a wordy writer; they are usually redundant: *to really understand* is *to understand.* The quickest cure for split infinitives is to drop the adverb, giving *try* and *understand* their full weight. Or you can spell out your adverbial thought in a phrase.

Even the splitters do not recommend splitting as a rule. The rule remains DON'T SPLIT; and if you must, learn what you are doing—a little deviltry is better for the soul than ignorance. But I am convinced that you can always mend the split for a gain in grace, and often for a saving of words. You can sometimes change the adverb to an adjective, gaining force; saving letters and words:

POOR	IMPROVED
to better understand	to understand completely
to really try	to try, harder than ever

POOR	IMPROVED
to adequately think out solutions	*to think* out *adequate* solutions

to enable us *to effectively plan* our advertising	to enable us *to plan effective* advertising

Or you can drop the adverb, or bring it forward, or move it along, or spell out your meaning in a phrase:

POOR	IMPROVED
I cannot bring myself *to really like* the fellow.	I cannot bring myself *to like* the fellow.
	I cannot bring myself *really to* like the fellow.
	I *really* cannot bring myself *to* like the fellow.
	I cannot bring myself *to like* the fellow, *though I really have tried.*

George O. Curme gives the following examples from eminent splitters, arguing that usage makes them right.* But each of them can be improved:

EXAMPLE	IMPROVED
I wish the reader to clearly understand this. (Ruskin)	I wish the reader to understand this.
	I wish the reader to understand this clearly.
I would have overburdened the text to there incorporate many details. (Hempl, *Mod. Lang. Notes*)	Details there would have overburdened the text.
. . . without permitting himself to actually mention the name. (Arnold)	. . . without permitting himself to mention the name.
. . . of a kind to directly stimulate curiosity. (Pater)	. . . of a kind to stimulate curiosity.

English Grammar (New York: Barnes and Noble, 1947), p. 269.

. . . things which few except parents can be expected to really understand. (Oliver Wendell Holmes)	. . . things only parents can understand.
. . . to bravely disbelieve (Browning, *The Ring and the Book,* Cambridge ed., p. 570)	. . . bravely to disbelieve

Browning's full line, in fact, would have thumped somewhat less if he had dared bravely to vary his meter and mend his infinitive:

Whence need bravely to disbelieve report.

Stationary, stationery. Sometimes confused. Remember that you get your stationery from a stationer.

Structure. A darling of the jargoneer, often meaning nothing more frame-like than "unity" or "coherence." *Plot structure* usually means *plot,* with little idea of beams and girders. Use it only for something you could diagram, like the ribs of a snake, and never use it as a verb. See *Jargon.*

POOR	IMPROVED
He *structured* the meeting.	He *organized* (planned, arranged) the meeting.

Such. Overused as a colloquial intensive: *She is such a good organizer.* Complete the implied relative clause: *She is such a good organizer that no one need worry.*

Note that as a demonstrative pronoun *such* may be followed by *that,* since meanings are now distinct:

The applause was *such* that he decided to run for governor.

Such is an effective demonstrative pronoun to conclude a summary or demonstration:

Such is life.
Such were the effects of unwarranted suspicion.

Such that. An awkward slippage from *such . . . that.* Write *so.*

AWKWARD	IMPROVED
He wrote mannered poetry, *such that* his audience was small.	He wrote mannered poetry, *so* his audience was small.
	He wrote *such* mannered poetry *that* his audience was small.

Sure. Too colloquial for writing: "It is *sure* a good plan." Use *surely* or *certainly*, or otherwise rephrase.

Tautology. Several words serving where fewer—usually one—are needed, or wanted: useless repetition. Drop the bracketed words in these habitual tautologies:

attach [together]	mix [together]
[basic] essentials	[pair of] twins
consecutive days [in a row]	(but, two *sets* of twins)
[early] beginnings	[past] history
[final] completion	refer [back]
[final] upshot	repeat [again]
[first] beginnings	sufficient [enough]
[just] merely	whether [or not]

That, which, who. *That* defines and restricts; *which* is explanatory and nonrestrictive; *who* stands for people, and may be restrictive or non-restrictive. See *Restrictive, nonrestrictive*; see also *Who, which, that*.

The faucet *that* drips is in the basement.
The faucet, *which* drips badly, needs attention.
Of all the Democrats *who* supported him at first, none was more ardent than Jones.
Of all the Democrats, *who* supported him at first, none was more ardent than Jones.

Here is the distinction: only some Democrats supported him in the first sentence, but all did in the second.

The, a (an). *The* is the *definite* article, specifying particulars:

the book you want
the secretary in charge

A (an) is the *indefinite* article. It is *indefinite* because it makes a single item represent its whole general ("indefinite") class:

A tree gives shade.
A woman lives longer than *a* man.
A few people reverse *the* stastics
An apple *a* day keeps *the* doctor away.
Not *a* penny in *the* house.

The progression from general to specific runs *books, a book, the book:*

Books can teach much.
A book can teach much.
The book sold millions of copies.

There is, there are, it is. However natural and convenient—it is WORDY. Notice that *it* here refers to something specific, differing distinctly from the *it* in "It is *easy* to write badly." This indefinite subject, like *there is* and *there are*, gives the trouble. Of course, you will occasionally need an *it* or a *there* to assert existences:

There are ants in the cupboard.
There is only one Kenneth.
There are craters on the moon.
It is too bad.

But avoid *There is* and *It is,* and you will avoid some sludgy traps. They are part of the spoken language, like clearing the throat, and they frequently add just as little, especially when entailing a *that* or a *which:*

WORDY	IMPROVED
There are three men on duty.	Three men *are* on duty. [5 words for 6]
There is nothing wrong with this.	Nothing *is* wrong with this. [5 words for 6]
There are two things *which are* important here.	Two things *are* important here. [5 words for 8]

It is a habit *which* few can break.	Few can break *this* habit. [5 words for 8]
It is a shame that they had no lawyer.	*Unfortunately*, they had no lawyer. [5 words for 9]

These kind, these sort. Should be *this kind, this sort.*

They. A loose indefinite pronoun; tighten it:

POOR	IMPROVED
They are all against us, you know.	*Everyone* is against us, you know.
They launch our rockets at Cape Kennedy.	The *United States* launches its rockets from Cape Kennedy.

Do not use *they* with a singular antecedent:

WRONG	RIGHT
Everyone knows *they* should write correctly.	*Everyone* knows *he* should write correctly.
Every one of the students assumes *they* will pass.	*Every one* of the students assumes *he* will pass.

Too. Awful as a conjunctive adverb: "Too, it was unjust." Also poor as an intensive: "They did not do too well" (note the difference in Shakespeare's "not wisely but too well"—he really means it). Use *very,* or (better) nothing: "They did not do well" (notice the nice understated irony).

Tool. Overused for *means.* Also try *method, instrument.*

Toward, towards. *Toward* is the better, though both are acceptable.

Transition. A word or phrase helping the reader to make the step from one paragraph to the next, or from one sentence to the next: *also, of course, but, to be sure,* and the like. See pp. 55–57; 59–61.

Transitive. A verb that takes an object: "He *hit* him."

Trite. From Latin *tritus:* "worn out." Many words get temporarily worn out and unusable: *emasculated, viable, situation,* to name a few. And many phrases are permanently frayed; see *Clichés.*

Try and. Write *try to. To try and do* means "to try and to do," which is probably not what you mean. *Come and, go and, be sure and,* and so forth, should all likewise take *to: come to see, go to look, be sure to ask.*

Type. Banish it, abolish it. If you must use it, insert *of:* not *that type person* but *that type OF person,* though even this is really jargon for *that kind of person, a person like that.* The newspapers have succumbed, and we hear of *commando-type forces* for *commando forces,* of *a Castro-type dictator* for *another Castro,* of *the force of a Hiroshima-type bomb* for *the force of the Hiroshima bomb.* The most accurate translations of *-type* are *-like, -ish, -esque,* and *-ate,* depending on sense and euphony: *Castro-like, Castro-ish, Russianesque, Italianate.* English has many ways of saying it:

WRONG	RIGHT
essay-*type* question	essay question
Mondrian's checkerboard-*type* painting	Mondrian's checkerboard painting
French-*type* dressing	French dressing
Italian-*type* spaghetti	Italian spaghetti [Be bold!—we neither know nor care whether it's imported.]
atomic-*type* submarine	atomic submarine
She was a Chris Evert-*type* girl.	She was *like* Chris Evert.
	She was a Chris Evert *kind of* girl.
	She was a Chris Evert *type.*
an apprentice-*type* situation	apprenticeship
a Puck-*type* person	a *Puckish* person, a *Puck-like* person

Unique. Something *unique* has nothing in the world like it.

WRONG	RIGHT
The more unique the organization. . . .	The more *nearly* unique . . . .
the most *unique* man I know	the most *unusual* man I know
a very unique personality	a unique personality

Use, use of. A dangerously wordy word. "Through [the use of] personification, he asserts a theme." "In this sense, [the use of] physical detail is significant."

POOR	IMPROVED
He *uses* personification	He personifies . . . .
He *uses* inductive reason- ing	He reasons inductively . . . .

Use to. A mistake for *used to.*

Utilize, utilization. Wordy. *Utilize* means *use* (verb). *Utilization* means *the use* (noun). And the whole idea of "using"—a basic, universal concept—is frequently contained in the other words of your sentence.

POOR	IMPROVED
He *utilizes* frequent dialogue to enliven his stories.	Frequent dialogue enlivens his stories.
The *utilization* of a scapegoat eases their guilt.	A scapegoat eases their guilt.

Viable. With *feasible,* overworked. Try *practicable, workable, possible.*

Very. Spare the *very* and the *quite, rather, pretty,* and *little.* I would hate to admit (and don't care to know) how many of these qualifiers I have cut from this text. You can do without them entirely, but they do ease a phrase now and then.

Virgule. Avoid it, except to mark lines of poetry (see p. 412). Replace it with a hyphen if you must use such lumps as "work/play problem," "science/religion controversy"—but rephrasing to avoid the jargon is better: "the choice of work or play."

Viz. Pronounced "vi-DEL-uh-sit," after *videlicet,* the Latin word it abbreviates. It means "that is" or "namely." Put commas before and after it; do not italicize. See "Abbreviations," pp. 414–416.

Wake, waken (awake, awaken). *Wake, woke, waked (awake, awoke, awaked)* are standard. *Waken, wakened, wakened (awaken, awakened, awakened)* are slightly different verbs meaning "to wake up" (intransitive) or "to cause to wake up" (transitive).

He *wakes* up early. He *woke* him up yesterday. He *has waked* them up every morning at seven.

Awake, awoke, awaked is usually intransitive:

> She *awakes* easily. They *awoke* with a start. The birds *have* already *awaked.*

Waken and *awaken* are most frequently used transitively: "He *wakened (awakened)* his roommate." And they are more frequent in the passive voice: "He *was awakened* by loud knocking." Figurative usages prefer *awake* and *awaken: He was awake to the risk; his fears were awakened.*

We (I, you, one). See discussion, pp. 18–20.

Ways. Avoid it. Means *way:* "He went a short *way* into the woods."

Weather, whether. *Weather,* which means storms or breezes, rain or shine, is sometimes mistakenly written for *whether.* Whether the reader will smile or wince is problematical.

Well. See *Good.*

Whereas. Now a useful subordinating conjunction, preceded by a comma: "Hamlet is partly responsible for the tragedy, *whereas* Ophelia is wholly an innocent victim."

Whether. See *If,* and *Weather.*

Which. See *Who, that, which.*

While. Reserve for time only, as in "*While* I was talking, she smoked constantly." Do not substitute for *although, whereas, and, but.*

WRONG	RIGHT
While I like her, I don't admire her.	*Although* I like her, I don't admire her.
The side roads were impassable, *while* the highways were clear.	The side roads were impassable, *but* the highways were clear.
The seniors eat in clubs, *while* the freshmen eat in their dormitories.	The seniors eat in clubs, *and* the freshmen eat in their dormitories.

Who, which, that. Relative pronouns, *relating* an additional and subordinate clause to some preceding noun or pronoun:

> She *who falls* falls far.
> The fall *that hurts least* is the last.
> The fall, *which was severe,* was not serious.

Who may be either restrictive or nonrestrictive (see *Restrictive*): "The ones *who win* are lucky"; "The players, *who are all outstanding,* win often." *Who* refers only to persons:

FAULTY	REPAIRED
The girl *that* so chooses may enter dentistry.	The girl *who* so chooses may enter dentistry.
Some of the characters *that* wander around the stage	Some of the characters *who* wander . . . .

Use *that* for all other restrictives; *which* for all other nonrestrictives. See "the *of*-and-*which* disease" (pp. 170–171), and the further discussion on pp. 371–372; see also *That, which, who.*

Avoid *which* in loose references to the whole idea preceding, rather than to a specific word, since you may be unclear:

FAULTY	IMPROVED
He never wore the hat, which his wife hated.	His wife hated his going bareheaded.
	He never wore the hat his wife hated.

Whom, whomever. The objective forms, after verbs and prepositions; but each is often wrongly put as the subject of a clause.

WRONG	RIGHT
Give the ticket to *whomever* wants it.	Give the ticket to *whoever* wants it. [The whole clause is the object of *to; whoever* is the subject of *wants.*]
The president, *whom* he said would be late	The president, *who* he said would be late . . . .[Commas around *he said* would clear the confusion.]
Whom shall I say called?	*Who* shall I say called?

BUT:
They did not know *whom* to elect. [The infinitive takes an objective subject; see p. 334.]

Who's, whose. Sometimes confused in writing. *Who's* means "who is?" in conversational questions: "*Who's* going?" Never use it in writing (except in dialogue), and you can't miss. *Whose* is the regular possessive of *who:* "The committee, *whose* work was finished, adjourned."

Will. See *Shall.*

-wise. Avoid all confections like *marketwise, customerwise, pricewise, gradewise, confectionwise*—except for humor.

Would. For habitual acts, the simple past is more economical:

POOR	IMPROVED
The parliament *would meet* only when called by the king.	The parliament *met* only when called by the king.
Every hour, the watchman *would make* his round.	Every hour, the watchman *made* his round.

Would sometimes seeps into the premise of a supposition. Rule: Don't use *would* in an *if* clause.

WRONG	RIGHT
If he *would have* gone, he would have succeeded.	If he *had* gone, he would have succeeded.
	Had he gone, he would have succeeded [more economical].
I wish I *would have* learned it.	I wish I *had* learned it.

Would of. See *Could of, would of.*

You (I, we, one). See discussion, pp. 18–20.

INDEX

A, an, 424
Abbreviations, 414–416
  period used with, 387, 414–416
  research paper, 265, 272, 280–283
Ablative absolute, 150–151
Above, 424
Abrogated, arrogated, 424
Absolutes, 149–151
Abstract words, 188–191
Accents, 412–413
Accept, except, 424
Acronyms, 414–415
Active voice, 135–137
  in place of passive voice, 135, 165–169
  use of, 342, 344–345
Acute accent, 412
Adapt, adopt, 424
Adjectival phrase, 145, 146–147, 333
Adjectives
  defined, 333
  misused and misplaced, 359–363
  parallel, 152, 155
  in series, punctuation of, 374, 375
Adverbs
  conjunctive, 139

defined, 333–334
  misused and misplaced, 359–363
  subordinating by, 141–142
Adverse, averse, 424
Advice, advise, 424
Aeneid (Virgil), 327
Aesthetic, 424
Affect, effect, 424
After, 137
Aggravate, 424
Agreement, 340–342, 425
Albee, Edward, quoted, 233–235
All, all of, 425
All in all, 58
Alliteration, 215, 425
All ready, already, 425
All right, alright, 425
Allusion, 196–197, 222–224
Allusion, illusion, disillusion, 425
Almanacs, 252–253, 255, 256
Alot, 425
Alphabetization, 261–263, 283–284
Also, 425
Although, 137
Ambiguous writing, 425–426

American Dream, The (Albee), 233–235
American English, 320–329
Among, 426
Amount of, number of, 426
Amplification, 139–140
Analogy, 95–97, 121–122
Analysis
  definition by, 112, 114–115
Anapestic tetrameter, 217
And, 59, 137, 138–139, 154, 368–370
And/or, 426
Anglo-Saxon language, 197–200, 310–314
Ante-, anti-, 426
Antecedents, 332–333, 356–358
Anxious, 426
Any, 426
Anybody, 426
Any more, 426
Anyone, 426
Anyplace, someplace, 427
Apostrophe, uses of 406–408, 427
Appear, appearing, 427
Appositives, 144–145, 352, 353, 374
Appreciate, 427
Apt to, likely to, liable to, 427
Area, 427
Argument
  in essay subject, 6–12
  pro-and-con pattern of, 30–37, 59,
    247–248
Argumentative edge, 6–8
Aristotle, 134, 177, 197, 375, 422
Around, 427
As, as...as, 428
As far as, 428
As if, 428
As of, as of now, 429
Aspect, 429
Aspern Papers, The (James), 225
Assignment, assignation, 429
Assonance, 215
Assumptions, 108–110
As to, 429
As well as, 154–155, 429
At, 429
Attitude, 13–15
Auden, W. H., quoted, 324–325
Audience, 14–15
Audubon, John James, quoted,
  79–80

Austen, Jane, 194, 227–228, 232
  quoted, 148
Authority, citing, 116–117
Averages, as documentary evidence,
  119–120
Awake, awakes, 429
Awhile, a while, 429

Back of, in back of, 429
Bacon, Sir Francis, 121
  quoted, 156–157, 158
Bad, badly, 429
Balance, bulk, 429–430
Baldwin, Hanson W., quoted, 83–85
Baldwin, James, quoted, 56–57
Bartleby, the Scrivener (Melville), 225
Basis, 430
Because, 88, 137
Because of, due to, 430
Begging the question, 11, 124
Behalf, in your behalf, on your behalf, 430
Belief in subject, 105–106
Beside, besides, 430
Be sure and, 430
Better than, 430
Between, among, 430
Bible, books of
  abbreviation of, 282
  punctuation of, 282
  quoted, 316–318
Bibliographies in research, 249,
  252–253, 255, 257, 263–269,
  283–284
  form of, 283–284, 304
Bimonthly, biweekly, 430–431
Bittner, William, quoted, 196
Black English, 321, 323–324
Black Prince, The (Murdoch), 225
Book of Common Prayer, 142
Both/and, 154–155
Brackets, use of, 390–391
Browning, Robert, 222, 224, 225
But, 41–43, 56, 59, 137, 138, 154, 155,
  334, 366, 369, 370,
  372–373
But, cannot but, 431
But rather, 431
But that, but what, 431

C., ca., use of, 281, 415, 431

Caesura, 217
Can, may (could, might), 431–432
Cannot, can not, 432
Canterbury Tales (Chaucer), 315–316
Can't hardly, couldn't hardly, 432
Can't help but, 432
Capability, 432
Capital, capitol, 432
Capitalization, 45, 417–419, 432–433
   abstract nouns, 418
   after colon, 385, 418–419
   after hyphen, 418
   proper names, 417–419
   prepositions and articles in proper
     names, 419
   quotations, 385, 418
   titles of works, 417–418
Card catalogs, 255, 256, 258–263
Cary, Joyce, "Evangelist," 240–242
Case, as deadwood, 433
Catcher in the Rye, The (Salinger),
   237–239
Cat's Cradle, The (Vonnegut), 219, 222
Catullus, 422
Cause, result, 433
Cause and effect, order of, 88–92
Cause-and-effect relationship, 433
Caxton, William, 318–319
   quoted, 327–328
Cedilla, 413
Censor, censure, 433
Center around, 433
Centum languages, 309–310
cf., use of, 280
Ch., Chs., use of, 281
Character development, 433–434
Characters in literature, analysis of,
   228–230
Charlotte's Web (White), 142
Chaucer, Geoffrey, 228
   quoted, 315–316
Chesterton, G. K., quoted, 279
Chicago *Manual of Style,* 284
Cicero, 422
Circumflex accent, 413
Circumstances, 434
Cite, 434
Clichés, 434
Coherence
   of paragraphs, 57–63, 64, 65

transitional devices, 59–61
Collective nouns, 332, 340–341
Colloquial, colloquialism, 434
Colon, uses of, 138, 139–140,
   384–386
Come and, try and, go and, be sure and,
   434
Comedy, 219
Comma
   in compound sentences, 138–139
   before conjunctions, 368–370
   introductory, 366–368
   joining clauses, 368–370, 375
   with parenthetical elements, 370–373
   in series, 374–375
   use of, 366–381
Comma splice, 375–379, 434
Compare to, compare with, 435
Comparisons, 361–362, 435
   analogy, 95–97, 121–122
   and contrasts, order of, 35–36, 95–100
   definition by, 112–114
   paragraph development by, 112–113
   point by point, 35
Compleat Angler, The (Walton), 17
Complected, 435
Complement, compliment, 435
Complex sentences, 137–138
   defined, 141–151, 337
Compound-complex sentences, 337
Compound sentences, 137–141, 337–338
Comprise, compose, is comprised of, 435
Concept, 435
Concrete words, 188–191
Conjunctions
   abverbial, 139, 378
   coordinating, 137–141, 154–157, 334
   defined, 334
   in parallel construction, 154
   subordinating, 137, 141–151, 335
Connected with, in connection with,
   435–436
Connectives, 141. *See also* Conjunctions;
   Prepositions
   paralleling, 154
Connotation, denotation, 438
Conrad, Joseph, 225
Consensus, 436
Consider, consider as, 436
Consonance, 215

Contact, 436
Contemptible, contemptuous, 436
Continual, continuous, 436
Contractions, 436
Contrast
  and comparison, order of, 35–36,
    95–100, 436
  in compound sentences, 139–140
  paragraph development by,
    112–113
Convince, persuade, 436
Coordinating conjunctions
  in compound sentences, 137–141
  defined, 334
  in parallel construction, 154–157
Could, might, 437
Could care less, 437
Couldn't hardly, 437
Could of, would of, 437
Council, counsel, consul, 437
Couple, 437
Cowley, Malcolm, quoted, 193–194
Cowper, William, quoted, 217
Credible, creditable, 437
Criticism. *See* Literature, writing about
Curriculum, 437

Dactylic hexameter, 217
Dahlberg, Edward, quoted, 178
Dangling modifiers, 147–149,
    363–365, 437–438
Dash, use of, 388–390
Data, 438
Death in the Afternoon (Hemingway), 151,
    152
Deduction, 120–125
  fallacies, 124–125
  standard rules, 124–125
  syllogism, 121
Deductive-inductive order, 129–133
Deductive order, 127–129
Defies, deifies, 438
Definitely, 438
Definition, 110–115
  four steps in achieving, 113–115
  kinds of, 111–112
  paragraph development by, 111–114
  pitfalls in, 113–114
Defoe, Daniel, 225, 236
De la Mare, Walter, quoted, 212–213, 216

"Democracy and Anti-intellectualism in
    America'' (Hofstadter),
    110–111
Denotation, connotation, 438
Depreciate, deprecate, 438
Description, 76–81, 101–103
Desert, dessert, 438
Details
  selection of, 82–83
  use of, 60–63
De Vries, Peter, quoted, 196–197
Dewey Decimal System, 259, 260–261
Diacritical marks, use of, 412–413
Dialectic order, 30–37
Dialects, 320–321, 322–325
Dialogue, punctuation of, 373
Dickens, Charles, 222–223
Dickinson, Emily, quoted, 207–208
Diction, 197–200
Dictionaries, 252–253, 255, 400
Dictionary (1755) (Johnson), 319
Dieresis, 412
Different from, different than,
    438–439
Dilemma, 439
Direct object, 346, 352–353
Discreet, discrete, 439
Disinterested, 439
Disprove, disapprove, 439
Dissemble, disassemble, 439
Documentary evidence, 118–120
Documents, punctuation of, 394
Double appositions, 374
Double negative, 439–440
Drama, writing about, 222–235
  analysis of names, 222–223
  characters, 228–230
  determination of setting, 226
  narration and scene, 230–231
  plot description, 226–227
  plotting, 227–228
  structure, 231–232
  symbols, 223–224
  titles, 222–223
  written voice, 224–226
DuBois, W. E. B., quoted, 63–64
Due to, 440
Due to the fact that, 440

E.g., 441

Economic, economical, 440–441
Ed., use of, 281
Effect, 441
Eiseley, Loren, quoted, 62
Either, neither, 441
Either/or, 124, 154–155, 341–342
Eliot, T. S., quoted, 13, 189, 442
Ellipsis, use of, 394–397
Eminent, imminent, immanent, 441
Emma (Austen), 227–228, 232
Encyclopaedia Britannica, 245, 255, 287
Encyclopedias, use of, 252–253, 255, 256
Eneydos (Caxton from Virgil),
   327–328
English language, 307–329
   American English, 320–329
   Anglo-Saxon, 310–314
   Black English, 321, 323–324
   Indo-European, 308–310
   Middle English, 314–318
   modern English, 318–320
   standardization of, 321–325
Enormity, 441
Enthuse, 441
Environment, 441–442
Equally as good, 442
Ergo propter hoc, 89
Erring, errant, 442
Eruption, irruption, 442
Essay, *See* Writing the Essay
Et al., use of, 280
Etc., 415, 442
Ethic, 442
Evaluation, 235–244
Everyday, every day, 442
Everyone, everybody, 442
Evoke, invoke, 442
"Evolution of Ethics, The" (Schweitzer),
   86–87
Exalt, exult, 442
Example, definition by, 112, 114
Except, 442
Exclamation, 442
Exists, 443
Expletive, 341
Explication, 202–208
Exposition, 7–8
   citing authority, 116–117
   comparisons, 95–97
   contrasts, 97–100

definition, 101–103
illustration, 86–88
paragraph development by, 86–103

F., ff., use of, 281
Facet, 443
Fact, 104–105, 109–110
   opinion and, 106–107
Factor, 443
Fallacies, logical, 115–120
Fantasy, 219
Farther, further, 443
Faulkner, William, 223, 232
   quoted, 192–193, 198
Faze, phase, 444
Feasible, 444
Fewer, less, 444
Fielding, Henry, 222
   quoted, 231
Firstly, 444
Fitzgerald, F. Scott, 225, 228
Fix, 444
Flaunt, flout, 444
Folks, 444
Foot (meter), 203, 215–219
Footnotes
   abbreviation of, 272, 282–283
   bibliography matched to, 283–284
   form of, 273–279
   punctuation of, 274–279
   spacing, 273–274
For, 369–370, 444
Former, latter, 444
Forster, E. M., 228–229
Forward, foreword, 444
Four Quartets (Eliot), 189
Fragments, grammatical and rhetorical,
   159–161, 162, 375–379, 445
Frequently, 58
Freud, Sigmund, quoted, 156
Frost, Robert, quoted, 221–222
Fun, 445
Function, definition by, 112, 114
Funny, 445
Further, 445
Fused sentence. *See* Run-on sentences

Genre, determination of, 219–222
Gerunds, 334, 355, 445
Gibbs, Wolcott, quoted, 142–143

Giovanni, Nikki, quoted, 206–207
*Go and see, come and see, be sure and
    see, try and see,* 445
Good, well, 445
Got, gotten, 445
Grammar, 330–365. *See also* specific
    subjects
Grave accent, 412–413
Gray, 445
Great Gatsby, The (Fitzgerald), 225
Guide to Reference Books (Winchell), 254,
    256
Gullah, 323

Haircut (Lardner), 225
Hand, on (the) one, 445
Hanged, hung, 445
Hardley, 446
Hardy, Thomas, 77
Healthy, healthful, 446
Heart of Darkness, The (Conrad), 225
Height, 446
Hemingway, Ernest, quoted, 151, 152
Heretics (Chesterton), 279
Herrick, Robert, quoted, 202–203, 224
His/her, his (her), 446
Historic, historical, 446
Historically, 446
Historical present, 343
History, 446
Hodgson, Ralph, quoted, 217–219
Hofstadter, Richard, quoted, 67, 110–111
Homogenous, homogeneous, 446
Honorable, 446
Hopefully, 446
Horace, 442
Host, 446
However, 32–33, 61, 372–373,
    446–447
Hughes, Ted, quoted, 211–212
Humanism, 447
Hung, 447
Hyperbole, 193
Hyphen, use of, 409–411, 477
Hypothesis, 120–123

I.e., 415, 448
I (we, you, one), 18–20
Iambic meter, 203, 215–216
Ibid., 280

Identify, 447–448
If, 137, 144
If, whether, 448
If-then, 124
Illustration, paragraph development by,
    86–88
Image, 448
Imperative mood, 337, 345
Implications, 108–110
Imply, infer, 448
Importantly, 448
In back of, 448
Includes, 448
Indeed, 56
Indefinite pronouns, 333, 341–342
Indentation, 68–69
Indexes, 252–253, 255, 256–257
Indicative mood, 345
Indirect object, 352–353
Indite, indict, 448
Individual, 448
Indo-European languages, 308–310
Induction, 120–124
Inductive leap, 122–124
Inductive order, 125–127
Inequity, iniquity, 448
Infer, 448
Infinitives, 334, 353, 449
    parallel, 152
    split, 470–472
Ingenious, ingenuous, 449
Inside of, outside of, 449
Instances, 449
Interesting, 449
Interjections, defined, 335
Intransitive verbs, 333, 346, 347, 449
Irony, 108–109, 449
Irregardless, 450
Irregular verbs, 346–350. *See also* Trou-
    blesome verbs
Is when, is where, 450
Italics, use of, 393–394, 415, 450
It is, 169, 341, 450
It's, its, 450
-ize, 450

James, Henry, 225
Jane Austen and Her Art (Laselles), 194
Jargon, 450–451
Jeans, Sir James, quoted, 66

Jingles, 451
Johnson, Samuel, 319
  quoted, 158–159, 189–190, 442
Joseph Andrews (Fielding), 231
Jotted outlines, 38–40
Joyce, James, 229
Judgment, judgement, 451

Kazin, Alfred, quoted, 85–86
Kentum languages, 310–311
Kind of, sort of, 451

L., ll., use of, 281
Lardner, Ring, 225
Laselles, Mary, 194
Lawrence, D. H., quoted, 78, 193,
  229–231
Lay, 451–452
Lend, loan, 452
Less, few, 452
Letter-writing, 452–453
Level, 453
Library, use of, 245–269
  almanacs, 252–253, 255, 256
  bibliographies, 252–253, 255,
    263–269
  card catalogs, 258–263
  encyclopedias, 252–253, 255, 256
  indexes, 252–253, 255, 257
Library of Congress System,
  249–250, 259, 260–261
Lie, lay, 346–350, 453
Lighted, lit, 453–454
Light in August (Faulkner), 232
Like, as, as if, 454
Linking verbs, 333, 336
Literally, 454
Literature, writing about, 201–244
  analysis of names, 222–223
  characters, 228–230
  determination of setting, 226
  drama, 222–235
  evaluation, 235–244
  explication, 202–208
  metaphor, 211–214
  narration and scene, 230–231
  novels, 222–235
  paraphrasing, 208–210
  parody, 210–211

past tense, 232–235
plot description, 226–227
plotting, 227–228
present tense, 232–235
question formulation, 208–214
structure, 231–232
symbols, 223–224
thesis, 235–236
versification, 215–222
written voice, 224–226
Loan, 452
Loath, loathe, 454
Loc. cit., 280
Logic, 15–16, 38, 113–114
Logical proof, 115–120
  deduction, 120–125, 127–133
  induction, 120–124, 129–133
Longfellow, William Wadsworth, quoted,
  217
Loose, lose, 454
Lots, lots of, a lot of, 455
Lowell, Amy, quoted, 212–213, 214
Lowth, Robert, 319

Macaulay, Thomas Babington, quoted, 157
Macbeth (Shakespeare), 198, 223
Machiavelli, Niccolo, quoted,
  131–133
Majority, 455
Mallarmé, Stéphane, quoted, 422
Manner, 455
Mannerism, in writing, 199–200
*Manual for Writers of Term Papers,
  Theses, and Dissertations, A* (Tura-
  bian), 284
Manuscript form, 24–26
Martial, marital, 455–456
Marvell, Andrew, quoted, 216
Maximum (minimum) amount, 456
May, 456
Maybe, 456
Me, 456
Medium, media, 456
Melville, Herman, 225
  quoted, 328–329
Metaphor, 191–195, 211–214
Meter, 203, 215–219
Middle English, 314–318
Might, 456
Mislead, misled, 456

Misspelling, categories of, remedies for, 399–401, 406–408
Misplaced modifier, 456
Miss Julie (Strindberg), 232
MLA Handbook for Writers of Research Papers, Theses, and Dissertations, The (1977), 284
Modern English, 318–320
Modifiers
  in complex sentences, 144–151
  dangling, 147–149, 363–365, 437–438
  misused and misplaced, 359–363
Moll Flanders (Defoe), 236
Mood (grammar), 344–346
Most, 457
Ms, mss, use of, 281
Murdoch, Iris, 225
Murray, Sir James A. H., quoted 319
Must, a must, 457
"My Last Duchess" (Browning), 222
Myself, 457

N.d., use of, 281
N.p., use of, 281
Narrative, 81–86
Native Son (Wright), 147
Natural divisions, order of, 100–101
Nature, 457
Near, 457
Nevertheless, 32–33, 41, 56, 59, 139
None, 457
Nonrestrictives, 370–373, 458
Non sequitur, 125
No one, 457
Nor, 137
Not . . . as, not . . . so, 458
Not/but, 154–155
Note-taking for research paper, 248–251, 265–268, 290, 292
Not only/but also, 154–155
Not un-, 458
Nouns
  agreement, 340–349
  collective, 332, 340–341
  defined, 332
  overuse of, 173–176
  parallel, 152
  proper, common, 332
  phrase, clause, 332

Novels, writing about, 222–235
  analysis of names, 222–223
  characters, 228–230
  determination of setting, 226
  narration and scene, 230–231
  plot description, 226–227
  plotting, 227–228
  structure, 231–232
  symbols, 223–224
  titles, 222–223
  written voice, 224–226
Nowhere, noplace, 458
Nowhere near, 458–459
Number, 339
Number of, 459
Numbers, use of, 413–414, 459

Of, 170, 171
Of-and-which, 170–171
Of course, 56, 59
Off of, 459
Often, 58
On behalf, in behalf, 459
One, 459–460
One (I, we, you), 460
Only, 460
On (the) one hand, 459
On the part, 459
Op. cit., 280
Opinion, fact and, 106–107, 109–110
Or, 137, 138, 154, 155, 369
Ornithological Biography (Audubon), 79–80
Orwell, George, quoted, 81
Outline of Psychoanalysis, An (Freud), 156
Outlines, 37–49
  capitalization in, 45
  exam answer, 39–40
  headings, 40–43, 45
  jotted, 38–40
  punctuation in, 45
  for reading, 45–49
  research paper, 253–256, 270–272
  revision of, 41–43
  sentence, 43–44, 45, 47
  thesis in, 39–40, 45
  title, 44
  topic, 40–43, 45, 47
  value of, 37–38
Outside of, 460

Overall, 460
Oversimplification, 124

P., pp., use of, 281
Pairs, paralleling of, 154, 155
Paragraphs, 50–103
  beginning, 52–55, 64, 69–71
  coherence of, 57–63, 64, 65
  of definition, 110–115
  descriptive, 76–81
  details in, 60–63, 82–83
  development of, 69–103
  end, 65–68, 69–71
  expository, 86–103
  indentation, 68–69
  middle, 55–65, 69–71
  narrative, 81–86
  standard, 50–52
  structure of, 51–52
  topic sentences in, 52–53, 55–57, 63,
    64–65
  transitions between, 55–57, 59–61, 63
  transitions within, 65–68
Parallel construction, 152–159
  coordinators, 154–157
  pairs, 154, 155
  repetition of connectives, 154
  sentences, 152–159
Parallelism, 460
Paraphrasing poetry, 208–210
Parent, 460
Parenthesis, use of, 388–391
Parenthetical elements, commas used with,
  370–373
Parody, 210–211
Participle for gerund, 355, 461
Participles, 147–149, 334, 347–349, 460
Parts of speech, 332–335
Passim, use of, 281
Passive voice, 135–137
  elimination of, 135, 167–170
  ineffectiveness of, 165–166
  use of, 166, 342, 344–345
Past tense, 232–235, 237–238
Per, 461
Per cent, percent, percentage, 461
Percentages, as documentary evidence,
  119–120
Perfect, 461
Perhaps, 58

Period, use of, 386–388
Periodicals, indexes to, 256–257
Periodic sentences, 134–137
Persistence of belief, 188
Person, 339
Personal, 461
Personally, 462
Persuasion (Austen), 148
Phase, 462
Phenomena, 462
Phenomenal, 462
Picket, 462
Pidgin, 323–324
Plagiarism, 268–269
Plan on, 462
Plato, 422
Plot description, 226–227
Plot structure, 462
Plotting, 227–228
Plumed Serpent, The (Lawrence), 78–79,
  193
Poetry, punctuation of, 69, 395–396
Poetry, writing about, 202–222
  explication, 202–208
  metaphor, 211–214
  meter in, 203, 215–219
  paraphrasing, 208–210
  parody, 210–211
  question formulation, 208–214
  versification, 215–222
Point of view
  in essay, 18–20
  in literature, 224–225
Possessives, 355, 406–408, 462
Post hoc, ergo propter hoc error, 89, 125
Pound, Ezra, quoted, 214
Power vacuum, 462–463
Prawer, Jhabvala, R., quoted, 77
Predicate. *See* Verbs
Predominate, predominant, 463
Prefixes, 186–188, 400, 410
Prejudice, 463
Prepositional phrases, 149, 151
Prepositions
  avoiding strings of *ofs,* 171
  defined, 334
  parallel, 155
Presence, presents, 463
Presently, 463
Present tense, 232–235, 237–238

Primary sources, 251–252
Principle, principal, 463
Pro-and-con argument, 30–37, 59, 247–248
Problem and solution, order of, 92–95
Proceed, precede, procedure, 463–464
Process, 463–464
Pronouns
  agreement, 340–342, 425
  antecedents, 332–333, 356–358
  defined, 332–333
  indefinite, 341–342
  kinds of, 332–333
  relative, 141, 144–145, 146, 342
  as subjects and objects, 350–356
  use of, 19–20
Pronunciation. *See* Spelling
Proof, evidence, 464
Proved, proven, 464
Provide, 464
Providing that, 464
Punctuation, 366–397, 406–420
  abbreviations, 414–416
  apostrophe, 406–408, 427
  brackets, 390–391
  colon, 138, 139–140, 384–386
  comma. *See* Comma
  comma splice, 375–379, 434
  of compound sentences, 139–140
  dash, 388–390
  diacritical marks, 412–413
  of dialogue, 373
  ellipsis, 394–397
  of footnotes, 274–279
  hyphen, 409–411, 477
  italics, 393–394, 415, 450
  numbers, 413–414, 459
  in outlines, 45
  parenthesis, 388–391
  period, 386–388
  of poetry, 69, 395–396
  quotation marks, 68, 69, 382, 391–394
  of quotations, 382, 384–385, 391–394
  run-on sentence, 375–379, 468
  semicolon, 138–139, 381–384
  of titles, 393–394
  virgule, 69, 392, 412, 477

Puns, 183–184
Put across, 464

Quality, 464
Question mark
  with period, 387
  with single and double quotation marks, 392–393
Quite, 465
Quotation marks, 68, 69, 382, 391–394
  with colon, semicolon, 384, 392
  with comma, period, 392
  with exclamation, question mark, 392–393
  single, 392–394
Quotations
  capitals in, 385, 418
  indentation of, 68–69, 272–274
  punctuation of, 382, 384–385, 391–394
Quote, quotation, 465

Rambler (Johnson), 422
Rarely ever, 465
Reader's Guide to Periodical Literature, 257
Real, 465
Reason . . . is because, 465
Reference of pronouns. *See* Agreement; Antecedents
References. *See* Footnotes
Regarding, in regard to, 465
Regardless, 465
Reiteration, 215
Relative pronouns, 141, 144–145, 146, 333, 342
Repetition, 215, 466
Reputed, reputable, 466
Research paper, 245–304
  abbreviations in, 280–283
  analysis for, 250–251
  bibliographies, 249, 252–253, 255, 257, 263–269, 283–284
  card catalogs, library, 255, 256, 258–263
  distinguishing sources, 251–254
  final draft, 272–285
  first draft, 270–272
  footnotes, 272, 273–280, 283–284
  note-taking, 248–251, 265–268
  organizing resources, 248–257

outline for, 253–256, 270–272
plagiarism, 268–269
sample, 287–304
subject selection, 246–248
thesis, 246–247
Respective, respectively, 466
Restrictives, 371–373, 466
Rev., use of, 281
Reverend, Honorable, 466–467
Revision
   essay drafts, 20–26
   outlines, 41–43
Rhetoric
   concept of, 13–18
   defined, 12
Rhetorical fragments, 159–161,
   375–379, 445
Rhyme, 215
Rhythm in writing, 161–162
Richard III (Shakespeare), 196
Rise, raise, 346–350, 467
Romance, 219
Roman numerals, table of, 467
Round, 468
Rousseau, Jean-Jacques, quoted, 131–132
Run-on sentences, 375–379, 468

"Sailing to Byzantium" (Yeats), 100
Salinger, J. D., 237–239
Sanction, 468
Sanctuary (Faulkner), 210
Sandburg, Carl, quoted, 213–214
Sarcasm, 468
Satem languages, 309
Satire, 219
Schlesinger, Arthur, Jr., quoted, 326
Schweitzer, Albert, quoted, 86–87
Secondary sources, 251–252
Seldom ever, 468
Semicolon, uses of, 138–139,
   381–384
Sentence outline, 43–44, 45, 47
Sentences, 134–180, 335–338
   complex, 137–138, 141–151, 337
   compound, 137–141, 337–338
   compound-complex, 337
   correcting bad habits, 163–180
   fragments, 159–162, 375–379
   length of, 159–162
   loose, 134–136

outline, 43–44, 45, 47
parallel construction, 152–159
periodic, 134–137
run-on, 375–379, 468
simple, 135–137, 335–337
sliding, 331–332
topic, 52–53, 55–59, 63, 64–65, 67–68,
   87–88
wordiness, 163–180
Series, punctuation of, 374–375
Set, sit, 468
Setting, determination of, 226
Shakespeare, William, 118, 232
   quoted, 196, 198, 209, 210–211,
      216–217, 219–220, 223
Shall, will; should, would, 469
Shelley, Percy Bysshe, quoted, 100
"Shooting an Elephant" (Orwell), 81
Should of, 469
Sic, use of, 281, 469
Similarly, 59
Similar to, 469
Simile, 192–193, 195, 211–212
Simple sentence, 135–137, 335–337
Sit, set, 346–350, 469
Site, sight, cite, 469
Situate, 469
Situation, 469
Size, 469
Slash, slant-line (/), 470. *See also* Virgule
Slow, 470
So, 66, 470
So . . . as, 470
Someplace, somewhere, 470
Sometimes, 58
Sonnet, 219–222
Sort of, 470
Souls of Black Folk, The (DuBois), 63–64
Sound and the Fury, The (Faulkner),
   192–193, 198, 223
Space, order of, 76–81
Spelling, 399–406
   abbreviations, 414–416
   apostrophe, use of, 406–407
   diacritical marks, 412–413
   difficult words, 402–405
   hyphenation, 409–411
   numbers, 413–414
   principles of, 399–401
   virgule, use of, 412

Split infinitives, 470–472
Starting Out in the Thirties (Kazin), 85–86
Stationary, stationery, 472
Statistics as documentary evidence, 119–120, 253
Still, 139, 369
Strindberg, August, 232
Structure, 472
Style in writing, 3–4, 197, 199
Subjective complement, 351–352
Subject of infinitive, 354
Subject of verb
  agreement with verb, 340–342
  needless changes in, 338–340
  pronouns as, 350–352
  in sentences, 335–331
Subjects, selection of
  essay, 4–12
  research paper, 246–248
Subjunctive mood, 345–346
Subordinating conjunctions, 137, 141–151, 335
Subordination, 141–151
Such, 472
Such that, 472–473
Suffixes, 410
Summary, in note-taking, 266
Superlatives, 361, 362
Sure, 473
Syllogism, 121
Symbols, in literature, 223–224
Synonyms, definition by, 111, 113–114
Synthesis, definition by, 112, 114

Tautology, 164, 473
Tenses of verbs, 342–344
Tertiary sources, 251–252
That, which, who. See Who, which, that
That, which, restrictive, nonrestrictive, 170–171
The, a (an), 473–474
The fact that, 443
The field of, 444
The idea that, 447
There is, there are, it is, 169, 341, 474–475
Therefore, 56
There's, theirs, 404

"There Was a Child Went Forth" (Whitman), 69
Thesaurus, 187
These kind, these sort, 475
Thesis, 4–12
  in beginning paragraph, 52–55
  in outlines, 39–40, 45
  of research paper, 246–247
  summary in end paragraph, 65–68
  writing about literature, 235–236
They, 475
Thoreau, Henry David, quoted, 193, 194
Tilde, 413
Time magazine, quoted, 379
Time, order of, 77–81
Titles
  analysis of, 222–223
  punctuation of, 393–394
  selection of, 9
"To a Skylark" (Shelley), 100
Tone of voice, identifying, 226
Too, 475
Tool, 475
Topic outline, 40–43, 45, 47, 49
Topic sentences, 52–53, 55–59, 63, 64–65, 67–68, 87–88
  indentation, 68–69
  outlining by, 43–44, 45, 47
To the Lighthouse (Woolf), 232
Toward, towards, 475
Tr., trans., use of, 281
Tragedy, 219
Transition, 475
  between paragraphs, 55–59
  in paragraphs, 65–68
Transitional tags, 59–61
Transitive (verb), 333, 346, 347, 475
Trite, 475
Trochaic meter, 215
Trochaic tetrameter, 217
Troublesome verbs, 346–349
Try and, 475–476
Turabian, Kate L., 284
Type, overuse of, 175, 476
Typee (Melville), 328–329

Ulysses (Joyce), 229
Unique, 476

"Upon Julia's Clothes" (Herrick), 202–205, 224
Usage, 421–480
  defined, 421–422
  glossary of, 424–480
Use, use of, 172–173, 476–477
Use to, 477
Utilize, utilization, 173, 477

"Vale of Laughter, The" (De Vries), 196–197
Verbs, 340–350
  agreement, 340–342, 344–345
  defined, 333
  irregular, 346–350
  intransitive, 333, 346, 347, 449
  kinds of, 333
  linking, 333, 336
  mood, 344–346
  parallel, 152–153
  in sentence, with subject, 335–337
  tense, 342–350
  transitive, 333, 346, 347, 475
  voice, (active, passive), 135–136, 344–345
Versification, 215–222
  alliteration, 215, 425
  assonance, 215
  consonance, 215
  meter, 203, 215–219
  reiteration, 215
  rhyme, 215
Very, 477
Viable, 477
Viewpoint, shifting, in narrative, 83
Virgil, 327
Virgule, use of, 69, 392, 412, 477
Viz., 415, 477
Vocabulary, 185–188
Voice. *See* Active voice; Passive voice
Vol., vols., use of, 281
Vonnegut, Kurt, 219, 222
Vs., 415

Wake, waken (awake, awaken), 477–478
Walden (Thoreau), 194
Walton, Izaak, quoted, 17
Ways, 478

We (I, you, one), 18–20
Weather, whether, 478
Well, 478
When, 137, 142, 144
Where, 137, 142
Whereas, 478
Whether, 478
Which, who, that. See Who, which, that
Which, that, nonrestrictive, restrictive, 170–171
While, 478
White, E. B., quoted, 96, 142
Whitehead, Alfred North, quoted, 171
Whitman, Walt, quoted, 69, 126, 128
Who, which, that, 137, 141–142, 144–145, 146, 156, 163–164, 170–172, 342, 478–479
Whom, whomever, 479
Who's, whose, 480
Will, 480
Winchell, Constance M., 254
-wise, 480
Woolf, Virginia, 232
  quoted, 130, 161, 374
Wordiness, 163–180
Words, 181–200
  abstract, 188–191
  allusion, 196–197
  concrete, 188–191
  diction, 197–200
  metaphor, 191–195, 211–214
  multiple meanings, 182–184
  nouns into verbs, 164–165
  puns, 183–184
  vocabulary, 184–188
Would, 480
Would of, 480
Wright, Richard, quoted, 147
Writing the essay, 13–20. *See also* Literature, writing about; Research paper
  ascending interest of arguments, 28–29
  attitude, 13–15
  beginning structure, 52–55
  deductive order, 127–133
  end structure, 65–68
  inductive order, 125–127, 129–133
  mechanics, 23–24
  middle structure, 27–37, 55–65

Writing the essay (*Continued*)
  outlines, 37–49
  paragraphs, 50–103
  pro-con opposition, 30–36
  sentences, 134–160
  subjects. finding, 45
  thesis of, 4–12
Written voice, 15–20, 224–226

Wycliffe, John (Bible), 317
Wyzanski, Charles, Jr., quoted, 66–67

Yeats, W. B., quoted, 100
Yet, 137, 369
You, indefinite use of, 19
You (I, we, one), 18–20

79 80 81 82 83 84 9 8 7 6 5 4 3 2 1

CHECKLIST

1. Thesis stated in one sentence? (pp. 5, 8)

2. Thesis at end of first paragraph? (pp. 6, 27, 52–55)

3. Thesis clearly evident throughout paper? (p. 8)

4. Each paragraph begun with topic sentence? (pp. 52, 57–59)

5. Each with transitional tag? (pp. 55–57, 59–61)

6. Paragraphs four or five sentences long? (pp. 50–51)

7. Your best point last? (pp. 28–29)

8. Conclusion an inverted funnel? (pp. 53–54)

9. Generalizations, and thesis, free from fallacies? (pp. 11, 108–109, 115–125)

10. Sentences show some variety? (pp. 159–162)

11. Long sentences exhibit parallel construction? (pp. 152–157)

12. No passive, no *There is* . . . , no *It is* . . . ? (pp. 165–169)

13. Colons and semicolons properly used? (pp. 381–385)

14. Commas before every *and, but,* and *for* that needs them? (pp. 368–370)

15. A *pair* of commas around every inserted word, phrase, or clause? (pp. 370–372)

16. A comma before every *which?* Every *which* without comma changed to *that?* (pp. 170–171, 466, 473)

17. Every excess *of, which, that, -tion, to be,* and *the use of* dropped? (pp. 169–173)

18. Every noun-on-noun and *-type* revised? (pp. 173–176)

19. All excess wordage cut? (pp. 163–178)

20. No sentence that could be misread?

21. Have you said it as briefly and clearly as possible?

**SET ANY OF THESE POINTS ASIDE—
IF YOU HAVE AN IRRESISTIBLE RHETORICAL REASON.**